THE
SIERRA CLUB
GUIDE TO
THE
NATURAL AREAS
OF
CALIFORNIA

THE SIERRA CLUB GUIDES
TO THE NATURAL AREAS OF THE UNITED STATES

THE SIERRA CLUB GUIDE TO THE NATURAL AREAS OF CALIFORNIA

JOHN PERRY

AND

JANE GREVERUS PERRY

SIERRA CLUB BOOKS   SAN FRANCISCO

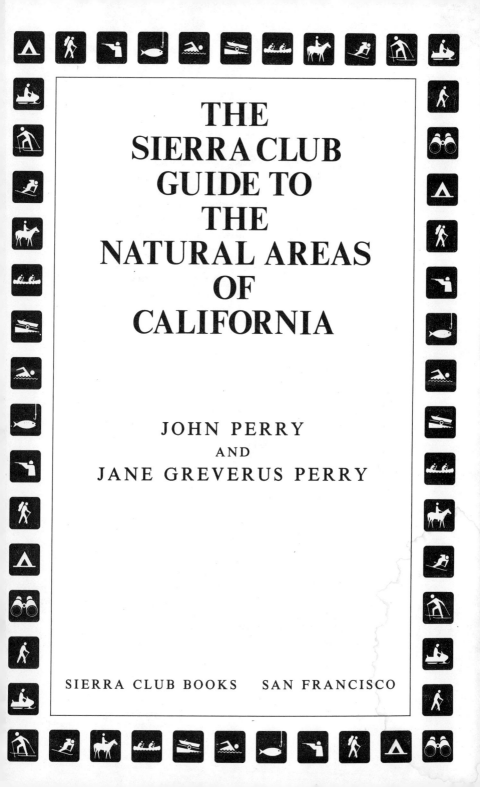

The Sierra Club, founded in 1892 by John Muir, has devoted itself to the study and protection of the earth's scenic and ecological resources—mountains, wetlands, woodlands, wild shores and rivers, deserts and plains. The publishing program of the Sierra Club offers books to the public as a nonprofit educational service in the hope that they may enlarge the public's understanding of the Club's basic concerns. The point of view expressed in each book, however, does not necessarily represent that of the Club. The Sierra Club has some sixty chapters coast to coast, in Canada, Hawaii, and Alaska. For information about how you may participate in its programs to preserve wilderness and the quality of life, please address inquiries to Sierra Club, 730 Polk Street, San Francisco, CA 94109.

Library of Congress Cataloging in Publication Data

Perry, John, 1914–
The Sierra Club guide to the natural areas of
California.

Includes bibliographical references and index.
1. Outdoor recreation—California—Guide-books.
2. Natural history—California. 3. Natural areas—
California—Guide-books. 4. California—Description
and travel—1981–   —Guide-books. I. Perry, Jane
Greverus. II. Title.
GV191.42.C2P47 1983   917.94   82-16936
ISBN 0-87156-333-9

Cover design by Gael Towey

Book design concept by Lilly Langotsky

Illustrations by Nancy Warner

Printed in the United States of America on acid-free paper
containing a minimum of 50% recovered waste paper, of which
at least 10% of the fiber content is post-consumer waste
20 19 18 17 16 15 14 13 12 11

TO THE RANGERS,
FORESTERS, NATURALISTS,
WILDLIFE BIOLOGISTS,
AND OTHER MEN AND WOMEN
WHO CARE FOR OUR FORESTS,
PARKS, AND PRESERVES

CONTENTS

The Natural Areas of California

ZONES OF CALIFORNIA

Del Norte
Siskiyou
Modoc
Humboldt
Trinity
Shasta
Lassen
①
②
Tehama
Plumas
Mendocino
Glenn
Butte
Sierra
Colusa
Nevada
Sutter
Yuba
④
Placer
Lake
Amador
Sonoma
Yolo
El Dorado
Alpine
③
Napa
Calaveras
Marin
Sol-ano
⑥
Sacramento
San Joaquin
Mono
San Francisco
Tuolumne
Contra Costa
Stani-slaus
Mari-posa
Alameda
Santa Clara
Inyo
San Mateo
Merced
Santa Cruz
⑤
Madera
San Benito
Fresno
Tulare
⑦
Monterey
Kings
San Luis Obispo
Kern
San Bernardino
⑧
Santa Barbara
Los Angeles
⑨
Ventura
Riverside
Orange
San Diego
Imperial

N

0 20 40 60 80 100
scale   miles

INTRODUCTION

This is a guide to California's quiet places, where plants grow, birds sing, and the signs of man are few.

Western friends warned that the quiet places have been overrun. One must make reservations weeks ahead to enter a wilderness. Beach parking is full by midmorning. Noisy off-road vehicles have driven off wildlife and hikers.

The western landscape has been much changed since we first saw it 50 years ago. Many hillsides have been stripped of timber, tundra trails beaten into muddy ditches by many boots, deserts permanently scarred by vehicle tracks.

Yet we had no difficulty finding quiet places. In the last phase of our research, we traveled 8,000 miles, camping every night. On most nights we were alone or with few neighbors. When we were too late for a backcountry permit at Yosemite, we found a lightly used trail in the nearby National Forest.

People congregate. Most seem to prefer the developed recreation sites, the publicized trails. Most come at certain seasons. Those who seek solitude can find it, often nearby. We camped alone in a vast marsh less than an hour's drive from a major city.

In the East, less than 10% of the land is publicly owned. Almost half of California remains in federal ownership, and the state has extensive landholdings. Most of these public lands are in the mountains and deserts, although California has kept much of its seacoast in public ownership.

Almost every description of California begins by remarking on its contrasts and extremes. The highest point in the conterminous United States is 14,495-ft. Mt. Whitney. The lowest point, in Death Valley, is only 85 miles distant. Temperatures have ranged between −45°F and +134° F. A desert rain gauge has recorded zero for a full year; one in a rain forest accumulated 161 in. One can ski in the mountains and swim in the ocean on the same day, or lunch at Fisherman's Wharf and hike in a wilderness that afternoon.

The state is 800 mi. long, but its coastline measures 1,340 mi. The Coast Range parallels the shore from the Oregon border to just N of the Los Angeles Basin. These mountains rise abruptly from the sea or from a narrow coastal plain, not to the heights of the Sierra Nevada, although some peaks in the N exceed 8,000 ft. In the N, the Coast Range merges with the Cascade Range, forming a high, rugged area more than 200 mi. wide.

California's Cascades rise to peaks and ridges 5,000 to 10,000 ft. high, Mt. Shasta towering over them at 14,161 ft. To the SE the Cascades merge with the Sierra Nevada, the largest mountain mass in the United States, more than 400 mi. long, 60 to 80 mi. wide. Elevations increase from N to S. In the N, few peaks exceed 8,000 ft., while S of Yosemite National Park the crest is above 11,000 ft.

The Coast Range and the Sierra are separated by a broad, flat valley, from which the Sierra foothills rise gradually. The W slopes are generally moderate, cut by many rivers and streams. The high country is not a single ridge but many ridges, some paralleling the main crest, others branching away from it. This is a spectacularly rugged region of mountain meadows, glacial lakes, ice fields, and tundra flowers, deep in snow for most of the year. The E slope drops steeply.

E of Bakersfield the Sierra meets the Tehachapi Mountains, which trend SW, meeting the Coast Range and closing the S end of the Central Valley. Beyond, minor ranges extend SE to Mexico. The mountain barrier denies rainfall to the land on the E side. The SE quarter of California is a vast and fascinating desert.

The Sierra is a formidable obstacle to travel as well as to moisture. From Lake Tahoe to the S tip of the mountains, no all-year road crosses the range. Highway maps show the few transmountain roads as "Closed in Winter." Strangers may not know that "winter" in this high country may extend to the Fourth of July. Don't expect to travel these roads in April!

California has 5,000 lakes, 30,000 mi. of rivers and streams, more than 40 million acres of forest land. California also has more participants in outdoor recreation than any other state. We were told that one household in three has some kind of recreation vehicle. Unfortunately, many of them are off-road vehicles (ORV's): 1 million dirt bikes, 0.5 million 4-wheel-drives, 0.25 million dune buggies. Their damage to flora, fauna, and artifacts is widespread and increasing. Control efforts are opposed by a vociferous, well-financed lobby.

Even wilderness areas are crowded in California, we were told. So many fragile places have been trampled that access to some areas is now rationed. More and more campgrounds are now "reservation only."

All true, but, wherever we traveled, we found the quiet places.

HOW WE SELECTED SITES

We use the term "natural area" broadly, generically. A few specialists have objected. They have appropriated the term and devised narrow definitions. "Federal Research Natural Areas," for example, are "lands on which various natural features are preserved in an undisturbed state solely for research and educational purposes."

We look for places where a visitor can enjoy nature. Most such places are not pristine. Some have been logged, farmed, mined, or otherwise disturbed, but the healing processes of nature are at work. Most wildlife refuges are not "natural," because their ponds and marshes are maintained by dikes and crops are planted to support waterfowl. Without such places few waterfowl would travel the flyways. When tens of thousands of geese and ducks endorse these places, they're good enough for us.

Large National Forests and National Parks were automatic selections. More than 20 million acres—one-fifth of California—is in 17 National Forests. Sites administered by the National Park Service total almost 4.5 million acres, National Wildlife Refuges another 0.25 million.

The State has many splendid sites and is acquiring more. The largest is 520,000-acre Anza-Borrego State Park. The Providence Mountains State Recreation Area has only 5,233 acres, but it is surrounded by a sweeping landscape of public lands, and no boundaries are visible.

California has been more determined than most states to maintain public ownership of and access to its ocean beaches, despite pressures for commercial development. Near cities and resorts, beaches are often unpleasantly crowded. But the Coast still has fine, unspoiled areas. The largest, wildest, and most remote is the King Range in zone 1.

We studied smaller sites more critically. We did not include a state park planned for intensive recreation unless, in addition to a developed area, it has a few hundred roadless acres of interest to hikers and birders.

In studying a small site, we considered its setting. A small seaside park may provide access to a dozen miles of uncluttered ocean beach. A park with little more than a campground may be a wilderness trailhead. A site that is intolerably crowded on the Fourth of July may offer splendid solitude in December.

THE PUBLIC DOMAIN

When we had screened every National Park, National Forest, and National Wildlife Refuge, we had 16.5 million acres of federal land left over, what remains of the original public domain: one-sixth of California. It sprawls over the landscape, sometimes in huge, solid blocks, sometimes in a checkerboard of 1-mi. squares, alternating with state and private land. It includes mountains, plains, canyons, rivers, lakes, and wetlands, but most of it is in the California Desert.

Its boundaries are not marked. It is not divided into neat packages, such as parks and forests. We looked for outstanding features, such as a mountain or canyon, then studied the surrounding area. Finally, we fixed arbitrary boundaries enclosing areas that seemed to fit together.

The U.S. Bureau of Land Management, which manages the public domain, was then engaged in a prodigious task mandated by Congress: identifying each roadless area of 5,000 or more acres, then gathering data to judge its suitability for wilderness status. This data and other documents in BLM District files were invaluable to us, as were our many talks with BLM specialists. We knew where to look when our field work began.

Our entries for BLM sites have local names and unmarked boundaries. The visitor will find no signs, no gates, and—except at a few recreation sites—no facilities. Only by chance will a BLM staff member be present. It is almost as unlikely that he or she will encounter other visitors.

These tens of millions of acres are yours to enjoy. Here you can drive, hike, backpack, ride horseback, and camp almost anywhere, hunt and fish subject to state laws. Except in a few developed recreation areas, you are unlikely to meet other visitors.

Much of this land has been leased, usually for grazing, and some of it fenced by cattle ranchers. This does not shut you out. Where public land is fenced and gated, you have the right to enter—and close the gate behind you.

How do you know you are on public land? In some areas, private and public lands are intermixed. Our entries are for areas with few private inholdings. If you have doubts or concerns, visit the BLM District Office.

What if a rancher tells you to get off his place? Go quietly. You could have strayed onto private land. But some ranchers have used the public land for so long they consider it their own. Perhaps previous visitors have misbehaved. However, such confrontations are rare even on private land. Should you have one, the BLM office would like to know about it.

OTHER PUBLIC LANDS

We reluctantly decided to omit county and regional parks. We had spent two days visiting and admiring units of the East Bay Regional Park District, across from San Francisco, and visited several parks in the Riverside and San Bernardino county systems. Several of these would be included were they state parks.

Inquiries convinced us that gathering data from 58 counties would be impossible. Few could supply the data we need. Some, we were told, would refuse our request, holding that their parks are for local taxpayers, not outsiders. At best, a prodigious task would have a small yield.

We have included no military reservations. Some of these are large, and many permit limited public use. However, the limits are usually strict, and they often change from day to day. The base nearest our home has a special number to call in order to hear whether visitors are permitted today. Most public use of these reservations is by hunters and fishermen, but if there is one near you, inquire. Some reservations have naturalists or wildlife managers who can tell you what's there and who may even offer a guided tour.

PRIVATE LANDS

Some of the largest private holdings are those of timber companies. In the past some companies permitted or invited public use. We wrote to the largest and asked if this is still the case. Only two replied. Both asked that we not mention their lands. Neither answered our question.

Off the record, company officials said, "We allow public use, but we don't want publicity. If many more people come, we'll have to close the gates. And we must be able to close them at any time, without notice, for operating reasons."

A state wildlife official confirmed this. Most timber company lands are used by hunters and fishermen, he said, and sometimes by hikers. Some owners require permits. A few charge fees. He advised prospective visitors to inquire at the nearest federal or state forestry office. Our advice: Forget it, unless you have a special interest in an area.

The Nature Conservancy
Western Regional Office
425 Bush St.
San Francisco, CA 94108
(415) 989-3056

The Conservancy is a national nonprofit organization devoted solely to the acquisition and management of ecologically significant land. It has helped preserve over 2 million acres of such land.

TNC preserves are, for the most part, small and fragile. Few have full-time managers, and visitors are asked to write or call for permission. We met with TNC staff members and agreed that only the Coast Range Preserve (California zone 1) should be an entry.

HOW TO USE THIS BOOK

We divided the state into zones. Zone boundaries generally follow county lines. A map showing these zones appears on page ix. An alphabetical list of the sites appears in the index.

At the beginning of each zone section is a zone map on which sites are spotted, with key numbers. Sites are listed in numerical order.

- If you plan to visit an area, find the corresponding zone and see what other sites in the zone would interest you.
- If you plan to visit—say—a National Park, locate its key number on the zone map and see what other sites are nearby.
- Entries are arranged alphabetically within zones.
- Information in entries is presented in a standard sequence.

SITE NAMES

Parks are for people. Most parks have formal entrances. Most parks are closed to logging and hunting. Most parks have developed recreation sites. Parks have more facilities, more supervision, more rules, and more visitors than forests or refuges.

Forests are for trees and water. National Forests are managed for wood, water, wildlife, and recreation, although critics charge imbalance. Timber is often harvested on the more humid western slopes, vegetation maintained in semiarid areas. Hunting and fishing on National Forests are governed by state law. Recreation has a high priority in many National Forests. Although there are campgrounds, one can make camp almost anywhere.

Wildlife management areas, state operated, are for birds and beasts, fishes included. In the past, most visits were by hunters and fishermen, whose license fees supported the state system. Now visits by "nonconsumptive users," such as hikers and birdwatchers, are welcomed, especially outside hunting season.

National Wildlife Refuges are also for birds and beasts, but many have visitor facilities: auto tour routes, exhibits, information centers. Hunting is usually permitted, though often restricted to certain parts of the refuge and with special rules.

Public domain lands, managed by the BLM, have many uses, including grazing, mining, forestry, and geothermal development. Most areas are open to public use. Large areas are far from any paved roads, and access often requires 4-wheel drive or a sturdy pickup truck. In the many roadless areas, travel is by foot or horseback. Most BLM lands are arid or semiarid.

ADMINISTERING AGENCY

Entries name the agencies with management responsibility, not parent departments.

ACREAGE

Many National Forests and some other sites have "inholdings," privately owned land within their boundaries. If these are significant, the entry gives both the acreage within the boundaries and the acreage of publicly owned land.

HOW TO GET THERE

Routings begin from points easily found on ordinary highway maps. For large sites, the route is one most visitors use.

OPEN HOURS

Most National Parks are open 24 hours. Many State Parks are closed at night, though campers may be able to leave or enter. National Wildlife Refuges and many state wildlife management areas are closed at night. Forests don't have gates.

SYMBOLS

Symbols tell at a glance if a site offers camping, swimming, etc. Most symbols have obvious meanings:

 Without the pack, this means "hiking," with it, "backpacking." The entry for a small site carries the backpacking symbol if it serves as trailhead.

 In addition to canoeable waters, this symbol is also used for white water requiring rafts.

 Used for ski touring, usually includes snowshoeing.

 We used this sightseeing symbol in our *Guide to the Natural Areas of the Eastern United States* to indicate places of special scenic value. It doesn't appear here because of its wide application in the west. Almost every natural area is worth seeing.

In many cases, the symbols correspond to items in the "Activities" part of the entry. If there is no useful information to report, the symbol stands alone.

DESCRIPTION

Each site is briefly characterized: terrain, main physical features, climate, vegetation, wildlife. Subheads such as *"Plants"* and *"Birds"* do not appear in all entries, usually because no one has studied these areas.

Even if complete flora and fauna lists were available, reproducing them would require a library, rather than a volume. Using whatever data we could gather, we have made selections of species, attempting to characterize the principal plant and animal communities. In some cases this has seemed best achieved by listing the most common species. In others it seemed useful to mention rarities.

Comprehensive mammal lists were less often available than bird lists. Information on reptiles and amphibians was scarce.

In entries, the singular is used to signify single species. Plurals signify more than one species. Example: ". . . mountain bluebird, woodpeckers . . ."

Note: Authorities often decree changes in common names. "Myrtle warbler" and "Audubon's warbler" have become "yellow-rumped warbler." But "Traill's flycatcher" has been split into "willow flycatcher" and "alder flycatcher." Most species checklists supplied to us include some of the old names. Our purpose has been to use the names most readers now use.

FEATURES

Noted first are wilderness areas, primitive areas, and other large and note-worthy portions of sites.

For several years all federal land-managing agencies have, at the direction of Congress, been identifying and studying roadless areas of 5,000 or more acres and recommending those that meet the criteria for wilderness designation. Final designation is by Congress. Wilderness areas are closed to virtually all entry except by visitors on foot or horseback.

We gathered our data while this process was going on, and while Secretary of the Interior Watt was proposing some highly controversial curtailments in the wilderness scheme. Although the decision by Congress determines the future of an area, it does not transform it. Thus we have not been limited by pending Congressional decisions but have based our choices on what sites are today.

This portion of entries also mentions other noteworthy site features, such as waterfalls, canyons, major rivers, and caverns. It also mentions the principal recreation sites.

Because our concern is with natural areas, we give little or no attention to forts and other historical features.

INTERPRETATION

Here we note visitor centers, museums, nature trails, campfire programs, guided hikes, and other naturalist programs.

ACTIVITIES

Camping: Entries note numbers of sites, seasons of operation, and whether reservations are required. (Reservation requirements and systems change from year to year.)

Camping in parks is limited to campgrounds.

One can camp almost anywhere in National Forests. Along some heavily traveled routes, camping is restricted to campgrounds. In some Forest areas, camping is prohibited during periods of high fire danger.

One can camp almost anywhere on the public domain.

Most National Wildlife Refuges prohibit camping. Some state wildlife areas permit it. In some cases, hunters are allowed to park RV's overnight in parking areas.

Can one "camp"—park an RV overnight—in highway rest stops or roadside pullouts? In California, no.

Hiking, backpacking: The backpacking symbol is used where hiking with trailside camping is permitted and attractive. It is used for some small sites that serve as trailheads.

Trails in parks are more likely to be marked and maintained than trails in forests, although many National Forests have extensive trail systems. In California, many National Parks and Forests have connecting trails.

Over most of the public domain, you're on your own, although there are numerous unmapped trails and tracks.

If you plan a backcountry trip, visit the nearest Ranger Station or BLM

District Office for useful advice on routes, trail conditions, and whether many hikers are on the trail. You may be shown trail maps, even photographs of your destination.

We haven't tried to list all available trail guides. More appear each year, and many are available only locally.

The hiking season in the high country is short. Trails may be blocked by snow into July, and new snow may fall in October. Trail maintenance can't be performed until soil is reasonably dry, so expect problems if you follow the melt too closely. Streams one can ford later may be dangerous torrents during the runoff.

Some western hikers scorn all but the high country—and thus spend most of the year indoors. One can find delightful trails in any season. Spring and fall are the best times on the lower slopes and in the green valleys. Beach hiking can be good in any season.

Hunting: Except for the parks, portions of some wildlife refuges, and recreation areas, public lands are generally open to hunting. State regulations apply everywhere, as do federal regulations on migratory species. Wildlife management areas often have special rules limiting the number of hunters or permitting hunting only on certain days.

Fishing: Entries report whether fishing is possible and name the principal species. In some National Parks, stocking has been discontinued, in keeping with the policy of maintaining near-natural conditions.

Swimming: We report what we were told. Swimming from many Pacific beaches is said to be cold, rough, and dangerous. In some State Parks, swimming is permitted only when lifeguards are present. Responses from forests and BLM sites often failed to mention swimming even though lakes and rivers are present. Management is permissive: Swim where you wish, at your own risk.

Boating: The symbol is not used for bodies of water smaller than 100 acres.

Canoeing, kayaking, drift boating, rafting: It seemed impractical to have symbols for each, although each is the choice for certain streams. Usually the text makes the distinction.

Horse riding: The symbol is used where pack trips and other trail riding were reported. Horses can be ridden in many other places: on any suitable trail in a National Forest, for example, or anywhere on BLM land. If horse rentals were said to be available, this is noted in text, but the reader is warned that such enterprises come and go.

Skiing: Downhill ski areas are mentioned when they are on public land. Many ski areas are operated by concessioners.

Ski touring: Usually one can ski crosscountry wherever there's enough snow. We note where this was reported as a popular activity.

Snowmobiling: Noted where reported. Many National and State Parks restrict or prohibit snowmobiles. They are banned in wilderness areas.

RULES AND REGULATIONS

All sites have them. Parks have the most.

Pets: In parks, the general rule is that pets must be leashed. They are often prohibited on trails and beaches and in buildings. California requires proof of rabies vaccination, and pets must be confined to a tent or vehicle at night. A fee is charged for each dog.

Refuges and wildlife areas generally require that dogs be leashed, except while used in hunting.

Some sites ban pets altogether, and entries note this.

CAUTIONS

Some site managers thought you should be warned—about ocean currents, summer thunderstorms, rattlesnakes. We report their warnings. But keep in mind that other managers didn't mention similar hazards.

PUBLICATIONS

Entries list publications issued by sites or about sites. If a site has a descriptive leaflet, you may be able to have it sent to you, but fewer and fewer sites have sufficient manpower to respond to such requests. Most leaflets, species checklists, nature trail guides, etc., are available only on site.

California's State Parks now charge for leaflets, except where old leaflets are still in stock. We paid 25 cents for most, 50 cents for a few.

National Forests will send maps by mail. In 1981 the price was increased to $1.

"Checklist available" usually means copies can be obtained. Not always. At some sites we found supplies exhausted but were allowed to study file copies.

REFERENCES

These are publications pertaining to a site offered by commercial publishers or natural history associations.

WHAT'S NOT IN THE ENTRIES

Entries do not include information about:

Picnic grounds. One can picnic almost anywhere.

Campground facilities. Excellent directories are published.

Cabins, inns, lodges. We could not distinguish among lodgings on public land, lodgings on private inholdings, and lodgings just outside.

Restaurants and snack bars presented the same difficulty. Also, many close when crowds are absent.

Playgrounds, golf courses, etc.

Admission fees. Many parks charge fees. They change from year to year. Toll booths are often closed when visitors are few.

Rock climbing, rockhounding, spelunking, and scuba diving are too special-
ized for a general guide.

CHANGES

These are hard times for the public lands. For years budgets failed to keep
pace with increasing public use. Now federal and state agency budgets have
been cut, in some cases savagely. The permanent damage thus inflicted on
precious natural resources is of deep concern to us, but beyond the scope of
this book. Readers will encounter many reductions in opportunities and
services:

- Publications may be out of print. Others, once free, will be sold.
- Campfire programs, guided walks, and other interpretive programs
  may be curtailed.
- Some campgrounds may be closed, others operated for shorter
  seasons. Facilities may be reduced. Broken or vandalized equipment may not be replaced.
- Some wildlife refuges may be closed, perhaps seasonally or on
  certain days. Visitors may be restricted to smaller portions of refuges.
- Maintenance of hiking trails may be reduced.
- Snow plowing may be discontinued on some park roads.

PATHFINDING

To travel California, the first need is an ordinary highway map. The state
is so large one needs larger-scale maps to find your way locally. A fine series
of regional maps is available to members of the American Automobile Association (California State Automobile Association, 150 Van Ness Ave., San
Francisco, CA 94101; or Automobile Club of Southern California, 2601 S.
Figueroa St., Los Angeles, CA 90007.) The Los Angeles office also has 11 maps
of the southern counties.

Most surfaced roads shown on such maps are suitable for ordinary cars,
except mountain roads in winter. Map legends for other roads should be
heeded, especially "graded dirt," "dirt," and "poor or doubtful." Washouts,
mudslides, and other interruptions are common. Inquire locally about the
condition of unpaved roads, especially if you are driving an RV or towing a
trailer.

These maps do not show road networks in National Forests. Each National
Forest has its own map.

Pathfinding in the public domain can be adventurous. In the California
Desert Conservation Area are 15,000 mi. of paved and maintained roads,
21,000 mi. of unmaintained dirt roads, and 7,000 mi. of washes an ORV can
negotiate in dry weather. The best available maps, according to those who use

them, are AAA's county maps, but this set doesn't include sparsely populated Inyo and Mono counties. The Bureau of Land Management was planning a set of 22 maps covering the California desert area, but budget limitations made publication date uncertain. Inquire at a BLM office.

Backcountry travel can be hazardous. Some of the sites we describe can't be visited casually. One needs good maps, a reliable vehicle, local advice—and common sense. Especially in desert travel, two vehicles are far safer than one. If you travel alone, it's wise to drive in no further than you'd be able to walk out.

AGENCY OFFICES AND PUBLICATIONS

FEDERAL AGENCIES
U.S. Forest Service
Pacific Southwest Region
630 Sansome St.
San Francisco, CA 94111
(415) 556-0122

Publications Include:
Recreation Guide: National Forests in California
Map: National Forests in California
Wilderness on the National Forests in California
Obtaining Your Wilderness Permit
Campground reservations information
Checklist of Birds, Mammals, Fish, Reptiles, Amphibians
Present on Forest and Rangelands in California
Wintersport Recreation Areas
Stalking the Wilderness Experience
Your Wilderness Trip
The Wilderness Traveler
Wild and Scenic Rivers
Backpacking in the National Forests
Horse Sense on Backcountry Trips
Snow Avalanche
Winter Recreation Safety Guide

National Park Service
Western Regional Office
450 Golden Gate Ave.
San Francisco, CA 94102
(415) 556-4196

Publications Include:
Camping in the National Park System
Backcountry Travel in the National Park System
National Recreation Trails

U.S. Fish and Wildlife Service
Regional Office
500 N.E. Multnomah St.
Portland, OR 97232
(503) 231-6121

U.S. Bureau of Land Management
2800 Cottage Way
Sacramento, CA 95825
(916) 484-4217

Publications Include:
BLM in California
List of BLM campgrounds

STATE AGENCIES
California Department of Parks and Recreation
P.O. Box 2390
Sacramento, CA 95811
(916) 445-2358

Publications Include:
Leaflets describing each State Park were once issued free. When we visited,
a new generation of leaflets was in the making, but progress depended
on each Park's budget. Most of those that had appeared were sold for
25 cents, one or two for 50 cents. Some Parks were still handing out their
old leaflets.
Guide to the California State Park System. 50¢.
Rules and regulations.
Campground reservation information.

Note: Campground reservations are necessary for popular parks in season.
The list of Parks requiring reservations and their reservation seasons changes
from year to year. When we gathered our information, the Ticketron reservation system was in use statewide.

California Department of Fish and Game
1416 Ninth St.
Sacramento, CA 95814
(916) 445-7613

Publications Include:
  How the DFG Works
  Sport fishing regulations.
  Hunting regulations.
  Public Access Projects (list and map)
  Publications price list.

California Department of Forestry
1416 Ninth St.
Sacramento, CA 95814
(916) 445-5571

THE
SIERRA CLUB
GUIDE TO
THE
NATURAL AREAS
OF
CALIFORNIA

ZONE 1

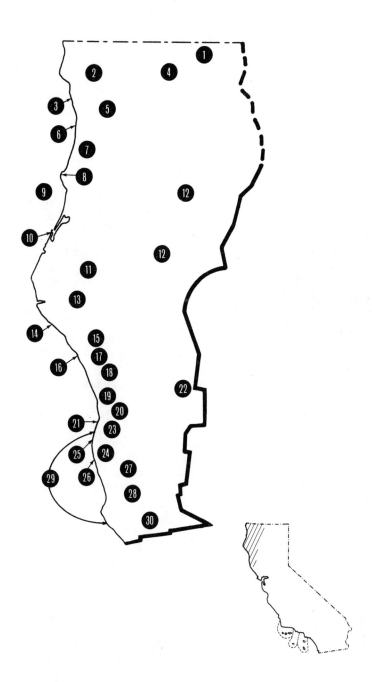

CALIFORNIA, ZONE 1

Includes these counties:

Del Norte	Humboldt	Mendocino
Siskiyou (W of I-5)	Trinity	

From Gualala N to Rockport, SR 1 is a scenic highway along a splendid coast: rocky headlands, sheer cliffs, haystack islands, sheltered coves, long sand beaches backed by dunes, salt marshes, shallow bays. Through traffic uses US 101 inland. The Coast Road is narrow, and it can be congested on holiday weekends, but much of the time driving can be relaxed and delightful. It's a trip to make without haste, for there are many places to stop for views of the Coast, a stroll along the headlands, or a hike up a moist canyon. Several State Parks are along the way. Points of interest include ancient marine terraces, a pygmy forest, groves of Coast redwoods.

Near Rockport, SR 1 turns inland, ending at its junction with US 101. For the next hundred-odd miles, the terrain was too forbidding to build a coastal road. This is California's "Lost Coast," remote, rugged, with only a few points reachable by any kind of road. Don't rely on your ordinary highway map here. See the entries for King Range, Sinkyone Wilderness, and Humboldt County Beaches.

Groves of Coast redwoods can be seen S of San Francisco, and several fine ones lie between SR 1 and US 101 before they join. From here N, however, one is much more aware of them. Redwood parks described in entries include Standish-Hickey, Smithe, Richardson, and Humboldt, largest in this area. Humboldt Bay is worth exploring before proceeding N of Eureka. Now US 101 becomes the Coast Road, at least the road nearest to the Coast, passing a number of State Beaches before arriving at Redwood National Park and associated State Parks.

In the N part of California, the Coast and Cascade ranges merge, creating a rugged, mountainous area more than 200 mi. from W to E. From the Oregon border S, most of the mountains in zone 1 are within National Forests: Six Rivers, Klamath, Shasta-Trinity, and Mendocino.

ADMIRAL WILLIAM STANDLEY STATE RECREATION AREA
California Department of Parks and Recreation
45 acres.

From Laytonville on US 101, W on Branscomb Rd. 14 mi.

A small park on a lightly traveled road. Fine stand of Coast redwoods. Over 3,000 ft. along the South Fork of the Eel River. Elevation 1,700 ft.

COAST RANGE PRESERVE
The Nature Conservancy; U.S. Bureau of Land Management
4,000 acres each.

From US 101 at Laytonville, W on Branscomb Rd. about 18 mi. N on Wilderness Lodge Rd. to HQ.

For reasons stated in the preface, we have not included sites owned by The Nature Conservancy, although they are fine natural areas. We make an exception here because the site is large, it has a resident manager, permission to visit is easily obtained, and the TNC and BLM portions are cooperatively managed.

This was the Conservancy's first CA project, established in 1956. Only 480 of TNC's 4,000 acres had been logged when they acquired the site. On the South Fork of the free-flowing Eel River. The boundaries contain several watersheds. One, Elder Creek, is completely within the Preserve and virtually pristine. Terrain is hilly to mountainous, elevations ranging from about 1,200 to 4,209 ft. in the BLM section. The two streams above and Fox Creek have white water, cascades, and falls.

The only practical access to the BLM land, which includes the higher elevations, is through the TNC site; even this is difficult because the terrain is rugged and there are no trails. Except for the elderly and disabled, visitors may not drive into the Preserve. They park outside and hike in. The interior road is narrow and winding, not suitable for vehicles with low clearance, high tops, or dual wheels.

Plants: 85% forested. Several thousand acres of old-growth Douglas-fir, undisturbed. Understory includes madrone, tan oak, California bay laurel, Oregon white oak, black oak, hazelnut, huckleberry. Also some black oak forest, knobcone pine community, chaparral, redwood groves, and meadows. Over 450 species of flowering plants have been identified, including various orchids, monkeyflower, brodiaea.

Birds: Checklist available. 120 species recorded. In fall and winter, ripening fruits of coffeeberry, poison oak, honeysuckle, and madrone attract many band-tailed pigeon, varied thrush, cedar waxwing, purple finch. Forest species include ruby-crowned and golden-crowned kinglets, Townsend's warbler, chestnut-backed chickadee, Hutton's vireo. Golden-crowned sparrow and dark-eyed junco are among the species frequenting the meadows. The checklist notes both season abundance and favored habitats.

Mammals: Checklist of 42 species available. Often seen: river otter, bear, cottontail, skunk, squirrel. Present but seldom seen: mountain lion, mink, gray fox.

Reptiles and amphibians: Checklist is being compiled.

INTERPRETATION

Small *visitor center* has displays.
Sugar Creek Nature Trail, 1/2 mi., with printed guide.
Guided hikes are offered occasionally on weekends. Inquire.

No pets, firearms, radios, ORV's.
Reservations, made by telephone, are necessary for all visits. Heavy rain can make winter visit inadvisable. High fire danger in Aug.

PUBLICATIONS

Bird checklist. 25¢.
Mammals of the Northern California Coast Range Preserve. $1.50.
Field Guide to the Shrubs of the Northern California Coast Range Preserve. $1.50.
Field Guide to the Trees of the Northern California Coast Range Preserve. $1.50.
Nature trail guide.
Leaflet with map.
Miscellaneous natural history pages.

HEADQUARTERS: 42101 Wilderness Rd., Branscomb, CA 95417; (707) 984-6653.

DEL NORTE COAST REDWOODS STATE PARK
See Redwood National Park.

GRIZZLY CREEK REDWOODS STATE PARK
California Department of Parks and Recreation
234 acres.

35 mi. SE of Eureka. From US 101 near Alton, 18 mi. E on SR 36.

Smallest and furthest inland of the state redwood parks, seldom crowded, visited chiefly by campers. In Van Duzen River Valley, near base of the Coastal Range. Elevation 375 ft. Almost 1 mi. of river frontage.

Plants: About 85% forested. Several groves of Coast redwood, "partially virgin stands." Other tree species: Douglas-fir, lowland fir, California bay laurel, tan oak, cottonwood, bigleaf maple. Understory includes thimbleberry, huckleberry, Oregon grape, poison oak, ceanothus, salal, oxalis, ferns.

Wildlife: Although the park is small, the surroundings are sufficiently undeveloped to support populations of deer, skunk, raccoon, pine squirrel, and river otter, as well as seldom-seen bobcat, mountain lion, black bear, and porcupine.

INTERPRETATION

Visitor center has information on local wildlife.

Campfire programs 2–3 times weekly, mid-June to Labor Day.

Guided hikes in summer.

Nature trail, 3/4 mi., self-guided.

ACTIVITIES

Camping: 30 sites, all year. Reservations Apr. 27–Oct. 1.

Hiking: 3 mi. of trails, longest 1 1/4 mi.

Fishing: Stream. Salmon, steelhead, trout.

Swimming: Stream, unsupervised.

HEADQUARTERS: Star Route, Box 75, Carlotta, CA 95528; (707) 777-3683.

HENDY WOODS STATE PARK
California Department of Parks and Recreation
605 acres.

From Cloverdale on US 101, NW about 37 mi. on SR 128, then left on Greenwood Rd.

Two virgin redwood groves. Park is on N slope of Greenwood Ridge, elevation 200 ft. Navarro River runs the length of the park, quiet in summer, a torrent after heavy winter rains. N portion of SR 128 is a scenic drive.

Plants: Big Hendy (80 acres) and Little Hendy (20 acres) have enormous old-growth redwoods, up to 16 ft. diameter, over 300 ft. tall. Other species include Douglas-fir, California bay laurel.

Birds: Include Steller's jay, varied thrush, olive-sided flycatcher, pileated woodpecker, great horned owl.

INTERPRETATION
> *Campfire programs* and *guided walks* in summer.
> *Nature trail,* with leaflet, in Big Hendy Grove.

ACTIVITIES
> *Camping:* 92 sites, all year. Reservations May 1–Sept. 30.
> *Hiking:* 3 mi. of trails.
> *Fishing:* Steelhead, salmon; fall and winter.
> *Swimming:* Marginal. River is too low by late summer.

PUBLICATION: Leaflet with map.

HEADQUARTERS: c/o Mendocino Area, Department of Parks and Recreation, Star Route, Mendocino, CA 95460; (707) 937-5804.

HUMBOLDT BAY

> At Eureka. For S spit, take Hookton Rd. W from US 101, at S end of bay, to Table Bluff Rd.

The shallow bay, about 10 mi. long, is a concentration area for waterfowl and shorebirds. The S spit, about 4 1/2 mi. long, is undeveloped. From a small county park at Table Bluff, overlooking the sea, the road drops down to the spit, running behind low dunes to the jetty at the harbor entrance. Dunes are partially covered with vegetation, but strong winds drive sand over the road. Past storms have washed heavy driftwood across the road.

Portions of the area between the road and the bay are fenced and posted by private owners, but there are many points of access to the bayshore. Ownership of other bayshore land and the seaward dunes is unannounced, but the land is used as public. The "Do Not" signs that decorate so many landscapes are absent.

Boaters and fishermen congregate at the jetty.

The N spit is heavily developed with industries, airport, Coast Guard station, and other installations.

Birds: Pacific black brant, as many as 40,000 at one time, stop here in spring and fall migrations. Many wigeon, teal, pintail, loon, and other waterfowl are winter residents. The large numbers of shorebirds include dunlin, willet, turnstone, marbled godwit, least sandpiper. Seabirds include scoters, cormorants, brown pelicans.

Mammals: Numerous harbor seal. Porpoise and sea lion often seen in bay, gray whale offshore during migration.

ACTIVITIES

Camping: No campground, but (as of 1980) no posted prohibition. Tents were pitched on the beach, RV's pulled off among the dunes and at the bayshore.

Hiking, backpacking: Almost 9 mi. of beach available, from the jetty to Table Bluff and S to Eel River Wildlife Area (see note in Humboldt County Beaches entry).

Fishing: Surf and bay.

Boating: Ramp at jetty.

HUMBOLDT COUNTY BEACHES

See also King Range National Conservation Area, Humboldt Bay, Patrick's Point State Park, Redwood National Park.

SR 1 turns away from the Coast near Humboldt County's S border. The next 90 mi. N are California's "Lost Coast." Mountains rise steeply from the sea, so rugged as to discourage roadbuilding. Hillsides are forested, although some slopes have been logged or burned in recent years.

From Garberville, a steep but well-kept paved road crosses the mountains to Shelter Cove. From Dyerville, also on US 101, a longer paved road crosses the Humboldt Redwoods State Park, passes through Honeydew and Petrolia, and meets the Coast S of Cape Mendocino. Near the Cape it turns inland again, rejoining US 101 NE of Ferndale.

The beach is wilderness, with few access points. Impassable below Shelter Cove, it can be hiked N, although some points are blocked by very high tides. Much land above the high-tide mark is privately owned, although un-developed, but other sections are within the King Range National Conservation Area.

From Ferndale to Trinidad, a coastal plain extends as much as 5 mi. inland, with extensive salt marshes at Humboldt and Arcata bays.

Near Trinidad, the hills again come down to meet the sea. US 101 follows the Coast to Orick. Beyond, to the county's N boundary, the Coast is within national and state redwood parks.

INCLUDES

Eel River Wildlife Area (California Department of Fish and Game), 168 acres. S of Eureka. From US 101, Loleta exit. W on Cannibal Rd. to Crab Park; boat necessary to cross McNulty Slough. Or hike S along beach from Table Bluff (see entry for Humboldt Bay), about 2 mi.

Narrow spit of land, about 2 1/4 mi. long, between the ocean and slough, at mouth of Eel River. Dunes to 25 ft. high. Much large driftwood. Many waterfowl in season, including pintail, wigeon, teal, scaup, scoter, loon. *Hiking, hunting,* and *fishing.*

Caution: 4-wheel-drive vehicles and dune buggies can often travel the beach from Table Bluff, but abrupt dropoff on surf side, rising tides, and sand traps are hazards.

Clam Beach/Little River State Beach. About 13 mi. N of Eureka, on US 101. Marked exits from US 101 lead to a parallel service road back of the dunes. Numerous trails cross the dunes, some of which are almost 100 ft. high. Dune vegetation includes brush, scrub trees. Sea is cold; few people swim. Fishing is said to be good in Little River, and children splash in the lagoon. Beach is undeveloped but popular on warm weekends. *Hiking* and *fishing.*

Trinidad State Beach, 159 acres. At Trinidad, on US 101. Popular small park in a busy resort community, crowded with picnic parties on fine weekends. Sandy beach backed by high bluffs. Pewetole Island is close to the shore. Two short trails to scenic coves. Headlands overlook sea lion rock and puffin rookery, whale migration route. *Fishing.*

Dry Lagoon State Beach, 1,036 acres. On US 101, 31 mi. N of Eureka. 5 mi. of sand beach, including a long sand spit enclosing Dig Lagoon. Much driftwood. Agate and black jade sometimes found. Surf usually heavy. *Camping,* 30 primitive sites; *hiking,* beach trails, S toward Patrick's Point State Park, N toward Redwood Creek; *fishing,* surf and lagoon.

HUMBOLDT REDWOODS STATE PARK
California Department of Parks and Recreation
50,692 acres.

On US 101 45 mi. S of Eureka.

Largest of the redwood State Parks, and, in relation to its size, relatively underused. Most visitors see the Avenue of the Giants Parkway, a 33-mi. route paralleling US 101 along the South Fork of the Eel River. Many of the principal redwood groves, as well as campgrounds, are on or near this route. Most of the park acreage is W of US 101, crossed by a single secondary road and several trails.

Much of the forest is open and sunlit, mixed conifers and oaks. Entering a redwood grove, one is suddenly in deep shadow. The giant trees grow close together, the canopy blocking off the sun.

Elevation at the Avenue is about 150 ft. Highest point is Grasshopper Peak, 3,379 ft. Rainfall averages 64 in. per year, most of it Nov.–Apr. The river runs high and muddy until Apr.; thereafter it may be too shallow for rafts or kayaks. Snow is a rarity; winter temperatures are usually above freezing.

Park officials would like to encourage greater use of the backcountry, to relieve visitor pressure on redwood groves close to main highways.

Plants: Chief interest is the Coast redwood, many specimens over 300 ft. high, occurring both in pure stands and with other tree species such as Douglas-fir, lowland white fir, madrone, tan oak, bigleaf maple, California bay laurel. Dyerville Giant in Founder's Grove measures 362 ft. Spring flowers include dogwood, azalea, rhododendron, trillium, oxalis, fairy lantern, calypso.

Birds: Include great and snowy egrets, great blue heron, golden eagle, turkey vulture, raven, osprey, common merganser, water ouzel, Steller's jay, varied and hermit thrushes, brown creeper, rufous-sided and brown towhees, Oregon junco, pine siskin, winter wren, hermit warbler. Recent sighting of wild turkey.

Mammals: Include mule deer, bobcat, skunk, raccoon, tree and ground squirrels, ringtail, river otter, chipmunk. Cougar, mink, fisher considered probable.

Reptiles, amphibians: Mountain and common kingsnakes, Pacific rattlesnake, common garter snake, Pacific giant salamander, clouded salamander, western fence and alligator lizards, California and rough-skinned newts, redlegged and yellow-legged frogs, tree frog.

FEATURES

Rockefeller Forest, 9,000 acres, largest of the groves, includes one of the world's tallest trees.

Founder's Grove is dedicated to the early leaders of the Save-the-Redwoods League, organized in 1918.

Other groves along the Avenue of the Giants and elsewhere in the Park are named for sponsoring organizations and individuals.

The Bull Creek area, upstream, was outside the Park and had been logged. Damaging floods demonstrated that redwoods in the Park could not be saved unless the upper watershed was rehabilitated. Most of the watershed has been acquired, young redwoods planted. It is now good deer habitat.

Luke Prairie, an open, grassy ridge, has fine spring wildflowers, is a good place to look for hawks.

INTERPRETATION

Visitor center has natural history exhibits, information, publications. *Naturalist* is on site all year.

Campfire programs and *guided hikes* are offered occasionally in June, regularly July 1–Labor Day. Schedules are posted.

Nature trail at Founder's Grove.

ACTIVITIES

Camping: 3 campgrounds, at least one open all year. 247 sites. Reservations May 1–Sept. 15.

Hiking: 55 mi. of trails, most shown on park leaflet map. Grasshopper Peak trail is a 12-mi. round trip from E. Backpacking has been prohibited, but a limited trial is under consideration.

Fishing: Winter steelhead and salmon runs.

Swimming: River, unsupervised.

Horse riding: About 30 mi. of old logging and fire roads. Group horse camp.

Bicycling: On "bikecentennial" route. Hike and bike camp near Weott.

PUBLICATIONS

Leaflet with map.

Founder's Grove Nature Trail guide.

Species checklists.

Publications of Humboldt Redwoods Interpretive Association.

HEADQUARTERS: P.O. Box 100, Weott, CA 95571; (707) 946-2311.

JACKSON STATE FOREST
California Department of Forestry
50,000 acres.

Along SR 20; E of Fort Bragg on SR 1, W of Willits on US 101.

Mountainous; elevations from 200 to 1,948 ft. 90% forested: Coast redwood, Douglas-fir, tan oak, madrone, hemlock, beach and Bishop pines, red alder. Two areas of old-growth redwood. Logging has been continuous since the 1850s.

A Forest map is essential. Forest roads are not shown on highway road maps, and no signs on public roads identify the Forest land or Forest roads. The office is at Fort Bragg, not in the Forest.

Several streams, notably the South Fork of the Noyo River and North Fork of Big River.

Condition of the forest differs from area to area, because of past and current logging. However, recreation is one of the management considerations, and logging is planned to maintain scenic, wildlife, and general recreation values.

FEATURES AND INTERPRETATION

Pygmy Forest, a Registered Natural Landmark, an area of cypress and pine stunted by high soil acidity and poor drainage.

Forest Management Demonstration Trail. Two loops: 15-minute and 45-minute walks.

ACTIVITIES

Camping: 20 campgrounds, 50 sites. All year. Permit must be obtained from HQ.

Hiking: Chiefly on Forest roads and old logging roads.

Hunting: Deer.

Some Forest roads may be muddy and rutted in wet weather, unsuitable for RV's.

Pets must be leashed in campgrounds.

Crowding is probable on opening weekend of deer season, early Aug.

NEARBY: Russian Gulch State Park, Jug Handle State Reserve (see entries). Both have common boundaries with the Forest, but no formal trails link them. Also see entry for Van Damme State Park.

PUBLICATIONS

Forest leaflet with map.

Forest Management Demonstration Trail Guide.

HEADQUARTERS: 820 N. Main St., P.O. Box 1185, Fort Bragg, CA 95437; (707) 964-5674.

JEDEDIAH SMITH REDWOODS STATE PARK
See Redwood National Park.

JUG HANDLE STATE RESERVE
California Department of Parks and Recreation
1,800 acres.

From Mendocino, N about 6 mi. on SR 1.

Parking area on W side of highway, just S of bridge over Jug Handle Creek. Highway sign reads "Ecological Staircase and Beach Parking." Trail from parking lot to small, sandy beach.

Exhibit explains that the "staircase" is a series of uplifted marine terraces, each about 100 ft. above the one before. Each step has a distinctive plant community. Unusual pygmy forest appears at fourth step.

Guided hikes are usually offered on Saturday, weather permitting, beginning 10 A.M. at parking area, returning about 3 P.M. Bring lunch. Advisable to check schedule with HQ: (707) 937-5804.

Hiking: About 5 mi. of trails. Staircase trail from parking area goes underneath highway bridge. Trail map on bulletin board. Water on trail made boots a necessity.

PUBLICATION: A leaflet was said to be in production.

KING RANGE NATIONAL CONSERVATION AREA
U.S. Bureau of Land Management
54,200 acres.

From US 101 just N of Garberville, W through Redway and about 20 mi. toward Shelter Cove.

On California's "Lost Coast," where rugged topography forces the Coast Road far inland. The King Range extends about 35 mi. between the Mattole River and Whale Gulch. For most of this area, the coastal mountains rise steeply from the sea. The Coast has miles of sandy beaches, some strewn with boulders, about a dozen coves where streams flowing through canyons meet the sea, and rocky headlands where breaking waves send spray high on the cliffs.

The road just mentioned crosses the ridge to Shelter Cove, a small seaside resort community. Grades are steep, but the road is paved and well maintained. Near the crest, it meets Kings Peak Rd., running N along the ridge, and Chemise Mountain Rd. running S. Both are classed as all-weather surfaces. Neither is suitable for trailers or large RV's. Both are scenic. Two BLM campgrounds are on each of them. Just outside the site boundary the Kings Peak Rd. meets Wilder Ridge Rd., which ends at Mattole Rd. A right turn leads through Humboldt Redwoods State Park. Those who like adventures on wheels should turn left. The 45 mi. from the Humboldt Redwoods to Ferndale is a scenic route known to a few Californians who would prefer others not know about it. Mountain driving.

Highest point in the King Range area is Kings Peak, 4,087 ft. The crest is generally above 2,000 ft., numerous peaks higher than 2,500 ft. Terrain is rugged, the mountains deeply cut by drainages. On the W slopes, many short streams drop rapidly to the sea. Many cliffs, huge rock slides, talus piles. The E slopes, although also steep and rugged, are not so precipitous as the W side. Here streams drain into the Mattole River.

From Oct. to Apr., the King Range is one of the wettest places on the Pacific Coast, receiving about 100 in. of rain per year, more at higher elevations. Yet the appearance is not that of rain forest. Indeed, only three-fifths of the acreage is forested. The area has broad expanses of grass, especially in the N, and slopes covered with coastal chaparral. The vegetation is the product of thin soils, rapid runoff, and long, hot summers. Winter temperatures rarely drop below freezing. Snow sometimes falls on the higher slopes but little accumulates.

Most of the site is N of the road to Shelter Cove. Only two all-weather roads descend to the coastline. Most of the area between the sea and the upper slopes is roadless, the shoreline a true wilderness beach.

The late Congressman Clem Miller introduced the legislation to preserve this wild area, legislation that was enacted in 1970, after his untimely death. The BLM is authorized to buy most of the private inholdings if owners offer to sell or exchange. The legislation restrains conflicting uses of tracts remaining in private hands.

Plants: Forest is mixed conifers and hardwoods. Principal species are Douglas-fir, tan oak, madrone, California bay laurel. Understory includes blueblossom, manzanita, black huckleberry, poison oak, ferns. The area includes a number of old-growth Douglas-fir and a unique stand of mature sugar pine on the E slopes. We asked about a recent burn near the Shelter Cove road and learned it had covered 14,000 acres, since replanted in Douglas-fir.

Plants of the coastal grassland and chaparral include wild oats, poison oak, filaree, annual rye. Beach strand has mostly annual forbs, sand verbena. Succulents along W-flowing streams with some alder-willow.

Prominent flowering species include ceanothus, madrone, dogwood, poppy, monkeyflower, lupine.

Birds: BLM office has a bird list. Species noted include blue grouse, bandtailed pigeon, Steller's and scrub jays, kinglets, gnatcatchers, flycatchers, golden eagle, spotted owl, turkey vulture, red-tailed hawk, Oregon junco, towhees, osprey, California murre, pigeon guillemot, mountain and valley quail, brown pelican. Bald eagle on offshore rocks.

Mammals: Species recorded include Columbian black-tailed deer, raccoon, black bear, coyote, marten, weasel, ground squirrels, river otter, mink. Present but seldom seen: mountain lion, ringtail, bobcat, gray fox. Offshore: Steller sea lion, harbor seal, porpoise, gray and killer whales. Offshore rocks at Punta Gorda are a rookery for Steller sea lion and marine birds.

Reptiles and amphibians: Species include Pacific rattlesnake, gopher snake, kingsnake, Pacific giant salamander, northern rough-skinned newt, Pacific tree frog, tailed frog, speckled black salamander, Pacific mud turtle, garter snake, rubber boa, yellow-bellied racer.

ACTIVITIES

Camping: 4 campgrounds. 48 sites. Primitive. Camping elsewhere on BLM land is permitted, but suitable level sites are few.

Hiking, backpacking: Hiking the wilderness beach is one of the main attractions. The BLM recommends hiking N to S, with the prevailing winds. From Mattole River trailhead to Telegraph Creek, near Shelter Cove, is 24 mi. Several points cannot be passed at very high tides. Rattlesnakes are common in driftwood and rocky areas. Much land above the mean high-tide mark is privately owned, but BLM lands are sufficient to offer campsites. The King Crest Trail is part of a trail system in the higher country. Loop hikes of up to 34 mi. are feasible. W-slope streams are untested but probably safe to drink. Water is scarce and hard to find on the upper slopes, as are level campsites.

Hunting: Chiefly deer, bear.

Boating: Launching at Shelter Cove, one of the few protected harbors along the N CA Coast.

Some dirt roads required 4-wheel-drive vehicles. All dirt roads should be approached with caution in wet weather. Winter driving can be hazardous because of extremely high rainfall, slides, washouts, mud, occasional snow. Vehicles should be in excellent condition, as repair facilities are miles away.

NEARBY: Sinkyone Wilderness (see entry).

PUBLICATION: Map. $1.50.

HEADQUARTERS: BLM, Ukiah District Office, P.O. Box 940, Ukiah, CA 95482; (707) 462-3873.

KLAMATH NATIONAL FOREST
U.S. Forest Service
1,671,053 acres; 1,891,724 acres within boundaries. (Additional 26,564 acres in OR.)

From the OR border S, occupying most of Siskiyou County W of I-5. Another large section is E of Yreka on US 97.

Part of a huge complex of National Forests and other public lands covering much of N CA. The Klamath Forest is mountainous, within the Coast Range system. It includes portions of the Klamath, Salmon, Siskiyou, Marble, and Scott ranges. It adjoins the Shasta-Trinity National Forest on the S, Modoc National Forest on the E, Six Rivers National Forest on the W, and two OR National Forests, Rogue River and Siskiyou, on the N.

Elevations range from about 600 ft. to over 8,500 ft. The mountain ranges are generally narrow ridges, 5,000 to 8,000 ft. high, separated by deep canyons with steep walls. Principal rivers are the Klamath, Scott, and Salmon, swift streams flowing through rugged canyons and mountain valleys. The Forest has many lesser streams and small, clear lakes.

Climate is generally moderate. Below-freezing temperatures are common in winter, especially at higher altitudes. Snowfall in the valleys is usually light. Some of the high passes have snow from early Nov. to mid-May, but roads are usually kept open. June–Oct. weather is usually fine: bright, warm days and cool nights.

The Forest's Public Information Officer told us: "The Forest is too remote for many people except the hard-core backpacker and camper . . . the visitors seeking peace, quiet, and remoteness."

Plants: The complex terrain produces a mosaic of life zones. Principal timber trees are the ponderosa, sugar, western white, and Jeffrey pines; Douglas-fir; white and red firs; incense cedar, lodgepole pine, Port Orford cedar. Other tree species include vine, dwarf, and bigleaf maples; live, Oregon white, and California black oaks; box, red, and white alders; Brewer and Engelmann spruces. Other plant species range from sagebrushes of dry slopes to ferns and mosses of moist canyons. A 33-pp. checklist of plant species is available.

Birds: 284 species identified. Include such waterfowl as western, horned, eared, red-necked, and pied-billed grebes; whistling swan; Canada, white-fronted, Ross's, and snow geese; wigeon, shoveler; blue-winged, green-winged, and cinnamon teals; wood duck, redhead, canvasback, bufflehead; greater and lesser scaups; common, red-breasted, and hooded mergansers. Birds of prey include bald and golden eagles; Cooper's, sharp-shinned, marsh, rough-legged, ferruginous, red-tailed, red-shouldered, and Swainson's hawks; many shorebird species. Broad-tailed, calliope, Anna's, Allen's, rufous, and black-chinned hummingbirds. Many woodpeckers, sapsuckers, swallows, flycatchers, swallows, jays, chickadees, nuthatches, thrushes, blackbirds, orioles, sparrows, wood warblers.

Mammals: Checklist of 98 species includes elk, mule deer, mountain lion, bobcat, black bear, wolverine, coyote, red and gray foxes, otter, mink, marten, fisher, numerous shrews, moles, bats, squirrels, gophers, mice, voles, etc.

FEATURES

Marble Mountain Wilderness Area, 213,363 acres plus proposed additions, is almost entirely forested. Trails have moderate grades; foot travel is relatively easy. Abundant wildlife. Fishing said to be excellent. Fine displays of alpine flowers.

Red Butte roadless area. This proposed wilderness includes 25,900 acres straddling the Siskiyou Mountains at the N end of the Forest and the SW corner of the Rogue River National Forest. Terrain is highly dissected, steep slopes, scenic.

Salmon-Trinity Alps Primitive Area is shared with Shasta-Trinity National Forest and is described in that entry.

ACTIVITIES

Camping: 28 campgrounds, 419 sites. Only 2 open all year. Others open May 10, June 10, one as late as July 9. Most campgrounds are along SR 96, SR 93, Scott River Road.

Hiking, backpacking: Many miles of trails and unimproved roads. Pacific Crest Trail through the Forest was to be completed in 1980. High trails normally snow-free by July 1, but this varies from June 1 to Aug. 1.

Hunting: Principally deer, bear, small game.

Fishing: Klamath is best known as fishing country. Salmon and steelhead in the principal rivers fall and winter, rainbow trout in summer. Many smaller trout streams.

Swimming: River swimming at several campgrounds.

Canoeing, kayaking, rafting: Klamath River. Class 3 water from Ash Creek bridge to Beaver Creek; class 2 to confluence of Scott River; class 3 to Happy Camp, except class 4 at points near Hamburg and Fort Goff. Careful trip planning recommended.

Horse riding: HQ can supply the names of outfitter-guides. Some trails may be too wet for horse travel until Aug.

PUBLICATIONS

Forest map.
Marble Mountain Wilderness map.
General Information.
Campground information.
Camping on the Klamath.
Packers' List for Outfitter-Guides.
Klamath Boating and Rafting Guide.
Available from California Department of Fish and Game:
 Anglers' Guide to the Lakes and Streams of the Marble Mountains.
 Anglers' Guide to the Lakes and Streams of the Salmon and Scott Mountains.
 Anglers' Guide to the Klamath River.

REFERENCES

Green, David. *Marble Mountain Wilderness.* Berkeley, CA: Wilderness Press, 1980.
Forest HQ wrote that *Hiking Trails on the Klamath* is available in shops catering to backpackers. Author and publisher not given.

HEADQUARTERS: 1312 Fairlane Rd., Yreka, CA 96097; (916) 842-6131.

RANGER DISTRICTS: Oak Knoll R.D., Klamath River, CA 96050; (916) 465-2241. Happy Camp R.D., Happy Camp, CA 96039; (916) 493-2243. Salmon River R.D., Sawyers Bar, CA 96027; Sawyers Bar 4600. Scott

River R.D., Fort Jones, CA 96032; (916) 468-5351. Goosenest R.D., Star
Route 3, Box 175, Weed, CA 96094; (916) 398-4391 or 4343. Ukonom
R.D., Somes Bar, CA 95568; (916) 469-3331.

MACKERRICHER STATE PARK
California Department of Parks and Recreation
1,135 acres.

On SR 1, 3 mi. N of Fort Bragg.

Seacoast. 7 mi. of varied ocean frontage: some sheer cliffs, rocky areas, broad
sandy beaches, small islands close to shore. Highest point about 50 ft. Many
tidepools. Several mi. of sand dunes N of the developed area, reached by
hiking along beach.

Coastal prairie along the headlands. 25-acre Lake Cleone is within the
developed area. About 20% of the site, on higher ground, is forested.

Plants: Great variety of wildflowers in season, including sea rocket, yellow
sand verbena, baby blue eyes, ice plant, sea pink, cinquefoil, California poppy,
paintbrush, wallflower, iris, buttercup. (Wildflower checklist in preparation.)
Forest species include Bishop, beach, and Monterey pines; tan oak; wax
myrtle. Understory includes salal, thimbleberry, huckleberry, blackberry.

Birds: Park is not on a main flyway, but about a hundred species recorded.
Migratory sea- and shorebirds, many visiting Lake Cleone. Upland species
include valley quail, scrub and Steller's jays, osprey, white-tailed kite, red-
shafted flicker, mountain bluebird, kingfisher, Wilson's and Audubon's warblers.

Mammals: Harbor seal live on the rocks just offshore, not far from the Seal
Watching Station on the headland. Gray whale seen during migration. Deer,
raccoon, spotted and striped skunks, weasel, mink, gray fox, jackrabbit, chipmunk, gray and ground squirrels.

Tidepools: Great variety of marine fauna and flora, including sea and brittle
stars, sea anemone, sea urchin, hermit crab, turban snail, limpet, chiton,
abalone, periwinkle, mussel, kelp crab.

INTERPRETATION
Scenic drive: Georgia-Pacific haul road along 7 mi. of beach and dunes is
open to public weekends and holidays.

Nature trail around Lake Cleone, half of it usually under water in winter,
early spring.

Campfire programs weekly in summer. *Guided hikes* and *tidepool walks* once or twice a week in summer. Notices posted.

ACTIVITIES

Camping: 14 sites. Reservations May 1–Sept. 30.
Hiking: Beach and headlands.
Fishing: Surf. Lake stocked with trout.
Horse riding: Trail along beach. But horses may not be kept in the park.

Crowding: Campground usually full from end of school to mid-Sept.
Caution: High winds can cause tree hazards. Portions of campground may be closed during high winds, most common winter and spring.

PUBLICATION: Leaflet with map.

HEADQUARTERS: c/o Department of Parks and Recreation, Mendocino Area, P.O. Box 440, Mendocino, CA 95460; (707) 937-5804 or 964-9112.

MAILLIARD REDWOODS STATE RESERVE
California Department of Parks and Recreation
242 acres.

From Cloverdale on US 101, 20 mi. NW on SR 128; left on Fish Rock Rd.

200-acre grove of Coast redwoods. Forested site crossed by creek that is source of Garcia River.

NEARBY: Hendy Woods State Park (see entry), another small park with redwood groves, and Paul M. Dimmick Wayside Campground, which has large second-growth redwoods, are also along this route from Cloverdale to the Coast.

MENDOCINO COUNTY BEACHES
See also entries for Van Damme State Park, Russian Gulch State Park, MacKerricher State Park.

From the county's S boundary, SR 1 closely follows the Coast. Most through traffic uses US 101, further inland, leaving the coastal route to those with time to enjoy its spectacular views of the sea.

For much of the distance, headlands rise abruptly from the shore. Sandy beaches are isolated between rocky points. Back of the headlands is a plateau, often quite narrow, usually grassy, occasionally wooded, hills rising to the E. At times a fringe of trees forms a screen between the road and the sea, but soon the road is again near the edge. Close to shore are many small islands that attract seals, sea lions, and seabirds.

Large sections of the plateau are privately owned and posted against tres-
passing. Although there are available routes to many beaches, the scalloped
shoreline limits hiking; rocky points are effective barriers. A few beaches are
more extensive, offering opportunities to hike for several miles. In several
places, headlands are replaced by sand dunes.

Coastal hillside forests include such species as Bishop pine, madrone, and
Coast live oak. River canyons are moister; here are Coast redwood with dense
growths of ferns and mosses.

INCLUDES

Gualala Point Regional Park, 150 acres. 1 mi. S of Gualala on SR 1. Sand
spit at mouth of Gualala River. *Camping,* 18 sites.

Manchester State Beach, 760 acres. Central area, including campground:
from Manchester, 1 mi. N on SR 1, then W on Kinney Lane. Dunes area: about
1 mi. S of Manchester, then W on Stonesboro Road. Alder Creek area: about
2 mi. N of Manchester, then NW on Alder Creek Road. *Camping, fishing,
swimming, boating.*

3 1/2 mi. of sand beach. Much driftwood. Sand dunes, stabilized by plants,
slowly evolving into prairie grassland. Spring wildflowers include sea pinks,
poppies, lupines, baby blue eyes, wild iris. Central portion is popular picnic
area, often crowded on weekends. *Camping,* 46 sites; *hiking; fishing.*

Mendocino Headlands State Park, 131 acres. Coast, at town of Mendocino.
Wave action has cut deeply into the headlands, forming caves, arches, and
small islands separated from the mainland and each other by narrow channels. Waves pile high in these channels, breaking over the lower islands,
sending white water high on the cliffs. Prairie back of the headlands is
trampled in places, elsewhere has abundant wildflowers. Sweeping vistas up
and down the Coast. Essentially a town park, but scenic, a pleasant place to
walk a mile or so. *Hiking* and *fishing.*

Westport-Union Landing State Beach, 41 acres. 1 1/2 mi. N of Westport on
SR 1. About 2 1/2 mi. of moderately rugged coast. Long roadside parking
area, an extended overlook. No facilities. At the time of our visit (1980), no
sign identified this as state land. No signs prohibited roadside camping, and
several RV's had parked overnight. *Fishing.*

MENDOCINO NATIONAL FOREST
U.S. Forest Service

About 170,000 acres of this Forest are in zone 1. The entry appears in zone
3, where most of the Forest is located. The zone 1 portion is on the W slope
of the Coast Range, chiefly in Mendocino County, crossed by a secondary
road E from Covelo.

MONTGOMERY WOODS STATE RESERVE
California Department of Parks and Recreation
1,142 acres.

From Ukiah on US 101, about 11 mi. NW on Comptche Rd.

On Big River headwaters. One of the finest groves of Coast redwoods. No development except trails. An exceptional display of woodwardia ferns, 7–8 ft. tall. Road continues 34 mi. to Van Damme State Park (see entry).

PATRICK'S POINT STATE PARK
California Department of Parks and Recreation
443 acres.

25 mi. N of Eureka on US 101.

Headland of forest and meadow with broad, sandy beach jutting into the sea. Main portion is up to 200 ft. above the sea. Steep bluffs, constantly eroded by sea, rain, wind. Agate Beach, reached by short, steep trail, extends 2 mi. N. Semiprecious stones often found. Much driftwood. To S are steep, craggy inlets, rugged promontories. Steep trails down the cliffs.

Temperatures moderate all year, but ocean too cold for swimming.

Plants: Forest of spruce, hemlock, pine, fir, red alder. Dense understory of salal, huckleberry, blackberry, azalea, rhododendron.

Birds: Include Steller's jay, Wilson's warbler, chestnut-backed chickadee, wrentit, many shorebirds.

Mammals: Include sea lions on islands close inshore, mule deer. Whale often seen during migration.

FEATURES AND INTERPRETATION

Ceremonial Rock, viewpoint, 100-ft. climb from meadow. Trails to promontories: *Wedding Rock, Rocky Point, Abalone Point, Palmer Point.*

Museum has rocks, semiprecious stones, Indian artifacts. *Naturalist programs,* mid-June through Labor Day. *Nature trail.*

ACTIVITIES

Camping: 3 campgrounds, 123 sites. All year. Reservations May 25–Oct. 1.

Hiking: 2-mi. Rim Trail. Forest trails. Agate Beach.

PUBLICATION: Leaflet with map.

HEADQUARTERS: Trinidad, CA 95570; (707) 677-3570.

PRAIRIE CREEK REDWOODS STATE PARK
See Redwood National Park.

REDWOOD NATIONAL PARK
U.S. National Park Service

JEDEDIAH SMITH REDWOODS STATE PARK

PRAIRIE CREEK REDWOODS STATE PARK

DEL NORTE COAST REDWOODS STATE PARK
California Department of Parks and Recreation

106,562 acres.

US 101 between Orick and Crescent City.

These four redwoods parks are contiguous. The State Parks are separately managed, but the federal and state agencies cooperate. For example, a single leaflet describes all four units. (Transfer of ownership or management of the state units to the National Park Service has been discussed, but it seemed to be a remote possibility when we visited.)

The great Coast redwoods once covered about 2,000,000 acres. Less than 135,000 acres of original growth remain. The Save-the-Redwoods League, organized in 1918, has raised over $25 million to purchase redwood forestland, now in these and 28 other State Parks. About 75,000 acres of redwoods have thus been preserved. The 60,000 acres still in private ownership are being logged at close to 10,000 acres per year.

The park area is long and narrow with about 30 mi. of coastline. Rolling hills and coastal bluffs. Some sandy beaches, others rocky and inaccessible. Numerous streams, including Redwood Creek, Prairie Creek, Smith River. Climate is mild and humid. Annual precipitation is 80–100 in., most of it Nov.–Mar.

Many of the magnificent redwood groves can be seen from US 101 and US 199, or by a short stroll from a parking area. Much more can be seen away from these main highways. Although there is no wilderness area, one can find quiet trails.

Plants: Redwoods occur both in pure stands and with other species. Redwoods grow rapidly, live up to 2,000 years. Average mature trees are 200–240 ft. tall, 10–15 ft. in diameter. Exceptional specimens attain 350 ft. in height, diameter over 20 ft. Coast redwoods are the world's tallest trees. In groves they grow surprisingly close together, their canopy casting deep shade on the forest floor.

Associated species are Douglas-fir, western hemlock, tan oak, madrone, California bay laurel. Inland, redwoods are replaced by Douglas-fir or Jeffrey pine. Understory includes redwood sorrel, rhododendron, huckleberry, salal, many ferns. Prairies, naturally occurring "balds," form openings on hillsides favorable for wildlife.

Rivers and streams often lined with alder, bigleaf maple, vine maple. Coastal scrub vegetation is diverse, including wild strawberry, lupine, cow parsnip, paintbrush, stonecrop, silk tassel, ceanothus, coyote brush, with thick strands of red alder, Sitka spruce.

Birds: Checklists available for Redwood National Park and Prairie Creek Redwoods State Park. Common residents include pied-billed grebe, cormorants, mallard, cinnamon teal, common merganser, white-tailed kite; Cooper's, marsh, and red-tailed hawks; kestrel; blue grouse, California quail, great blue heron, Virginia rail, black oystercatcher, killdeer, spotted sandpiper, western gull, common murre, pigeon guillemot, Cassin's auklet, marbled murrelet (seen over Boyes Prairie July, Aug., early Sept.); screech, great horned, and barn owls; flicker, black phoebe, Steller's jay, raven, chestnut-backed chickadee; winter, Bewick's, and long-billed marsh wrens; robin, varied thrush, purple and house finches, savannah and white-crowned sparrows. Many migrants.

Mammals: Checklist available. Includes among common residents: Trowbridge, vagrant, Pacific, and marsh shrews; Townsend mole, little brown myotis, brush rabbit, beaver, California ground squirrel, Townsend chipmunk, pocket gopher, various mice, porcupine, coyote, gray fox, raccoon, skunks, bobcat, Roosevelt elk, mule deer, some bear. Also harbor seal, river otter. Regular visitors include elephant seal, California sea lion, Steller sea lion.

Elk herd often seen along highway and near campground at Prairie Creek Redwoods State Park.

Tidepools: Variety of marine fauna and flora seen at low tides, including sea cucumber, crab, snails, etc.

FEATURES

Tall Trees Grove, reached by Redwood Creek Trail or, in summer, by shuttle bus. *Lady Bird Johnson Grove* on Bald Hill Rd. Several groves in Prairie Creek Redwoods State Park reached by short trails from parking lot near main entrance. Many other groves along highway and foot trails. Jedediah Smith Redwoods State Park has 36 memorial groves, including 5,000-acre *National Tribute Grove.*

Fern Canyon, reached by Davison Rd., near Coast, has 50-ft. walls, masses of ferns. Nearby is *Gold Bluffs Beach.*

Scenic drives, in addition to US 101 and US 199: *Bald Hill Rd.,* N of Orick, E of US 101; *Davison Rd.,* to Fern Canyon; *Coastal Drive,* about 8 mi., from US 101 S of Klamath; *Requa Rd.,* W of US 101, to trailhead for Coastal Trail, exhibits; *Enderts Beach Rd.,* S of Crescent City, to Crescent Beach, Enderts Beach; *Howland Hill Rd.,* in Jedediah Smith Redwoods State Park, through old-growth redwood forest. Several of these roads are unpaved, narrow, unsuitable for trailers, large RV's.

INTERPRETATION

Information at Ranger Station on US 101 in Orick; open daily, 8 A.M.–5 P.M., until 8 P.M. in summer. Exhibits, publications.

Park HQ is at Crescent City, Second and K Sts.; open weekdays 8 A.M.–5 P.M.; daily Apr.–Nov.; until 7 P.M. in summer.

Hiouchi Ranger Station on US 199, open 8 A.M.–5 P.M., to 7 P.M. in summer.

Prairie Creek HQ also has information, exhibits.

Nature trails: at Lady Bird Johnson Grove; Yurok Loop Trail near Lagoon Creek; Revelation Trail, near Prairie Creek HQ, for both blind and sighted people.

Campfire programs and *guided hikes* at campgrounds in summer. Notices posted.

Shuttle bus tours in summer.

ACTIVITIES

Camping: In State Parks only. 4 campgrounds, 378 sites. All year. Reservations May 25–Oct. 1.

Hiking; backpacking: Limited backpacking opportunities; inquire. Over 150 mi. of foot trails, round trips of a few minutes to 8 hrs. Trails through redwood groves, other forest, along bluffs, beach. Leaflets of all 4 parks show some trails; trail map for sale.

Fishing: Surf, river. Steelhead, salmon, trout.

Swimming: Smith River, in Jedediah Smith unit.

Canoeing, kayaking: Seasonally in Smith River. Organized daily kayak trips in summer.

Campgrounds generally full July–Sept. 15.

ADJACENT: Six Rivers National Forest (see entry).

PUBLICATIONS

Leaflets with maps, all 4 units.

Trail map.

Redwood National Park Visitor Guide, published seasonally.
Nature trail guides, available at sites.
Interpretive folder.
Forest rehabilitation folder.

REFERENCES: Numerous publications of Save-the-Redwoods League, 114 Sansome St., San Francisco, CA 94104.

HEADQUARTERS: Redwood National Park, 111 Second St., Crescent City, CA
95531; (707) 464-6101. Prairie Creek Redwoods State Park, Orick, CA
95555; (707) 488-2171. Del Norte Coast Redwoods State Park, P.O.
Drawer J, Crescent City, CA 95531; (707) 458-3115. Jedediah Smith Redwoods State Park, P.O. Drawer J, Crescent City, CA 95531; (707) 464-
9533.

RICHARDSON GROVE STATE PARK
California Department of Parks and Recreation
815 acres.

On US 101, 8 mi. S of Garberville.

Fine groves of giant redwoods, the tallest 320 ft., diameter 15 ft. About 200
mi. N of San Francisco on a major highway. Park attracts half a million
visitors annually. Campground is often full. A concession (restaurant, grocer-
ies, gifts) is on E side of highway, some fine trees with exhibits across the road.
Richardson Grove Trail begins here. A minority of visitors hike the Lookout
and Toumey Trails, on opposite side of the South Fork, Eel River. (Bridge
at N end of Toumey Trail is removed Oct.–May.)

Plants: Associated tree species include Douglas-fir, incense cedar, tan oak,
canyon oak, madrone; bigleaf maple, red alder, willow along stream. Understory includes ceanothus, salal, California bay laurel, blackberry, raspberry,
toyon, dogwood. Wildflowers include calypso orchid, bush monkeyflower,
inside-out flower, trillium, redwood lily, firecracker flower, fairy bells, oxalis,
spring beauty. Ferns 3–4 ft. tall.

Birds: Include osprey, great blue heron, water ouzel, bald eagle, American
merganser, robin, varied thrush, meadowlark, western tanager, black phoebe,
California towhee, brown creeper, chestnut-backed chickadee, Oregon junco,
hermit thrush, great egret, red-tailed hawk, California quail, spotted sandpiper, spotted owl, pileated woodpecker, common flicker, belted kingfisher.

Mammals: Pacific and other shrews, long-eared myotis, gray fox, ground squirrel, deer mouse, brush rabbit, black-tailed jackrabbit, redwood white-footed mouse, Townsend chipmunk, chickaree, western gray squirrel, pocket gopher, flying squirrel, otter, spotted skunk, raccoon, mule deer, coyote, mink.

Reptiles, amphibians: Ranger reports many snakes, salamanders, newts, lizards, frogs.

INTERPRETATION: *Interpretive center* has literature, card file of species observed. Announcements of hikes, etc., are posted. Active program.

Camping: 3 campgrounds; one open all year. 169 sites. Reservations May 25–Sept. 17.

NEARBY: Standish-Hickey State Recreation Area, Smithe Redwoods State Reserve (see entries).

PUBLICATION: Leaflet with map.

HEADQUARTERS: P.O. Box E, Garberville, CA 95440; (707) 247-3318.

ROGUE RIVER NATIONAL FOREST
U.S. Forest Service
54,016 acres in CA.

No practical road access from CA.

Most of this 630,000-acre Forest is in Oregon. A portion extends into California, where it has a common boundary with the Klamath National Forest (see entry). A section of the Pacific Crest Trail lies along this boundary. Only foot and jeep trails enter from California. Best access is from Oregon SR 238, turning S at Ruch, entering the Forest at McKee Bridge, and continuing S into California to the trailhead at Cook and Green. The campground here is a popular base for backpacking, trail riding, and hunting.

The region is mountainous. The highest peaks, between 6,000 and 7,000 ft., are on the boundary between the two National Forests. Numerous creeks and intermittent streams flow generally N.

PUBLICATION: Forest map. $1.00.

HEADQUARTERS: P.O. Box 250, Medford, OR 97501; (503) 776-3579.

RUSSIAN GULCH STATE PARK

California Department of Parks and Recreation
1,209 acres.

2 mi. N of Mendocino on SR 1.

Remarkable diversity in a relatively small area: coastal headlands, sand beach, redwood forest, fern canyon, abundant wildlife. Site is a long oblong extending inland for about 3 mi. along Russian Gulch. Broken headlands, cliffs up to 100 ft., fine views up and down the Coast. Devil's Punch Bowl: a sea-cut tunnel about 200 ft. long has collapsed at inland end to form a blowhole—although "blowing" occurs only in storms. Some tidepools.

Plants: Canyon is deep, moist, with second-growth, large Coast redwood and Douglas-fir. Associated species: tan oak, hemlock, California bay laurel; alder and bigleaf maple beside stream. Many rhododendron, ferns, spring wildflowers.

Birds: Include osprey, red-tailed hawk, kingfisher, band-tailed pigeon, great blue heron, California quail, raven, Steller's jay, sea- and shorebirds.

Mammals: Include raccoon, rabbit, chipmunk, mule deer, skunk, bobcat, gray fox.

FEATURE: *Russian Gulch Falls,* 36 ft., reached by Falls Loop Trail.

ACTIVITIES

Camping: 30 sites. All year. Reservations Mar. 1–Sept. 30.

Hiking: Several trails can be combined in a 9-mi. loop, through canyon, forest.

Fishing: Trout. (Steelhead fishing prohibited.) Surf.

Swimming: Sheltered beach. Cold water.

Bicycling: Canyon Bike Trail, 2 1/2 mi.

ADJACENT: Jackson State Forest (see entry). No formal trails link the two sites.

NEARBY: Van Damme State Park, Jug Handle State Reserve (see entries).

PUBLICATION: Leaflet with map. (The Fern Canyon Discovery Trail leaflet prepared for Van Damme State Park is applicable to Russian Gulch.)

HEADQUARTERS: Mendocino, CA 95460; (707) 937-5804.

SHASTA-TRINITY NATIONAL FOREST
U.S. Forest Service
2,159,001 acres. 2,862,101 acres within boundaries.

NE and S and W of Redding. W portion is crossed by SR 299, E portion by SR 89. Many access routes E and W of I-5.

A vast area, part of a complex of 5 contiguous National Forests in N CA. Several large sections of the Forest are a checkerboard, private and Forest lands alternating in 1-mi. squares, but this is not conspicuous on site. Forest roads and foot trails cross both private and public land. An occasional house or commercial establishment is the principal indication of inholdings.

Terrain includes gently rolling plateaus, river valleys, steep-walled canyons, ridges, high mountains. Highest point is Mt. Shasta, 14,161 ft. Forest includes 131 natural lakes, 11 reservoirs, 1,900 mi. of fishable rivers and streams.

Although the Forest receives over 5 million visitors annually, they concentrate in several popular recreation sites in the warm months. At any season it is possible to find quiet, secluded areas.

Climate in lower sections is moderate: warm, dry summers; cool, wet winters. More than half the annual precipitation is in Dec.–Feb. Snowfall is light; depth of 6 in. is seen only once in 25 years. Much more cold and snow at higher elevations.

Whiskeytown-Shasta-Trinity National Recreation Area has three units. Clair Engle and Lewiston Lakes unit and Shasta Lake unit are within National Forest boundaries and administered by Forest Service. Whiskeytown unit (see entry zone 2) is outside the boundaries and administered by National Park Service.

Plants: Ponderosa pine and Douglas-fir are the principal tree species of the Forest, but many other conifer species occur. Digger pine, for example, is found below 4,500 ft. elevation, incense cedar at 3,500 to 6,000, Jeffrey pine 3,500 to 7,000, knobcone pine 1,000 to 5,600, whitebark pine 7,000 to 10,000. Others, also with characteristic ranges, are foxtail pine, lodgepole pine, mountain hemlock, Pacific yew, Port Orford cedar, red fir, sugar pine, western juniper, western white pine, white fir. Hardwood species include black oak, white oak, tan oak, canyon live oak, bigleaf maple, black cottonwood, Pacific madrone.

Widely distributed shrubs include ceanothus, deerbrush, snowbush, mountain lilac, poison oak. Many wildflower species including tiger lily, pitcher plant, columbine, Indian pink, Indian paintbrush, spreading phlox, bleeding heart, fireweed, shooting star, mountain pennyroyal, mountain violet, buttercup, monkeyflower. Great variety of alpine plants; over 400 species identified on Mt. Shasta.

Birds: No checklist available. Common species include bald eagle, osprey; red-tailed, red-shouldered, Cooper's, and sharp-shinned hawks; goshawk, kestrel, turkey vulture, raven, Steller's and scrub jays, red-winged blackbird; acorn, hairy, downy, and Lewis' woodpeckers; robin; California and mountain quails; savannah, rufous-crowned, white-crowned, golden-crowned, fox, song, and house sparrows; Oregon junco, western tanager; black-capped, mountain, and chestnut-backed chickadees; Nashville, yellow, hermit, Wilson's, and McGillivray's warblers; calliope, Anna's, and rufous hummingbirds; killdeer, great blue heron, water ouzel.

Mammals: No checklist available. Include black bear, mule deer, raccoon, ringtail, beaver, striped skunk, bobcat, mountain lion, coyote, gray fox, Townsend chipmunk, golden-mantled squirrel, western gray squirrel, northern flying squirrel, chickaree.

FEATURES

Yolla Bolly-Middle Eel Wilderness, 111,000 acres. Includes a portion of the Mendocino National Forest (see entry). Wild, rugged country on the headwaters of the Middle Fork, Eel River, bounded by the North and South Yolla Bolly Mountains. Mountains are rounded, heavily forested. The area is scenic, though not dramatic. Average elevations 2,000–4,000 ft., with peaks over 8,000 ft. For those who seek solitude, this area is choice. Visitor use is light. Yet most of the area is open for hiking by late May, earlier than most CA wildernesses. Ridges have a mixture of dense stands of pine and fir with open meadows. Lower slopes are a combination of conifers and chaparral. Good fishing in several creeks, but water is generally scarce and springs are usually dry by late summer. Trail map available. Wilderness permit required.

Salmon-Trinity Alps Primitive Area, 225,200 acres. Along the headwaters of the Salmon and Trinity Rivers in the NW sector of the Forest, partially within the Klamath National Forest (see entry). Various access routes from SR 299 and SR 3 near Weaverville. This is the second largest wilderness area in CA. Spectacular scenery. High, rough mountain ridges, deep glacial canyons, peaks from 7,000 to 9,000 ft. Mixed stands of timber; some brush-covered slopes; huge talus boulders above timberline. Annual precipitation is about 50 in., snowfall in some high places up to 12 ft. Frost-free period is usually July 1–Sept. 15. Wildflower blooming peak July–Aug. Many lakes and streams. Good hunting, fishing. Wilderness permit required.

Mt. Shasta, 14,162 ft., rising over 10,000 ft. from its base, 7,000 ft. higher than nearby peaks in the Cascade Range. Everitt Memorial Highway, from

Mt. Shasta City, 14 mi. to just below the 7,800-ft. level. Timberline at about 8,000 ft. About 16,700 acres, largely above timberline, proposed for wilderness status. Area includes 5 living glaciers, hot spring, Shastina Crater, Clarence King Lake. A variety of hiking trails to the top. Map information available at Ranger District office.

Castle Crags roadless area, 7,300 acres. Noted for the unique granite spires found here and in adjacent Castle Crags State Park. Numerous streams, 6 alpine lakes. Wide range of elevation; highest point 7,078 ft. Near Pacific Crest Trail.

Medicine Lake Volcanic Highlands. NE sector. A 2-hr. drive from McCloud to Medicine Lake. Miles of colorful volcanic formations. Volcanic glass mountain, spatter cones, ice caves. Fine vista from fire tower on Little Mt. Hoffman. Check at Ranger Station in McCloud before entering the Highlands sector.

Shasta Lake is California's largest artificial lake, with a 370-mi. shoreline. Water-based recreation attracts many visitors, and shore points reached by road are crowded in season. However, regulations have kept the water clean, and it is one of the few large CA lakes where shoreline camping is permitted away from established campgrounds. More than 90 Forest Service campgrounds around the shoreline, including 10 that can be reached only by boat. Several foot trails leave from or link shore points. Houseboating is popular. Fishing is popular, best in cool weather.

Clair Engle Lake, 150 mi. of shoreline, is also a focus for water-based recreation. Nearby, smaller Lewiston Lake is mostly for fishing, boat speed limited to 10 mph. The lakes are the center of the Trinity unit, National Recreation Area. Many campgrounds. Trails lead into the nearby Salmon Trinity Alps Primitive Area.

Black Butte, 6,325 ft., N of Mt. Shasta, is a cinder cone. 2 1/2-mi. trail leads past various volcanic formations to fire lookout at peak. Visitors welcome but must bring own water.

Castle Lake is 11 mi. from Mt. Shasta City by adequate road. Camping, fishing. Short trail to Little Castle Lake, scenic area. Pacific Crest Trail is nearby.

Scenic drives: Many Forest roads have high scenic value. Outstanding is SR 299 along the Trinity River.

INTERPRETATION

Interpretive programs chiefly at the two National Recreation Areas, Shasta Lake and Trinity.

Visitor information at U.S. Forest Service, Weaverville. *Visitor center* at S end of Clair Engle Lake, Trinity area. At Lake Shasta, visitor information at Salt Creek station, Salt Creek exit from I-5; Shasta Lake Ranger District, Mountain Gate exit from I-5. *Taped information by telephone:* (916) 246-5338.

Campfire programs at several campgrounds in Recreation Areas. Schedules posted. Also *guided hikes, nature trails.*

ACTIVITIES

Camping: More than 100 campgrounds, 1,591 sites. Most sites open May 15–Sept. 15, and, according to Forest Service, "as needed or as the weather permits during the balance of the year." Forest has several campgrounds available on Ticketron reservation system; inquire if you plan summer visit. Camping outside campgrounds is permitted subject to area restrictions and required fire permit.

Hiking, backpacking: About 3,100 mi. of trails. 150 mi. of Pacific Crest Trail nearing completion. Trail is generally E–W, elevations 2,400–7,200 ft. Crosses Salmon-Trinity Alps Primitive Area where wilderness permit is required. Trail map shows current trail conditions. 400-mi. trail system in Salmon-Trinity Alps area. Yolla Bolly area also has many trails. Maps of both available. Many trails for day hiking; those most heavily used begin at the National Recreation Areas. An interesting new trail, Sisson-Callahan, begins at Siskiyou Lake, SW of Mt. Shasta City, follows North Fork of Sacramento River W, meeting Pacific Crest Trail near Deadfall Lakes. Map available.

Weaverville Ranger District office has a large loose-leaf book describing trails and destinations: topo maps, color photos, precise information on trail conditions, water, campsites. Many destinations are small lakes.

Backpacking begins in spring, but snow limits access to high country. In early May 1980, upper slopes still had 10 ft.

Forest map does not show contours. Topo maps are essential for backcountry travel. Points that appear close together on Forest map may be separated by sawtooth ridges, a difficult day's climb.

Hunting: Deer, bear, small game.

Fishing: Many opportunities: lakes, rivers, streams. Trout, bass, other species.

Swimming: Mostly in lakes. Unsupervised.

Boating: Marinas, ramps, rentals, other facilities at Shasta and Clair Engle lakes. Small motors, 10 mph limit, on Lewiston Lake.

Canoeing: On smaller lakes, some rivers. Whitewater opportunities on South Fork of the Trinity River.

Pack trips, horse riding: Forest Service says "six pack stations serving the area." If you bring your own stock, consult District Ranger; it may be necessary to carry feed. Hundreds of miles of trails suitable for horses.

Ski touring: Special area on Mt. Shasta. Elsewhere as conditions permit.

Snowmobiling: Good terrain in McCloud-Mt. Shasta area.

In dry periods, when fire hazard is high, special restrictions apply. Under extreme conditions, some Forest areas are closed; low-risk areas are exempt.

ADJACENT: Mendocino, Lassen, Klamath, Six Rivers National Forests (see entries). Castle Crags State Park (see entry).

NEARBY: Whiskeytown unit, Whiskeytown-Shasta-Trinity National Recreation Area (see entry, zone 2).

PUBLICATIONS
Forest map. $1.00.
Visitor information map.
Campground information and directory.
Information sheets
Yolla Bolly-Middle Eel and Salmon-Trinity Alps area.
Yolla Bolly leaflet with map.
Leaflets
Trees of the Trinity.
Wildflowers of the Trinity.
Birds of the Trinity.
Wildlife of the Trinity.
Conifers of the Mt. Shasta District.
Tabulation of Tree Range for the Mt. Shasta District.
Geology of the Mount Shasta Area.
Leaflet, Shasta Lake Recreation Area.
Leaflet, Trinity Recreation Area.
Pacific Crest Trail, current information, trail maps.
Sisson-Callahan trail map.
Restricted use and emergency closure plan.
Mt. Shasta Ski Touring Trail Map.
Mt. Shasta, A Climber's Guide, leaflet.

HEADQUARTERS: 2400 Washington Ave., Redding, CA 96001; (916) 246-5222. After-hours information, recorded: (916) 246-5338.

RANGER DISTRICTS: Yolla Bolly R.D., Platina, CA 96076; (916) 352-4211. Hayfork R.D., P.O. Box 159, Hayfork, CA 96041; (916) 628-5227. Big Bar R.D., Big Bar, CA; (916) 623-6106. Weaverville R.D., P.O. Box T, Weaverville, CA 96063; (916) 623-2121. Shasta Lake R.D., 6543 Holiday Dr., Redding, CA 96001. (916) 257-1587. Mt. Shasta R.D., 204 W. Alma, Mt. Shasta, CA 96067; (916) 926-4596. McCloud R.D., Drawer I, McCloud, CA 96057; (916) 964-2184 and 2185.

SINKYONE WILDERNESS STATE PARK
California Department of Parks and Recreation
3,500 acres.

From US 101 just N of Garberville, W through Redway. Briceland Thorne Rd. through Briceland to Thorn Junction, then S to Four Corners. From here both Usal Rd. and Briceland Rd., generally S, enter site. Latter continues to Bear Harbor, within boundaries.

Day use only; no camping or backpacking. Both possible in nearby King Range Conservation Area (see entry). Rugged, undeveloped coastline, steep coastal mountains. About 5 1/2 mi. of seacoast. Coastal bench is grassland, inland areas heavily forested, mixed conifers, Coast redwood. Whitethorn, chamise, huckleberry in understory.

No facilities. This, the day-use limitation, and relative inaccessibility mean few visitors. (Further land acquisition is possible, to be followed by a new management plan.)

Ranching, grazing, and logging preceded state acquisition in 1975. A rail spur to Bear Harbor ceased operating in 1906.

Wildlife much the same as that of King Range. Good area for raptors, sea- and shorebirds. Mammals include deer, fox, squirrel, raccoon, porcupine, occasional bear.

ACTIVITIES
Hiking: About 15 mi. of trails, unmarked.
Fishing: Surf.
Horse riding: No stable nearby.

Caution: The last 15 mi. of access road are narrow, unpaved. In wet weather, 4-wheel-drive vehicle necessary. Visitors are advised to consult Ranger at Richardson Grove State Park about road and trail conditions, etc.

NEARBY: King Range National Conservation Area (see entry).

HEADQUARTERS: c/o Richardson Grove State Park, P.O. Box E, Garberville, CA 05440; (707) 247-3318.

SIX RIVERS NATIONAL FOREST
U.S. Forest Service
980,285 acres. 1,118,366 acres within boundaries.

From OR border to a point E of Garberville. Crossed by SR 199, SR 96, SR 299, SR 36.

Long, narrow site, part of a huge complex of National Forests in N CA. Extends 140 mi. S from OR border, a short distance inland from several redwood parks. Coastal mountains cut by the valleys of six major streams: Smith, Klamath, Trinity, Mad, Van Duzen, Eel. Many smaller streams. Ruth Lake, 9 mi. long, 1,150 acres. Range of elevations: 250 ft. to 6,424 ft. at Bear Mountain. Winter climate is more moderate than in forests further inland.

Although there are hiking trails, most visitor use is river-based: fishing, swimming, boating. Indeed, some mapped trails have been abandoned for lack of use.

Plants: Predominant tree species is Douglas-fir. Others: sugar, Jeffrey, and ponderosa pines; white and red firs, Port Orford and incense cedars, tan oak, madrone, canyon live oak. Many wildflowers late Apr. and May; plant list in preparation, tree checklist available. Poison oak is common. Notable display of fall colors mid to late Oct.

Birds: Checklist available. Common and abundant residents include turkey vulture, red-tailed hawk, kestrel, California and mountain quails, band-tailed pigeon, mourning dove, screech owl, nighthawk, Vaux's swift, Anna's and Allen's hummingbirds, kingfisher, flicker, acorn and hairy woodpeckers, western and olive-sided flycatchers; violet-green, barn, and cliff swallows; Steller's and scrub jays, raven, chickadee, red-breasted nuthatch, wrentit, winter and Bewick's wrens, robin, golden-crowned kinglet, vireos; Nashville, yellow-rumped, Townsend's, and hermit warblers.

Mammals: Checklist available. Common and abundant species include Trowbridge shrew, Townsend mole, little brown myotis, silver-haired bat, black bear, raccoon, striped skunk, coyote, gray fox, California ground squirrel, western gray and golden-mantled squirrels, Townsend chipmunk, chickaree, deer and pinyon mice, California vole, porcupine, black-tailed jackrabbit, brush rabbit, mule deer.

Reptiles, amphibians: Checklist available. Common and abundant species include western toad, Pacific tree frog, bullfrog, rough-skinned newt, salamander, western fence lizard, western skink, alligator lizard, gopher snake, racer, garter snake, pond turtle.

INTERPRETATION

Scenic drives include road around Ruth Lake, US 199 along Smith River.

Lookout towers offer many vistas. Towers are marked on Forest map and

Off-Road & Vehicle Travel Plan map. Check with Ranger District office to determine whether lookout is open.

Nature trails at Gray's Falls, on US 299 12 mi. E of Willow Creek, and Fir Cove, between Fir Cove and Bailey Canyon campgrounds.

ACTIVITIES

Camping: 15 campgrounds, 384 sites. Most close to rivers or lakes. Fees $2–$3. At least one campground in each area open all year. No reservations. Camping is permitted almost anywhere outside campgrounds; fire permit required for any fire, including camp stove, outside an enclosed vehicle.

Hiking, backpacking: 195 mi. of trails, plus unpaved Forest roads. Some trails shown on maps are not maintained; a few have virtually disappeared. Backpacking is not a major activity here, in part because of the Forest's long, narrow shape. Thus it offers opportunities for weekend outings when trails in other forests may be busy. Check trail conditions with a Ranger District.

Recommended trails include South Kelsey (Gasquet Ranger District) and Horse Trail Ridge (Lower Trinity Ranger District), both designated National Recreation Trails. HQ may have information page describing other trails.

Hunting: Deer, bear, squirrel, quail, blue grouse, dove.

Fishing: The principal visitor activity. Rivers, streams, lakes. Salmon, steelhead, trout.

Swimming: Rivers, lake. Unsupervised.

Boating: Power boating on Ruth Lake. Commercial facilities.

Canoeing, kayaking: On all main rivers, chiefly Klamath and Trinity. Inflated rafts generally preferred. Inquire about conditions. Canoe camping; fire permit needed.

Ski touring: South Fork Mountain ridge, off SR 36. Wherever conditions permit.

Skiing: Commercial facility at Horse Mtn.

Snowmobiling: As conditions permit, subject to Forest regulations. *(See Off-Road & Vehicle Travel Plan.)*

ADJACENT: Klamath, Shasta-Trinity, Mendocino National Forests (see entries). Redwood National Park (see entry). Hoopa Valley Indian Reservation.

PUBLICATIONS

Forest map. $1.00.

Off-Road & Vehicle Travel Plan, map and regulations. Shows all Forest roads, many trails.

Forest information sheet.

Species checklists: trees, birds, mammals, reptiles and amphibians.

Camping Guide. Directory.

Nature trail leaflets.

River trips information sheet.

HEADQUARTERS: 507 F St., Eureka, CA 95501; (707) 442-1721.

RANGER STATIONS: Gasquet R.S., P.O. Box 228, Gasquet, CA 95543; (707) 457-3131. Orleans R.S., Drawer B, Orleans, CA 95556; (916) 627-3291. Lower Trinity R.S., P.O. Box 668, Willow Creek, CA 95573; (916) 629-2118. Mad River R.S., Star Route Box 300, Bridgeville, CA 95526; (707) 574-6233.

SMITHE REDWOODS STATE RESERVE
California Department of Parks and Recreation
622 acres.

4 mi. N of Leggett on US 101.

On South Fork, Eel River. A splendid grove of giant redwoods is on W side of highway. Short trails through the grove and to the river. This is a small portion of the site, but the larger portion, across the highway, is not open to visitors.

NEARBY: Standish-Hickey State Recreation Area, Richardson Grove State Park (see entries).

STANDISH-HICKEY STATE RECREATION AREA
California Department of Parks and Recreation
1,009 acres.

1 mi. N of Leggett on US 101.

A redwood park, but only one tree is old growth. Scarred by fire and saw cuts, this one stands 225 ft. tall, 13 ft. diameter. Within the canyon of South Fork, Eel River; steep cliffs. Ranger described it as a "transient and overflow park, not a destination."

Plants: Forest of Coast redwood, Douglas-fir, tan oak, California bay laurel, Oregon and other oaks, bigleaf maple, alder. Shrubs include toyon, manzanita, huckleberry, ceanothus. Many ferns. Wildflowers include brodiaea, Indian pink, redwood sorrel, shooting star, lupine, buttercup.

Birds: Include Steller's jay, raven, quail, Oregon junco, osprey, merganser, great blue heron.

Mammals: Include mule deer, raccoon, bobcat, ground squirrel, gray squirrel.

INTERPRETATION: *Campfire programs* 3 evenings weekly in summer.

ACTIVITIES
Camping: 3 campgrounds, 162 sites. One campground open all year. Reservations May 25–Sept 3.
Hiking: 4 loop trails, longest 4.7 mi. Steep sections.
Fishing: Steelhead, salmon.
Swimming: River. Unsupervised. Deep holes.

NEARBY: Smithe Redwoods State Reserve, Richardson Grove State Park (see entries).

PUBLICATION: Leaflet with map.

HEADQUARTERS: Leggett, CA 95455; (707) 925-6482.

VAN DAMME STATE PARK
California Department of Parks and Recreation
1,930 acres.

3 mi. S of Mendocino on SR 1.

Coast, extending about 3 mi. inland. Ocean beach, forest, river canyon, meadows, bog. Once a virgin redwood forest, but logged off; sawmill was closed in 1893.
Plants: Second-growth forest now has trees of impressive size. Coast redwood, Douglas-fir, Pacific hemlock, Bishop pine, shore pine, lowland fir. In *Fern Canyon,* luxuriant growth of trees and ferns; sword, five-finger, lady, licorice, wood, bird's-foot, deer ferns. Many rhododendrons, spring wildflowers. *Pygmy Forest,* reached by Fern Canyon Trail, has mature cypress and pine trees stunted by acid soil. Pygmy Forest can also be reached by Airport Road, S of Park. *Cabbage Patch* is a bog with skunk cabbage.

Tidepools can be seen at low tide. Beach is used for picnicking, beachcombing, scuba; swimming is inadvisable, with water seldom above 52°F.

ACTIVITIES
Camping: 74 sites. All year. Reservations May 1–Sept. 30.
Hiking: Fern Canyon trail, 2 1/2 mi. from campground to junction with Old Logging Trail. 6 mi. round trip. Bog Trail near visitor center.

NEARBY: Russian Gulch State Park, Jackson State Forest (see entries).

PUBLICATIONS
Leaflet with map.
Fern Canyon Discovery Trail.
Pygmy Forest Discovery Trail.

HEADQUARTERS: P.O. Box 440, Mendocino, CA 95460; (707) 937-5804.

ZONE 2

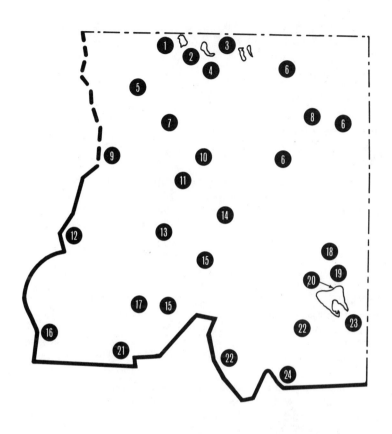

CALIFORNIA, ZONE 2

Includes these counties:

Siskiyou (E of I-5)   Lassen   Plumas
Shasta   Tehama

The Cascade Range extends into this zone from the N, the Sierra Nevada
from the S. In the SW is the upper part of the Sacramento Valley and the E
slope of the Coast Range. The far NE is within the Great Basin.

The forests, parks, and wildlife areas described in these entries make up
more than half of the zone's land area. Most of the remainder is crop and
grazing land, much of it in the fertile Sacramento Valley. By far the largest
public areas are the National Forests, and these, for the most part, occupy
the mountains.

Elevations range from around 200 ft. in the Valley to 14,161-ft. Mt. Shasta.
Although there is much rugged terrain, the mountain slopes are generally less
steep than in the Sierra to the S, and the high country is not quite as high.

In the far N are wetlands that attract vast numbers of waterfowl. The zone
has many lakes, rivers, and streams, as well as semiarid regions where travelers must bring their own water.

Some mountain areas are open for hiking by late May, others blocked by
snow until July. Snow closes some passes. The road through Lassen Volcanic
National Park is usually closed by snow from the end of Oct. until early June.
Snowfall is generally light at lower elevations.

The zone offers a great array of scenic features: volcanic craters and peaks,
lava caves, waterfalls, cascades, virgin forests, seasonal wildflower displays.
Hiking trails range from easy to difficult. Quiet isolation in splendid surroundings is available to anyone willing to walk a few miles. The National Forests
have large wilderness areas, and some of the long trails have only moderate
grades. Many trails are suitable for horses.

Many popular resorts are within the zone, and some public recreation areas
are crowded at times. A few wilderness trails have become so popular that
some fragile areas are now closed to overnight camping.

Ordinary road maps will take you to the zone. Within the zone, National
Forest maps are indispensable.

BISCAR WILDLIFE AREA
U.S. Bureau of Land Management/California Department of Fish and Game
5,433 acres.

From Susanville, E and N on US 395 about 35 mi. SW on county road
through Karlo. Site boundary just beyond SP railroad tracks.

Isolated, high desert country, seldom visited except by hunters in season.
Federal and state areas are cooperatively managed, but separate. A sweeping
plateau cut by steep-walled canyon of Snowstorm Creek, an intermittent
stream. Canyon walls are lava rimrock. Annual precipitation about 10 in.,
winter snowfall scant. Impoundments.

Plants: Typical of Great Basin: scattered juniper; rabbitbrush, sage, black
greasewood, saltbush. Less common: bitterbrush, curl-leaf mountain mahogany, squaw apple.

Birds: Chukar, quail, sage grouse, dove; migrant waterfowl on creek.

Mammals: Cottontail, black-tailed jackrabbit, coyote, bobcat, badger, marmot. Summer antelope range. Some mule deer.

No designated campground, but no apparent objection to RV's overnighting. Travel over much of the area on foot only.

Bring your own water.

Winter road conditions variable. Advisable to consult BLM office in Susanville or DFG office in Redding.

HEADQUARTERS: Department of Fish and Game, P.O. Box 1480, Redding,
CA 96001; (916) 246-6511.

CASTLE CRAGS STATE PARK
California Department of Parks and Recreation
6,216 acres.

6 mi. S of Dunsmuir on I-5.

In the Klamath Mountains, along the Sacramento River. Feature is group of
soaring crags, 4,000-ft. granite spires, sheer faces with rounded domes. 2-mi.
frontage on the river, across I-5 from main portion of park.

Plants: About 80% forested: ponderosa pine, Douglas-fir, incense cedar, black oak, sugar pine, alder. Understory species include California hazelnut, California blackberry, green- and white-leaf manzanita, vine maple, poison oak. Flowering plants include azalea, tiger lily, columbine, flowering dogwood, orchids, larkspur. Plant checklist available.

Birds: Waterfowl, water ouzel, kingfisher, at river. Steller's jay, red-shafted flicker, Oregon junco, red-tailed hawk, other raptors, woodpeckers, songbirds.

Mammals: Mule deer, coyote, black bear, striped skunk, opossum, gray squirrel. Present but seldom seen: porcupine, mink, river otter, mountain lion.

INTERPRETATION: *Campfire programs,* nightly, June 15–Labor Day. *Nature trail,* 1/2 mi., forest and chaparral plants.

ACTIVITIES

Camping: 64 sites. All year. Reservations May 18–Sept. 16.

Hiking, backpacking: On the Pacific Crest Trail. Hikers often stop here for mail, supplies. Trailside camping in National Forest, not Park.

Park trail to Castle Dome, one of the lowest promontories. Round trip 5 1/2 mi., rise of 2,000 ft. Hikers are warned not to go beyond trail: cliffs with sheer drops of almost 2,000 ft., no markers or warning signs. For experienced climbers only.

Fishing: River.

Swimming: River.

Canoeing: River navigable by canoe or kayak late spring to early or mid-summer, depending on runoff.

ADJACENT: Shasta-Trinity National Forest (see entry).

PUBLICATIONS

Information sheet.

Plant list.

Nature trail guide.

HEADQUARTERS: Castella, CA 96017; (916) 235-2684.

CLEAR LAKE NATIONAL WILDLIFE REFUGE
U.S. Fish and Wildlife Service
33,440 acres.

About 15 mi. SE of Tulelake. From SR 139, 23 mi. SE of Tulelake, 9 mi. NE on Clear Lake Reservoir Rd. Access to N side of lake: from Makin, OR, 4 mi. E and S on Old Alturas Highway, then E on Kowoloski Rd. (Rd. 108).

20,000-acre lake surrounded by dry grasslands. Clear Lake is a unit of the Klamath Basin Refuges (see entry). Two other CA units, Tule Lake and Lower Klamath, are more accessible and offer better opportunities for viewing wildlife. Clear Lake level is low when irrigation water is released.

Grassland is habitat for pronghorn, sage grouse. White pelican, cormorant, other colonial species nest on small islands. Waterfowl during migration, but not in such large numbers as at the two other units.

Access roads are impassable in wet weather.

HEADQUARTERS: c/o Klamath Basin National Wildlife Refuges, Route 1, Box 74, Tulelake, CA 96134; (916) 667-2231.

DOYLE WILDLIFE AREA
California Department of Fish and Game
14,013 acres.

From Doyle on US 395 (SE of Susanville), N on Herlong road. Area adjoins US 395, N and E of Doyle.

Foothills and flatland on Long Valley Creek. Creek, in a deep cut, flows N to Honey Lake, dry only in extreme drought. Wildlife Area was established to provide winter deer habitat. Purpose now is to maintain all wildlife resources. Climate is dry, about 10 in. of precipitation a year; hot summers, cold winters.

Plants: Typical of Great Basin. Exclusion of domestic livestock has brought recovery of browse species, notably bitterbrush. Also curl-leaf mountain mahogany, big sage, California juniper.

Fauna: Include mule deer, coyote, bobcat, badger, raccoon, skunk, cottontail, mourning dove, chukar, California quail, various raptors and passerines, some waterfowl.

ACTIVITIES
Camping: No campground or sanitary facilities.
Hunting: Obtain regulations.

Vehicles must stay on maintained roads. Soft sand.

NEARBY: Plumas National Forest (see entry).

PUBLICATION: Leaflet with map.

HEADQUARTERS: Department of Fish and Game, P.O. Box 1480, Redding, CA; (916) 246-6511.

HONEY LAKE WILDLIFE AREA
California Department of Fish and Game
4,980 acres.

From Susanville, E on US 395 through Litchfield. 3 mi. beyond Litchfield, right 2 mi. on Mapes Rd., then left 1 mi. to HQ.

Two units, both on N shore of Honey Lake. Lake is in a large natural sink. Surface water is mostly drainage from irrigated farmland. Surrounding area was once largely wetlands, supporting vast waterfowl populations. Only a few federal and state refuges now provide nesting, resting, and feeding habitat. Impoundments and cultivation of feed crops increase carrying capacity.

Elevation 4,000 ft. Ponds and marshes, plus cropland.

Birds: More than 150 species recorded. Nesting area of Great Basin Canada goose, only goose nesting in CA. Snow, white-fronted, cackling, and Ross's geese are migrants, as are mallard, pintail, scoter, coot, merganser. Nesting species include sandhill crane, avocet, black-necked stilt, willet, curlew. Pheasant introduced. Said to be spectacular opportunities to observe newly hatched geese and ducks.

Mammals: Include mule deer, muskrat, mink, beaver, weasel, porcupine, raccoon, coyote, bobcat, occasional pronghorn.

ACTIVITIES

Camping: 15 sites; expansion planned. Limited facilities. Water in summer only. Obtain use permit on arrival.

Hunting: In designated areas, on designated days in season; number of hunters limited. Waterfowl, pheasant.

Fishing: Termed "modest." Bass, catfish, sunfish, mostly fall and spring.

Capacity crowds on opening weekend of waterfowl hunting season and pheasant season.

NEARBY: Plumas National Forest (see entry).

PUBLICATION: Leaflet with map.

HEADQUARTERS: Wendel, CA 96136; (916) 253-2573.

KLAMATH BASIN NATIONAL WILDLIFE REFUGES: TULE LAKE AND LOWER KLAMATH UNITS
U.S. Fish and Wildlife Service
85,700 acres.

From Tulelake on SR 139, W on East-West Rd. 5 mi. to Hill Rd. Left to HQ and Tule Lake. For Lower Klamath, NW from Tulelake about 4 mi. on SR 139, then W on SR 161 10 mi. to beginning of tour route.

The Klamath Basin, almost a million acres in CA and OR, was once a region of vast shallow lakes and marshes, one of the world's chief waterfowl areas. Dams, ditches, and other alterations have eliminated most of the wetlands. Lower Klamath became a Refuge in 1908, Tule Lake not until 1928. Clear Lake, a storage reservoir (see entry in CA zone 2), was brought into the system in 1911.

Reclamation destroyed the Lower Klamath, and for a time two federal agencies, the Reclamation Service and the Biological Survey, fought angrily over water management. Eventually they compromised and cooperated. Although the basin as a whole will never be restored to its primitive condition, the 5 units of the Klamath Basin Refuge—two of them in Oregon—support great numbers of waterfowl. Both the Tule Lake and Lower Klamath units support peak waterfowl populations of more than a million.

Lower Klamath includes water, marsh, and upland. Marshes are maintained by water pumped from Tule Lake by a 6,600-ft. tunnel through an intervening ridge and by water diverted from the Klamath River. Part of the upland is farmed by permittees who must leave 1/3 of the grain crop for waterfowl.

Tule Lake is surrounded by rich grainlands that were once part of the lakebed. The original 100,000-acre lake is now only 13,000 acres, but it produces a rich crop of aquatic plants and attracts vast numbers of waterfowl.

Birds: Spring is a fine season here, the population of migrants usually peaking in early March, but the fall migration is phenomenal, producing the largest concentration of waterfowl on the North American continent. The five Klamath units are likely to have 1 to 2 million birds, including 500,000 pintail, 100,000 mallard, 200,000 wigeon, 100,000 white-fronted goose, 100,000 cackling Canada goose, 200,000 snow goose. An estimated 70–80% of all the waterfowl on the Pacific Flyway pass through here.

More than 275 bird species have been recorded, including 170 nesting on one or more of the units. The complex produces 50,000 to 70,000 ducks and geese per year. Many redhead nesting. Also gadwall, mallard, cinnamon teal, ruddy duck; with lesser numbers of shoveler, pintail, scaup, and canvasback. In July and August, broods can be observed from SR 161.

Duck populations usually peak in the last half of October, geese one to two weeks later.

Many bald eagle winter here. Sandhill crane nest at Lower Klamath. Eared, western, and pied-billed grebe nest at Tule Lake and Lower Klamath.

The Refuge checklist includes many shorebirds, hawks, owls, woodpeckers, songbirds.

Mammals: Include mule deer, coyote, pronghorn, marmot.

Auto tour routes are available on both units. Lower Klamath has two, 6 and 16 mi. Tule Lake has a 10-mile tour. All are on graded gravel roads. Your car is a good blind.

ACTIVITIES

Hiking: On unpaved roads, some of which are on the auto tour route.
Hunting: Designated areas; special rules, Inquire.

Interior roads may be in poor condition in wet weather. Inquire.

NEARBY. Lava Beds National Monument (see entry).

PUBLICATIONS
Leaflet with map.
Bird checklist.
Beginners Check List.
Hunting maps.

HEADQUARTERS: Route 1, Box 74, Tulelake, CA 96134; (916) 667-2231.

KLAMATH NATIONAL FOREST
See entry in zone 1.

LASSEN NATIONAL FOREST
U.S. Forest Service
1,060,588 acres; 1,375,067 acres within boundaries.

Surrounds Lassen Volcanic National Park. Crossed by SRs 89, 44, 36, 32.

Lassen Peak, in the National Park, is the S outpost of the Cascade Range. The N tip of the Sierra is near Lake Almanor, SE of the Park. In the National Forest, although elevations range to 9,000 ft., peaks are rather widely separated and most slopes are moderate. Steeper slopes occur in the SW sector, but even these are less rugged than many to the S and N.

Because of inholdings, the Forest land is patchy in some sectors, and there are scattered bits on the periphery. However, there are large, solid blocks, largely N of the Park, but also to the E, S, and SW.

Some frontage on Lake Almanor, almost 15 mi. long, and on S end of Eagle Lake, slightly shorter. Numerous smaller lakes and ponds, many formed by volcanic action. Streams, mostly small (except for Mill, Deer, and Hot creeks), some intermittent.

Plants: Largely forested, up to timberline. In general, lower slopes have white fir, ponderosa and Jeffrey pines, hemlock, some Douglas-fir, sugar pine, incense cedar. Higher, red fir, dense stands of lodgepole. Alder, willow, aspen along streams. Common shrubs include ceanothus, mountain mahogany, manzanita. Some open meadows with grasses, bromegrass, meadow barley, sedges, rushes.

Wildflowers include lupine, buttercup, filaree, violet, penstemon, aster, yarrow, dandelion.

Birds: Canada goose common on lakes in summer. Other waterfowl include mallard, teal. Osprey Management Area at Eagle Lake. Several hawk species, golden eagle. Bald eagle rare but present. Some California and mountain quail. Turkey introduced. Band-tailed pigeon, mourning dove. Numerous blackbirds, woodpeckers, Steller's jay, killdeer. No checklist.

Mammals: Include mule deer, pronghorn, coyote, fox, cottontail, bobcat, jackrabbit, chipmunk, western gray squirrel. Uncommon: black bear, mountain lion.

FEATURES

Thousand Lakes Wilderness: 15,695 acres. 7,000-acre addition proposed. NW of the National Park. Access from four trailheads on Forest Roads. Popular area for short trips; long trail across the area is about 6 air mi. Open enough for off-trail hiking, with topo and compass. Elevations 5,000–9,000 ft. Open and barren above timberline, forest and meadow below. Some gentle slopes with recent lava flows, sparse vegetation. Thousand Lakes Valley is the principal attraction, a level, glacier-carved valley with many small lakes and ponds. Difficult trail to top of Magee Peak, 8,550 ft. Wilderness permit required.

Caribou Wilderness: 19,080 acres. 1,800-acre addition proposed. On E boundary of National Park. Access from three trailheads on Forest Roads. Gently rolling forested plateau with many tree-fringed lakes. Trails well maintained. Highest point is Red Cinder Cone, 8,370 ft. Forest cover mostly Jeffrey and lodgepole pines, with white and red fir, western white pine, hemlock, on lower slopes. Wilderness permit required.

Cinder Butte roadless area: 15,500 acres. NW corner of Forest, E of Burney. Encompasses, almost entirely, a volcano active within the past 2,000 years. Numerous cinder cones, caves, shallow water-filled potholes. Rising River, large volcanic spring, near NW corner.

Cinder Butte is 4,288 ft., highest point, panoramic views. Vegetative cover is sparse, as is wildlife. Ground surface is rocky, irregular.

Ishi roadless area: 41,600 acres. SW corner of Forest. Transition zone between Sacramento Valley and upper slopes of Sierra. Elevations 2,000–3,000 ft. Network of steep ravines separated by sharp ridges. Most slopes have annual grasses or dense brush with scattered digger pine, black oak. Several small, flat plateaus have stands of ponderosa pine. Drained by Mill Creek. Jeep and foot trails.

Timbered Crater roadless area: 4,400 acres. Near SE corner of Siskiyou County. Three parcels of Forest land adjacent to a larger area, administered by the Bureau of Land Management, that is concurrently being considered for wilderness status. Timbered Crater rim elevation almost 4,000 ft. Area elevations 3,600–3,900 ft. Lava flows and shallow depressions are principal landscape features. Sparse vegetation.

Eagle Lake: Forest Service campgrounds, boat rentals.

Subway Cave: On SR 89 near junction with SR 44. Lava tube 1,300 ft. long, formed less than 2,000 years ago. Stairs at both ends, but no lights; bring your own. Rough floor. Low ceiling in places, but only tall people need stoop. Always 46°F.

Antelope Mountain Lookout: W of Eagle Lake, reached by gravel road from Eagle Lake Road. Mountain is 7,684-ft. elevation. Lookout station open 8 A.M.–5 P.M. during fire season.

Scenic drives: Many attractive routes. On a paved road, SR 36 SW from its junction with SR 89, W of Lake Almanor, follows Deer Creek, in a steep-walled canyon. Dogwood and redbud blooms in spring. Many gravel roads in Forest for backcountry travel, plus many roads requiring 4-wheel drive.

ACTIVITIES

Camping: 39 campgrounds, 997 sites. Campgrounds vary in size (4 to 182 units) and facilities. A few have no water or only water taken from stream or lake. Seasons vary. Some are open all year. Others open Mar. 1–Jun. 1, close Oct. 1–Nov. 30.

Hiking, backpacking: Trails and unpaved roads. Pacific Crest Trail runs roughly N–S, through center of Forest, also crossing center of National Park. Parts of the Trail were still temporary when we visited. Crest Trail follows the ridges, where snow limits travel to season beginning mid-July, ending Oct. Crest Trail elevations 2,900–7,000 ft. When Trail is completed, at least part will be open in winter.

Many trails and back roads are good hiking possibilities in addition to the Crest Trail and wilderness routes. Example: shoreline meadows around Eagle Lake. Several trails link the Forest and National Park.

Trailside camping is permitted almost everywhere. Special permit required in wilderness areas. Campfire permit is required for any type of fire, including stove, outside campgrounds.

Hunting: Deer, bear, game birds. Not outstanding.

Fishing: Lakes and streams.

Swimming: Beaches, unsupervised, at several campgrounds. Elsewhere as settings permit.

Boating: Lake Almanor, Eagle Lake. On both, most shoreline is privately owned, with much development.

Pack trips: Pleasant routes, most of them rather short. Because forage is limited, wilderness users must pack in feed for their stock.

ADJACENT: Lassen Volcanic National Park, Plumas National Forest, McArthur-Burney Falls Memorial State Park (see entries).

NEARBY: Honey Lake Wildlife Area (see entry).

PUBLICATIONS
Forest map. $1.00.
Visitor Guide.
Thousand Lakes Wilderness leaflet.
Caribou Wilderness leaflet.

HEADQUARTERS: 707 Nevada St., Susanville, CA 96130; (916) 257-2151.

RANGER DISTRICTS: Almanor R.D., P.O. Box 767, Chester, CA 96020; (916) 258-2141. Eagle Lake R.D., Johnstonville Rd., Susanville, CA 96100; (916) 257-2595. Hat Creek R.D., P.O. Box 220, Fall River Mills, CA 96028; (916) 336-5521.

LASSEN VOLCANIC NATIONAL PARK
U.S. National Park Service
106,000 acres.

Between Susanville and Redding. Access from SR's 44, 89, 36, 32. SR 89 crosses the Park; closed by snow from end of Oct. to early June.

Region of forest and lakes, dominated by 10,457-ft. Lassen Peak. Peak was formed by extrusion of lava from a vent in a larger extinct volcano. Beginning May 1914, eruptions occurred intermittently for more than 7 years. Other signs of volcanism: Cinder Cone, hot springs, steaming fumaroles, sulfurous vents.

Lowest elevation is 5,200 ft. The Transition life zone, up to 6,500 ft., has snow 4–5 months a year. The Canadian life zone, up to 8,000 ft., is under snow 6–7 months a year with depths up to 20 ft. or more. The Hudsonian life zone, up to the timberline at 9,000 ft., has snow cover 8–9 months a year with depths to more than 27 ft. Above 9,000 ft. is the Alpine zone, buried under snow 9–10 months a year with some patches the year around. High winds; wide daily temperature fluctuations.

A major portion of the Park is roadless wilderness. 50 lakes, the largest about 1 3/4 mi. long. Numerous clear streams. Almost 50 peaks, many over 8,000 ft.

Although the Park is open all year, winter use is chiefly ski touring and skiing. From the NW entrance, the road is kept open a short distance to Manzanita Lake. Winter sports area is near the SW entrance.

Plants: The Park is at the S end of the Cascade Range, just N of the Sierra, W of the Great Basin. Thus there is intermingling of species. Because of comparatively recent volcanic action, the forest community is in an early stage of succession. Each life zone has typical species: TRANSITION ZONE: ponderosa pine with associated sugar pine, white fir, incense cedar. Typical wildflowers: snowplant, Washington lily, blue-eyed grass, dwarf larkspur, sneezeweed. CANADIAN ZONE: red fir with associated lodgepole, Jeffrey, and western white pines; bush chinquapin, Labrador tea. Typical wildflowers: Lewis monkeyflower, bog kalmia, subalpine spiraea, western pasque flower, Lassen paintbrush. HUDSONIAN ZONE: mountain hemlock in lower portion, dwarf whitebark pine above. Shrubs: Brewer mountainheath, Mertens cassiope, pinemat manzanita. Typical wildflowers: rose willowweed, phacelia, Shasta knotweed, tolmie saxifrage. ALPINE ZONE: low or creeping plants, often with hairy leaves: dwarf hulsea, golden draba, polemonium.

Birds: No checklist. Common species include Steller's jay, robin, water ouzel, Clark's nutcracker, Lewis's and three-toed woodpeckers, purple finch, pygmy nuthatch, Swainson's thrush, Nashville warbler, sharp-shinned hawk, Williamson's sapsucker, green-tailed towhee, fox sparrow. Species present but rare include bald eagle, peregrine falcon.

Mammals: Common species include chipmunk, golden-mantled ground squirrel, chickaree. Less often seen: black bear, pika, marmot, marten, weasel, coyote, mountain beaver, porcupine, mountain lion, flying squirrel, Columbian black-tailed deer.

FEATURES

Wilderness area, where travel is by foot or horse only, is more than 3/4 of the Park. The Caribou Wilderness of Lassen National Forest is adjacent. This is a popular area, and regulations are designed to minimize environmental damage. A wilderness permit is required for overnight stays. Either Park or Forest will issue a permit good for the combined areas.

Lassen Park Road (SR 89) winds around three sides of the peak, offering many views of the mountain and the volcanic landscape. Features on or near the road include Manzanita Lake, Chaos Jumbles and Dwarf Forest, Devastated Area, Summit Lake, Lake Helen, Bumpass Hell, Sulphur Works. *Color Road Guide* available at entrances.

Unpaved roads from outside Park boundaries lead to Butte Lake, Juniper Lake, Warner Valley.

INTERPRETATION

Manzanita Lake visitor center, NW entrance, open daily, 8 A.M.–7:30 P.M., early June–late Sept. Information, exhibits, slide program, publications. *Southwest visitor center,* SW entrance, open daily 8 A.M.–5 P.M., same season. Information, exhibits, publications.

Guided hikes of many kinds: short nature walks, half-day hikes to points of interest, all-day Saturday hikes, night hikes. Details in *Summer Naturalist Program.*

Nature trails at Bumpass Hell, Lassen Peak, Cinder Cone, Boiling Springs Lake, Sulphur Works.

Evening talks at Manzanita Lake and Summit Lake amphitheaters.

ACTIVITIES

Camping: 6 campgrounds, 449 sites, plus one campground with 21 walk-in sites. Seasons differ: earliest opening some time in May; latest closing Oct. 15. 7-day limit within Park.

Hiking, backpacking: 150 mi. of trails, throughout Park. 17-mi. section of Pacific Crest Trail. Other trail connections into Lassen National Forest. No trailside camping within 1 mi. of developed area or road or within 1/4 mi. of a long list of areas considered fragile.

Fishing: Rainbow, brook, and brown trout. Some restricted zones.

Swimming: Especially at Butte, Bathtub, Juniper Lakes.

Canoeing: Canoes, other nonpowered craft permitted on all waters except Reflection, Emerald, Helen, Boiling Springs lakes.

Horse riding: Pack and saddle stock may not overnight in Park except in corrals at Buttle Lake, Summit Lake, and Juniper Lake. Reservations required. No grazing allowed. Wilderness permit required. A small corral near N boundary is available for those using Pacific Crest Trail.

Ski touring: Winter snow conditions usually good, but backcountry is closed when there is danger of avalanches. Downhill ski area near SW entrance.

If planning a visit in May or Oct., inquire to make sure road is open. Backcountry may be closed when fire danger is high.

Visitor use is heavy, even in backcountry, during most of the Jun.–Sept. season.

ADJACENT: Lassen National Forest (see entry).

PUBLICATIONS

Leaflet with map.
Backcountry Information.
Campground Information.

Lassen's Plants and Animals.
Summer Naturalist Program.

REFERENCES: Loomis Museum Association, Lassen Volcanic National Park, Mineral, CA 96063, issues list of publications for sale. Includes illustrated guide, trail leaflets, pamphlets on geology, fauna, flora, history, etc.

HEADQUARTERS: Mineral, CA 96063; (916) 595-4444.

LATOUR STATE FOREST
California Department of Forestry
9,033 acres.

50 mi. E of Redding. SR 44 E to Whitmore Rd., E on Whitmore to Bateman Rd. Normally accessible to vehicles late Jun. to Nov. High winds, wet snow, extreme cold are common winter and spring.

On W edge of Lassen National Forest (see entry), near Thousand Lakes Wilderness. Part of the Cascade Range, elevations 3,800–6,740 ft. Primarily forested, some brushfields and small meadows. Somewhat out of the way, it attracts more hunters than hikers or campers.

Plants: Pines: sugar, ponderosa, Jeffrey, western white, and lodgepole. Also white and red fir, Douglas-fir, incense cedar. All age classes. Shrubs: mountain snowberry, manzanitas, chinquapin, serviceberry, mountain ash, Oregon grape, mountain heather, etc. Wildflowers include scarlet fritillary, Washington lily, fairybell, pink pussy paws, shooting star, anemone, star flower, slim solomon. Plant checklists available.

Birds: Resident species include goshawk, sharp-shinned hawk, blue grouse, mountain quail, screech and spotted owls, flicker; pileated, hairy, downy, and white-headed woodpeckers; scrub and Steller's jays, white-breasted nuthatch, California thrasher, golden-crowned kinglet, Cassin's finch, red crossbill, pine siskin. Checklist available.

Mammals: Resident species include shrews, California mole, big brown bat, pika, snowshoe hare, mountain beaver, squirrels, yellow-bellied marmot, porcupine, coyote, red and gray foxes, bobcat, mountain lion, black bear, fisher, long-tailed weasel, striped skunk. Mule deer in summer. Checklist available.

ACTIVITIES
Camping: 3 campgrounds. Primitive.
Hiking: No trails, but miles of forest roads.
Fishing: Rainbow and German brook trout.

Horse riding: Riders must bring own horse feed; grazing is limited.

PUBLICATIONS
  Leaflet with map.
  Species checklists.

HEADQUARTERS: 1000 W. Cypress St., P.O. Box 2238, Redding, CA 96001;
  (916) 243-1436. Latour Station: (916) 474-3197.

LAVA BEDS NATIONAL MONUMENT
U.S. National Park Service
46,821 acres.

Near OR border. From Tulelake, 5 mi. S, then S on County Road III. 1.3
mi. unpaved. Open all year.

Rugged lava landscape; gentle slopes on the side of a dormant volcano; lava
fields grading into high desert flats, the fields area honeycombed with lava
tubes. Elevations 4,000–5,700 ft. Snow has been recorded in all seasons; but,
because annual precipitation is only 11–13 in., accumulations are small. Summer climate is moderate.

Features are cinder and spatter cones, craters, lava-tube caves. 21 caves are
officially open to visitors; others may be explored by notifying a ranger. Some
tubes extend 1 1/2 mi. The most recent lava flow was about 500 years ago.

Plants: Grassland-sagebrush community at lower altitudes; juniper-cha-
parral above; small amounts of ponderosa pine higher. Semiarid species; over
200 recorded. Prominent species include western juniper, curl-leaf mountain
mahogany, northern antelope bush, greenleaf manzanita, basin sagebrush,
gray ball sage, bitter cherry, rabbitbrush. Flowering plants include sagebrush
buttercup, western blue flax, blazing star, desert phlox, gilia, phacelia, paintbrush, pussytoes.

Birds: Checklist available. Although the varied plant communities are
generally rather dry, the Monument shares a long boundary with the Tule
Lake National Wildlife Refuge (see entry), which is mostly lake and marsh.
The bird list carries a number of species, including the bald eagle, white
pelican, bittern, and herons, that are most likely to be seen in the Refuge.
Among the permanent residents in the Monument itself are goshawk; sharp-
shinned, red-tailed, and marsh hawks; golden eagle, prairie falcon, kestrel,
blue grouse, mountain and California quail, pheasant; barn, screech, great
horned, saw-whet, and short-eared owls (as well as the long-eared, burrowing,
and great gray owls, which are less likely to be seen). Also kingfisher, flicker;

hairy, downy, and white-headed woodpeckers; horned lark; Steller's and scrub jays; black-billed magpie; raven; Clark's nutcracker; 3 nuthatches; brown creeper; Bewick's and canyon wrens; hermit thrush; western and mountain bluebirds; Townsend's solitaire; ruby- and golden-crowned kinglets; loggerhead shrike; yellow-rumped warbler; red-winged, tricolored, and Brewer's blackbirds; evening grosbeak; purple, Cassin's, and house finches; pine siskin; Oregon junco; song sparrow.

Summer residents include turkey vulture, Swainson's hawk, poorwill, nighthawk, Vaux's swift, several hummingbirds, flycatchers, swallows, and vireos, house wren, blue-gray gnatcatcher, yellow-headed blackbird, Bullock's oriole, cowbird, black-headed and evening grosbeaks, lazuli bunting, green-tailed towhee, sparrows.

Many other species in migration.

Mammals: Mule deer common in winter, scarce in summer. Often seen: yellow-bellied marmot, Belding ground squirrel, golden-mantled ground squirrel, chipmunk, cottontail, black-tailed jackrabbit, pika. Often seen along roads at night: porcupine, kangaroo rat, coyote, mice. Pronghorn, bobcat, mountain lion rarely seen.

Reptiles and amphibians: Western rattlesnake fairly common; visitors are advised to watch their footsteps on trails early morning and evening, use light at night. Seven nonpoisonous snakes, four species of lizards, one frog, one toad recorded; most take shelter during summer middays.

FEATURES

Wilderness areas include 28,460 acres, 3/5 of the Monument. Travel by foot or horse only. Water must be carried. Cold weather is possible at any time. Register before entering.

Cave Loop Road, near HQ, passes near many caves.

Symbol Bridge, 3/4-mi. hike from Skull Ice Cave road, is site of Indian pictographs.

Mammoth Crater, main source of lava, is near S boundary.

Schonchin Fire Tower, reached by 3/4-mi. trail; viewpoint.

INTERPRETATION

Visitor center: geology, history, natural history exhibits and publications. 8 A.M.–5:30 P.M. in summer.

Summer naturalist programs include movies, cave walks, demonstrations, evening talks. Announcements posted.

Nature trail at Black Crater.

ACTIVITIES

Camping: One campground, 46 sites. All year, but no water Oct. 15–May 14.

Hiking, backpacking: 55 mi. of trails, chiefly in wilderness areas. Map shows trails leading into Modoc National Forest, but ask about conditions.

Only one cave is lighted. Adequate lights (more than one), good walking shoes, hard hats, and jackets are needed in caves. Lights and hats available at visitor center.

Crowding limited to occasional holiday weekends.

ADJACENT: Tule Lake National Wildlife Refuge (see entry, Klamath Basin National Wildlife Refuges); Modoc National Forest (see entry).

PUBLICATIONS
Leaflet with map.
Species checklists: plants, birds, mammals, reptiles and amphibians.
Things to See and Do (leaflet).
Wilderness Hiking and Camping (leaflet).
Cave Information (leaflet).
Captain Jack's Stronghold Historical Trail (pamphlet).
Rock Art (leaflet).
Summary of Geology (leaflet).

HEADQUARTERS: P.O. Box 867, Tulelake, CA 96134; (916) 667-2283.

LOWER KLAMATH NATIONAL WILDLIFE REFUGE
See Klamath Basin National Wildlife Refuges.

MCARTHUR-BURNEY FALLS MEMORIAL STATE PARK
California Department of Parks and Recreation
853 acres.

From Burney, 11 mi. NE on SR 89.

Midway between Mt. Shasta and Lassen Peak. Most visitors stop here to see the falls, once called by Theodore Roosevelt the eighth wonder of the world. The 129-ft. falls are supplied by giant springs a few hundred yards upstream, flowing full even in dry weather.

Almost 2 mi. frontage on 9-mi.-long Lake Britton and Burney Creek. Elevations from 2,762 to 3,140 ft. Predominantly ponderosa pine forest with Douglas-fir, incense cedar, willows, aspen, black oak. Sparse understory includes manzanita, squaw carpet, squaw brush. Relatively few wildflowers.

Birds: 132 species recorded. Noteworthy are black swift nesting in the cliff. Bald eagles nest. Others recorded include western, eared, and pied-billed grebes; great blue heron, Canada goose, mallard, common merganser, ruddy duck, barn and great horned owls, belted kingfisher, common flicker, black-headed and evening grosbeaks, Oregon junco.

INTERPRETATION: *Campfire programs* and *guided hikes,* Jun.–Aug. *Nature trail,* 1 mi.; leaflet.

ACTIVITIES
    Camping: 2 campgrounds, 118 sites. All year. Reservations accepted May 25–Sept. 8.
    Hiking, backpacking: 4 mi. of trails. Connection with Pacific Crest Trail; Park often used as stopover.
    Fishing: Lake and stream. Bass, brown trout in lake. Streams have rainbow, brown, and brook trout.
    Swimming: Lake. Unsupervised. Usual season Jun.–Sept.
    Boating: Ramp. Rentals.

NEARBY: Portion of Shasta National Forest that is administered by Lassen National Forest. Forest map shows some primitive roads that may offer good hiking, but inquire.

PUBLICATIONS
    Leaflet with map.
    Nature trail guide.
    Bird checklist.

HEADQUARTERS: Route 1, Box 1260, Burney, CA 96013; (916) 335-2777.

MENDOCINO NATIONAL FOREST
U.S. Forest Service

About 125,000 acres of this Forest, in Tehama County, is in zone 2. The largest part is in zone 3, where the entry appears.

MODOC NATIONAL FOREST
U.S. Forest Service
1,651,232 acres; 1,979,407 acres within boundaries.

NE CA. Largest portion extends S from OR border, from Lava Beds National Monument on W to Goose Lake on E. Another block, from 5 to 15 mi. wide, extends 60 mi. S from OR border, E of Goose Lake. S portion is irregular, fragmented, with many inholdings. US 395 is between major sections. Forest is crossed by SR 299, SR 139.

Large, diverse, scenic region of California, less visited than mountain areas to S. Climate relatively dry. Elevations from 4,200–9,892 ft. Mountain slopes from gentle to precipitous. Obsidian cliffs, craters, lava caves. Extensive forested plateaus, meadows, open rangeland. Lakes, reservoirs, and streams.

Doublehead Ranger District, NW sector, adjoins Lava Beds National Monument (see entry) on W, S, and E, has similar volcanic features: glass and lava flows, caves, tubes, chimneys, craters. W portion has mountains with moderate to steep slopes. *Plants:* Sugar pine and red and white firs; understory of bitterbrush, manzanita, showbrush. At higher elevations, pure stands of lodgepole pine. To the E, sagebrush and juniper slopes. Medicine, Little Medicine, Bullseye, and Blanche lakes offer the only fishing. This Ranger District completely surrounds the Clear Lake National Wildlife Refuge (see entry).

Devil's Garden Ranger District, W of Goose Lake, S to the Pit River. Gentle to moderate slopes. Average elevation 4,800 ft. Although much of the District, like Modoc County as a whole, is semiarid, it contains the 6,000-acre Big Sage Reservoir and a number of smaller ones. It also contains some 34,000 acres of wetland habitat, 15,000 of which are permanent water and 19,000 are intermittent wetlands. The basins in this area are characterized by heavy clay soils, with meadow, grasses, forbs, and silver sage communities. The characteristic vegetation of the associated uplands is low sagebrush and bluegrasses, or juniper, low sagebrush, and grasses. These lands are being managed for wildlife, including pronghorn, feral horse, sage grouse, and waterfowl. Grazing is a continuing use. One of the largest continuous stands of juniper in the western United States, 800 acres preserved in *Devil's Garden Natural Area.* Juniper areas have big, black, and silver sagebrushes; rabbitbrush, bunchgrass. Also stands of ponderosa and Jeffrey pines, with white fir and incense cedar on N slopes above 5,500 ft.

Big Valley Ranger District, SW and S central portions. Basalt-capped plateaus and steep, mountainous uplands. Elevations 4,500–7,000 ft. At lower elevations: sage-bunchgrass, juniper-bunchgrass, with some bitterbrush, curl-leaf mahogany. Higher, ponderosa and Jeffrey pines, with white fir and incense cedar on N slopes above 5,500 ft.

Warner Mountain Ranger District includes South Warner Wilderness (see Features section). Mountain range moderately sloping on W side, very steep on E. Several high peaks, including 9,892-ft. Eagle Peak. Sage, bunchgrass, juniper at lower elevations, with bitterbrush and curl-leaf mahogany. At intermediate altitudes: pure and mixed stands of ponderosa and Jeffrey pines, white fir. Above, lodgepole and western white pines. Small lakes, streams. The best fishing is outside the Wilderness, at East Creek, Patterson, and Lily Lake.

Plants: Ponderosa and Jeffrey pines, incense cedar, western juniper. Associated species include oaks, quaking aspen, mountain mahogany, manzanita, chokecherry and bitter cherry, blueberry, snowberry, currant, Sierra plum, mountain misery, fern bush, squaw apple, sagebrush, rabbitbrush, bitterbrush, squaw carpet, serviceberry. Wildflowers include wild onion, camas, Indian paintbrush, low larkspur, shooting star, daisy, strawberry, lupines, tarweed, bluebell, phlox, buttercup, pansy, wooly mule's ear. Monkeyflower, evening primrose, peony, gilia, fireweed are among the species less commonly seen.

Birds: List available. Common shorebirds and waterfowl include red-necked and pied-billed grebes, double-crested cormorant, great blue heron, Canada goose, mallard, gadwall, pintail, shoveler. Sandhill crane rare. Raptors include hawks, golden and bald eagles, osprey, and goshawk. Coot, killdeer, willet, greater and lesser yellowlegs, spotted sandpiper, American avocet, Wilson's phalarope. Black-necked stilt less common. Ring-billed gull, Forster's tern, and black tern are common, with Caspian tern less so. Owls, hummingbirds, woodpeckers, kingbirds, and flycatchers are represented by several species each. Six swallow species are numerous.

Mammals: Common species include mule deer, pronghorn, coyote, striped skunk, raccoon, cottontail, muskrat, beaver, porcupine, feral horse, many mice, voles, and ground squirrels. Black bear, bobcat, cougar, badger, fisher, marten, mink, weasels, marmot, jackrabbit, snowshoe hare, and several squirrel species are here, but less common.

FEATURES

South Warner Wilderness, 68,540 acres. Spectacular alpine and subalpine area. Highest point is Eagle Peak. Patches of timber, grassy basins, slopes, meadows. Tumbling streams, a few small lakes, many springs. Area is unusual in that the trails are designed for access and penetration only. Once in the area, travel is by bushwhacking, so topo map and compass are essential. Wilderness permit is required. Subfreezing temperatures can occur in any month. Thunderstorms common in summer; snow not uncommon late spring and early fall; strong winds late Aug. and Sept.

Medicine Lake Highlands, 9,000 acres. Lies within a loosely defined boundary S of Lava Beds National Monument. Points of interest are Medicine Lake, crystal-clear in an old crater; Glass Mountain, unique glassy dacite and rhyolitic obsidian flow estimated to be about 1,400 years old; Burnt Lava Flow, picturesque flow of jumbled black lava surrounding islands of timber; Medicine Lake Glass Flow, composed of dull, stony-gray dacite, which covers a square mile, and ranges 50–150 ft. in height; Little Mount Hoffman Lookout, seldom used lookout affording spectacular view N toward Lava Beds National Monument.

ACTIVITIES

Camping: 20 campgrounds, about 320 sites. A few campgrounds are easily accessible, with vault toilets and piped water. Others are primitive, access roads not suitable for larger RV's. As in other National Forests, one can camp almost anywhere, subject to fire permits and special regulations. Camping season generally May 15–Oct. 1. Many campgrounds are on or near lakes or streams.

Hiking, backpacking: About 140 mi. of trails, 2,000 mi. of maintained Forest roads, all suitable for hiking. Off-trail hiking is possible in many areas.

Hunting: Mule deer for both rifle and bow hunters; pronghorn, waterfowl, migratory birds other than waterfowl, quail.

Fishing: Variety of lakes and streams. Brook and rainbow trout, bass, catfish, arctic grayling.

Swimming: Medicine Lake, Blue Lake, elsewhere.

Boating, canoeing: Power boating on Blue Lake, Big Sage, Medicine Lake. Canoeing on a few smaller lakes.

Horse riding: Some horse parties use the Forest, especially the South Warner Wilderness. Ask Forest HQ about local outfitters.

Downhill skiing: Cedar Pass area.

Ski touring: Warner Mountains and Medicine Lake Highlands.

Call HQ if planning trip in May or after mid-Sept. for advice on late or early snow. If press reports forest fires, check for advice on possible closure.

PUBLICATIONS

Forest map. $1.00.

Off-road vehicle map.

South Warner Wilderness brochure with map.

Medicine Lake Highlands brochure with map.

HEADQUARTERS: P.O. Box 611, Alturas, CA 96101; (916) 233-3521.

RANGER DISTRICTS: Big Valley R.D., Adin, CA 96006; (916) 299-3215. Devil's Garden R.D., Canby, CA 96015; (916) 233-4611. Doublehead R.D., Tulelake, CA 96134; (916) 667-2246. Warner Mountain R.D., Cedarville, CA 96014; (916) 279-6116.

MODOC NATIONAL WILDLIFE REFUGE
U.S. Fish and Wildlife Service
6,203 acres.

From just S of Alturas on US 395, E on County Road 56 for 0.6 mi., then S on County Road 115 and follow Refuge signs.

Open: Daylight hours. Dorris Reservoir closed Oct.–Feb.

Waterfowl area 60 mi. SE of the Klamath Basin marshes. At the W base of the Warner Mountains. Elevation about 4,400 ft. Area is flat to rolling.

Numerous lakes, ponds, with many islands for breeding. South Fork of Pit River flows through. Dorris Reservoir, about 3 mi. E of the main portion, supplies water by canal for irrigation. About 700 acres of impoundments, 500 of marsh, 40 of river bottom; the balance is cropland and sagebrush-juniper. Area is semiarid, with dry summers.

Large concentrations of waterfowl spring and fall. Many nesting species, so birding is also good in summer.

Birds: More than 187 species recorded. Peak fall population about 15,000 geese, 25,000 ducks. Nesting flock of Canada goose as well as migrants. Other nesting waterfowl: eared, western, and pied-billed grebes; mallard, gadwall, pintail, ruddy duck, green-winged and cinnamon teals, shoveler. Migrants include white-fronted and snow geese, wigeon, bufflehead. Sandhill crane sometimes seen in courtship dance; approximately 10 young a year are produced on the Refuge. White pelican present in summer, not nesting here. Whistling swans stop over during migration.

Snipe, avocet, willet, Wilson's phalarope, black-necked stilt, pheasant, bitterns, Virginia rail, owls, flicker, and many swallow species nest here. Migratory species include long-billed dowitcher, greater yellowlegs. Other species often seen include raptors, egrets, flycatchers, mountain chickadee, mountain bluebird, warblers, sparrows.

Checklist available.

Mammals: Include mule deer, pronghorn, coyote, bobcat, badger, skunk, raccoon, mink, muskrat, ground squirrel, cottontail, black-tailed jackrabbit.

Entrance road overlooks several ponds. *Birding,* including upland species, is good in HQ area. Short *auto tour route* around a marsh.

ACTIVITIES

Hunting: Waterfowl. Designated area. Special rules may change from year to year. Inquire.

Fishing: Reservoir. Bass, catfish, trout.

Boating: For fishing only; hp limited.

NEARBY: Modoc National Forest (see entry).

PUBLICATION: Hunting leaflet with map.

HEADQUARTERS: P.O. Box 1610, Alturas, CA 96101; (916) 233-3572.

PLUMAS-EUREKA STATE PARK

California Department of Parks and Recreation
6,600 acres.
Within Plumas National Forest.

From Lake Tahoe, 80 mi. N on SR 89 to Graeagle, then 5 mi. W on County A-14.

Scenic and historic park on E slopes of the Sierra Nevada. Mountainous. Elevations from 4,000–7,500 ft. Eureka Peak, 7,447 ft., is the natural focal point of the Park. Two small lakes; several creeks. Cascades and falls on Jamison Creek. Park is open all year, campground seasonally.

Plants: Lower slopes forested, tree species including red and white firs, Douglas-fir, incense cedar; ponderosa, sugar, and Jeffrey pines; with alder, black cottonwood, aspen, willow along streams. Brushy areas, especially at higher elevations, have manzanita, chinquapin, ceanothus, buckthorn. No wildflower list, but local flora index is available at the museum.

Birds: No checklist. Species noted include Steller's jay, band-tailed pigeon, robin, golden eagle, common flicker, white-headed and pileated woodpeckers, red-tailed hawk, great blue heron.

Mammals: Include deer, squirrel, chipmunk, gopher, raccoon, porcupine, striped and spotted skunks, muskrat, beaver. In more remote sections: coyote, mountain lion, bobcat, black bear, marten, weasel.

FEATURES: Scenic drives: to parking area near Eureka Lake, 6,300-ft. elevation; Red Dirt Road into National Forest and to the isolated N section of the Park.

INTERPRETATION: *Visitor center/museum.* Natural and cultural history. *Campfire programs* and *guided hikes,* Jun.–Sept. *"Talking Forest"* nature trail.

ACTIVITIES
Camping: 67 sites. Approx. May 15–Oct. 15. Reservations accepted June 9–Sept. 3.
Hiking, backpacking: Trails to Eureka Peak, around Madora Lake, along Jamison Creek to falls. Trails into National Forest backcountry. Trailside camping in the Forest.
Fishing: Rainbow, brook, brown trout.
Ski touring: 6 mi. of trail. Usual snow season: Dec. 15–Mar. 30.

Crowding often occurs July–Aug.

PUBLICATION: Leaflet with map. 25¢.

HEADQUARTERS: Johnsville Star Route, Blairsden, CA 96103; (916) 836-2380.

PLUMAS NATIONAL FOREST
U.S. Forest Service
1,154,754 acres; 1,409,986 acres within boundaries.

US 395 approximates the NE boundary. SR 70 crosses the Forest from the E, approximating its W boundary just N of Lake Oroville. Bullards Bar Reservoir is at the S tip. SR 89 crosses, SE to NW.

Part of the huge block of public land in E California, adjoining the Lassen National Forest on the N, the Tahoe National Forest on the S. In the transition zone where the Sierra Nevada and Cascade Range merge. Elevations from 1,000 ft. to 8,372 ft. About a hundred lakes, more than 1,000 mi. of streams with canyons, waterfalls, cascades. Forest, brushfields, meadows.

Our source at HQ commented that the area is not as popular as other National Forests along the Sierra, and that most people think it less scenic. Presumably the comment applies to the N portion, above SR 70. The views may be less dramatic, but it's attractive country. Trails are not heavily traveled.

The Forest includes most of the Feather River watershed, and this area is undeniably popular. The quarter-million acres of Forest inholdings include numerous commercial resorts, summer homes, and tourist enterprises. Many of the lakes have developed private land as well as Forest land along their shores. Some parts of the Forest, especially around lakes, are heavily used, and restrictions have been adopted to minimize damage to the environment.

The Forest map shows relatively few hiking trails but an extensive road network, including many miles of primitive roads, some of which are more suitable for quiet hiking than for driving with an ordinary car. The network also includes many miles of gravel and regularly maintained dirt roads. Many of these follow streams. Some lead to relatively isolated lakeside campgrounds.

At Quincy, elevation about 3,500 ft., at the junction of SR 70 and SR 89, annual precipitation is about 43 in. per year, most of it in winter. Temperatures here are mild, seldom below freezing in winter. SR 70 W of Quincy is below the snow line most of the time. On the higher slopes, of course, snowfall is heavier and freezing temperatures more common. Campgrounds at lower elevations generally open in May, those higher about June 1. High trails are usually open by mid-June.

Plants: About two-thirds of the area is forested, the other third mostly in manzanita, sagebrush, and sagebrush-juniper, with some meadows and rocky places. Of the forest area, mixed conifers dominate the zone from about 2,000 ft.–6,000 ft. of elevation, red fir in the zone next above. Together these make up about half of the forested acreage. Ponderosa pine is on the hotter, drier slopes, white fir where conditions are somewhat cooler and moister. Other species include incense cedar, sugar pine, black oak. Douglas-fir in some areas. A rarity is the Baker cypress, found at 6,500–7,000 ft. on Wheeler and

Eisenheimer peaks. The champion is a specimen 70 ft. high, 21-ft. diameter. Virtually the entire forest has been logged from time to time, but isolated old-growth specimens remain.

No wildflower checklist is available. Notable displays are redbud in Apr., dogwood in May and June.

Birds: Checklist on file at HQ. 223 species recorded, including common loon; western, eared, pied-billed, and horned grebes; white pelican, great blue and black-crowned night herons, great and snowy egrets, many waterfowl species, many birds of prey; blue and sage grouse, California and mountain quail, many shorebirds, many gulls and terns, 9 species of owls, 10 species of woodpeckers, 12 species of flycatchers, 6 swallow species; Steller's, scrub, and pinyon jays; black-billed magpie, Clark's nutcracker; black-capped, mountain, and chestnut-backed chickadees; 5 wren species, western and mountain bluebirds, northern and loggerhead shrikes, 12 wood warbler species; black-headed, evening, and rose-breasted grosbeaks; 15 species of sparrows and towhees.

Mammals: Checklist on file at HQ. Species recorded include black bear, raccoon, ringtail, bobcat, mountain lion, long- and short-tailed weasels, mink, pine marten, river otter, badger, striped and spotted skunks, red and gray foxes, coyote, mule deer, yellow-bellied marmot, chickaree, ground squirrels, chipmunks, beavers, porcupine, mice, snowshoe and black-tailed hares, mountain cottontail, pika, Trowbridge shrew, little brown bat, long-eared myotis.

Reptiles and amphibians: Include long-toed salamander, California newt, western toad, Pacific treefrog, California red-legged frog, mountain yellow-legged frog, 5 lizard species, 10 snake species including western ringneck, Pacific gopher, rubber boa, western rattlesnake.

FEATURES

Feather Falls Scenic Area: 15,000 acres, including portions of Middle Fork of the Feather River and three tributaries. Wide variety of topography, vegetation, wildlife. Spectacular granite domes, picturesque waterfalls. Feather Falls, 640 ft., is sixth highest in continental United States; reached by self-guiding trail, 7 mi. round trip. Hiking and riding trails. *Caution: Sheer cliffs. Stay back of guard rails.*

Middle Fork, Feather River: 93 mi. long. Designated a National Wild and Scenic River. Designated land, a narrow band, along river includes 13,200 acres of National Forest land, 12,000 acres privately owned. Five zones include

- *Bald Rock Canyon Wild River Zone.* Rugged, scenic. Massive boulders, cliffs, waterfalls, canyon walls. Access is difficult. End-to-end travel seldom possible, rarely accomplished. Portions can be visited by day or overnight hikes.
- *Upper Canyon Wild River Zone.* River is rugged, rocky. Slopes

vegetated but steep. Three trails to river for 4-wheel-drive vehicles or trail bikes. Also foot trails.

- *Milsap Bar Scenic River Zone.* Scenic, rugged. Automobile bridge crosses river within this zone; campground nearby. *South Branch Falls,* also known as Seven Falls, has 9 falls of 130–150 ft. About 1 mi. upstream from campground, but no trail. A primitive road from Brush Creek is nearby. A scenic area, but rough country.
- *English Bar Scenic River Zone.* Scenic, less rugged than other zones. Timber stands closer to river. Automobile bridge crosses at Nelson Point. Access also from unimproved roads. Unimproved campsites.
- *Recreational River Zone* includes a variety of scenic types, notably Mohawk Valley. Many inholdings, commercial developments including motels, resorts, stables.

Caution: Wild River zones are not for the inexperienced. Scenic River zones are not for the unprepared. Although portions of the river can be floated, sections are treacherous, and access in or out of some sections is nearly impossible. Check with rangers before undertaking a river trip.

Lake Davis Recreation Area. Elevation 5,575 ft. Camping, hiking, fishing, hunting, boating, ski touring. No swimming because of snail parasites in lake water.

Bucks Lake Recreation Area. Elevation 5,155 ft. Camping, hiking, fishing, hunting, swimming, boating, horse riding, and also ski touring. Commercial resorts and private homes occupy part of lakeshore. Good trails in area; Pacific Crest Trail is nearby. Unusual botanical feature is the brilliant red snow plant seen May–July. Beaver ponds and dams in Haskins Valley and Bucks Creek.

Little Grass Valley Recreation Area. Reservoir at 5,046-ft. elevation. Upper Canyon Wild River Zone of Middle Fork is N of lake. Feather River Falls Scenic Area is SW of lake. Camping, hiking, hunting, fishing, swimming, boating, ski touring. Although there are some inholdings, the entire shoreline is accessible. The snow plant is seen in this vicinity also.

Antelope Lake Recreation Area. Elevation 5,002 ft. Camping, hiking, hunting, fishing, swimming, boating. Scenic drive from here to timberline near crest of Diamond Mountain, ending at Red Rock Lookout; 25 mi. Road usually passable by late June.

INCLUDES: Plumas-Eureka State Park (see entry).

ACTIVITIES

Camping: 41 campgrounds. 1,008 sites. Open June 1–Oct. 31, those at lower elevations may open mid-May. Camping is generally permitted elsewhere except for specified areas around lakes, subject to obtaining fire permit.

Hiking, backpacking: 67 mi. of the Pacific Crest Trail will be in the Forest.

Temporary sections will be in use. Trail guides available for this and other trails.

Hunting: Deer, bear, squirrel, rabbit, waterfowl, quail, chukar, dove.

Fishing: Many lakes and streams. Rainbow and brown trout, kokanee and coho salmon, bass, catfish, bluegill.

Swimming: Beaches at several lakes. Elsewhere as you choose.

Boating: Ramps on several lakes.

Canoeing, kayaking: Attempting the Middle Fork by raft or kayak is inadvisable. Tubing in the recreation zone and English Bar Scenic Zone is feasible in June and July.

Horse riding: Rentals at Blairsden. Some trails are unsuitable for horses. Few riders make overnight trips.

ADJACENT: Lassen National Forest, Tahoe National Forest (see entries).

PUBLICATIONS
Forest map. $1.00.
Forest information sheet.
Campground information.
Trail information: Quincy Ranger District.
Pacific Crest Trail route description.
Pacific Crest Trail fact sheet.
Trail guide: Feather River Canyon.
Leaflets with maps
    Feather Falls Scenic Area.
    Middle Fork, Feather River.
    Lake Davis Recreation Area.
    Bucks Lake Recreation Area.
    Little Grass Valley Recreation Area.
    Antelope Lake Recreation Area.
Plumas National Forest off-road vehicle control plan.

HEADQUARTERS: Box 1500, Quincy, CA 95971; (916) 283-2050.

RANGER DISTRICTS: Beckwourth R.D., Box 7, Blairsden, CA 96103; (916) 836-2575. Greenville R.D., Box 329, Greenville, CA 95947; (916) 284-7126. La Porte R.D., Box F, Challenge, CA 95925; (916) 675-2462. Oroville R.D., 875 Mitchell Ave., Oroville, CA 95965; (916) 534-6500. Milford R.D., USFS, Milford, CA 96121; (916) 253-2223. Quincy R.D., Box 69, Quincy, CA 95971; (916) 283-0555.

SHASTA-TRINITY NATIONAL FOREST
U.S. Forest Service

See entry in zone 1. Although a large portion of the Forest is in zone 2, most is in zone 1, and a unified entry seemed best.

The Whiskeytown-Shasta-Trinity National Recreation Area has three units. Two of them, Clair Engle Lake and Shasta Lake, are within the Shasta-Trinity National Forest and described in that entry. The Whiskeytown unit stands alone and is an entry in zone 2.

SKEDADDLE-AMEDEE MOUNTAINS
U.S. Bureau of Land Management
63,130 acres.

From Susanville, E 18 mi. on US 395, then E on Wendel, the SW boundary. E boundary is Skedaddle Rd. Several dead-end roads lead N into the area.

Rugged vertical cliffs and canyons, peaks, and basins of the Amedee and Skedaddle Mountains. The high (up to 7,552 ft.) elevations of the Skedaddles support scattered aspen groves and patches of large berry shrubs. Riparian vegetation (willows, wild rose, berry shrubs) in the deep canyons, and small grass meadows in the basins. The rugged core unit is surrounded by open, sagebrush-covered flats at about 3,250-ft. elevation. Numerous springs. Unusual rock formations in scenic Wendel Canyon.

Wildlife abounds in the unit, including mule deer, pronghorn, and the seldom-seen mountain lion. Prairie and peregrine falcon nest.

HEADQUARTERS: BLM, Susanville District Office, P.O. Box 1090, 705 Hall St., Susanville, CA 92507; (916) 257-5385.

TEHAMA WILDLIFE AREA
California Department of Fish and Game
43,605 acres.

From Red Bluff on I-5, E 3 mi. on SR 99, then 15 mi. E on Hogsback Rd. Or 20 mi. N and E from SR 99 to Paynes Creek, then S on Plum Creek Rd.

Winter range for Columbian black-tailed deer. Sierra Nevada foothills, a broad bench sloping from 4,000 ft. down toward the Sacramento River Valley, cut by steep-sided canyons with prominent rimrocks and lava outcroppings. The herd migrates over 100 mi. from summer range in and around Lassen National Park, arriving here mid-Oct. and remaining until early Apr. Woodland, grass, and brush. Primary deer forage is wedgeleaf ceanothus, along with acorn mast, oak leafage, mountain mahogany, live oak, redberry.

A major portion of the Wildlife Area, that S of Hogsback Rd., is closed Dec. 31 through first Friday in Apr. to prevent harassment of deer in breeding season.

On the E, the area adjoins a lightly used section of Lassen National Forest (see entry). Map shows jeep roads crossing into the Forest.

ACTIVITIES

Camping: Two campgrounds. Primitive; no water.

Hiking: Trails and primitive roads.

Hunting: Chiefly deer. Also feral hog, valley quail, some mountain quail, turkey, squirrel. Poor waterfowl hunting.

Fishing: Rainbow and brown trout; bass in lower portion of Antelope Creek.

Caution: Visitors are advised to be extremely cautious using roads and trails. ORV use is prohibited.

PUBLICATION: Leaflet with map.

HEADQUARTERS: P.O. Box 188, Paynes Creek, CA 96075; (916) 597-2201.

TIMBERED CRATER
U.S. Bureau of Land Management
18,690 acres.

From Fall River Mills on US 299, E 7 mi., then 8 mi. N on road to Day.

The Day road passes through private and National Forest land to an area of private land in Little Hot Spring Valley. This site lies to the W and adjoins Shasta National Forest land on the W and SE. It takes its name from a large crater on the W boundary, its slopes covered with grasses, manzanita brush, and ponderosa pine. Most of the area is a large lava flow that has not yet developed deep soils and is rocky, rough, and difficult to traverse. Terrain includes low buttes, shallow depressions and drainages. Natural vegetation includes ponderosa and digger pine, oak, juniper, and dense to scattered mountain shrub. Much of the area burned in 1977.

The BLM reports that more than 200 bird species have been identified in the area, including bald eagle, mourning dove, band-tailed pigeon, valley and mountain quail, turkey, pheasant, blue grouse. Mammals include black bear, Columbian black-tailed deer, mule deer, cottontail, western gray squirrel, chickaree, mountain lion, Rocky Mountain elk. Wolverine reported. The site includes the Baker Cypress-Lava Rock Natural Area, 1,148 acres, designated to protect a stand of Baker cypress. Elevation here is 3,400–3,600 ft.

Most of the Timbered Crater area and adjoining National Forest land has been recommended for wilderness study. Just S of the boundary, maps show a wetlands complex: Eastman Lake, Big Lake, Tule Lake, the Tule and Little Tule rivers, swamp, and meandering creeks. The BLM bird information included waterfowl, and presumably this is where they occur. The area is said to be a combination of private and state-owned land. From Fall River Mills, Glenburn Road leads toward this area, and it would seem worth exploring, especially by birders.

TULE LAKE NATIONAL WILDLIFE REFUGE

See Klamath Basin National Wildlife Refuges.

WHISKEYTOWN UNIT; WHISKEYTOWN-SHASTA-TRINITY NATIONAL RECREATION AREA

U.S. National Park Service
42,503 acres.

From Redding, 8 mi. W on SR 299.

Other units of this National Recreation Area are within the Shasta-Trinity National Forest (see entry, zone 1). This one stands alone. Chief attraction is the 3,250-acre lake. Unlike Shasta and Clair Engle Lakes, it is not drawn down in summer. Thus it can have sandy beaches fine for swimming. Its size and shape favor canoeing and sailing rather than high-speed motorboating.

Surrounded by hills. Highest point 6,029 ft. The original forest was logged off in recent years with little heed for reforestation. Now under management, gradual recovery is occurring. Stands of young trees and extensive shrub cover have promoted development of wildlife populations.

People come here because of the lake. Few except hunters use the upcountry. The map shows no foot trails, but there are 50 mi. of backcountry dirt and gravel roads.

ACTIVITIES

Camping: 2 campgrounds; 193 sites. All year.

Hunting: Deer, bear, squirrel, rabbit, fox, dove, pigeon, quail, some water-fowl.

Fishing: Brown and rainbow trout, bass, bluegill, kokanee salmon.

Boating, canoeing: Ramps, marina, rentals.

Swimming: 2 supervised beaches.

PUBLICATION: Leaflet with map.

HEADQUARTERS: Box 188, Whiskeytown, CA 96095; (916) 241-6584.

WOODSON BRIDGE STATE RECREATION AREA
California Department of Parks and Recreation
414 acres.

From Corning on I-5, 6 mi. E on South Ave.

On the Sacramento River. Small park much used by local groups for nature study. Over 100 plant species identified. Prominent trees include valley oak, California black walnut, Oregon ash, black cottonwood. Many shrubs, wild-flowers. Vivid fall colors.

Many bird species; checklist available. Deer often seen, as well as small mammals.

A portion of the site across the river, not accessible by land, has been set aside as a natural preserve.

ACTIVITIES

Camping: 46 sites. All year. Reservations available May 25–Sept. 14.

Fishing: Boat and bank. King salmon, shad, steelhead, striped bass, catfish, occasional sturgeon.

Boating: Ramp at adjacent county park.

PUBLICATION: Leaflet with map.

HEADQUARTERS: Route 1, Box 325, Corning, CA 96021; (916) 839-2112.

ZONE 3

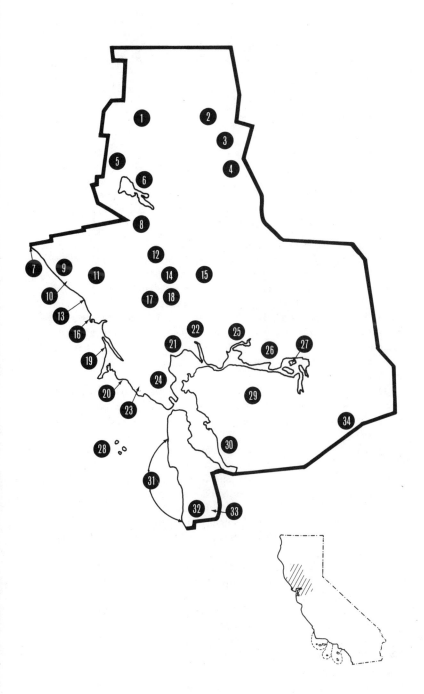

CALIFORNIA, ZONE 3

Includes these counties:

Glenn	Yolo	San Joaquin
Lake	Marin	San Francisco
Colusa	Solano	San Mateo
Sonoma	Sacramento	Alameda
Napa	Contra Costa	

Few cities have as much diverse, scenic, wild country nearby as does San Francisco. Zone 3 includes the Bay Area and the counties to the N and E. Those to the S are in zone 5.

The Bay itself is surrounded by fascinating wetlands, only a fraction of what was once here but none the less impressive. The largest, the Grizzly Island Wildlife Area, is relatively little known, but it is one of America's great marshes, in the same league as Brigantine, Blackwater, Merritt Island, and Bear River. Wetlands near the confluence of Sacramento and San Joaquin rivers are best explored by boat, although some areas are accessible by car and on foot.

The ocean beaches S of the city are attractive but heavily used, with few sections one could call natural. We have written a collective entry: San Mateo State Beaches. Inland are two of the redwood State Parks: Portola and Butano.

To the N is the Golden Gate National Recreation Area, at least a part of which merits the name "the wilderness next door." This National Recreation Area is a complex of city, state, and federal sites, knitted together in an imaginative management scheme. Included are some of San Francisco's city parks. Across the bridge are the Marin Highlands, Muir Woods, Mt. Tamalpais, and other areas. Under the plan, development will be limited, large sections left wild. Adjoining is Point Reyes National Seashore, a large part of it wilderness.

Still further N are Bodega Harbor and the Sonoma Coast State Beaches, a spectacular coastline. A bit inland is another redwood State Park, Armstrong.

Directly N of the city, out SR 29, is the Napa Valley, famous for its wine grapes. Several State Parks offer easy and pleasant hiking: Annadel, Bothe-Napa Valley, Robert Louis Stevenson, with Boggs Mountain State Forest a bit beyond. The valley floor is rolling rather than flat. The mountains on either side are not high but steep, with many canyons. Cross-mountain roads are likely to be scenic but steep and narrow.

W and N of Clear Lake, the W boundary of the zone is the crest of the Coast Range. The mountains are largely occupied by the Mendocino National Forest, a major part of which is in zone 3.

I-5, near the E boundary of the zone, runs through the Sacramento Valley. Once a great wetlands, supporting millions of waterfowl, the valley is now agricultural. In recent years, the swing has been to rice. Fields are surrounded by low dikes. Many operations are performed by low-flying planes. The Sacramento National Wildlife Refuges have the dual role of accommodating large numbers of wintering waterfowl and reducing their predation on farm crops.

Here we had to give further thought to our earlier decision not to include municipal and county parks. The East Bay Regional Parks District has a magnificent array of sites, 40 or more units totaling 51,000 acres, the largest 5,086 acres, 14 of them with more than 1,000 acres. Although some of these sites are heavily developed, with golf courses, playgrounds, and other facilities, a number are carefully protected natural areas, comparable to many of the State Parks we select as entries. We spent two days visiting and admiring them. In the end, we reaffirmed our decision not to include. The reasons are explained in the Preface.

ANGEL ISLAND STATE PARK
See Golden Gate National Recreation Area.

ANNADEL STATE PARK
California Department of Parks and Recreation
Approximately 5,000 acres.

> From Santa Rosa, E on SR 12 about 6 mi.; S on Los Alamos; W on Montgomery Dr.; S on Channel Dr.

A day-use park for hiking, about 50 mi. N of San Francisco. Flat to rolling terrain. Elevations from 300 ft. to 1,887 at top of Bennett Mountain. (The peak is just outside the Park boundary.) Some steep-sided canyons, rock outcroppings on knolls. Intermittent streams. Includes 30-acre Lake Ilsanjo; 1 1/2-mi. shoreline, a 35-acre marsh. A 30-ft. waterfall is usually dry. Parking, office, picnic facilities, trails. No other development.

Plants: About 70% forested: mixed evergreen and oak-deciduous. Trees include Douglas-fir, bay, madrone, California black oak, Oregon oak, Oregon ash, California buckeye, Coast live oak, bigleaf maple. Small stand of redwood, a few old growth. Understory includes wood fern, hazelnut, abundant poison oak. About 1/4 of the area is chaparral-shrub, including manzanita, chamise, toyon. About 200 species of flowering plants including brodiaea, lupine, California poppy, goldfields, shooting star, linanthus, mule ears, Douglas iris, hound's tongue. The rare and endangered white fritillary blooms Feb.–Apr.

Birds: Checklist of 130 species available. Includes Cooper's hawk, great blue heron, screech owl, western bluebird, pileated woodpecker, white-crowned sparrow.

Mammals: Include wild pig, fox, raccoon, muskrat, skunk, bobcat, Columbian black-tailed deer.

Reptiles and amphibians: Include western fence and alligator lizards, California newt, gopher snake, kingsnake, western yellow-bellied racer, rattlesnake (occasional), ring-necked snake.

ACTIVITIES
Hiking: 35 mi. of trails. Most have moderate grades. Ledson Marsh is a good birding area; at least 10 different plant community types.
Fishing: Black bass, bluegill. Live bait prohibited.
Horse riding: Permitted on trails.
No drinking water. No fires allowed; this includes charcoal grills.
Dogs are prohibited except at parking lot and outer drive.

PUBLICATIONS
Leaflet with map.
Trail map.
Bird list.

HEADQUARTERS: 6201 Channel Dr., Santa Rosa, CA 95405; (707) 539-3911.

ARMSTRONG REDWOODS STATE RESERVE/AUSTIN CREEK STATE RECREATION AREA
California Department of Parks and Recreation
680 acres/4,236 acres.

W of Healdsburg. From Cotati on US 101, NW on SR 116 to Guerneville. N 2 mi. on Armstrong Woods Rd.

Access to Austin Creek is through Armstrong. Armstrong is a popular, heavily used redwoods park. First and second-growth Coast redwoods, the largest specimen 308 ft. tall, 14 1/2 ft. in diameter.

The adjacent Austin Creek area is hilly, elevations 150 ft. to almost 2,000 ft. Attractive canyons; many springs; several streams. Second-growth Coast redwoods, not so impressive as the Armstrong groves. Also Douglas-fir with madrone, oak, red alder, azalea, Oregon ash. Some open grassland. Annual rainfall about 50 in. Many wildflowers in the two areas, including hawkweed, balsamroot, heartleaf arnica, scarlet gilia, yellow globe lily, trillium.

Outdoor theater at Armstrong.

ACTIVITIES
Camping: 25 sites. All year. Trailers, RV's over 20 ft. can't use the access road, which may be closed to autos in bad weather. Also two primitive campgrounds for horse riders and hikers.
Hiking: 16 mi. of trails.
Horse riding: Horse trailer parking at entrance. Horse camps.

HEADQUARTERS: 17000 Armstrong Woods Rd., Guerneville, CA 95446; (707) 869-2015.

BODEGA HARBOR
Mixed ownerships, including state and county lands.

At Bodega Bay on SR 1.

On the N and W, the harbor is enclosed by a cape about 3 1/2 mi. long ending in a high promontory, Bodega Head. On the S it is separated from the larger and more open Bodega Bay by a long sand spit. The harbor has a large fishing fleet.

A road leads along the N shore of the harbor to parking areas on the Head. Birding along the shore is excellent. In March we saw large numbers of loons, horned grebe, coot, bufflehead, marbled godwit, surf scoter. Fine views from the Head. The coast below is rocky, with tidepools.

One can also drive part-way out on the S sand spit, where there is a campground and Coast Guard facility. We found good birding here, too.

ACTIVITIES
Camping: West Shore Park Campground, a county facility, is on the N shore road. We don't find it listed in directories, but we camped there. Doran Park, on the S shore, also a county facility, seemed larger, more open and windswept; 128 sites, all year; first come, first served. A state campground, Bodega Dunes, is 1/2 mi. N of Bodega Bay on SR 1; 98 sites, all year, reservations through Ticketron only.
Hiking: Fine hiking along the bayshore, over the dunes of the S shore,

around the Head. A 5-mi. trail system in the N dunes begins at West Bay Rd., at the N end of the bay.

Swimming: At Doran Park.

Boating: Ramps at both county parks.

Horse riding: The 5-mi. dunes trail system is open to horses.

HEADQUARTERS: Doran Park, P. O. Box 372, Bodega Bay, CA 94923; (707) 875-3540. Bodega Dunes, Sonoma Coast State Beach, Department of Parks and Recreation, Bodega Bay, CA 94923; (707) 875-3483.

BOGGS MOUNTAIN STATE FOREST
California Department of Forestry
3,460 acres.

From I-80, N on SR 29 through Napa to Middletown. Left on SR 175 through Cobb. Entrance is on SR 175, 1 mi. N of Cobb.

An experimental and demonstration forest acquired in 1949 after all merchantable timber had been cut except a few seed trees and scattered, inaccessible patches. Under management, forest has regenerated and harvesting has resumed. Rolling to mountainous terrain. Elevations from 2,400 ft. to 3,750 ft. on Boggs Mountain, a viewpoint. Annual precipitation is about 70 in. Summers are dry. This is resort country; numerous developments along SR 175.

The Forest map is needed. We had some difficulty even with the map; roads are not well marked. When we visited in spring, roads were muddy. In extreme wet weather many are impassable. One campground was flooded. The only mapped trail is in the NW corner of the Forest. Most hiking and horse riding are on secondary roads.

Plants: 90% forested: ponderosa and sugar pines, Douglas-fir. Understory includes manzanita, dogwood, coffeeberry, madrone, live oak, black oak.

Birds: No checklist. Species mentioned: mountain and valley quail, band-tailed pigeon.

Mammals: Include gray squirrel, gray fox, coyote, raccoon, mink, bobcat, black bear, mule deer.

ACTIVITIES
Camping: 12 primitive campgrounds. All year. No water except at Big Springs and Houghton Spring. Permit required. No HQ on site. During summer months permits can be obtained from heliport station near entrance to Forest on Road 500.

Hiking: 3-mi. loop trail up Boggs Mountain begins at Hobergs Resort.
Hunting: Heaviest use is in deer hunting season, Aug. 15–Sept. 15. Dates set by California Fish and Game Department, may vary from year to year.

PUBLICATION: Leaflet with map.

HEADQUARTERS: P.O. Box 670, 135 Ridgeway Ave., Santa Rosa, CA 95402; (707) 542-1331.

BOTHE-NAPA VALLEY STATE PARK
California Department of Parks and Recreation
1,887 acres.

From St. Helena, N 4 1/2 mi. on SR 29.

The Park extends about 2 1/2 mi. W from the highway, along the canyon of Ritchie Creek. About 1/2 mi. wide. All development is at the E end. Only foot and horse travel beyond the parking area and campground. The campground is popular, often used by people sightseeing in the Napa Valley and as a one-night stopover. A minority of the campers uses the trails.

Elevations from 320 ft. to 2,000 ft. Steep hillsides. One of the most E stands of Coast redwoods. The original trees were logged off some years ago. Second-growth trees are now of good size.

Plants: In woodland areas: Coast redwood, Douglas-fir, Pacific madrone, bigleaf maple, and oaks: black, Oregon, Coast live, valley. Understory has Pacific poison oak, sweet shrub, creambush ocean spray. In chaparral areas: chamise, ceanothus, manzanita, scrub oak. Many wildflowers.

Birds: About 100 species recorded, including turkey vulture, red-tailed and red-shouldered hawks, California quail, Anna's hummingbird, common flicker; pileated, acorn, hairy, downy, and Nuttall's woodpeckers; black phoebe, western and olive-sided flycatchers, violet-green swallow, Steller's and scrub jays, chestnut-backed chickadee, plain titmouse, common bushtit, brown creeper, varied and hermit thrushes, western bluebird, ruby-crowned kinglet, orange-crowned and Wilson's warblers, solitary vireo, pine siskin; chipping, golden-crowned, and song sparrows.

Mammals: Include squirrel, raccoon, deer.

INTERPRETATION: *Campfire programs* and *guided hikes* in summer. Guided hikes are sometimes organized here for Robert Louis Stevenson State Park (see entry).

ACTIVITIES
Camping: 50 sites. Reservations May 1–Oct. 31. Also hiker-biker camp.
Hiking: 10 mi. of trails.
Horse riding: 6 mi. of trails.

PUBLICATION: Leaflet.

HEADQUARTERS: 3801 St. Helena Highway N, Calistoga, CA 94515; (707) 942-4575.

BRANNAN ISLAND STATE RECREATION AREA
California Department of Parks and Recreation
336 acres.

3 mi. S of Rio Vista on SR 160.

The park, on the Sacramento River just above its junction with the San Joaquin River, is not a natural area. Popular with swimmers, fishermen, boaters, campers, and sure to be crowded on any fine weekend. We include it because it is a good base for exploring the many channels and sloughs in the delta region.

INTERPRETATION: *Campfire programs* once or twice weekly in summer.

ACTIVITIES
Camping: 100 sites. All year. Reservations Mar. 2–Oct. 28.
Fishing: Striped bass, bluegill, crappie, perch, bullhead.
Swimming: Beach, lifeguards in season.
Boating: 6-lane ramp; ample parking. 30 slips for overnighting. Walk-in camps available with slips.

NEARBY: Franks Tract State Recreation Area, 3,508 acres. 5 mi. SE of Brannan Island by boat. Just N of Bethel Island. This was rich delta farmland until the levee broke. Now most of the area is water. Little Franks Tract, 330 acres, is a freshwater marsh protected by a levee. Boat access only. Waterfowl, beaver, muskrat, fox, raccoon, river otter, mink.

PUBLICATION: Leaflet, Brannan Island and Franks Tract, with area map.

HEADQUARTERS: Star Route, Box 75 A, Rio Vista, CA 94571; (916) 777-6671.

BUTANO STATE PARK
California Department of Parks and Recreation
2,186 acres.

From Half Moon Bay, S 15 mi. on SR 1. Turn inland to Pescadero, then
S 5 mi. on Cloverdale Rd.

A redwood park in the Santa Cruz Mountains, planned for hiking. Includes
most of the Little Butano Creek watershed. Park is about 4 mi. E–W, 1 mi.
N–S. The developed area is at the W end. Elevations from 220 ft. to 1,714 ft.

Plants: About 80% forested: Coast redwood, Douglas-fir, tan oak, madrone. All second-growth redwood except for a small virgin stand in a relatively inaccessible area. Understory of redwood sorrel, thimbleberry, huckleberry, California swordfern. Chaparral along the upper ridges. Wildflowers
include California poppy, trillium, Douglas iris, skunk cabbage, clintonia.

Birds: No checklist. 114 species recorded, including Steller's jay, winter
wren, robin, varied thrush, song sparrow, great horned owl, red-tailed hawk,
California quail, brown towhee, chestnut-backed chickadee.

Mammals: Include gray squirrel, raccoon, coyote, gray fox, bobcat, mule
deer.

Reptiles and amphibians: Include California newt, ensatina, gopher snake,
coast garter snake, Pacific tree frog, western fence lizard, Pacific giant salamander, ringneck snake.

INTERPRETATION: Small *exhibit area* at park office. *Campfire programs,* Sat.
nights, Memorial Day–Labor Day. Also *guided hikes,* Sundays.

ACTIVITIES
Camping: 40 sites, 19 of them walk-in. All year. Reservations Apr. 27–Sept.
30.

Hiking, backpacking: 20 mi. of trails. Trail camp for backpackers in old-
growth forest. About a 5-mi. hike with elevation gain of 1,600 ft. Reservations
required for trail camp. Make them by telephone at the park, not by Ticketron. Only 6 campsites.

Dogs are permitted in campground, not on trails or in trail camp.
Campground is full Fri., Sat., and holidays, May–Sept.

PUBLICATIONS
Leaflet with map.
Trail camp information.

HEADQUARTERS: P.O. Box 9, Pescadero, CA 94060; (415) 879-0173.

CASWELL MEMORIAL STATE PARK
California Department of Parks and Recreation
258 acres.

From Ripon on SR 99, 6 mi. S on Austin Rd.

A small park with 4 mi. of frontage on the meandering Stanislaus River. Noted for a 138-acre stand of valley oak, remnant of the large hardwood forest that once covered much of the Central Valley's flood plains. Some trees with girths over 17 ft. Camping and day use areas are at the S end of the park, foot trails beyond.

Oak Forest Nature Trail winds through the oak stand. Elsewhere are wild rose thickets, blackberry, wild grape, wild currant. Observation point for a great blue heron rookery. River is too shallow for boating.

Camping: 66 sites. All year. No reservations.

PUBLICATION: Leaflet with map.

HEADQUARTERS: 28000 S. Austin Rd., Ripon, CA 95366; (209) 599-3810.

CEDAR ROUGHS
U.S. Bureau of Land Management
7,183 acres.

N of Napa. About 2 mi. W of Rancho Monticello on Lake Berryessa, Berryessa-Knoxville Rd. No public road or trail access; site is surrounded by private land. Ask at BLM office for routing.

A large serpentine mound extending NW–SE. Elevation of Lake Berryessa, near E boundary, is 440 ft. Site elevations from 1,000 ft. to 2,287 on Iron Mountain at SE corner of the site. Trout Creek drains the E slope. Noted for a large, almost pure stand of Sargent cypress. Such a stand is unusual on ridgetops, more frequent on lower slopes and in canyons. On the lower slopes, chaparral with scattered live oak, digger pine, native grasses.

Selected as a wilderness study area, where human impact is substantially unnoticeable.

HEADQUARTERS: Ukiah District, Bureau of Land Management, 555 Leslie St., Ukiah, CA 95482; (707) 462-3873.

CHINA CAMP STATE PARK
California Department of Parks and Recreation
1,512 acres.

From San Francisco, N on US 101 to San Rafael. Turn right at Marin County Civic Center; 4 mi. on North San Pedro Rd.

Open: 8 A.M.–sunset.

Site has not been intensively developed, but a campground is planned. 2 mi. of shoreline on San Pablo Bay. About 500 acres of salt marsh, 200 of grassland, 800 of forest. Elevations to 1,000 ft. Site includes China Camp Village Historical Area.

Forest tree species include California bay laurel, Coast live oak, valley oak, and madrone. Pickleweed, cordgrass, and saltgrass in marsh. No bird checklist; marshes attract waterfowl, shorebirds. Park Ranger reports mule deer, gray fox, raccoon.

ACTIVITIES
Hiking: 6 mi. of trails.
Fishing: Bay. Striped bass, flounder, sturgeon.
Swimming: Unsupervised.

Picnic and swimming areas sometimes crowded on weekends.

HEADQUARTERS: Rt. 1, Box 244, San Rafael, CA 94901; (415) 456-0766.

CLEAR LAKE STATE PARK
California Department of Parks and Recreation
565 acres.

From Cloverdale, N 15 mi. on US 101 to Hopland. E on SR 175 to SR 29 and S to Kelseyville. NE 3 1/2 mi. on Soda Bay Rd.

Clear Lake, 45,000 acres, is the largest natural lake wholly within California. A popular resort area, much of the shoreline developed. Vineyards and orchards around Kelseyville. The Park is also popular, the campground full on pleasant weekends, daily in summer. Hillside trails are not heavily used, especially fall to spring.

2 mi. frontage on the lake. Elevations from 1,320 ft. to 2,800 ft. Site is 75%

forested. On high ground: digger pine, blue oak, valley oak. Lower: box elder, cottonwoods, black walnut, California white oak, Oregon ash, California bay laurel, willow. Spring display of western redbud with California buckeye. Shrubs include manzanita, mountain mahogany, coyote bush.

Birds: Checklist available. Species "seen on most days" in season include pied-billed and western grebes, great blue heron, mallard, green-winged teal, ruddy duck, bufflehead, American coot, killdeer, California and Bonaparte's gulls, red-tailed hawk, American kestrel, turkey vulture, California quail, Anna's hummingbird, belted kingfisher, red-shafted flicker, acorn woodpecker, black phoebe; violet-green, tree, and barn swallows; plain titmouse, common bushtit, white-breasted nuthatch, mourning dove, ruby-crowned kinglet, western meadowlark, red-winged blackbird, house finch, lesser goldfinch, brown and rufous-sided towhees, dark-eyed junco, white-crowned and golden-crowned sparrows.

Mammals: Include black-tailed jackrabbit, brush rabbit, ground squirrel, chipmunk, raccoon, mink, gray fox, mule deer. Occasional bobcat.

INTERPRETATION: *Nature trail. Campfire programs* and *guided walks* July and Aug., as requested.

ACTIVITIES
Camping: 2 campgrounds. 82 sites. All year. Reservations May 13–Sept. 7.
Hiking: 3 mi. of trails.
Boating: Ramp.

PUBLICATIONS
Leaflet with map.
Bird checklist.
Nature trail guide.

HEADQUARTERS: 5300 Soda Bay Rd., Kelseyville, CA 95451; (707) 279-4293.

COLUSA NATIONAL WILDLIFE REFUGE
See Sacramento National Wildlife Refuges, zone 3.

COW MOUNTAIN AREA
U.S. Bureau of Land Management
60,000 acres.

From Ukiah, E on Milk Creek road toward Lakeport.

In the Mayacmas Mountains. Elevations from 800 to 4,000 ft. Steep chaparral-covered slopes with small stands of fir, pine, and oak. In 1927, Congress set aside 50,000 acres of Cow Mountain for hunting, fishing, public recreation, and watershed protection. Roads in the area are steep and narrow, not suitable for trailers and large RV's. Several perennial and intermittent streams, and a number of small reservoirs. In summer, hot, dry days and cool nights. Winters are moderate with frequent rain. Annual rainfall is about 40 in. Hunting is the principal visitor activity.

The area has been divided into two parts. In the N, ORV's are limited to the main road. In the S, they may use all roads and trails. The leaflet map does not show trails.

Birds: No checklist or detailed reports. Mentioned: vulture, hawks, owls, quail, dove, jays, swallows, woodpeckers, eagles.

Mammals: Said to include mule deer, black bear, mountain lion, bobcat, wild pig, coyote, raccoon, skunk, badger, porcupine.

Reptiles and amphibians: Mentioned: garter snake, rubber boa, kingsnake, western rattlesnake.

ACTIVITIES

Camping: 4 campgrounds, 34 sites, with water, pit toilets. Other unimproved campgrounds, and trailside camping is not prohibited.

Hunting: Quail, dove, squirrel, rabbit, wild pig, deer, bear.

Fishing: Rainbow trout in some streams. Sunfish in reservoirs.

PUBLICATION: Leaflet with map.

HEADQUARTERS: Ukiah District, BLM, P. O. Box 940, 555 Leslie St., Ukiah, CA 95482; (707) 462-3873.

DELEVAN NATIONAL WILDLIFE REFUGE
See Sacramento National Wildlife Refuges, zone 3.

DEL MAR LANDING ECOLOGICAL RESERVE
California Department of Fish and Game
48 acres.

On the Pacific Coast about 3 1/2 mi. S of the mouth of the Gualala River. From a marker on Del Mar Point S about 3,000 ft. A public access route is planned but was not available in 1981. Visitors may request permission to enter through the private Sea Ranch development.

A relatively virgin bit of coastline. Exposed outer rocks, deep channels, tidepools. An undisturbed assemblage of plants and animals native to rocky shores. Harbor seal often seen on the outer rocks.

HEADQUARTERS: Department of Fish and Game, 1416 Ninth St., Sacramento, CA 98514; (916) 445-7613.

FARALLON NATIONAL WILDLIFE REFUGE
U.S. Fish and Wildlife Service
211 acres.

In the Pacific Ocean about 30 mi. W of San Francisco.

A cluster of offshore islands with the largest colonial seabird rookery S of Alaska, upward of a quarter-million breeding birds each summer. Breeding species include western gull, Cassin's and rhinoceros auklets, common murre; Brandt's, double-crested, and pelagic cormorants; pigeon guillemot, ashy and Leach's storm-petrels, tufted puffin, black oystercatcher. Breeding marine mammals include California and Steller sea lions, elephant and harbor seals. Northern fur seals and gray and humpback whales are occasionally seen around the islands.

Visitors may not go ashore. Bay Area birding organizations sponsor seasonal boat trips around the islands.

HEADQUARTERS: San Francisco Bay National Wildlife Refuge Complex, 9800 Thornton Ave., Fremont, CA 94536. (By mail: P.O. Box 524, Newark, CA 94560.) (415) 792-0222.

FORT ROSS STATE HISTORIC PARK
California Department of Parks and Recreation
446 acres.

12 1/2 mi. N of Jenner on SR 1.
Open: 10 A.M.–4:30 P.M.

Russians built a fort here in 1812. One original structure still stands; others have been restored or reconstructed. The fort is on a flat 90 ft. above the sea, below a cypress grove. One can hike over the grassy flat, down into the ravine where ships once landed. Fine views from the edge of the bluffs. Several steep trails down to rocky beaches with tidepools. Many wildflowers.

GOLDEN GATE NATIONAL RECREATION AREA
U.S. National Park Service
20,015 acres of federal land; 14,923 acres nonfederal.

In San Francisco, the city's N and W edge. Across the bridge in Marin County, most of the seacoast to Bolinas Bay and along SR 1 to Olema.

Together with the adjacent Point Reyes National Seashore, this is the world's largest urban park. Many areas are either undisturbed or returning to a natural state, and these will be preserved. This National Recreation Area is composed of municipal, county, and federal sites, transferred to the National Park Service for management. This entry describes the sites N of the Golden Gate Bridge. The complex includes the Marin Headlands, Tennessee Valley, Muir Woods, Mt. Tamalpais, Muir Beach, Stinson Beach, and Olema Valley. The extensive Marin Municipal Water District lands, Samuel P. Taylor State Park, and Angel Island are nearby open space.

This National Recreation Area includes museums, Cliff House, and Alcatraz Island (once a Prison), which are not natural areas, and are thus not within the scope of this Guide.

Highest point in the area is Mt. Tamalpais, 2,586 ft. The Marin Headlands rise steeply from the sea. Much of the terrain is rolling to mountainous, with many valleys and canyons. Especially near the city, many of the slopes are open, windswept, and grassy, with areas of brush and scattered trees. The Mount Tamalpais area includes open grasslands and redwood forests. Muir Woods is noted for its stand of gigantic Coast redwoods. The National Recreation Area includes no large lakes but numerous streams, ponds, freshwater marshes, salt marshes, and several lagoons.

Immediately on crossing the Golden Gate Bridge, Vista Point is on the right. At the next right turn, a road loops back under the highway and to Conzelman Road. This part of the Headlands was for many years the site of forts and guns defending the Golden Gate. The road is scenic, part of it one-way, steep, closed to trailers and RV's. After several turns, the route rounds Rodeo Lagoon and ends at a Ranger Station that offers information and a few exhibits. One can return to SR 1 via Bunker Road. Between this circuit and the Shoreline Highway, 3 mi. N, the area is roadless except for a stub road at the head of Tennessee Valley. This is hiking country, with coastal, valley, and mountain trails, some to elevations 1,000 ft. above the ocean.

SR 1, here called the Shoreline Highway, turns seaward and follows the Coast from Muir Beach to Stinson Beach and Bolinas Lagoon. It forms part of the SW boundary of Mount Tamalpais State Park (see following Features section). An alternate route, Panoramic Highway and Stinson Beach Highway, follows part of the State Park's N boundary, passes the access road to Muir Woods (see Features), then cuts across the State Park on its way to the ocean. Trails from the Marin Headlands area link with the Mt. Tamalpais trail system.

Beyond Bolinas Lagoon, SR 1 is the approximate boundary between the Point Reyes National Seashore (see entry) and the upper end of the Golden Gate National Recreation Area in the Olema Valley. The Valley itself is pastoral, and continuation of some cattle grazing may become part of the land-use plan. The area also has forested canyons, tree-lined ridges, open grassy slopes. Fine hiking trails, some long and steep.

Plants: Primary plant communities of the Headlands and similar areas are coastal scrub and grasslands. Common plants are coyote bush, sagebrush, lupine, poison oak, cow parsnip, blackberry, poison hemlock. Willow and elderberry found along streams; other trees in this area are exotics, planted around Coast artillery installations.

Forest in the Mt. Tamalpais area includes some virgin redwood in Steep Ravine Canyon. Generally mixed forest: Douglas-fir, California live oak, sitka spruce, California bay laurel, western hemlock. Oak woodlands have interior live oak, tan oak, California bay laurel. The rare Sargent cypress is associated with serpentine rock formations. Also areas of chaparral: manzanita, ceanothus, chaparral pea.

Wildflowers include lupine, California poppy, buttercup, shooting star, sticky monkeyflower, Douglas iris, hound's tongue, deer orchid, many others. 786 species of plants have been identified in the Mt. Tamalpais area alone.

Birds: No checklist is yet available, but Ranger Stations are informative. Many seabirds along the coast. Brown pelican. Waterfowl and shorebirds in lagoons, marshes, ponds. Species noted include turkey vulture, red-tailed and marsh hawks, golden eagle, American kestrel, scrub jay, common flicker, goldfinch, brown wrentit, house finch, great and snowy egrets.

Mammals: Include deer mouse, pocket gopher, gray squirrel, jackrabbit, brush rabbit, striped skunk, ground squirrel, raccoon, gray fox, bobcat, badger, mountain lion, mule deer.

Reptiles and amphibians: Include various salamanders, ensatina, rough-skinned newt, Pacific giant salamander, bullfrog, kingsnake, gopher snake, garter snake, rubber boa, striped racer, rattlesnake.

FEATURES

Mount Tamalpais State Park, 6,233 acres. Long a popular sightseeing, hiking, and horse riding area. Scenic road to the summit. Loop trail around the peak. More than 200 mi. of marked trails. A nature trail begins behind the Ranger Station. The Park surrounds Muir Woods. *Stinson Beach,* at the seaward base of the mountain, has 4,500 ft. of sand beach with low dunes, large rock masses at the S end. Swimming is said to be good during the season when lifeguards are on duty, otherwise hazardous because of riptides.

Muir Woods National Monument, 514 acres, has trails through cathedral-like groves of giant redwoods. Visitor center.

Samuel P. Taylor State Park, 2,576 acres. From San Rafael, 15 mi. W on Sir Francis Drake Blvd. Two quite different sections on opposite sides of the Boulevard, one cool, damp forest, the other dry, sparsely vegetated hillsides. Trails from other parts of the National Recreation Area, including horse trails. Papermill Creek crosses the area, and a pool offers limited swimming.

Angel Island State Park, 740 acres. In San Francisco Bay. Ferries from Tiburon and San Francisco, or private boat. Trails to top of 781-ft. Mt. Caroline S. Livermore. Island is partially wooded, but native trees were almost all cut years ago, exotics introduced. Native plant species include California bay laurel, ceanothus, Coast live oak, buckeye. Birds include valley quail, hermit thrush, hawks, lesser goldfinch, Anna's and Allen's hummingbirds, Steller's jay, great blue heron, great egret, brown pelican, western crow, numerous warblers, waterbirds. Deer and raccoon are common. Visitor center, naturalist programs. Private boats may land at Ayala Cove only. Finger piers, sheltered.

Camping: Except for group camps, the only campgrounds are at Mt. Tamalpais, with 18 primitive sites, and Samuel P. Taylor State Park, which has 65 sites; reservations Mar. 2–Oct. 1. In an area so close to a major city, this is next to nothing. Additional campgrounds are being considered in National Recreation Area planning.

ADJACENT: Pt. Reyes National Seashore (see entry).

PUBLICATIONS
Golden Gate National Recreation Area leaflet.
Muir Woods National Monument leaflet.
Mount Tamalpais State Park
Leaflet.
Nature trail guide.

REFERENCE
Hart, John. *San Francisco's Wilderness Next Door.* Presidio Press, Box 3515SC, San Rafael, CA 94902. $9.95, + $0.75 shipping and handling.

HEADQUARTERS: Golden Gate National Recreation Area, Building 201, Fort Mason, San Francisco, CA 94123; (415) 556-0560. Muir Woods National Monument, Mill Valley, CA 94941; (415) 388-2595. Mount Tamalpais State Park, 801 Panoramic Highway, Mill Valley, CA 94941; (415) 388-2070. Samuel P. Taylor State Park, P.O. Box 251, Lagunitas, CA 94952; (415) 488-9897.

GRIZZLY ISLAND WILDLIFE AREA
California Department of Fish and Game
10,487 acres.

From I-80, exit to Fairfield on SR 12. About 1 mi. beyond Fairfield, turn
right on Grizzly Island Rd. About 9 mi. to HQ.

The Suisun Marsh is a remnant of the 750,000 acres of marshlands that once
occupied the Sacramento-San Joaquin Delta. The Marsh, encompassing 55,-
000 acres of wetlands and 29,000 acres of bays and sloughs, is the largest
remaining contiguous area of coastal wetland in California. A leaflet declares,
"Although it lacks the national fame of the Everglades of Florida, the Dismal
Swamps of Louisiana or the Bear River Marshes of Utah, in most ways it is
the peer, and in many ways the superior, of these famous wetlands." Perhaps
one reason for nonrecognition is that most of the Marsh is privately owned.
Both federal and state government have been seeking ways to preserve the
remaining wetlands by purchase, easement, cooperative agreements, and
other means.

Waterfowl are the principal attraction of the Marsh, up to 1.5 million birds
feeding and resting here in winter. In dry years, 1/4 of California's entire
wintering waterfowl population may be concentrated here.

Strictly speaking, the Marsh is not an undisturbed natural area. More than
3/4 of the wetlands have been enclosed and protected by levees. Most of this
area is at or slightly below mean tide level. The area is crossed by a network
of sloughs and drainage channels open to the tidewaters. Roads run along
many of the levees. In the late 1800s, extensive efforts were made to drain and
reclaim the wetlands for farming. Poor drainage and salty soils doomed these
efforts. A large part of the private area is now owned or leased by waterfowl
hunting clubs. The principal threat to the Marsh today is diversion of river
water for agricultural, municipal, and industrial use, reducing by more than
half the flow of fresh water to San Francisco Bay. Thus salt water intrudes
further and further into the Marsh, increasing salinity beyond the tolerance
of the food plants on which the waterfowl depend.

The Grizzly Island Wildlife Area has two units, 1,887-acre Joice Island, to
the right on the road to HQ, and 8,600-acre Grizzly Island, immediately
beyond the HQ. Both units border on Montezuma Slough. Most areas are
open to the public with some restrictions on nonhunters in the hunting season.
Joice Island and most of Grizzly Island are closed to fishing from Oct. 1 to
Feb. 1. Grizzly Island is open to waterfowl hunters on Wed., Sat., and Sun.
in season, and nonhunters are asked to keep out on those days. All visitors
must register on entering.

Birds: About 220 species of birds recorded. Checklist available. Ducks and geese begin to arrive in Aug. Some 200,000 may be present by mid-Sept. Most early arrivals are pintail. At peak population in mid-winter, about 75–85% of the ducks present are pintail. Other species include gadwall, wigeon, green-winged teal, shoveler, and mallard. The Marsh has relatively few diving ducks. Common winter species include tule white-fronted goose, eared and pied-billed grebes, great and snowy egrets, black-crowned night heron, American bittern, cinnamon teal, canvasback, goldeneye, bufflehead, white-tailed kite, red-tailed and rough-legged hawks; barn, short-eared, and great horned owls; pheasant; California, ring-billed, and Bonaparte's gulls. Warblers are common. The birding here is good at any season.

Mammals: A small herd of tule elk. Numerous bat species, black-tailed jackrabbit, cottontail, pocket gopher, beaver, deer mouse, muskrat, gray fox, raccoon, long-tailed weasel, mink, badger, spotted and striped skunks, river otter, bobcat.

ACTIVITIES

Hiking: No special trails but many opportunities. When we visited in Mar., travel on Joice Island was by foot only.

Hunting: Special rules; by permit issued at headquarters.

Fishing: Striped bass, catfish, crappie, sturgeon.

Boating: Ramp provides access to Montezuma Slough and Honker Bay.

PUBLICATIONS

Grizzly Island Wildlife Area.
Wildlife of Suisun Marsh.
Bird checklist.
Hunting maps and regulations.

HEADQUARTERS: Department of Fish and Game, Region 3 Headquarters, P.O. Box 47, Yountville, CA 94599; (707) 944-2443.

LOWER SHERMAN ISLAND WILDLIFE AREA

California Department of Fish and Game
3,100 acres.

From West Pittsburg, E on SR 4, continuing N across Antioch Bridge and SR 160 to Emmaton. Left on Sherman Island Rd. to parking area.

At the confluence of the Sacramento and San Joaquin rivers. The island is partially flooded, and there is boat access only beyond the parking lot and boat ramp. Several past attempts to reclaim the area with levees and cultivate the drained land failed. The state acquired the island in 1920. Open water, extensive marshes, and a small area of tidal flats at the tip. Willow thickets; dense stands of tule reeds.

The site is much used by waterfowl hunters. Needless to say, nonhunters should avoid the site in the waterfowl hunting season. Fishing is the largest use, with an average of more than 100 fishermen per day.

Wildlife is abundant. No checklists are available, but the DFG estimates that 75–100 bird species occur here, including many waterfowl, mourning dove, pheasant, and valley quail. Mammals include beaver, mink, muskrat, opossum, raccoon, striped skunk, cottontail, and river otter.

Outside hunting season, it should be an interesting area to explore by small boat or canoe, although visitors are warned that strong winds often come up rapidly, especially in late afternoon, and there is strong tidal action. The area has a maze of channels and shallows. The N levee on the Sacramento River is a favorite picnic site.

PUBLICATION. Site map.

HEADQUARTERS: Region 2, Department of Fish and Game, 1701 Nimbus Road, Suite "A," Rancho Cordova, CA 95670; (916) 355-7010.

MENDOCINO NATIONAL FOREST
U.S. Forest Service
876,236 acres; 1,079,459 acres within boundaries.

From just N of Clear Lake, extends N about 65 mi. About 35 mi. wide. Access from I-5, to E, or US 101, to W, by secondary and Forest roads.

Southernmost of a continuous block of National Forests extending N into Oregon. Rolling to mountainous terrain on E side of the Pacific Coast Range. Elevations from 1,100 ft. to 8,092 ft. About 2/3 forested, remainder brush-covered hills. Lake Pillsbury, about 2,000 acres; several smaller lakes, ponds. Numerous streams, including tributaries of Eel River. At lower elevations temperatures range from 20°F winter low to 110°F summer high; cooler in high country.

No main roads penetrate the Forest. Several secondary roads, as well as Forest Roads not shown on highway maps.

Plants: Principal tree species include Douglas-fir, white fir, ponderosa pine, incense cedar. Old-growth stands in Big Butte-Shinbone area and Yolla Bolly-Middle Eel Wilderness. Understory includes black oak, mixed conifers. Other tree species include Shasta red fir; Jeffrey, sugar, foxtail, digger, knobcone, and western white pines; Sargent and McNab cypresses; several live oak species and other oaks; golden chinquapin, madrone, red alder, cottonwoods, willows. Chaparral species include chamise, mahoganies, toyon, cascara sagrada, bitter cherry, western chokecherry, wood and California wild roses, raspberry, blackberry, several manzanita species, many others. Long list of flowering plants includes golden fairy lantern, pussy ears, mariposa lilies, several brodiaeas, false hellebore, several lilies, several orchids, buttercups, many more. Plant checklists available.

Birds: Checklist of 131 species available. Residents include golden and bald eagles; Cooper's, sharp-shinned, red-tailed, and Swainson's hawks; merlin, kestrel, mountain and California valley quails, blue grouse, belted kingfisher, Anna's and calliope hummingbirds; white-breasted, red-breasted, and pygmy nuthatches; Bewick's and winter wrens, Hutton's vireo; American, lesser, and Lawrence's goldfinches; savannah and lark sparrows.

Mammals: Checklist available. Abundant and common species include mule deer, bobcat, coyote, porcupine, raccoon, gray fox, striped skunk; Douglas, gray, and northern flying squirrels; Townsend, Sonoma, and yellow pine chipmunks; Heermann kangaroo rat, pocket gophers. Also mice: western harvest, deer, pinyon, brush, California meadow, long-tailed meadow, creeping meadow. Black bear, mountain lion, badger, tule elk, bison reported but rare or uncommon.

Reptiles: Include mountain swift, western fence and alligator lizards; Pacific pond turtle, western skink. Also snakes: rubber boa, Pacific ringneck, California striped racer, sharp-tail, California mountain kingsnake, rattlesnake. Reptile and amphibian checklists available.

FEATURES

Yolla Bolly-Middle Eel Wilderness, 111,000 acres. Includes portion of Shasta-Trinity National Forest (see entry). Wild, rugged country on the headwaters of Middle Fork, Eel River; bounded by North and South Yolla Bolly Mountains. Forest Roads to trailheads are not the best, so visitor use is light. Average elevations, 2,000–4,000 ft., with peaks over 8,000 ft. Most of the area is available for hiking by late May, earlier than most other California wildernesses. Fall storms common from early Oct., but heavy snows are rare before Dec. Ridges have dense stands of pine and fir; lower slopes are chaparral. Good fishing in several creeks, but water is generally scarce and springs usually dry by late summer. Trail map available. Wilderness permit required; obtain from HQ or Ranger Districts.

Snow Mountain roadless area, 25,000 acres on Lake County-Colusa County boundary, E side of Forest. Snow Mountain is S-most peak in North Coast Range; twin peaks, both over 7,000 ft. A minimum of 65 plant species here reach their S range limit. Near crests, open stands of red fir in protected areas; exposed sites treeless. Red and white fir, Douglas-fir, and ponderosa pine at middle elevations, chaparral, brush, and oaks below. Wildlife is abundant, with frequent reports of bear and cougar. This area also provides opportunity for early season activity. Wilderness status proposed.

Lookouts: Visitors are invited to fire lookouts when they are manned, daylight hours, June to mid-Oct. Several can be reached by road, in some cases with a short walk at the end. However, road conditions change seasonally, and it's advisable to ask about routing at any Ranger post.

Recreation areas: At Letts Lake, Hammerhorn Lake, Plaskett Lake, Lake Pillsbury.

INTERPRETATION

Campfire programs, summer, at Letts Lake. Occasional *guided hikes.* Notices posted.

Nature trail, 3/4 mi., at Lake Pillsbury.

Exhibits on Forest Road 6 mi. W of Stonyford.

ACTIVITIES

Camping: 24 campgrounds, 400 sites. Usual season May–Oct., but most campgrounds open all year. No reservations. Camping outside designated sites is permitted in most areas, but fire permit is necessary.

Hiking, backpacking: Over 160 mi. of mapped trails. Easy hikes of 1/2 to 4 mi. from recreation areas. Backpacking popular in the wilderness areas, but many other parts of the Forest offer attractive long hikes, on trails and lightly used unpaved roads.

Pack trips: No commercial packers or stables in Forest. Camping along trails permitted, but horses not permitted at campgrounds. Bring feed for entire trip; natural feed is insufficient. Good horse trails.

Hunting: Except in State Game Refuge, recreation areas, near campgrounds. Mule deer, wild pig, squirrel, quail, pigeon, grouse, turkey, bear.

Fishing: Chiefly trout, lakes and streams.

Swimming: Streams and small lakes, chiefly at recreation areas. Unsupervised.

Boating, canoeing: Power boats on Lake Pillsbury only. Tubing on Stony Creek. Spring kayaking, Mill Creek Campground to Mine Camp. Rafting and canoeing on Eel River just outside Forest boundary.

Ski touring, snowmobiling: Forest Highway 7 to the snow line. Some ski touring. Snowmobiling from Covelo side in Mendocino Pass and Anthony Peak areas.

Caution: Most Forest roads are unpaved; some are narrow, steep, rocky. Dust, mud, and snow are seasonal hazards. Be alert for logging trucks, cattle. Poison oak is common, potent all year.

ADJACENT: Six Rivers National Forest, Shasta-Trinity National Forest (see entries).

PUBLICATIONS
Forest map. $1.00.
Wilderness map. $1.00.
Meet the Mendocino.
Plants and Animals of the Mendocino National Forest.
The Yolla Bolly-Middle Eel Wilderness.
Hoofin' It in the Yolla Bollys. Brochure.
Trail map, Yolla Bolly-Middle Eel Wilderness.
Snow Mountain proposed wilderness.
Off Roading, map and regulations.

HEADQUARTERS: 420 E. Laurel St., Willows, CA 95988; (916) 934-3316. Recorded recreation message: (916) 934-2350.

RANGER DISTRICTS: Corning R.D., 1120 Solano St., Corning, CA 96021; (916) 824-5196. Covelo R.D., Route 1, Box 62 C, Covelo, CA 95428; (707) 983-2941. Stonyford R.D., Lodoga Rd., Stonyford, CA 95979; (916) 963-3128. Upper Lake R.D., P.O. Box 96, Upper Lake, CA 95485; (707) 275-2361.

MOUNT DIABLO STATE PARK
California Department of Parks and Recreation
14,500 acres.

E of Oakland. From Danville, E 5 mi. on Diablo Rd.

Many sightseers drive to the top of Mt. Diablo for the view, said by some to encompass more land area than any other point in California; others make the claim even broader. That's on a clear day, after a N wind has blown away the prevailing smog. Many fewer people take to the trails, but don't expect solitude on a fine weekend. The peak's elevation is 3,849 ft., more than 3,600 ft. above the base.

Plants: Most of the hillsides are forested: Coast, blue, and black oaks and digger pine in open woodlands. On sunny slopes: madrone, California bay laurel, buckeye. In shady canyons: bigleaf maple, western sycamore, cottonwood, white alder. Wildflowers include wyethia, California poppy, wallflower, trillium, fairy lantern, monkeyflower, giant red paintbrush, shooting star, wild rose, delphinium.

Birds: Checklist available. Species reported include barn, screech, and great horned owls; golden eagle, red-tailed hawk, American kestrel, yellow-bellied sapsucker, horned lark, western tanager, violet-green and cliff swallows, Anna's hummingbird, cedar waxwing, western bluebird, blue-gray gnatcatcher, orange-crowned warbler, house finch.

Mammals: Include squirrel, raccoon, brush rabbit, skunk, mule deer, bobcat. Mountain lion rarely seen.

ACTIVITIES

Camping: 50 sites. All year, except in periods of high fire danger. First come, first served.

Hiking: Over 50 mi. of trails.

Entrance road gates at bottom locked to incoming and outgoing traffic at 5:30 P.M. (N side), sunset (S side).

PUBLICATIONS

Leaflet with map.

Bird checklist. 20¢.

HEADQUARTERS: P.O. Box 250, Diablo, CA 94528; (415) 837-2525.

MOUNT TAMALPAIS STATE PARK
See Golden Gate National Recreation Area.

MUIR WOODS NATIONAL MONUMENT
See Golden Gate National Recreation Area.

NAPA MARSHES
Mixed ownerships. California Department of Fish and Game management.

On the Napa River. Boat access only. Various sloughs on W side of river N of SR 37, Sears Point Rd.

A complex of sloughs, marshes, and islands, many of the islands partially or wholly inundated by high tides. Portions of the area are owned by private gun clubs, most of the rest by the Leslie Salt Co. The Department of Fish and Game has a cooperative agreement opening the Leslie land to hunting, by permit, in season.

The Coon Island Ecological Reserve, 250 acres, is on the river at the N of the area about 1 1/4 mi. S of the Southern Pacific railroad bridge. Established to preserve a representative marsh area. Cordgrass on the frequently flooded areas. California bulrush and tules on slightly higher elevations. Pickleweed on land seldom flooded.

Birds: Marshes attract many waterfowl. Exposed mudflats are feeding areas for snowy egret, great egret, great blue heron. Marsh hawk, white-tailed kite, and red-tailed hawk often seen. Also present: California clapper rail.

PUBLICATION: Site map.

HEADQUARTERS: Department of Fish and Game, 1416 Ninth St., Sacramento, CA 98514; (916) 445-7613.

POINT REYES NATIONAL SEASHORE
National Park Service
65,303 acres.

From Olema on SR 1, turn seaward on Bear Valley Rd.

The site is a rough triangle, about 18 mi. on its N–S base, its hooked tip projecting into the sea. The triangle is partially separated from the mainland by Tomales Bay, less obviously by the San Andreas Fault. Many bays, streams, and lagoons penetrate the triangle. The Inverness Ridge parallels the base, with elevations to 1,470 ft. on Mt. Wittenberg. W of the ridge are rolling hills. The Point has tall cliffs rising from the sea. The S portion has 5 small lakes near the shore.

More than 2/5 of the area is classed as wilderness, open to foot, horse, and bicycle travel only. Outside this roadless area, several roads lead to the Point, to beaches, to an overlook on Pt. Reyes Hill, and to other points of interest.

No car camping. Four campgrounds are available to hikers.

Warm, dry summers; cool, rainy winters. The exposed headlands and outer beaches have constant moderate to strong winds. The E side of Inverness Ridge is sheltered from the winds; the inland valleys have less fog; summer temperatures are usually 8 to 10 degrees F higher on the E side. In winter, night temperatures are usually higher along the beaches than inland. At the Point, rainfall averages about 12 in. per year, Dec.–Feb. having the most. At Bear Valley, annual average is about 34 in.

Plants: Several habitats. On the ridge, stands of Douglas-fir and Bishop pine, not often found together. At lower elevations, groves of California bay laurel, madrone, tan oak, live oak, maple, and wax myrtle, with many shrubs such as blue blossom, rhododendron, honeysuckle, wild rose, and huckleberry. Bordering the forest, an extensive belt of grassland with a scattering of California buckeye. Many wildflowers on the coastal dunes.

Birds: Checklist available at visitor centers. Along the shoreline, curlew, oystercatcher, sandpipers, godwit, yellowlegs, as well as gulls, various waterfowl, white and brown pelicans. Egrets and great blue heron are among the marsh birds. Inland, red-tailed hawk, marsh hawk, American kestrel, white-tailed kite, California quail, great horned owl.

Mammals: Include gray fox, raccoon, long-tailed weasel, badger, striped and spotted skunks, mountain lion, bobcat, brush rabbit, black-tailed jackrabbit, mountain beaver, Sonoma chipmunk, southern pocket gopher, western gray squirrel, Pt. Reyes jumping mouse, mule deer, and two exotics: fallow and axis deer. Offshore: northern fur seal, Steller and California sea lions, harbor seal, elephant seal, gray whale in migration.

FEATURES
Bear Valley, visitor center and Park HQ, near the entrance. *Earthquake Trail* along the San Andreas Fault. *Woodpecker Trail.* Also replica of native Indian village.

Limantour Beach for swimming. Bird watching at nearby Limantour Estero.

Pt. Reyes Beach, with two road access points, is fine for hiking and beachcombing, not swimming.

McClure's Beach is one of several with good tidepools.

Tule Elk Range has a small herd of free-ranging tule elk, reintroduced a century after they were eliminated here.

ACTIVITIES
Backpacking: Many miles of trails, especially in the central and S portions. Four hike-in campgrounds. Permits are required, and limit is one night per campground. Trail map shows trailheads, destinations, distances, the longest one-way route 13.1 mi. Hikers must bring their own water; stream water is not safe. Fog, wind, and cold occur in July as well as Dec.

Swimming: The beaches N of the Point are unsafe. On the E side of the Point, Drakes Beach and Limantour Beach are sheltered.

ADJACENT: Golden Gate National Recreation Area and Tomales Bay State Park (see entries).

Dogs are prohibited in campgrounds, on designated beaches, and on trails. Elsewhere they must be leashed.

PUBLICATIONS
Leaflet with map.
Trail map.
Backpack campsite reservation request.
Information pages on climate, vegetation types, wildlife, geology, gray whales, deer, harbor seals.

HEADQUARTERS: Point Reyes, CA 94956; (415) 663-1092

PORTOLA STATE PARK
California Department of Parks and Recreation
2,000 acres.

From I-280 W of Palo Alto, exit W on SR 84 7 mi. to SR 35. S on SR 35 to Alpine Rd. W 3 mi. to Portola State Park Rd.

Just over the hill from the Bay Area, a redwood park in the rugged terrain of a deep canyon between Skyline and Butano ridges. The Park is a natural basin forested with Coast redwoods and associated flora. Elevations from 300 ft. to 1,000 ft. Annual precipitation is about 48 inches, chiefly in fall and winter. Peters Creek and Pescadero Creek flow in faults.

The Park is irregular in shape. Developments are clustered near the W boundary. For about 2 mi. to the E, the Park is roadless, open only to foot traffic.

Plants: Several groves of virgin Coast redwoods. One specimen, burned hollow but still living, is 20 ft. in diameter. The Park is almost entirely forested. Douglas-fir and tan oak on ridges and S slopes. Understory includes California huckleberry, ferns. Wildflowers include redwood violet, trillium, hound's tongue, western azalea.

Birds: Checklist available, with habitats. All-year residents include marbled murrelet, red-tailed and Cooper's hawks; horned, screech, and pygmy owls; common flicker, acorn woodpecker, Steller's and scrub jays, chestnut-backed chickadee, wrentit, dipper, pine siskin, band-tailed pigeon.

Mammals: Include raccoon, ringtail, coyote, bobcat, mule deer.

Reptiles and amphibians: Include western salamander, Pacific tree frog, garter snake, gopher snake, rubber boa.

INTERPRETATION
Visitor center and museum.
Campfire programs, seasonally.
Sequoia Nature Trail, 1/2 mi.

ACTIVITIES
Camping: 52 sites. All year. Reservations Mar. 30–Oct. 1, through Ticketron.
Hiking, backpacking: 14 mi. of trails. 5 1/2-mi. Coyote Ridge-Slate Creek loop. Trails pass redwood groves, other points of interest. Trail camp for backpackers. Make reservations at Park.

PUBLICATIONS
Leaflet with map.
Nature trail guide.

HEADQUARTERS: Star Route 2, La Honda, CA 94020; (415) 948-9098.

ROBERT LOUIS STEVENSON STATE PARK
California Department of Parks and Recreation
3,178 acres.

From Calistoga, 8 mi. N on SR 29.
Open: Daylight hours.

An undeveloped parkland; limited parking, no restrooms or water. Includes Mt. St. Helena, 4,343 ft., highest point this close to San Francisco. The summit and fire lookout tower are a private inholding, but public access is permitted at present. Mostly steep, rocky, brush-covered slopes with wooded canyons. Some N-facing slopes are also wooded. A fire road, power line, and communications installation impair what is otherwise wilderness quality.

Plants: Only about 10% forested: Douglas-fir, tan oak, canyon live oak, ponderosa and knobcone pines, madrone. Mostly chaparral with manzanita, chamise, scrub oak, poison oak.

Birds: No checklist. Species reported include turkey vulture; red-tailed, Cooper's, and sharp-shinned hawks; American kestrel, golden eagle, band-tailed pigeon, mourning dove, scrub jay, mountain quail, screech and barn owls, Vaux's swift, common flicker, western kingbird, canyon wren, orange-crowned warbler, house finch, Oregon junco, golden-crowned and white-crowned sparrows.

Mammals: Include California ground squirrel, spotted skunk, black-tailed jackrabbit, western gray squirrel, ringtail, pocket mouse, bobcat.

Reptiles and amphibians: Include Pacific tree frog, western toad, Pacific ringneck snake, Mt. St. Helena mountain kingsnake, Pacific gopher snake, California striped racer, rubber boa.

INTERPRETATION
Guided hikes are sometimes held in summer, originating at Bothe-Napa Valley State Park.
Nature trail, 1 mi., includes old silver mine.

Hiking: 6 mi. of trails, including trail to the summit.

PUBLICATION: Nature trail guide.

HEADQUARTERS: Napa Area, Department of Parks and Recreation, 3801 N. St. Helena Highway, Calistoga, CA 94515; (707) 942-4575.

SACRAMENTO NATIONAL WILDLIFE REFUGES
U.S. Fish and Wildlife Service
23,480 acres.

5 units. For Sacramento National Wildlife Refuge unit, 6 mi. S of Willows on old US 99W, which parallels and is E of I-5.

The Sacramento Valley is the major wintering area for waterfowl of the Pacific Flyway. Most of the wetlands were drained and cultivated. Waterfowl became dependent on farm crops. Beginning in 1937, these refuges were established, attracting waterfowl so successfully that crop losses to ducks and geese are now minor. The Sacramento Complex has 5 units: Sacramento, Colusa, Delevan, Sutter, and Butte Sink. Portions of all but the last are open to visitors. The California Department of Fish and Game's Gray Lodge Wildlife Area (see entry in zone 4) is nearby and serves the same general function.

These are not undisturbed natural areas. Intensive management includes dikes and other water control structures; cultivating rice, millet, and other feed crops; fertilizing and weed control. The objectives are to provide feeding and resting areas during the fall and winter seasons; providing nesting and rearing habitats for ducks that remain through the spring.

Numbers of wintering waterfowl may exceed 2 million by December. The areas are also used by many other bird and mammal species.

Sacramento National Wildlife Refuge, 10,783 acres, is the largest unit. Refuge HQ is here. Hundreds of thousands of ducks and geese are here Sept.–Feb., marsh birds Aug.–Apr. About 6 mi. long, 3 mi. wide, the refuge is divided by dikes and ditches into ponds, marshes, and fields. Visitors can drive on the dikes, following an auto tour route, hike on designated trails. When we visited, birding here was better than at any of the other units.

Colusa National Wildlife Refuge, 4,040 acres, on SR 20, 1/2 mi. W of Colusa. Long, rather narrow site, somewhat similar to Sacramento unit in managed habitats and species present. The auto tour route seemed to have fewer visitors and, we thought, was likely to be closed in wet weather. Hiking on designated trails.

Delevan National Wildlife Refuge, 5,634 acres; from Willows, 10 mi. S on US 99W to Maxwell, then 4 mi. E on Maxwell Rd. No auto tour route. In hunting season, nonhunters are restricted to public roads bordering the site.

Sutter National Wildlife Refuge, 2,591 acres. From Yuba City, S to Oswald Rd., then W. Croplands and marshes. No auto tour route.

Butte Sink, 1,154 acres, is closed to visitors.

Hunters may prefer the smaller units. Other visitors, we suggest, should go first to the Sacramento unit, consider visiting Colusa and the state's Gray Lodge Wildlife Area but ask advice at Sacramento. Also, there is much good sightseeing and birding along the back roads of the area. To the E of Colusa are the Sutter Buttes, the highest 2,132 ft., unique upthrusts. W of the buttes are about 10,000 acres of privately owned prime waterfowl habitat.

Birds: Checklist available. About 175 species recorded. Ducks begin arriving in Sept., geese in Oct., populations peaking in Jan. In the goose population, lesser snow goose is most numerous, white-fronted and cackling geese next in order. Ross's and Canada geese also present. Of the ducks, pintails are most numerous, followed by mallard, wigeon, green-winged teal, shoveler, cinnamon teal, gadwall, and ruddy duck. Also canvasback, common merganser. Also common: western and pied-billed grebes, great blue heron, great and snowy egrets, black-crowned night heron, American bittern, whistling swan, turkey vulture, white-tailed kite, red-tailed and marsh hawks, kestrel, California quail, pheasant, Virginia rail, common gallinule, coot, greater yellowlegs, dowitcher, least and western sandpipers, American avocet, black-necked stilt, ring-billed gull, Forster's and black terns.

Songbirds are largely restricted to the cottonwoods and willows bordering irrigation ditches. Waterfowl numbers gradually decline after early Jan. A few thousand mallard, cinnamon teal, and other species nest. Shorebirds are present all year.

Mammals: Include striped and spotted skunk, jackrabbit, cottontail, ground squirrel, raccoon, red fox, muskrat, opossum, California ground squirrel. Ringtail, mink, beaver, river otter, and coyote are present, but uncommon.

ACTIVITIES

Hunting: Portions of each refuge are open to hunting in season. Special regulations; inquire.

Fishing: Designated areas during the nonhunting period. Mostly in drain ditches.

NEARBY: Gray Lodge Wildlife Area (see entry, CA zone 4).

PUBLICATIONS
Recreation Guide.
Bird checklist.
Young People's Bird List.
Hunting and fishing maps.
Hunting regulations.
Tour Routes (Colusa).

HEADQUARTERS: Route 1, Box 311, Willows, CA 95988; (916) 934-2801.

SALT POINT STATE PARK
California Department of Parks and Recreation
4,114 acres.

20 mi. N of Jenner on SR 1.

On the Coast. SR 1 runs about 1/10 to 1/4 mi. inland. The developed park area is between SR 1 and the ocean. A much larger area, with hiking trails and fire roads, is across the highway.

The Coast includes protected, sandy beach coves as well as sharp bluffs and sheer sandstone cliffs plunging into the waves. Headlands are generally grassy, but in places the forest is near the sea. Inland, the terrain rises, coastal brush and grassland giving way to lush forest of Bishop pine, Douglas-fir, madrone, tan oak, a few redwoods. At the top of the coastal ridge, about 1,000-ft. elevation, is a large open "prairie" and pygmy forest, where stands of cypress, pine, and even redwood grow in stunted profusion.

From the highway, a short access road leads to the campground and a parking area. The campground is set back, with no ocean view. From the parking area, one can hike N along the Coast, in several places dropping down to a beach or cove. Many tidepools. The site includes one of California's first underwater parks, where marine organisms are given special protection, although fishing is allowed.

Many wildflowers. Some, such as calla lily and red-hot poker, are signs of a former residence. No bird list is available. Mammals noted include mule deer, long-tailed weasel, raccoon, coyote, bobcat, striped skunk, numerous rodents. Gray whale often seen offshore between Dec. and Mar.

ACTIVITIES
Camping: 31 sites. All year.
Hiking: 14 mi. of trails, mostly inland. Coast trail to Kruse Reserve (see section headed "Nearby").
Swimming: Divers enjoy the underwater park.
Horse riding: Marked trails E of the highway.

NEARBY: Kruse Rhododendron State Reserve is just N of the site. 317 acres. Second-growth redwood, Douglas-fir, tan oak, and an exceptional display of rhododendron, plants to 20 or more ft. tall, usually blooming May through early June. 5 mi. of trails.

PUBLICATION: Leaflet with map.

HEADQUARTERS: 25050 Coast Highway 1, Jenner, CA 95450; (707) 847-3221.

SAMUEL P. TAYLOR STATE PARK
See Golden Gate National Recreation Area.

SAN FRANCISCO BAY NATIONAL WILDLIFE REFUGE
U.S. Fish and Wildlife Service
15,499 acres.

From San Francisco, Bayshore Freeway (US 101) S to Palo Alto-Menlo Park area. E on SR 84 (Willow Rd.) across Dumbarton Bridge to HQ and interpretive center.

Diking, dredging, and filling have greatly reduced the area of San Francisco Bay, a rich estuarine system supporting large fish and wildlife populations. Since 1972, South Bay wetlands have been acquired for this refuge. Two-thirds of the authorized acreage has been acquired. More will be leased from the state.

Only selected portions of the area are now open to visitors, chiefly the interpretive center and a 1 1/3-mi. trail loop through a representative sample of the habitat and several mi. of hiking trails. More trails are planned, as well as fishing piers.

The site includes salt evaporator ponds, salt marsh, tidal mudflats, open water, and a small upland area. Pickleweed and cordgrass are the primary marsh vegetation.

Birds: Checklist of 248 species is a guide to the birds of the South Bay, not a record for the refuge only. However, most of the species can be expected here. The South Bay wetlands are visited annually by most of the shorebirds of the Pacific Flyway as well as many waterfowl. Important habitat for four endangered bird species: California clapper rail, least tern, brown pelican, peregrine falcon. Winter is the best season for birding.

INTERPRETATION

The refuge is the base for an extensive interpretive program: Bay Adventure Seminars, sponsored by the Coastal Parks Association. These are formal classes requiring registration and fee; college credits can be earned. Most seminars are for one or two days and feature field trips.

The Interpretive Center is on a hill overlooking the Bay, near the Dumbarton Bridge toll plaza. Open 10 A.M.–5 P.M. Closed Mon., Tues., and most federal holidays.

PUBLICATIONS
Leaflets.

Trail map.
Bird checklist.
Seminar program schedule.

HEADQUARTERS: P.O. Box 524, Newark, CA 94560; (415) 792-3178. Recorded information: (415) 792-3178. Bay Adventure Seminars: (415) 792-3271.

SAN MATEO STATE BEACHES

California Department of Parks and Recreation
2,786 acres.

Seacoast, along SR 1, from Thornton Beach at Daly City to Año Nuevo Point, 27 mi. S of Half Moon Bay.

State beaches occupy 19 mi. of this 51-mi. stretch of Coast S of San Francisco. These are not swimming beaches, because of rough surf and strong currents, and this somewhat limits the weekend crowds. Most of the beaches are sand, backed by bluffs 10–200 ft. high. Some rocky areas; some offshore rocks. Many of the beaches are at points where creeks flow into the sea; here there are small coves and lagoons. The principal units, N to S, are

Thornton State Beach, 50 acres, is nearest to the city, a popular fishing and picnicking spot. 3,100 ft. of sandy beach. Offshore rocks. Nature trail.

Gray Whale Cove State Beach, 93 acres. Surf fishing. Concession operated.

Montara State Beach, 13 acres, is rather narrow, partially rocky, 11,000 ft. ocean frontage, 4,287 ft. sandy beach. Hiking.

Half Moon Bay State Beach, 170 acres. The HQ beach, and the only one with camping. In the city of Half Moon Bay.

San Gregorio State Beach, 165 acres. Creek, high cliffs, sand bar at the creek mouth. 1 mi. of beach.

Pomponio State Beach, 80 acres. Over 1 mi. of ocean front. Small lagoon.

Pescadero State Beach, 290 acres, adjoins the 584-acre Pescadero Marsh Natural Preserve, one of the few remaining natural marsh areas on the central California coast. Good birding. Great blue heron rookery.

Bean Hollow State Beach, 44 acres. 2 mi. of ocean frontage. Only 1,300 ft. of sandy beach. Tidepools.

Año Nuevo State Reserve, 420 acres. Año Nuevo Point is the only mainland breeding ground of the northern elephant seal. Access in breeding season (Dec.–Apr.) is restricted to daily tours; reservations required. For tour information: (415) 879-0227. 7 1/2 mi. of ocean frontage, including 3 mi. of sandy beach, open May 1–Dec. 1.

Año Nuevo Island, just offshore, has resident and migratory harbor seal, California and Steller sea lions, many seabirds. No public access.

Other beaches: The units just mentioned account for about half the acreage of state land. Other areas are undeveloped. Along the Coast are numerous unsigned, informal beach access points where people pull off the highway and make their way down to secluded beaches. Some of these access points are on private land whose owners consent to public use, but land that is obviously private should not be crossed without owner consent.

Camping: Half Moon Bay, 50 sites. All year. Reservations Mar. 3–Oct. 29.

HEADQUARTERS: 95 Kelly Ave., Half Moon Bay, CA 94019; (415) 726-6238.

SAN PABLO NATIONAL WILDLIFE REFUGE
U.S. Fish and Wildlife Service
11,700 acres.

On San Pablo Bay W of Vallejo. Part of the N boundary is SR 37.

Of the total protected acreage, 11,200 is leased from the state. Most of it is open water and tidelands on the N shore of San Pablo Bay. Less than 50 acres are above the maximum high tide. Nearly 5,000 acres are tidal mudflats, 1,700 acres of salt marsh, 300 acres of salt-brackish marsh.

Winter home for, on the average, half of the canvasbacks on the Pacific Flyway. Many loons, grebes, cormorants, terns, pintail, shoveler, wigeon, scaup, bufflehead, scoter, ruddy duck. Wading birds and shorebirds also winter here.

SONOMA COAST STATE BEACHES
California Department of Parks and Recreation
2,220 acres.

Pacific Coast, along SR 1, from the Russian River near Jenner S to Bodega Bay.

The state owns most of this 13 mi. of spectacular coastline, one of the most scenic sections of the Coast Highway. Along it are frequent overlook points, some high above the sea. Rugged headlands with rocky bluffs and natural arches divide the coast into a series of beaches, some long enough for an hour of hiking, others small, secluded coves. Many offshore rocks. Many tidepools. The sea is not for swimming: heavy surf, strong undertow, sudden groundswells. Bluffs, slopes, and dunes have a hardy cover of shrubs, grasses, and wildflowers. Spring display of yellow and blue lupine, sea pink, Indian paintbrush, western wallflower, wild strawberry, monkeyflower. Many gulls, cormorants, pelican, other seabirds, as well as goldfinch, swallows, valley quail, raven, hawks, wrens. Mammals include raccoon, gray fox, cottontail, mule deer, skunk, ground squirrel.

Parking and trails to beaches have been provided at more than a dozen points.

Camping: Wright's Beach, 30 sites. Bodega Dunes, 98 sites. All year. Reservations all year through Ticketron. No reservations made at the Park.

PUBLICATION: Leaflet with map.

HEADQUARTERS: Bodega Bay, CA 94923; (707) 875-3483.

SUGARLOAF RIDGE STATE PARK
California Department of Parks and Recreation
2,200 acres.

From Santa Rosa, 7 mi. E on SR 12; N on Adobe Canyon Rd. Narrow, steep roads, not suitable for trailers or large RV's.

In the coastal mountains. Elevations from 600 ft. at the entrance to 2,729 ft. at the top of Bald Mountain. The office, campground, and other developments are clustered in the SW corner. Elsewhere the Park is open to foot and horse traffic only. Sonoma Creek, a perennial stream, begins in the Park and flows 3 mi. near its S boundary. There is a small waterfall.

Plants: Chaparral on the slopes and ridges: manzanita, chamise, ceanothus, poison oak, coyote bush, toyon, winebush. Meadows and groves of trees along the drainages. One of the state's largest bigleaf maples. Other tree species include Coast madrone, California laurel, digger pine, Douglas-fir, alder, California buckeye, Coast redwood, live oak. Wildflowers include California poppy, cream cups, lupine, penstemon, calochortus, thistle, farewell-to-spring, brodiaea, Indian pink, buttercup, coral root, zigadene, scarlet larkspur, mimulus, Indian warrior, iris, western azalea, spicebush, trillium, California fuchsia, shooting star, clarkia, fritillaria.

Birds: Checklist available. Species include great blue heron, turkey vulture, golden eagle; sharp-shinned, Cooper's, and red-tailed hawks; California and mountain quail; screech, great horned, and pygmy owls; Anna's, rufous, and Allen's hummingbirds; pileated and acorn woodpeckers; ash-throated, western, and olive-sided flycatchers; house and Bewick's wrens; varied, hermit, and Swainson's thrushes; Hutton's, solitary, and warbling vireos; orange-crowned, yellow, yellow-rumped, black-throated gray, hermit, and Wilson's warblers; black-headed grosbeak, lazuli bunting, purple and house finches, American and lesser goldfinches.

Mammals: Include rabbit, skunk, coyote, squirrel, weasel, raccoon, bobcat, gray fox, mule deer.

Reptiles and amphibians: Include rubber boa, kingsnake, gopher snake, ringneck snake, rattlesnake.

ACTIVITIES
Camping: 50 primitive sites.
Hiking: 25 mi. of trails. Trail to tops of Bald, Red Mountains and Brushy Peaks.
Horse riding: Horse travel permitted on most trails.

PUBLICATIONS
Leaflet with map.
Bird checklist.

HEADQUARTERS: 2605 Adobe Canyon Rd., Kenwood, CA 95452; (707) 833-5712.

SUISUN MARSH
See Grizzly Island Wildlife Area.

SUTTER NATIONAL WILDLIFE REFUGE
See Sacramento National Wildlife Refuge.

TOMALES BAY STATE PARK
California Department of Parks and Recreation
1,078 acres.

On Pt. Reyes Peninsula. From Inverness, N 3 mi. on Sir Francis Drake Blvd. Then right 1 1/2 mi. on Pierce Point Rd.

On the W shore of Tomales Bay, its land boundaries common with Pt. Reyes National Seashore (see entry). Sheltered by the Inverness Ridge, the Park's beaches are often warm and sunny while the outer Point experiences wind and fog. Rolling hills with elevations to 565 ft. Deep, rugged canyons. Rocky headlands on the Bay. Four sheltered beaches within the 2 mi. of waterfront. The gently sloping, surf-free beaches are the chief public attraction. The Park has 6 1/2 mi. of hiking trails, much less than the larger, adjacent National Seashore. For the naturalist, however, the Park has much to offer.

Plants: About 70% forested. The E slope of Inverness Ridge is steep, heavily wooded, with thick underbrush. The 310 acres of Bishop pine include one of the finest remaining virgin stands. The Jepson Trail crosses this grove. About 210 acres of mixed evergreen forest, 130 of oak-bay woodland, 160 acres of coastal scrub. Tree species include tan oak, toyon, Coast live oak, madrone, red alder. In the understory: ceanothus, huckleberry, hazelnut, salal, poison oak, coffeeberry, gooseberry, salmonberry, manzanita, mountain mahogany. Some shrubs grow to tree size. The many ferns include woodwardia, sword-fern, deer fern, lady fern, maidenhair, gold-back, five-finger, polypodium. About 300 species of spring wildflowers have been identified, including lilies, fritillaria, California poppy, wild strawberry, lupine, irises, monkeyflowers, rein orchid, violets, pussy's ear, trillium, hound's tongue, slim solomon, fairy bells, columbine, larkspurs, bleeding heart, western wallflower, rosy arabis, Indian paintbrush, heliotrope.

Birds: No checklist. Species reported include 5 species of owls, including the spotted owl, nesting here. Also murre, puffin, geese, scoters, ruddy duck, pelican, grebes, goldeneye, bufflehead, rails, sandpipers, band-tailed pigeon, horned lark, kingfisher, pygmy nuthatch, various warblers.

Mammals: Include fox, raccoon, badger, weasel, chipmunk, cottontail, skunk, wood rat, mule deer.

Reptiles and amphibians: Include granulated newt, Pacific giant salamander, slender salamander, garter snake, rubber boa.

INTERPRETATION: *Nature trail,* 1/2 mi., from Hearts Desire Beach to Indian Beach.

ACTIVITIES
Hiking: 6 1/2 mi. of trails linking the beaches.
Canoeing: No launching ramp. Hand-carried boats may be put in the water away from swimming areas.

PUBLICATIONS
Leaflet with map.
Nature trail guide. 75¢.

HEADQUARTERS: Star Route, Inverness, CA 94937; (415) 669-1140.

ZONE 4

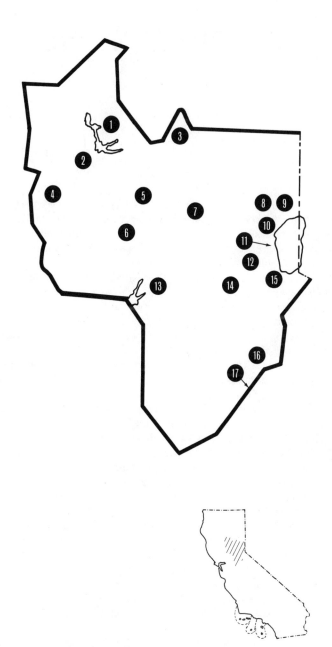

CALIFORNIA, ZONE 4

Includes these counties:

Butte	Sutter	El Dorado
Yuba	Placer	Amador
Sierra	Nevada	Calaveras

The zone includes a bit of the E portion of the Sacramento Valley, the foothills and W slope of the Sierra Nevada from near Yuba Pass to Bear Valley, and as much of the E slope as is in California. It includes the California side of Lake Tahoe. It is crossed by I-80, the main route from Sacramento to Reno, and US 50, from Sacramento to South Lake Tahoe.

By far the largest public sites are the National Forests that straddle the Sierra Nevada: Tahoe, Eldorado, and part of the Stanislaus. The Forests have many inholdings, chiefly along the principal roads, with summer and winter resorts. Proximity to major cities and easy access make this zone one of the state's most popular recreation areas. Many places are crowded in season, but we found quiet trails.

Many of those who saw Lake Tahoe pristine pronounced it the world's loveliest. Surely it should become a National Park. Early in the 20th century, legislation was introduced to achieve this. It failed to pass. Then, suddenly, it was too late. A National Park Service team sent there in the 1930s concluded the lake was a lost cause. Too much land had been sold, subdivided, and developed along the lakeshore. Commercial blight was far advanced.

From some vantage points the lake is still lovely, but there are not many. Along SR 89 one has only a few glimpses before reaching the lakeside State Parks. Pollution has become a serious concern.

At Emerald Bay State Park, everyone reaches for cameras; it is the lake's most-photographed scene. Other State Parks on or near the lake are Burton Creek, D. L. Bliss, Sugar Pine Point. The Lake Tahoe Basin Management Unit (see entry) is a Forest Service effort to salvage what remains of the undeveloped public lands near the lake.

The runoff from the W slope of the Sierra is precious, and many dams have been built to store the water for use in the dry season. Two of the largest impoundments, Lake Oroville and Folsom Lake, are State Recreation Areas. We have entries for them, but not for several other impoundments with developed shorelines.

In the Valley, two state Wildlife Areas, Gray Lodge and Spenceville, are of interest. Their function is much like that of the nearby Sacramento National Wildlife Refuges described in zone 3.

BURTON CREEK STATE PARK AND NATURAL PRESERVE
California Department of Parks and Recreation
1,800 acres.

2 mi. E of Tahoe City on SR 28.

A relatively new park, not yet shown on some highway maps. Near but not on the lake. Elevations from 6,270 ft. to 7,170 ft. About 90% forested, second-growth Jeffrey, lodgepole, and sugar pines; red and white firs. Understory includes manzanita, buckbrush, squaw carpet. Some montane meadow.

ACTIVITIES

Hiking: About 13 mi. of old logging roads, one or two of which lead into the National Forest.

Ski touring: About 3–4 mi. of track set in the Park by the adjacent Nordic Ski Center.

ADJACENT

National Forest land. (See entry, Lake Tahoe Basin Management Unit.)

Tahoe State Recreation Area, 13 acres. Camping, 39 sites; reservations May 25–Sept. 3. Swimming, fishing.

HEADQUARTERS: Sierra Area, North Sector, c/o Donner Memorial State Park, P.O. Box 549, Truckee, CA 95734; (916) 587-3789.

CALAVERAS BIG TREES STATE PARK
California Department of Parks and Recreation
5,994 acres.

From Angels Camp, NE on SR 4, about 4 mi. beyond Arnold. SR 4 is closed in winter at Lake Alpine, 25 mi. NE of the Park.

On both sides of the North Fork, Stanislaus River. Within the Stanislaus National Forest (see entry, zone 6), and adjoining the 380-acre Calaveras

Bigtree National Forest (described in the Stanislaus National Forest entry). On the west slope of the Sierra Nevada; elevations from 3,400 ft. to 5,500 ft. This is the only State Park with groves of the California big tree, the giant sequoia, largest of living things, the species seen in Sequoia National Park. (Coast redwoods are taller but less massive.)

Generally rugged terrain. 5 mi. of frontage on the Stanislaus River and Beaver Creek. The Stanislaus flows through a canyon, with rocky ledges, shallows with pebble beaches, a pool deep enough for swimming. Annual precipitation is about 51 in. The Park remains open all year. Usually, in winter, enough space has been plowed open to meet camping needs.

A scenic drive extends 10 mi. from the Park entrance to Beaver Creek, passing campgrounds, overlooks, and trailheads. This drive is closed in winter beyond the North Grove area.

Plants: The giant sequoia was first discovered here at the height of the Gold Rush. Visitors came from everywhere, and this site continued to be the chief attraction for some years after other groves were found. About a quarter-million people per year now walk the easy 1-mi. trail through the North Grove, where the first discovery was made. The South Grove is much larger, more primeval. It takes a bit more walking, and many fewer people see it. The Park is almost entirely forested. Giant sequoias grow in mixed stands with ponderosa and sugar pines, white fir, incense cedar, black and canyon live oaks. Understory species include Pacific dogwood, mountain alder, bigleaf maple, California bay laurel, hazelnut. Flowering species include western azalea, monkeyflower, snowplant, lupine, yarrow.

Birds: Checklist of 90+ species available. Included: Steller's jay, American robin, common flicker, white-headed woodpecker, mountain chickadee, red-breasted nuthatch, goshawk, brown creeper, western tanager, black-headed and evening grosbeaks, Oregon junco.

Mammals: Include California ground squirrel, chickaree, chipmunk, deer mouse, raccoon, coyote, black bear, mule deer. Present but seldom seen: mountain lion, bobcat, flying squirrel, gray fox.

Reptiles and amphibians: Include Sierra salamander, alligator lizard, Gilbert skink, garter snake, Pacific rattlesnake.

INTERPRETATION

Visitor center: museum, herbarium, publications. Open daily in summer, weekends and holidays in winter.

Campfire programs and *guided hikes* in summer. *Snowshoe hikes* in winter. *Three Senses Nature Trail* through North Grove.

ACTIVITIES

Camping: 2 campgrounds, 129 sites. All year; limited facilities off-season. Reservations May through Sept.; needed July–Aug.

Hiking: 40 mi. of trails.

Swimming: No supervision. Water can be cold, swift.

Ski touring, snowshoeing: 4 mi. of signed trail. Guided ski tours by arrangement. Check before coming; snow is often wet.

PUBLICATIONS
Leaflet with map. 25¢.
North and South Groves, guides.
Species checklists.
Hiking maps.
Winter activities information.
Campground information.

HEADQUARTERS: P. O. Box 120, Arnold, CA 95223; (209) 795-2334.

D. L. BLISS AND EMERALD BAY STATE PARKS
California Department of Parks and Recreation
1,830 acres.

19 mi. S of Tahoe City on SR 89.

On Lake Tahoe. Emerald Bay is one of the most photographed points on the shoreline drive. The Emerald Bay Overlook is often crowded. The Parks, with 6 mi. of lake frontage, are among the few remaining natural areas on the lake. Much of the shoreline is rugged, with massive rock outcroppings. The land rises steeply from 6,229 ft. at the shore to 7,400 ft. Eagle Falls, an impressive cascade of several hundred feet, is at the head of Emerald Bay. Other features include Fanette Island, a balancing rock, and Vikingsholm, reproduction of a Norse fortress. The two parks are contiguous, operate as a single unit, but have separate developed areas linked by trails.

Plants: 90% forested: Jeffrey, sugar, and lodgepole pines; red and white firs, incense cedar, western juniper, black cottonwood, aspen. Understory includes greenleaf manzanita, huckleberry oak, Sierra chinquapin, ceanothus. Flowering plants include red penstemon, snow plant, columbine, monkeyflower; peak blooming July–Aug.

Birds: No checklist. Reported: Canada goose (spring), common merganser, bald eagle (winter), goshawk, Cooper's hawk, Steller's jay, white-headed woodpecker, mountain chickadee, red-breasted nuthatch, Oregon junco.

Mammals: Include bats, California ground squirrel, chickaree, golden-mantled ground squirrel, chipmunk, white-footed mouse, beaver, coyote, raccoon.

Reptiles and amphibians: Reported: Pacific tree frog, yellow-legged frog, western fence lizard, garter snake.

INTERPRETATION: *Naturalist activities,* July–Labor Day, include *campfire programs, guided hikes.* Notices posted. 1-mi. *nature trail* around Balancing Rock.

ACTIVITIES
Camping: 3 campgrounds, 288 sites. Open June 26–Labor Day. Reservations. 20 primitive boat-in or hike-in sites on N shore of Emerald Bay.
Hiking: 10 mi. of trails. Rubicon Trail follows the shoreline from Vikingsholm to Calawee Cove, 4 1/2-mi. Vikingsholm Trail descends from Emerald Bay Overlook; closed when icy.
Fishing: Rainbow, lake, brown trout; kokanee salmon.
Swimming: Lester Beach, at extreme N of site.
Boating: No ramp within the site. Mooring buoys at boat-in camp.
Ski touring: 3 mi. of trails.

Very busy; campgrounds constantly full July–Aug

ADJACENT· National Forest land; Lake Tahoe Basin Management Unit. Nearby trails into Desolation Wilderness, Eldorado National Forest.

PUBLICATION: Leaflet with map.

HEADQUARTERS: P.O. Box 266, Tahoma, CA 95733; (916) 525-7277.

DONNER MEMORIAL STATE PARK
California Department of Parks and Recreation
353 acres.

From Truckee, 2 mi. W on old SR 40, just off I-80.

As the name suggests, the Park's theme is historical. Donner Lake is almost 3 mi. long, most of the shoreline privately owned and developed. Elevation about 6,000 ft. Forested site. Lake and river frontage.

ACTIVITIES
Camping: 154 sites, summer only. Reservations May 25–Sept. 3.
Fishing: Trout, kokanee.
Swimming: Cold water.
Boating: No ramp.

HEADQUARTERS: P.O. Box 549, Truckee, CA 95734; (916) 587-3789.

ELDORADO NATIONAL FOREST
U.S. Forest Service
668,947 acres; 884,779 acres within boundaries.

S and W of Lake Tahoe. US 50 crosses its center, SR 88 its S portion.

From the upper foothills to the Sierra Crest. Elevations from 2,000 ft. to 10,000 ft. The portion E of the Crest and nearest Lake Tahoe is now, for management purposes, part of the Lake Tahoe Basin Management Unit (see entry). Although this portion is the most heavily impacted by visitors, the entire Forest is described in one of its publications as "a vast outdoor backyard for visitors from Sacramento, Stockton, and the San Francisco Bay Area."

As the acreage figures indicate, the Forest has many inholdings. From Lake Tahoe, a block about 20 mi. wide with relatively few inholdings extends SW to the Mokelumne River. The Forest land to the W and N is broken by many more inholdings, but the Forest map shows blocks where one can travel for 10 or 20 mi. without crossing private land. Furthermore, many of the inholdings are forested, and few owners of forested tracts have posted or marked their boundaries.

Annual precipitation varies from 40 to 75 in. The Forest has 890 mi. of fishing streams, 297 lakes and reservoirs. 14 lakes are over 1 mi. long. Most are surrounded by Forest land. In four cases, a major portion of the shoreline is privately owned. Forest campgrounds are beside most of these lakes.

Plants: The Forest is an important timber producer. Principal tree species are sugar pine, white and red firs, Douglas-fir, incense cedar, ponderosa and Jeffrey pines, interior live oak. A large part of the Forest is in the mixed conifer belt, where the understory includes deerbrush, ceanothus, mountain whitethorn, Sierra mountain misery, greenleaf manzanita, thimbleberry, and Sierra currant. The belt includes numerous meadows with perennial grasses and forbs.

Above the mixed conifer belt, from 6,500 ft. to 8,000 ft., is the true fir belt, characterized by red fir and by lodgepole, western white, and Jeffrey pines. Next above is the subalpine belt, with mountain hemlock, whitebark pine, alpine willow; here trees are scattered, and most vegetation is grasses, forbs, and shrubs.

An estimated 1,000 plant species occur in the Forest. Flowering species include California Indian pink, wild rose, western azalea, snowberry, elderberry, little prince's pine, snow plant, California harebell, false Solomon's seal, rattlesnake orchid, heartleaf arnica, larkspurs, wild peony, eriogonums, waterleaf phacelia, lupines, fireweed, beargrass, crimson columbine, violet, monkeyflower, penstemon.

Birds: Partial checklist available. Forest species include turkey vulture, goshawk; Cooper's, red-tailed, and Swainson's hawks; golden and bald eagles, blue grouse, mountain quail, band-tailed pigeon; great horned, pygmy, great gray, and saw-whet owls; pileated, Lewis', hairy, downy, white-headed, acorn, and black-backed three-toed woodpeckers; yellow-bellied and Williamson's sapsuckers, Hammond's and olive-sided flycatchers, gray and Steller's jays, Clark's nutcracker, mountain and chestnut-backed chickadees, brown creeper, varied and Swainson's thrushes, western and mountain bluebirds, golden-crowned and ruby-crowned kinglets, solitary vireo. Warblers include Nashville, magnolia, yellow-rumped, Townsend's, hermit. Also western tanager, black-headed grosbeak, purple and Cassin's finches, pine siskin, rufous-crowned, and chipping sparrows, Oregon and gray-headed juncos.

Mammals: Forest species include Mount Lyell, Trowbridge, and dusky shrews; 15 bat species; black bear, mule deer, marten, fisher, coyote, red and gray foxes, mountain lion, bobcat, mountain beaver, yellow-bellied marmot; California, Belding, and golden-mantled ground squirrels; least, Townsend, yellow pine, long-eared, and lodgepole chipmunks; western gray squirrel, chickaree, northern flying squirrel, deer mouse, mountain vole, porcupine, pika, snowshoe hare.

FEATURES

Desolation Wilderness, 63,475 acres. On both sides of the Sierra Nevada, just W of Lake Tahoe. One of the most N sections of glaciated High Sierra-type scenic lands. Elevations from 6,500 ft. to 10,000 ft. Pyramid Peak, 9,983 ft., is one of a group of four summits on the S boundary. Many small streams. About 130 lakes, some as large as 900 acres. Because it is spectacularly lovely and readily accessible, the area attracted so many people that serious damage was occurring. In 1978 a rationing scheme was adopted: only 700 overnight visitors per day, June 15–Sept. 8. Half the permits issued up to 90 days in advance, half on the date. We recommend avoiding this area. If you do visit, Rangers will tell you which trails and destinations are least used.

Mokelumne Wilderness, 49,460 acres, between SR 88 and SR 4, just W of the Sierra Crest. Mokelumne Peak, 9,332 ft., dominates the area. The Mokelumne River, flowing SW, has cut a canyon down to the 4,000-ft. elevation. Many small, scenic lakes in the shallow valleys N of the Peak. Wildflowers are abundant during the hiking season. The Pacific Crest Trail is near the E boundary. Permits are required, but rationing use has not yet been thought necessary. Rangers can advise which areas are least used.

The principal road-access recreation areas of the Forest are as follows. These areas attract the most people, in season:

Crystal Basin. From US 50 at Riverton, N on Forest road toward Cleveland Corral, information station, Ice House, Loon Lake, Union Valley and Hell Hole Reservoirs. This is a busy area with numerous campgrounds, a private resort, lakeside developments.

Silver and Caples Lakes area, along SR 88 W of Carson Pass, just N of the Mokelumne Wilderness. Water-based recreation, 5 private resorts, campgrounds, a major winter sports facility for downhill and cross-country skiing.

Highway 50 area, E of Riverton. Numerous streams flows into the South Fork of the American River beside the highway. Small lakes. Many recreation residences on private and Forest land. Two downhill ski areas; one ski-touring center.

Bear River, S of SR 88. Lower Bear River Reservoir is one of the Forest's largest lakes. Two campgrounds; one private resort.

INTERPRETATION
Information at Ranger Stations, Cleveland Corral information station.
Nature trail at Lake Edson Burn.
Mormon Emigrant Trail auto tour, 13 mi.
Campfire programs are infrequent. No guided hikes.

ACTIVITIES
Camping: 32 campgrounds, 1,053 sites. One campground is open all year. Others open May 1–July 1, close Sept. 15–Nov. 1. A reservation system has been in effect at 4 of the larger campgrounds; inquire.
Hiking, backpacking: 350 mi. of trail, 72 mi. of 4-wheel-drive roads. The most popular trails are those in the two wilderness areas, but there are good trails and little-used logging roads in all parts of the Forest.
Hunting: Deer, bear, quail.
Fishing: 800 mi. of fishable streams. Nearly 12,000 acres of reservoirs and lakes; 11 of these account for 9,000 acres; the remainder is in small lakes near the Crest. Rainbow, brown, and eastern brook trout.
Swimming: Especially in Crystal Basin.
Boating: Ramps on all major reservoirs.
Skiing: E of Riverton, 2 downhill and 1 ski-tour area. Silver and Caples Lakes area has a major downhill and ski-tour area.
Ski touring: Kirkwood Meadows, Carson Pass, Echo Summit, Echo Lakes, Loon Lake.

ADJACENT: Tahoe National Forest, Stanislaus National Forest, Toiyabe National Forest (see entries).

PUBLICATIONS
Forest map. $1.00.
Desolation Wilderness map. $1.00.
Mokelumne Wilderness map. $1.00.
Crystal Basin Recreation Area map.
Off-Road and Vehicle Travel Plan.
Leek Springs Lookout. Leaflet.
Mormon Emigrant Trail Auto Tour map.
Lake Edson Burn Self-Guided Trail. Leaflet.

HEADQUARTERS: 100 Forni Rd., Placerville, CA 95667; (916) 622-5061.

RANGER DISTRICTS: Amador R.D., Jackson, CA 95642; winter (209) 223-1623; summer at Lumberyard Ranger Station (209) 295-4251. Georgetown Ranger District, Georgetown, CA 95634; (916) 333-4312; Pacific Ranger District, Pollock Pines, CA 95726; (916) 644-2348. Placerville Ranger District, 3491 Carson Ct., Placerville, CA 95667; (916) 644-2324.

EMERALD BAY STATE PARK
See D. L. Bliss State Park.

FOLSOM LAKE STATE RECREATION AREA
California Department of Parks and Recreation
17,545 acres, including 11,500 acres of water.

From Folsom, the Folsom-Auburn Rd.

25 mi. E of Sacramento. Called the most popular all-year multiple-use State Park in California. Chief Ranger reports very heavy use on weekends and holidays, May–Sept. We visited on a fine weekend in Mar., and few people were there. The remote areas of the Park are attractive and uncrowded in spring and fall.

Folsom Lake, larger of two, has 120 mi. of shoreline at high water, Lake Natoma, 18 mi. Lakes are about 450 ft. above sealevel. Reservoir is generally full in June, lowest in Nov.–Dec. In the Sierra foothills; rolling oak woodlands. Steep canyons up the N and S forks of the lake. Highest point: 1,200 ft.

Annual precipitation about 18 in. Climate is hot and dry in summer. Fire hazard is sometimes extreme.

Plants: Oak and chaparral. Some of the finest examples of blue oak woodlands remaining in CA, in the Peninsula area. Poison oak and toyon prominent in the understory. The many wildflowers include brodiaea, California poppy, California lilac, Douglas iris, shooting star, vetch, zigadene, monkeyflower, Indian paintbrush, larkspur, lupine, fiddleneck, morning glory. Some areas of chaparral are impenetrable.

Birds: Some waterfowl, including Canada goose, winter here. Three large great blue heron rookeries. Species noted include common flicker, acorn woodpecker, western kingbird, western wood pewee, Say's phoebe, common bushtit, kestrel, meadowlark, Bewick's wren, western bluebird, Swainson's thrush, yellowthroat, western tanager, lesser goldfinch; savannah, chipping, fox, and white-crowned sparrows.

Mammals: Ground squirrel, raccoon, black-tailed jackrabbit, opossum, coyote, skunk, gray fox, bobcat.

FEATURE: *Anderson Island Natural Preserve* is site of heron rookery. Visitors not permitted ashore in nesting season.

INTERPRETATION: *Campfire programs* and *guided hikes,* at campgrounds, by request.

ACTIVITIES
  Camping: 3 campgrounds, 150 sites. All year. Reservations May 25–Sept. 3.
  Hiking, backpacking: 65 mi. of trails. Map available. Western State National Recreation Trail passes through the Park, to the mountains.
  Fishing: Trout, bass, kokanee, catfish.
  Swimming: Usually May–Sept.
  Boating: Marina. No hp limit, but 5 mph within 200 ft. of shore. Dangerous in high winds. Hazards when lake is low.
  Horse riding: Popular. Horses allowed on most trails. Rentals nearby.

PUBLICATION: *Fauna and Flora of Folsom Lake.* $2.00.

HEADQUARTERS: 7806 Folsom-Auburn Rd., Folsom, CA 95630; (916) 988-0205.

GRAY LODGE WILDLIFE AREA
California Department of Fish and Game
7,500 acres.

8 mi. SW of Gridley; 2 mi. N of Pennington.

See the entry for Sacramento National Wildlife Refuges in zone 3. This state area is part of the same system, a waterfowl wintering area that reduces the crop losses on surrounding farms. We found less of interest here (after the waterfowl season) than at the Sacramento refuge, but a stop here is part of an interesting Valley tour.

The best time to see waterfowl here is during the hunting season, generally from mid-Oct. to mid-Jan. The main goose flights come in early Nov. On public shooting days (Sat., Sun., Wed.) you must obtain a pass at the checking station, but the visitor tour route is open for nonhunters.

Birds: At peaks, more than 2 million waterfowl have been observed here.

Waterfowl populations build from an average of 20,000 in Aug. to 250,000 in mid-Oct. to a peak in Dec. or Jan. About 40% of the ducks are pintail, followed by mallard, baldpate, shoveler, green-winged teal, gadwall. Snows are the most numerous geese, followed by white-fronted, cackling, Ross's, lesser Canada, and Canada. This appears to be the main wintering area for Ross's goose. The marshlands support many other bird species. Over 200 have been recorded.

Mammals: Include black-tailed jackrabbit, cottontail, deer, opossum, raccoon, striped skunk, muskrat, gray fox, ground squirrel.

The tour route, 2 1/2 mi. long, has a load limit that excludes large RV's. Except in hunting season, visitors can hike on service roads closed to autos.

Hunting: Permit system limits the number of hunters. Issued at checking stations just prior to hunting.

PUBLICATIONS
Leaflet.
Bird checklist.

HEADQUARTERS: Area Headquarters, Department of Fish and Game, P.O. Box 37, Gridley, CA 95948; (916) 846-3315.

LAKE OROVILLE STATE RECREATION AREA

California Department of Parks and Recreation
16,400 acres of water; 12,060 land acres. State property extends at least 300 ft. and as much as 1 mi. from the high-water line.

From Oroville, 7 mi. E on SR 162.

Lake Oroville is a Department of Water Resources project, built for water supply, flood control, and power generation. At full pool it has 167 mi. of shoreline, with four long arms. Although it is a popular recreation site, management reports capacity crowds only on major summer holidays. It is least crowded Sept.–May. The most popular recreation is water-based. Even in summer, however, someone with a small boat can find quiet waters up the tributaries, where boat speed is restricted to 5 mph.

Most of the area is within the foothills of the Sierra Nevada. The dam is on the Feather River. Upstream the site adjoins the Feather Falls Scenic Area of the Plumas National Forest (see entry, zone 2). Lake elevation at maximum is 900 ft. Elevations within the site range from 140 ft. to 1,300 ft. Annual precipitation ranges from 15 to 50 in.

Plants: Checklist in preparation. From valley grasslands to chaparral. Principal trees are digger pine, valley oak, blue oak, live oak, black oak, madrone, cedar, ponderosa pine. Great variety of chaparral plants, including manzanita, buck brush, ceanothus, poison oak. Wildflowers include California poppy, mariposa lily, brodiaea, thistles, Indian paintbrush, buttercup, spring vetch, shooting star.

Birds: Partial checklist available. Species include Canada and snow geese, western grebe, red-breasted merganser, American coot, Arctic and common loons, double-crested cormorant, mallard, wood duck, golden and bald eagles, osprey, red-tailed and Swainson's hawks, great blue heron, burrowing and pygmy owls, Caspian tern, acorn and downy woodpeckers, mountain quail, belted kingfisher, cedar waxwing, rock wren, bushtit, plain titmouse, scrub jay, western bluebird, violet-green swallow.

Mammals: Partial checklist. Species include coyote, raccoon, porcupine, black-tailed jackrabbit, California ground squirrel, ringtail, gray fox, black bear, beaver, mule deer.

FEATURE: *Feather Falls*—when the lake is high, one can boat to within 1/4 mi. of the 640-ft. high falls, spectacular in spring runoff. No trail from the lake, but the route is not difficult. (The falls are within the Plumas National Forest.)

INTERPRETATION
Visitor center themes include natural and cultural history, as well as the dam.
Campfire programs Wed., Sat., and Sun., June–Sept.
Guided hikes, June–Sept.
Nature trails: self-guided trail at Loafer Creek campground, on Indian uses of native plants. Also a self-guided trail at the visitor center, on chaparral fauna and flora. At Bidwell Canyon campground, a new trail is being developed.

ACTIVITIES
Camping: 2 campgrounds, 187 sites. All year. Reservations Apr. 27–Sept. 3. Also 109 primitive boat-in sites.
Hiking: 7 mi. of horse and hiking trail, from downtown Oroville to the visitor center.
Hunting: Designated areas. Upland small game and waterfowl only.
Fishing: Rainbow and German brown trout, bass, silver salmon, kokanee.
Swimming: Supervised May–Sept.
Boating: Marina, ramps. No hp limit but special zones. On-board boat camping in many areas if boat is properly equipped. Boat rentals at Lime Saddle Marina.

ADJACENT OR NEARBY
  Plumas National Forest (see entry, zone 2).
  Oroville Wildlife Area (see entry).

PUBLICATIONS
  Leaflet with map.
  Bird checklist.
  Chaparral Trail and Maidu Trail guides.
  Boating information.
  Fishing brochure.

HEADQUARTERS: 400 Glen Dr., Oroville, CA 95965; (916) 534-2409.

LAKE TAHOE BASIN MANAGEMENT UNIT

U.S. Forest Service
148,193 acres; 205,250 acres within boundaries.

National Forest land near Lake Tahoe, in CA and NV.

Lake Tahoe is 21 1/2 mi. long, 12 mi. at its widest, at an elevation of 6,225 ft. When pristine, it was called one of the world's loveliest sights. Development began early. Most of the shoreline is privately owned. In 1979 an official basin-wide assessment concluded what many environmentalists and local residents had said before: every element of the environment was deteriorating at an alarming rate.

Since then, the League to Save Lake Tahoe, other private groups, and various local, state, and federal agencies have achieved considerable progress. Stricter controls govern new construction. Road salting is out. Erosion control is improving.

Although only a few short sections of lake shore are federally owned, parts of three National Forests are nearby, and these parts have had heavy visitor use. The Lake Tahoe Basin Management Unit was established by the Forest Service to bring these areas into the general scheme for protecting the lake and its environs.

Most of the acreage within the Unit is around the S half of the lake, extending almost as far S as SR 88. Forest Service land around the N half of the lake is a patchwork. Other National Forest lands, of course, lie outside the Unit boundaries. Within the Unit are the trails, campgrounds, and other features visitors reach from the roads surrounding the lake.

FEATURES AND INTERPRETATION

The *Lake Tahoe Visitor Center* is just W of South Lake Tahoe on SR 89, just N of the turnoff for Fallen Leaf Lake. This is a good place to begin a tour. Open daily in summer. *Guided walks, nature trails,* other activities, including an *auto cassette tour, stream profile chamber, campfire programs.*

Angora Lookout is near the S end of Fallen Leaf Lake, reached by 3 mi. of mountain road. Views of the lakes and Desolation Wilderness.

Desolation Wilderness is described in the Eldorado National Forest entry. Wilderness permits are required and the number is limited. The most heavily used portion of the Wilderness is in the Management Unit.

Granite Chief Area is W and NW of Tahoe City, a backcountry area within which all vehicles are banned. Steep, rugged ridges, peaks between 8,000 and 9,000 ft. Glacial valleys. Small lakes and streams.

Meiss Area is reached by a trailhead on SR 89, 4 1/2 mi. S of the junction with US 50, S of South Lake Tahoe. Said to be one of the most beautiful hiking areas in the Basin: a rugged alpine area, with alpine lakes, meadows, overlooks. The Forest Service says the Granite Chief and Meiss areas are similar to the Desolation Wilderness, and use is not so heavy.

ACTIVITIES

Camping: 2 campgrounds, 264 sites. Summer months. Reservations.

Hunting: Said to be generally poor in this area.

Fishing: Many lakes, streams.

Swimming: Three day-use areas with beaches W of South Lake Tahoe. (Plus one in NV.)

Boating: Other public facilities on Lake Tahoe. Ramps on Fallen Leaf Lake, the Echo Lakes.

Horse riding: Outfitters offer horses, trail rides in summer.

Skiing: Concession-operated ski areas.

Ski touring: Forest Service may offer guided trips, Jan.–Feb. Inquire.

PUBLICATION: Map.

HEADQUARTERS: P.O. Box 8465, 870 Emerald Bay Rd., South Lake Tahoe, CA 95731; (916) 544-6420. Summer information station: (916) 583-3642.

MARTIS CREEK LAKE
U.S. Army Corps of Engineers
1,050-acre wildlife area; 770-acre lake.

Off SR 267, about 3 mi. SE of Truckee.

The reservoir is usually kept near-empty to provide space for floodwaters. The site is interesting because of the wildlife management area, where vehicles are excluded and land is kept in more or less natural condition.

Camping: 25 sites.

PUBLICATION: Leaflet.

HEADQUARTERS: c/o Englebright Lake Park, Smartville, CA 95977; (916) 639-2342.

OROVILLE WILDLIFE AREA
California Department of Fish and Game
5,500 acres.

Just W of Oroville on SR 162, Oroville Dam Blvd.

An interesting demonstration of wetlands restoration. This site on the Feather River showed the effects of half a century of gold dredging: ridges of rock intermixed with sand and gravel tailings. It became a borrow area during construction of Oroville Dam. Most of the rock piles were removed, land levels lowered, creating wetlands and riparian habitat. Plantings and natural plant dispersal turned the area green, and wildlife moved in.

The site is about 9 1/2 mi. long, extending S from SR 162. Improved dirt roads generally follow the river's course. Some may, at times, be closed to vehicles. The site includes over 350 acres of ponds and canals open to fishing.

Plants: Typical of valley riparian communities. Trees include Fremont cottonwood, willow, valley oak, western sycamore. Common groundcover species include yellow sweet clover, western ragweed, annual grasses.

Birds: No checklist. 171 species recorded. Many species of waterfowl winter on the river and ponds. Common game birds include mourning dove, California quail, ring-necked pheasant, band-tailed pigeon. Other species include marsh hawk, green heron, white-tailed kite, osprey.

Mammals: Include muskrat, beaver, striped skunk, coyote, raccoon, black-tailed jackrabbit, gray fox, mule deer.

NEARBY: Lake Oroville State Recreation Area (see entry).

PUBLICATION: Leaflet with map.

HEADQUARTERS: 945 West Oro-Dam Blvd., Oroville, CA 95965; (916) 534-0888.

PLUMAS NATIONAL FOREST
U.S. Forest Service

87% of this Forest is in zone 2, where the entry appears. About 157,000 acres
is in the N of zone 4. This includes the lower part of the Middle Fork, Feather
River, and the Feather Falls Scenic Area above Lake Oroville. It adjoins the
Tahoe National Forest at Canyon Creek.

SOUTH YUBA RIVER RECREATION AREA
U.S. Bureau of Land Management
10,560 acres.

From Nevada City, 12 mi. N on SR 49; right on Tyler Foote county road.

The South Yuba River, with a rugged canyon, cuts through the center of this
irregularly shaped site. Terrain varies from rough and mountainous to gentle
slopes and flat lands. In the far E of the site it adjoins Malakoff Diggins State
Park; on the S a piece of the Tahoe National Forest. The setting is mostly
forested: ponderosa pine, Douglas-fir, California oak. Annual precipitation is
about 55 in. Snowfall is usually light, and campgrounds can be used all year.

A feature is the South Yuba Trail, a National Recreation Trail, recently
expanded to 13 1/2 mi., linking with trail systems of the State Park and
National Forest.

A 1 1/2 mi. nature trail is near the campground.

Camping: 14-unit campground at about 2,600 ft. elevation. 2 primitive sites
along the river. Within the Recreation Area, camping is restricted to designated sites.

HEADQUARTERS: BLM, Folsom Resource Area, 63 Natoma St., Folsom, CA
95630; (916) 985-4474.

SPENCEVILLE WILDLIFE AREA
California Department of Fish and Game
11,213 acres.

From Smartville on SR 20, S on Smartville Rd.

The main body of the site is a narrow corridor for about 3 mi. along the Smartville Road S of Hammonton Road. It then broadens, about 4 mi. to the E. The W boundary is the Beale Air Force Base, of which the site was once a part. The only permanent stream is, inappropriately, named "Dry Creek." The creek has a waterfall. The site has 40 springs, several seasonal streams, three small reservoirs. Vegetation is predominantly blue oak, followed by live oak and valley oak. Ground cover of annual grasses, filaree, bur clover. Cottonwood, willow, and alder along the stream.

Birds: No checklist. Mentioned: valley quail, mourning dove, band-tailed pigeon, wild turkey. Great blue heron rookery.

Mammals: Cottontail, gray squirrel, coyote, bobcat, mule deer, gray fox, raccoon.

Camping, 8 sites.

No drinking water. Fire hazard often high May–Oct.

PUBLICATION: Leaflet with map.

HEADQUARTERS: Region 2, Department of Fish and Game, 1701 Nimbus Rd., Suite "A," Rancho Cordova, CA 95819; (916) 355-7010.

STANISLAUS NATIONAL FOREST
85,056 acres of this Forest are in Calaveras County of zone 4, adjoining the Eldorado National Forest. 9,097 acres of the Mokelumne Wilderness, described in the Eldorado entry, are in the Stanislaus. Most of the Stanislaus is in zone 6, and the entry appears there.

SUGAR PINE POINT STATE PARK
California Department of Parks and Recreation
2,011 acres.

On Lake Tahoe 10 mi. S of Tahoe City.

See the entry for Lake Tahoe Basin Management Unit. This is a crowded resort area. SR 89, following the lakeshore, offers few glimpses of the lake until it reaches Emerald Bay. This park is heavily used from Memorial Day to Labor Day. It is nonetheless a most attractive area, a welcome contrast to the surrounding development.

On a gently sloping, forested promontory, with 1 3/4 mi. of lake frontage, including several small sandy beaches. The site extends 3 1/2 mi. up the General Creek watershed, with trail access to the Desolation Wilderness (see entry, Eldorado National Forest). S of General Creek are the Ehrman Mansion, built in 1903, now part of the park, and a pioneer-built historic structure. N of the creek is the Edwin L. Z'berg Natural Preserve, where the mature forest of the Tahoe Basin extends to the water's edge. The campground is on the inland side of the highway.

Plants: Most of the site is forested. Principal tree species are sugar and Jeffrey pines, red and white firs, incense cedar. Lodgepole pine, quaking aspen, black cottonwood, and mountain alder in moister areas. A very large Sierra juniper near the Children's House (historic structure). Understory includes manzanita, chinquapin, deerbrush, willows, ferns. Flowering plants include lupine, Indian paintbrush, red columbine, penstemon, buckwheat.

Birds: No checklist. Reported: Steller's jay, American robin, flycatchers, woodpeckers, western tanager, belted kingfisher. Waterfowl on or near the lake.

Mammals: Include chickaree, chipmunk, California and golden-mantled ground squirrels, raccoon, deer, porcupine, coyote, weasel, bear, beaver, pine marten, fisher, snowshoe hare.

INTERPRETATION: *Park ranger* on site all year. *Campfire programs* and *guided hikes* in summer. *Nature trail* into the Natural Preserve.

ACTIVITIES

Camping: 150 sites. All year. (When we visited in March, snow was deep, but enough sites had been plowed for those seeking them.) Reservations June 15–Sept. 3.

Hiking: 8 mi. of trail, including trail into the National Forest. (Our informant commented that the National Forest trail is "very confusing" and backpackers prefer entering the Wilderness Area by the Meeks Creek trail.)

Swimming: Lake. Unsupervised.

Boating: No ramp. Boats may tie to pier in daylight. No overnight mooring.

Ski touring: 3 flagged trails: 1, 1 1/2, and 4 1/2 mi. Season usually late Nov.–late Apr.

PUBLICATION: Leaflet with map.

HEADQUARTERS: P.O. Drawer 266, Tahoma, CA 95733; (916) 525-7982.

TAHOE NATIONAL FOREST

U.S. Forest Service
811,740 acres of Forest land; 1,208,993 acres within boundaries.

W and N of Lake Tahoe. Crossed by I-80 and SR 89.

In the central Sierra Nevada. Extends from the Sacramento Valley across the mountains to the Great Basin. Elevations rise gradually on the W to about 8,687 ft. in the Sierra Buttes, then drop more steeply to about 6,000 ft. at Lake Tahoe. The area is scenic, diverse, with great contrasts in terrain and vegetation, many streams, rivers, and lakes.

A third of the land within the Forest boundaries is privately owned. The most extensive blocks of relatively solid Forest land are N of Truckee and N of the American River, Middle Fork. Because the area is attractive and accessible, it is heavily used for recreation all year. In the warm months, water is the chief attraction.

On the W side, annual precipitation is heavy, 50–80 in. per year. The E side, rain-shadowed, is drier, about 16 in. per year near Lake Tahoe. At the higher elevations, most precipitation falls as winter snow, and snow cover lasts from Oct. through Apr.

French Meadows Reservoir, on the upper reaches of the American River, Middle Fork, is nestled under the crest of the Sierra Nevada, at 5,200 ft. elevation. Almost entirely surrounded by Forest land, it provides a truly remote mountain environment.

Jackson Meadow Reservoir, NW of Truckee on the Yuba River, lies over 6,000 ft. elevation. Much of the shore is privately owned.

The New Bullards Bar Reservoir, at the W end of the Forest near Camptonville, is a large lake at about 2,000 ft. elevation, at the edge of the Sacramento Valley. It is heavily used by boaters, campers, fishermen, and hikers.

The area near Lake Tahoe is within the Lake Tahoe Basin Management Unit (see entry).

Plants: Largely forested, though with many open areas used for grazing.

The lower western slopes and canyons (elevations 2,000–4,000 ft.) are gently rolling ridges, cut by steep, highly dissected canyons. Vegetation is mostly canyon and interior live oak, black oak, scattered conifers, mixed brush species, and grasses.

The mixed conifer forest lies between 2,000 and 5,500 ft. Major species include ponderosa and sugar pines, incense cedar, Douglas-fir, and white fir. Some interspersed hardwoods are black oak, bigleaf maple, dogwood, interior live oak, California bay laurel, madrone, and tan oak. Understory includes deerbrush, white thorn, mountain misery, green and white leaf manzanitas, dwarf tan bark, and grasses. Alders, willows, and other water-loving species occupy riparian habitat.

The red fir community, between elevations of 5,500 and 9,500 ft., includes lodgepole, western white, and Jeffrey pines, red and white firs. Mountain hemlock and white-bark pine occur in isolated colder pockets or on harsh ridgetops. Bush chinquapin, snowbrush, huckleberry oak, bitter cherry, whitethorn, greenleaf manzanita, and wyethia are associated. Numerous meadows and seeps, with alders, willows, quaking aspen, sedges, and forbs occur throughout the community.

The northern juniper woodland plant community occurs below 6,500 ft. on the E side of the Forest. Tree species include Jeffrey pine, white fir, and, in drier locations, western juniper. Lodgepole pine, cottonwood, quaking aspen, alders, willows, sedges and forbs occur along drainways and in depressions. Other species include rabbitbrush, sagebrush, bitterbrush, wyethia, mountain mahogany, and perennial grasses.

Timber plantations occur at all levels, but are most prevalent in the mixed conifer and red fir forest communities. Ponderosa, white fir, sugar pine, and Douglas-fir are commonly planted below 5,500 ft., while Jeffrey pine, red fir, sugar pine, western white pine, and white fir are commonly planted above 5,500 ft.

Birds: Checklist available. Eared grebe, goldeneye, and merganser common fall through spring. Golden eagle, goshawk, red-tailed and Cooper's hawks, kestrel, great horned owl. California and mountain quail, coot in marshes and lakeshores. Band-tailed pigeon, scrub and Steller's jays, pileated and acorn woodpeckers, Clark's nutcracker, flicker. Flycatchers in the lodgepole and ponderosa pine areas. Violet-green, tree, barn, and cliff swallows; brown creeper, Bewick's wren, mountain bluebird, varied thrush, ruby-crowned kinglet, warbling vireo, black-throated gray and Wilson's warblers, western meadowlark, Brewer's blackbird, northern oriole, black-headed grosbeak, purple and house finches, pine siskin, green-tailed and rufous-sided towhees; white-crowned, Brewer's, and song sparrows.

Mammals: Mule deer, bear, coyote, pine marten, mountain lion, bobcat, fisher, weasel, red fox, raccoon, ringtail, spotted skunk, California and golden-mantled ground squirrels, Belding gray squirrel, marmot, porcupine. No checklist.

FEATURES: Scenic drives—several attractive routes. SR 89, N of Truckee, follows the Little Truckee River for some miles, later joins SR 49 and follows the Yuba River. South of Truckee, SR 49 follows the Truckee River in a steep-walled valley to Lake Tahoe. Many gravel roads in the Forest for backcountry travel, plus many roads requiring 4-wheel drive.

ACTIVITIES

Camping: 67 campgrounds, 1,400 sites. Campgrounds vary in size (1 to 200) and facilities. Seasons vary: 5 campgrounds are open all year. A few are open Apr.–Nov.; most June–Oct.

Hiking, backpacking: 300 mi. of trails and unpaved roads. Pacific Crest Trail, when completed, will extend for 93 mi. through the Forest. Parts of the Trail were still temporary when we visited. The Crest Trail follows the ridges, limiting the season to July–Oct.

Hunting: Deer, bear, game birds.

Fishing: Lakes, streams, reservoirs. Rainbow, kamloop, cutthroat, and brown trout stocked.

Swimming: Lakes and streams. Unsupervised.

Boating: On New Bullards Bar, Jackson Meadow, French Meadows, Stampede, and Boca reservoirs. Boat docks and launch ramps on several smaller lakes. Much of the shorelines privately owned.

Horse riding: Popular. Outfitters offer hourly, day, or extended trips. Information at HQ.

Ski touring, snowmobiling: 30 mi. of marked trails; also unplowed roads and trails. 67 mi. marked for snowmobiles.

ADJACENT: Plumas National Forest, Eldorado National Forest, Lake Tahoe Basin Management Unit (see entries).

Also about 30,000 acres of the Carson Ranger District, Toiyabe National Forest. Most of this widely scattered Forest is in NV. This CA portion adjoins the NE corner of the Tahoe National Forest, NE of Stampede Reservoir. It can be reached by Henness Pass Road from the Reservoir. Scenic Dog Valley, on the Emigrant Trail, is the chief feature of this area. Crystal Peak Campground takes its name from a nearby quartz outcropping. The area has 3 campgrounds with 36 sites, at elevations from 5,900 ft. to 6,700 ft., opening dates from May 15 to June 10.

PUBLICATIONS

Forest map. $1.00.
Birds of the Tahoe National Forest and Vicinity.
Tahoe National Forest: Camping and Picnicking.
Jackson Meadow Recreation Area, folder and map.
French Meadows and Hell Hole Recreation Areas, folder and map.
Bullards Bar Recreation Area, folder and map.
Washoe Snowmobile Area, folder and map.
Snowmobile Trails, folder and map.
Rock Creek Nature Trail, guided tour folder.
Glacier Meadow Loop Trail, tour guide.

HEADQUARTERS: Highway 49 and Coyote St., Nevada City, CA 95959; (916) 265-4531.

RANGER DISTRICTS: Downieville R.D., Downieville, CA 95936; (916) 289-3232. Foresthill R.D., Foresthill, CA 95631; (916) 367-2224. Nevada City R.D., 12012 Sutton Way, Grass Valley, CA 96126; (916) 994-3401. Sierraville R.D., Sierraville, CA 96126; (916) 994-3401. Truckee R.D., Truckee, CA 95734; (916) 587-3558.

ZONE 5

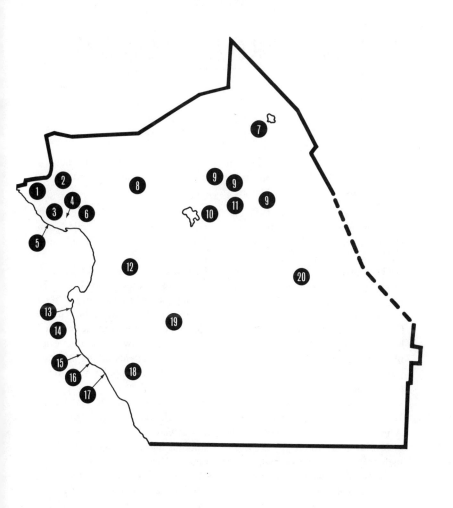

CALIFORNIA, ZONE 5

Includes these counties:

Santa Cruz	Monterey	Madera (W portion)
Santa Clara	San Benito	Fresno (W portion)
Stanislaus	Merced	Kings

This zone begins just S of the San Francisco Bay area, extending almost to San Simeon. It includes the ocean coast, the Santa Cruz and Santa Lucia Mountains near the Coast, the Salinas River Basin, the Diablo Range, and the W portion of the San Joaquin Valley.

The coastline is dramatically scenic. SR 1 hugs the Coast, often on high ledges. Along the way are frequent overlooks. Looking down at the kelp beds, one often sees sea otters. On the Coast are many public beaches, several State Parks, and Los Padres National Forest. On a fine weekend in March, we found the Coast Highway busy although not congested. Many of the park and beach parking lots were full or nearly so. Along the highway were numerous places where cars had parked off the road, their occupants taking informal trails down the cliffs to isolated beaches. The beaches are popular, though not for swimming.

The largest public area in the zone is a 300,000-acre unit of Los Padres National Forest, lying on or near the Coast in the Santa Lucia Mountains. A major portion of this unit is a wilderness area.

Several interesting areas are in the mountains and intermountain valleys, including the Pinnacles National Monument, Big Basin Redwoods State Park, Henry Cowell Redwoods State Park, and Pfeiffer Big Sur State Park, also a redwoods park. Henry W. Coe State Park and The Forest of Nisene Marks State Park are designed for hikers, with no roads beyond the developed areas.

The San Joaquin Valley is largely irrigated cropland. Before most of it was drained, natural ponds and marshes provided winter habitat for vast numbers of waterfowl. Wetlands are now preserved or restored in a number of federal and state refuges, all of them attractive to birds. They include the San Joaquin Valley National Wildlife Refuges and the Los Banos Wildlife Area Complex.

ANDREW MOLERA STATE PARK
California Department of Parks and Recreation
4,691 acres.

21 mi. S of Carmel on SR 1.

On the Pacific Ocean; Coastal Mountains on the E. Big Sur River flows through the site. Elevations from sealevel to 3,455 ft. at the top of the first coastal ridge. A highway sign warns, "No trailers." The unpaved parking area is next to the highway. All travel beyond is on foot. A path follows the river for about 1/4 mi. to an open meadow where camping is permitted. The path then goes through a wooded area toward the sea. One can choose a route to the top of the bluffs, about 100 ft. above the sea, or turn left where the river has formed a wide floodplain. The park has 2 1/2 mi. of ocean beach, mostly sandy, and about 2 1/2 mi. of river frontage.

When we visited in late March, on a Sunday, the parking lot was crowded, partly because of a large Scout encampment in the meadow, partly because a hot day had brought out day visitors for picnics and swimming. This was unusual, we were told. Crowding is usually limited to major summer holidays.

Plants: About 25% forested. Scattered stands of old-growth Coast redwood along the river and in canyons. Other trees: tan oak, California bay laurel, bigleaf maple, live oak, red alder, sycamore, cottonwood. Understory species include redwood sorrel, poison oak, blackberry, thimbleberry, ferns. Coastal prairie plants include wild oat, rattlesnake grass, little quaking grass, Italian rye, foxtail, ribgrass, common ice plant, dune eriogonum, yellow verbena, silverweed, primrose.

Birds: No checklist. Reported: horned, eared, western, and pied-billed grebes; Brandt's cormorant, great blue and green herons, turkey vulture, white-tailed kite, red-tailed and marsh hawks, snowy and great egrets, surf scoter, black oystercatcher, black turnstone, willet, sanderling, northern phalarope; western, California, and mew gulls; band-tailed pigeon, mourning dove, barn and great horned owls, dipper.

Mammals: Include gray squirrel, raccoon, sea otter, California and Steller sea lions, harbor seal, gray whale, coyote, bobcat, mule deer. Seldom seen but present: opossum, ringtail, weasel, brush rabbit.

INTERPRETATION: Guided hikes, July–Aug. Notices posted.

ACTIVITIES
Camping: Walk-in 1/4 mi. About 50 sites. All year.
Hiking: 10 mi. of trails.
Swimming: Ocean is cold and rough, river shallow.

HEADQUARTERS: P.O. Box A, Big Sur, CA 93920; (408) 667-2316.

BIG BASIN REDWOODS STATE PARK
California Department of Parks and Recreation
Over 16,000 acres.

From Santa Cruz, N 23 mi. on SR 9 and SR 236.

Close to the San Francisco metropolitan area and thus heavily used in season. However, it's larger than most State Parks, and except on peak holiday weekends one can find uncrowded trails. Most visitors come to walk the short trail through the redwood grove and to picnic or camp.

The Park straddles the watershed of Waddell Creek and its tributaries. Although the main body of the Park is inland, a neck follows the creek to the sea. The Park has 6,336 ft. of ocean frontage. Elevations from sealevel to 2,200 ft. The area is moderately humid, with 32 in. of precipitation yearly. The site has 4 waterfalls, of which Berry Creek Falls is 65 ft. and Sempervirens Fall 20 ft.

This is California's oldest State Park, established because of the old-growth redwoods, the largest 329 ft. tall. Several million visitors have walked the 0.6-mi. trail through the principal grove. Most of the site is forested: Coast redwood, Douglas-fir, tan oak, madrone. Flowering plants include California hazel, coffeeberry, inside-out flower, honeysuckle, western azalea, Douglas iris, huckleberry.

Birds: An exceptionally useful checklist tells what species can be seen, when and where. All-year residents include red-tailed and Cooper's hawks; horned, screech, and pygmy owls; common flicker; downy, hairy, and acorn woodpeckers; California quail, Bewick's wren, purple finch, common bushtit, wrentit, Steller's jay, American robin, chestnut-backed chickadee, Hutton's vireo, pine siskin, pygmy nuthatch, golden-crowned kinglet, Oregon junco, dipper.

INTERPRETATION
Nature lodge: exhibits and publications.
Campfire programs and *guided hikes:* mid-June to Labor Day.

ACTIVITIES
Camping: 4 campgrounds. 188 sites. Reservations May 1–Sept. 30.
Hiking, backpacking: 60 mi. of trails, including Skyline-to-the-Sea. Backpacking is by permit. The number of permits is limited. Reservations are recommended, all year; call HQ.
Horse riding: 14-mi. loop trail. No rentals. No camping.

PUBLICATIONS
Backpackers maps 1 and 2. 50¢ each.
Park map. 25¢.
Bird checklist.

HEADQUARTERS: Boulder Creek, CA 95006; (408) 338-6132.

CALIFORNIA SEA OTTER REFUGE
California Department of Fish and Game

Offshore, S of Pt. Lobos (below Monterey), seen from SR 1, the Cabrillo
Highway.

At the first overlook S of Pt. Lobos, we saw eight sea otters floating on their
backs amid the kelp. We stopped at other overlooks on our way S and saw
many more. Binoculars are useful.

CASTLE ROCK STATE PARK
California Department of Parks and Recreation
About 2,000 acres.

From Saratoga (SW of San Jose), SR 9 W to Saratoga Gap. S 2 mi. on
Skyline Blvd., SR 35.

As the single symbol indicates, this is a hiker's park. See the entry for Big
Basin Redwoods State Park. Castle Rock is linked to Big Basin by the
Skyline-to-Sea Trail. Terrain is steep, mountainous, with level areas only on
ridgetops. Elevations from 800 ft. at the San Lorenzo River to 3,214 ft. The
Park is a primitive wilderness, intended so to remain. Camping only in trail
camps.

Plants: Site is about 75% forested, 25% chaparral, the latter principally on
the S slope of the ridge. Principal tree species: Douglas-fir, Coast redwood,
knobcone pine, madrone; live, tan, and black oaks. Most of the redwoods are
second growth, but a few virgin specimens remain. The black oak woodland
has an exceptional wildflower display.

Birds: Checklists are being developed; HQ has records. Species include
red-tailed and Cooper's hawks; horned, screech, and pygmy owls; common
flicker; downy, hairy, and acorn woodpeckers; California quail, Bewick's
wren, purple finch, common bushtit, wrentit, Steller's and scrub jays, Ameri-

can robin, chestnut-backed chickadee, Hutton's vireo, pine siskin, pygmy nuthatch, golden-crowned kinglet, Oregon junco, dipper, fox sparrow.

Mammals: Include coyote, bobcat, gray fox, opossum; various bats, shrews, and moles; black-tailed jackrabbit, brush rabbit, cottontail, gray squirrel, raccoon, long-tailed weasel, striped skunk, mule deer. Occasional mountain lion.

Reptiles and amphibians: Western fence and alligator lizards, western skink, rubber boa, ring-necked snake, racer, gopher snake, common kingsnake, mountain kingsnake, common garter snake, western rattlesnake.

FEATURES
Several waterfalls notable during winter runoff. Castle Rock Falls drops 120 ft.

Goat Rock, 3,000-ft., 130-ft. S face, offers scenic views of Santa Cruz Mountains and Monterey Bay.

Skyline Boulevard, which crosses the Park, is a scenic highway.

Large outcroppings of Vaqueros Sandstone are much used by rock climbers. Sandstone caves.

INTERPRETATION: *Campfire programs* in trail camps, Sat. nights, spring to fall. Also *guided hikes.* Notices posted.

Hiking, backpacking: About 20 mi. of trails within the Park, 38 to the sea through Big Basin. Permits required for Skyline-to-Sea trail. Ranger commented the trail camps have never been full, "but the time will come."

Since dogs are prohibited on all CA State Park trails, they are banned here altogether.
Hazardous rocks; sheer cliffs. Stay on trails.
High fire hazard sometimes closes Park in midsummer.

PUBLICATIONS
Skyline-to-Sea trail maps (2). 50¢ each.
Park trails map.

HEADQUARTERS: 15000 Skyline Blvd., Los Gatos, CA 95030; (408) 867-2952.

FALL CREEK STATE PARK
California Department of Parks and Recreation
2,335 acres.

From Santa Cruz, N on SR 9 to Felton. Left 1/2 mi. on Felton Empire Rd. Parking on N side.
Open: daylight hours.

A subunit of nearby Henry Cowell Redwoods State Park (see entry). Roadless. A hiker's park. A trail camp is planned. On Ben Lomond Mountain. Elevations from 360 ft. to 1,920 ft. Steep-sided creek canyons, heavily forested. From the parking area, trails N and S forks of Fall Creek. Small falls.

Mostly forested, second-growth Coast redwood, Douglas-fir, with tan oak, madrone, California bay laurel, live oak. Some small upper areas are covered with chaparral.

Wildlife: See entry, Henry Cowell Redwoods.

Hiking: 7 mi. of trails.

PUBLICATION: Information page with map.

HEADQUARTERS: c/o Henry Cowell Redwoods State Park, P.O. Box P-1, Felton, CA 95018; (408) 335-4598.

FREMONT PEAK STATE PARK
California Department of Parks and Recreation
244 acres.

E of Salinas. From US 101, S on SR 156 to San Juan Bautista, then S 11 mi. on San Juan Canyon Rd.

A small, long, narrow park, somewhat isolated, in the Gabilan Mountains. Elevation 2,750 ft., at the end of a moderately steep, winding road. Rolling hills with oaks, madrone, and Coulter pine; the last bears the heaviest of all pine cones.

ACTIVITIES
Camping: 12 primitive sites.
Hiking: Trail to summit of Fremont Peak. Vista.

HEADQUARTERS: P.O. Box 1110, San Juan Bautista, CA 95045; (408) 623-4255.

HENRY COWELL REDWOODS STATE PARK
California Department of Parks and Recreation
1,737 acres.

From Santa Cruz, N on SR 9. For campground: from Santa Cruz, N on Graham Hill Rd.

Almost 7 mi. of the San Lorenzo River are within the Park, the land dropping from 1,100 ft. to 80 ft. elevation. The Park is best known for its Coast redwoods. Most of the area is second growth, but a large grove of virgin redwoods remains, at the N end of the site, near the day-use entrance. The largest tree is 285 ft. tall. The largest area of the Park, accessible only on foot or horseback, is mostly forested, redwood with tan oak, madrone, Douglas-fir, California bay laurel, California live oak, knobcone pine; huckleberry, ceanothus, manzanita in the understory. There is also a ponderosa pine forest, unusual at this elevation and nearness to the coast. Wildflowers include trillium, oxalis, wild ginger.

Birds: No checklist. Noted: mallard, kestrel, great horned owl, Cooper's and red-shouldered hawks, California quail, band-tailed pigeon, belted kingfisher, common flicker, acorn woodpecker, Steller's and scrub jays, golden-crowned kinglet, yellow-rumped warbler, Oregon junco.

Mammals: Noted: gray fox, ground squirrels, cottontail, opossum, raccoon, mule deer. Seldom seen but present: coyote, bobcat, ringtail.

FEATURES
Redwood grove, with self-guiding nature path.
Garden of Eden, scenic swimming area on the river.
Observation deck, on water tower. View of Monterey Bay.

INTERPRETATION: *Campfire programs* and *guided hikes* in summer; other seasons on request.

ACTIVITIES
Camping: 113 sites. All year. Reservations Mar. 3–Oct. 1. Needed in summer.
Hiking: 7 mi. of trails. (Also see entry, Fall Creek State Park.)
Swimming: River. Unsupervised.
Horse riding: 12 mi. of trails.

PUBLICATIONS
Leaflet with map.
Nature trail guide.

HEADQUARTERS: P.O. Box P-1, Felton, CA 95018; (408) 335-4598.

HENRY W. COE STATE PARK
California Department of Parks and Recreation
32,228 acres.

From Morgan Hill on US 101, 13 mi. E on E Dunne Ave. Road is paved
but steep, narrow, winding.

A wilderness park. Rugged, broken terrain. Deep canyons, ridges, wooded
hills. In the Diablo Range E of the Santa Clara Valley. Elevations from 1,040
ft. to 3,100 ft., with 3,216-ft. Mt. Sizer just outside the boundary. The entrance
road leads immediately to a small developed area: HQ, museum, parking, and
a small campground. Travel beyond this point is on foot or horseback.

The Coe family occupied this ranch from the late nineteenth century until
1953, when the family gave it to the state. Several of the ranch buildings are
in the HQ area. S- and W-facing slopes are mostly grassland; some chaparral
and oak woodlands on N- and E-facing slopes. Canyons are steep-sided below
gently rounded ridgetops. Annual precipitation is 24 in. Summers are hot and
dry. Much of the area is in the Coyote Creek drainage.

Plants: The site is about 60% forested. Mostly oak woodlands: valley, live,
and black oak with intermixed digger pine, laurel, madrone. Ridges are
crowned by an oddly sparse growth of large ponderosa pine, an unusual
location for the species. On Middle Ridge are exceptionally large manzanita
bushes, tree-size with large crowns. April is the peak month for wildflower
displays. Over 200 flowering species are here, including delphinium, globe
lily, mariposa lily, violets, sanicle, lupine, owl's clover, buttercup, poppy,
shooting star.

Birds: No site checklist, but the Santa Clara Valley Audubon Society
publishes one for the county, on sale at the Park. Typical of the site: scrub
and Steller's jays, California quail, red-tailed hawk, golden eagle, acorn woodpecker, mourning dove, white-breasted nuthatch, western bluebird, meadowlark, brown and rufous-sided towhees, Oregon junco.

Mammals: Include California ground squirrel, black-tailed jackrabbit, gray
fox, raccoon, coyote, bobcat. Mountain lion and badger are present, seldom
seen.

Reptiles and amphibians: Include western fence lizard, rough-skinned
newt, Pacific tree frog, western pond turtle, gopher snake, western ringneck
snake, common kingsnake, western garter snake, western rattlesnake. California mountain kingsnake is present, seldom seen.

FEATURES
Pine Ridge offers fine view of the Sierra Nevada and Pacific Ocean. *Blue
Ridge* also has viewpoints.

China Hole, reached by a 3.6-mi. hike, is a pool in Coyote Creek big enough for a swim.

INTERPRETATION
Visitor center and museum: ranch history and natural history exhibits. Publications.

Evening programs, Sat. nights, mid-Mar. through July 4. *Guided hikes* Sunday afternoons. Notices posted.

Corral Nature Trail, 1/2 mi.

ACTIVITIES
Camping: 20 primitive sites. (Group camping is popular, and the Park has 10 hike-in group sites.)

Hiking, backpacking: 45 mi. of trails and fire roads. Permits required for overnighting. Restricted to the number of campsites, 21. No fires at backpacking sites; stoves only. No other trailside camping. Day hikers planning more than a short walk should inform the Ranger. Carry water

Swimming. China Hole, a few other points in creek, until flow diminishes in early summer.

Horse riding: About 38 mi. of trails. No local rentals.

The Park, or parts thereof, may be closed at times of extreme fire danger. Summer hikers should be prepared for sun, heat, no water sources. Heavy rains may make some areas inaccessible because the creek can't be crossed.

PUBLICATIONS
Leaflet with map. 50¢.
Backcountry camping information.
Trail map.
Nature trail guide.

(The Pine Ridge Association has on sale at the Park a number of publications on the natural history of the area.)

HEADQUARTERS: P.O. Box 846, Morgan Hill, CA 95037; (408) 779-2728.

JULIA PFEIFFER BURNS STATE PARK
California Department of Parks and Recreation
2,405 acres and 1,680 acres of underwater park.

From Carmel, S 37 mi. on SR 1.

On the Big Sur coastline. Day-use area. Parking and picnic areas are in a redwood grove on the inland side of the highway. From here a trail follows McWay Canyon up toward the ridge, to about 1,500 ft. elevation. The Coast redwood is here near the S limit of its range and thrives only on cool, N-facing slopes of deep canyons with sufficient all-year moisture. With the redwoods: tan oak, madrone, California bay laurel, various ferns; flowering species include trillium, oxalis, baby blue eyes, wild columbine. Beyond the redwood grove is chaparral.

From the parking area, a path leads under the highway to the edge of a bluff about 100 ft. above the sea, offering a sweeping view. The water of McWay Creek drops 70 ft. from the cliff directly into the sea. A trail about 1,600 ft. long leads to an overlook. The area offshore became an underwater park in 1970. Access is limited to experienced diving groups, by permit.

PUBLICATION: Leaflet.

HEADQUARTERS: Route 1, Big Sur, CA 93920; (408) 667-2315.

KESTERSON NATIONAL WILDLIFE REFUGE
See San Joaquin Valley National Wildlife Refuges.

LOS BANOS WILDLIFE AREA
California Department of Fish and Game
3,208 acres.

From SR 165 N of Los Banos, E 0.8 mi. on Henry Miller Ave.

We visited several of the federal and state wildlife refuges in the San Joaquin Valley and enjoyed this one most. One reason was that camping is permitted. We parked our RV by a lake one April evening and, apparently, had the place to ourselves until next morning. Another reason is the natural appearances of the ponds and marshes, unlike the rectilinear flooded fields we saw elsewhere.

The area was, historically, an important waterfowl wintering area. Draining and cultivation of wetlands reduced habitat, and severe droughts in the late 1920s drastically reduced waterfowl populations. A number of refuges in the area now are managed to support maximum numbers of waterfowl and, incidentally, to minimize their predation on farm crops.

An auto tour route extends from the HQ area almost to the N boundary, about 5 mi. away. Other roads are also open to car and foot travel. Along the way are lakes, shallow ponds, marshes, ditches, and some upland. Trees and shrubs grow beside the lakes. Many places are available to park beside water, and a car makes a good blind.

Birds: Checklist of 203 species available. Seasonally common species include eared, western, and pied-billed grebes; great blue heron, great and snowy egrets, black-crowned night heron, American bittern, white-faced ibis, cackling Canada goose, white-fronted goose and lesser snow goose, mallard, gadwall, pintail, green-winged and cinnamon teals, American wigeon, shoveler, ruddy duck, turkey vulture, white-tailed kite, red-tailed and marsh hawks, kestrel, ring-necked pheasant, sandhill crane, Virginia rail, common gallinule, American coot, common snipe, long-billed curlew, killdeer, greater yellowlegs, least sandpiper, long-billed dowitcher, American avocet, black-necked stilt, common flicker, western kingbird, black phoebe, horned lark; tree, barn, and cliff swallows; yellow-billed magpie, long-billed marsh wren, mockingbird, water pipit, loggerhead shrike, yellow-rumped warbler, house sparrow, western meadowlark; yellow-headed, red-winged, and tricolored blackbirds; Brewer's blackbird, house finch; savannah, white-crowned, and song sparrows.

Mammals: Include coyote, gray fox, beaver, muskrat, mink, badger, raccoon, weasel, black-tailed jackrabbit, cottontail, spotted and striped skunks, opossum.

SATELLITES

Several other state Wildlife Areas are satellites of Los Banos. Information about them can be obtained here. We were advised that, for the ordinary visitor, Los Banos is the most interesting and accessible.

Volta Wildlife Area, 2,200 acres, is about 5 mi. NW of Los Banos on Ingomar Grade Road. Except in waterfowl season, foot access only. The Volta Wasteway, a large canal, crosses the site. Of interest chiefly to fishermen and hunters.

Cottonwood Creek Wildlife Area, 6,000 acres, is on the San Luis Reservoir N of SR 152. Foot access only.

The following areas are managed for big game, upland game, and waterfowl nesting habitat to mitigate losses occasioned by construction of San Luis Reservoir, which flooded over 15,000 acres.

O'Neill Forebay Wildlife Area, 700 acres, on SR 33. Foot access only.

San Luis Reservoir Wildlife Area, 900 acres, on Dinosaur Point Road, off SR 152. Foot access only.

Little Panoche Reservoir Wildlife Area, 780 acres, is further S, about 5 mi. W of I-5 on Little Panoche Rd. Foot access only.

ACTIVITIES

Camping: Between the end of the waterfowl season and Sept. 30. Los Banos only, not in satellites. No campground, but numerous suitable areas. Water available at HQ. Latrines in parking lots. Campers must register at HQ.

Hunting: Special regulations. Inquire.

Fishing: Between the end of the waterfowl season and Sept. 30.

NEARBY: San Joaquin Valley National Wildlife Refuges (see entry).

PUBLICATIONS

Leaflet with map.

The Los Banos Complex. Information pages, map.

Fishing, hunting regulations, map.

Bird checklist.

HEADQUARTERS: 18110 W. Henry Miller Ave., Los Banos, CA 93635; (209) 826-0463.

LOS PADRES NATIONAL FOREST
U.S. Forest Service

See entry in zone 8. 304,023 acres of this 1,750,857-acre Forest are in zone 5. This area, a unit somewhat separated from the main body of the Forest, is in the Santa Lucia Mountains. From Big Sur to just beyond Lucia on SR 1, the Forest boundary is 1–2 mi. inland, although there are two small bits on the Coast near Big Sur. From there S to the Monterey County line, the Forest is on the Coast, although there are a number of inholdings.

A large part of this Forest unit is in the Ventana Wilderness. Entry to this area is by permit only in fire season. Note that smoking is prohibited throughout the Forest except in designated sites.

MENDOTA WILDLIFE AREA
California Department of Fish and Game
9,500 acres.

From Mendota (W of Fresno), 3 mi. SE on Santa Fe Grade. E on SR 180 to entrance.

In the central San Joaquin Valley. Like other refuges in the Valley, once an extensive wetland habitat for wintering waterfowl, this one is managed to support optimum populations, reducing crop predation on neighboring farmlands. Management objectives now include fostering upland species.

From a point near the entrance, Fresno Slough cuts across the site to the SE. Unpaved all-weather roads provide access to most parts of the area. About 7,500 acres have been converted into marsh and mudflats attractive to waterfowl and shorebirds. Water level is manipulated to check the natural change of marshland into dense tule-cattail stands. About 1,500 acres are good upland habitat.

In recent years management has encouraged general recreational use of the area, outside of hunting season: fishing, sightseeing, nature study, picnicking, swimming, boating, and—the leaflet notes—an occasional baptism!

No species checklists are available, but common birds and mammals are much the same as at the San Joaquin Valley National Wildlife Refuges and the Los Banos Wildlife Area (see entries).

ACTIVITIES

Fishing: Open to fishing 24 hrs. a day, but only boat fishing is allowed in waterfowl hunting season.

Boating: On the Slough. Ramp near entrance.

NEARBY: San Joaquin Valley National Wildlife Refuges and Los Banos Wildlife Area (see entries).

PUBLICATION: Leaflet with map.

HEADQUARTERS: P.O. Box 37, Mendota, CA 93640; (209) 655-4645.

MERCED NATIONAL WILDLIFE REFUGE
See San Joaquin Valley National Wildlife Refuges.

PFEIFFER BIG SUR STATE PARK
California Department of Parks and Recreation
821 acres.

From Carmel, S 26 mi. on SR 1.

In a valley on both sides of the Big Sur River, within the Santa Lucia Mountains. A short distance from the Coast. Elevations from 215 ft. to 3,000 ft. Southernmost of the redwood parks. The Park is highly developed, with lodge, cabins, store. Heavily used in season. It adjoins the Ventana Wilderness of Los Padres National Forest (see entry); access is at a Ranger Station 1 mi.

S. Pfeiffer Beach, a detached bit of the National Forest, on the Coast, is nearby. (The ocean is not for swimming.) Pfeiffer Falls, within the Park, is in a fern-lined canyon.

Summers have warm days, cool, foggy evenings. Winters are mild; snow is rarely seen. Fall and spring have the best climate. Annual precipitation is about 40 in.

Plants: In the moister areas, Coast redwood with sycamore, black cotton-wood, bigleaf maple, alder, willow. Dry, S-facing slopes are covered with chaparral: Coast live oak, tan oak, California bay laurel, chamise, ceanothus, buckeye, toyon, coffeeberry, cascara, manzanita, yucca.

Birds: No checklist, but checklist for Los Padres National Forest is applicable. Species here include Steller's jay, valley quail, canyon wren, Oregon junco, chestnut-backed chickadee, band-tailed pigeon, turkey vulture, red-tailed hawk, dipper, belted kingfisher.

Mammals: Include opossum, gray squirrel, raccoon, wild boar, mule deer.

INTERPRETATION
Campfire programs and *nature walks* in summer. Also walks at nearby Julia Pfeiffer Burns State Park.
Exhibits at the lodge.
Nature trail, 1 mi.

ACTIVITIES
Camping: 218 sites. All year. Reservations May 29–Sept. 9.
Hiking: Trails to overlooks, other points of interest. Extensive trails in the National Forest. Trailhead is 1 mi. S.

NEARBY: Andrew Molera State Park (see entry).

PUBLICATION: Leaflet with map.

HEADQUARTERS: Big Sur, CA 93920; (408) 667-2315.

PINNACLES NATIONAL MONUMENT
U.S. National Park Service
16,251 acres.

From Hollister, 34 mi. S on SR 25, then S to entrance. A second entrance, on the W, is reached from Soledad via SR 146; this road is not recommended for large trailers and campers; it leads to the Chaparral Ranger Station and campground.

Noted for its many spirelike rock formations, 500–1,200 ft. high, with caves and other volcanic features. These are the last remains of an ancient volcano, eroded by rain, wind, heat, and frost. The spires rise from smoothly rolling hills. The site is on the W side of the San Andreas Fault, has moved N 195 mi. in 23.5 million years. Highest point is North Chalone Peak, 3,304 ft., in the SW corner of the Monument, reached by trail.

Precipitation is about 16 in. per year, mostly in winter and early spring, followed by a hot, dry summer and fall. Spring is the best time for a visit, when vegetation is green and many flowers bloom. Vegetation is chaparral, mostly chamise mixed with manzanita, buckbrush, hollyleaf cherry, and toyon.

The area is used almost entirely by day visitors. The only campground inside the Monument is small and on the W. A commercial campground is just outside the E entrance. The trail system is extensive, but the longest round trip is 9 mi.

Birds often seen include the acorn woodpecker, brown towhee, California quail, turkey vulture, scrub jay. Mammals include raccoon, mule deer, as well as the less commonly seen gray fox and bobcat.

FEATURES

High Peaks Trail, 5.4 mi., from Chalone Creek picnic area to Bear Gulch parking, a 1,650-ft. climb. Views of the entire park.

Condor Gulch Trail, 1.7 mi., ascends 1,100 ft., linking the visitor center and High Peaks Trail.

Chalone Peak Trail, 5 1/2 mi. each way, is the longest in the park, with a 2,150-ft. rise.

Old Pinnacles Trail, 2 mi., from Chalone Creek picnic area over fairly level terrain to *Balconies Caves.*

Balconies Caves can also be reached by a 1.2-mi. trail from the Chaparral Ranger Station.

Juniper Canyon Trail, 1.2 mi., links the Chaparral Ranger Station with High Peaks Trail.

Bench Trail, 1.2 mi., Pinnacle Campground to Bear Gulch Trail and Visitor Center.

INTERPRETATION

Bear Gulch Visitor Center, 3 mi. inside the E entrance, and Chaparral Ranger Station, 2 mi. inside W entrance. Naturalist, exhibits, publications.
Evening programs on weekends at both E and W campgrounds.

4 nature trails: Moses Spring, to Bear Gulch Caves. *Geology Hike,* up the Condor Gulch Trail. *Bear Gulch. Balconies Trail.* These are self-guiding. Leaflets on sale.

Camping: 24 sites. Tents. All year.

PUBLICATION: Leaflet with map.

REFERENCES

Offered by Southwestern Monuments Association, P.O. Box 1562, Globe, AZ 85501, or at the visitor center:
Guide to Plants of the Pinnacles. 75¢.
Natural History of Pinnacles. $1.75.
Pinnacles Topographic Map. $1.00.
Nature trail guides. 10¢ each.
Checklists of birds, mammals, amphibians, and reptiles.

HEADQUARTERS: Paicines, CA 95043; (408) 389-4578.

POINT LOBOS STATE RESERVE

California Department of Parks and Recreation
1,276 acres.

From Carmel, S 3 mi. on SR 1.
Open: 9 A.M.–7 P.M. in summer; otherwise 9 A.M.–5 P.M.

Maintained as a pristine site, a unique area scenically and in its flora and fauna. It includes the first underwater reserve. All the tide and submerged land surrounding the Reserve, 775 acres, are the Point Lobos Ecological Reserve, managed by the California Department of Fish and Game. The adjoining tide and submerged lands in Carmel Bay are the Carmel Bay Ecological Reserve, 1,642 acres, also managed by the DFG. This Reserve also includes the Pinnacles, a cluster of offshore rocks.

We visited the area on a fine, warm Sunday in March. It was impossible to enter, the road inside choked with cars, cars parked up and down the highway. All nearby beaches were crowded that day.

Pt. Lobos is a rugged peninsula of red-brown rock. Highest point is 260 ft. The site has 6 mi. of coastline in an irregular configuration. Strict rules protect the site: visitors must stay on trails; nothing may be collected from land or sea; scuba and skin diving require a permit; fishing is prohibited.

Plants: Monterey cypress and Gowen cypress occur naturally only here and in a small nearby area. (The Gowen cypress specimens are in a part of the site not yet open to visitors.) Also here are fine specimens of Monterey pine, a species gradually becoming extinct for natural causes in its native habitat, but one that is extensively planted commercially in South America, New Zealand, and Australia. Other terrestrial plant species include coastal sagebrush, chaparral broom, coyote brush, poison oak, bluff lettuce on cliffs, lace lichen on trees.

Over 300 species of wildflowers occur here. Some species are in bloom in almost every season, but spring is the peak. Species include sun-cups, California poppy, lizard-tail yarrow, Douglas iris, seaside painted cup, sea pink, star zigadene lily, Johnny-jump-up, cream-cup, wild lilac, brodiaea, Pacific blackberry, asters, lupine, blue-eyed grass.

Birds: 147 species recorded. Common residents include western gull, Brandt's cormorant, black phoebe, great blue heron, killdeer, black oystercatcher, great horned owl, hairy woodpecker, Steller's and scrub jays, wrentit, Bewick's wren, song sparrow, chestnut-backed chickadee, pygmy nuthatch, bushtit. Gulls and cormorants nest on offshore rocks. Brown pelican are summer visitors to the offshore. Common migrants include loons, grebes, scaup, surf scoter, red-breasted merganser, black turnstone.

Mammals: Good opportunities to see marine mammals. Sea otters are permanent residents. California and Steller sea lions are seasonal visitors. Harbor seal often seen. California gray whales pass in winter and early spring. Occasional killer whale. Dusky-footed woodrats build homes 3 ft. high in much of the Reserve. Other terrestrial species: California ground squirrel, western gray squirrel, California meadow mouse, gray fox, bobcat, raccoon. Occasional sightings of mountain lion, opossum, striped skunk.

INTERPRETATION
Naturalist programs daily in summer, weekends otherwise.
Nature trail.
Hiking. 7 1/2 mi. of trails.

HEADQUARTERS: c/o Monterey State Historical Park, 210 Olivier St., Monterey, CA 93940; (408) 624-4909.

SAN JOAQUIN VALLEY NATIONAL WILDLIFE REFUGES
U.S. Fish and Wildlife Service
Merced: 2,562 acres. Kesterson: 5,900 acres. San Luis: 7,430 acres.

Merced: From Merced, 8 mi. S on SR 59; 6 mi. W on Sandymush Rd.
Kesterson: From Merced, 39 mi. E on SR 140.
San Luis: From Los Banos, N 8 mi. on N. Mercy Springs Rd. (J-14), then NE 2 mi. on Wolfsen Rd.

The San Joaquin Valley was, historically, a great wintering area for waterfowl. Most of the wetlands have been drained and cultivated. State and federal refuges have been established both to support as many of these waterfowl as possible and to reduce their predation on farm crops. Waterfowl concentrations of 500,000 and more are common in winter.

The *Merced National Wildlife Refuge* looks much like the irrigated cropland that surrounds it. Intermittent marsh, grass upland, cultivated fields. Visitors drive on several miles of dikes. Two sloughs cut across the site. Its water supply, however, is pumped from deep wells, just enough in summer to irrigate feed crops. Cropland and marsh areas are flooded Oct.–Jan. to attract migrating and wintering waterfowl. Ring-necked pheasant are abundant here, as are cottontail.

We visited in the spring, after most of the waterfowl had departed. The site doesn't look like a natural area, but the birding is fine. In one quick trip around the tour route, we noted black-necked stilt, white-crowned sparrow, pheasant, killdeer, avocet, red-winged blackbird, great blue heron, meadowlark, red-tailed hawk, western tanager, nighthawk, coot, burrowing owl, western kingbird, black-crowned night heron, shoveler, snowy egret, pintail, cinnamon teal.

Kesterson National Wildlife Refuge is the newest of the three and its future is in doubt because of proposed projects of the Water and Power Resource Service. The site is on Bureau of Reclamation land. Visitors are now limited to Gun Club Road and Highway 140, which cross or border the area. Conservationists are opposing the threat to a natural area.

San Luis National Wildlife Refuge is the largest of the group and the most natural in appearance. Tree-lined Salt Slough and the meandering San Joaquin River nearly enclose the lush grasslands. Swales and depressions form a maze of ponds and marshes. Here the canals and water control structures make the most of natural contours. Here is a 1,000-acre block of native grassland, one of the largest fragments remaining in the Great Valley, with vernal pools and fine flower displays. The refuge has a herd of tule elk, numbering 26 in 1981. Visitors, whether in cars or on foot, are restricted to Tule Elk Drive, around the tule elk enclosure, and the main tour drive. The first is open daily. The main drive is open daily except Oct. 15–Jan. 20, when it is open only Mon., Tues., Thurs., and Fri.

Birds: Checklist available. Many species have been reported from all three Refuges. Merced has the largest pheasant population. Although it is the smallest of the three units, more than 350,000 ducks and 130,000 geese have been present at one time. White-fronted and snow geese are common, as well as the cackling Canada goose. Predominant ducks are pintail, mallard, wigeon, green-winged teal. Merced is the best of the three places to see sandhill crane and Ross's goose. San Luis is recommended as the place to see large concentrations of waterfowl. Populations at Kesterson are expected to increase year by year.

The checklist records 204 species. Peak population of sandhill crane is usually Oct.–Nov., with about 4,000 present. Many shorebirds pass through spring and fall, among them phalarope, yellowlegs, dowitchers, sandpipers, long-billed curlew. Many hawks and songbirds can be observed near woodland edges.

Mammals: Species reported include striped skunk, badger, cottontail, black-tailed jackrabbit, California ground squirrel, long-tailed weasel, muskrat, coyote.

ACTIVITIES

Hiking is restricted to designated routes.

Hunting: Waterfowl. Portions of all 3 units. Pheasant on portion of Merced. Special regulations; daily hunter quotas. Hunting Wed., Sat., Sun. in regular season.

Fishing: San Luis Refuge. Daylight hours, designated areas. Best Feb.–Apr.

NEARBY: Los Banos Wildlife Area (see entry).

PUBLICATIONS:
San Joaquin National Wildlife Refuge leaflet; area map.
Recreation Guide.
Maps of the 3 units.
Birds of the Merced National Wildlife Refuges.
Birds: San Luis, Merced, and Kesterson National Wildlife Refuges.
Young people's bird checklist.

HEADQUARTERS: P.O. Box 2176, Los Banos, CA 93635; (209) 826-3508.

SAN LUIS NATIONAL WILDLIFE REFUGE
See San Joaquin Valley National Wildlife Refuges.

SAN LUIS RESERVOIR STATE RECREATION AREA
California Department of Parks and Recreation
2,311 land acres; 15,800 water acres (at full pool) in two impoundments.

6 mi. W of I-5 on SR 152.

The Reservoir, part of the Central Valley Project, is formed by a dam 3 1/2 mi. long. It is an element in a complex of aqueducts, canals, forebays, pumping stations and reservoirs. The region is dry, about 8 in. of rain yearly, mostly in the winter months. The reservoir is surrounded by rolling hills, with some steep canyons. Slopes are sparsely vegetated, mostly grass. The site is heavily used for camping and water-based recreation.

On the N, on both sides of SR 152, are the San Luis Reservoir Wildlife Area and Cottonwood Creek Wildlife Area (see entry, Los Banos Wildlife Area). These are managed to develop winter waterfowl habitat in partial mitigation of the habitat loss caused by the dam.

Camping: Two campgrounds. One has 79 sites; reservations. The second is a primitive area with parking for up to 400 RV's.

PUBLICATION: Leaflet with map.

HEADQUARTERS: California Parks and Recreation, Four Rivers Area, 31426 West Highway 152, Santa Nella, CA 95322; (209) 826-1196.

THE FOREST OF NISENE MARKS STATE PARK
California Department of Parks and Recreation
9,917 acres.

From SR 1 E of Santa Cruz, Aptos-Seacliff exit. N on Aptos Creek Rd.

As the single symbol indicates, this is a hiker's park, although cars can be driven on a dirt road to the picnic areas. Steep coastal mountains, deeply carved by six creeks that originate within the Park. Elevations from 190 ft. to 2,600 ft. Maple Falls, 35 ft., flows all year. Aptos Creek has cascades between the 1,200-ft. and 600-ft. elevations. The Park was a gift from two brothers and a sister in honor of their mother; their wish was that it remain undeveloped.

Plants: 90% forested. Chiefly second-growth Coast redwoods with tan oak, Pacific madrone. The area was logged between 1870 and 1925. 20 old-growth redwoods remain. Riparian vegetation in drainages. Chaparral on ridges above 1,800 ft. Two freshwater sag ponds. Flowering species include redwood sorrel, trillium, starflower, toothwort, red clintonia, false Solomon's seal, fetid adder's tongue.

Birds: No checklist, but record cards at HQ. Noted: great horned owl, Steller's and scrub jays, California quail, band-tailed pigeon, brown creeper, golden-crowned kinglet, Oregon junco.

Mammals: Noted: opossum, black-tailed jackrabbit, cottontail, coyote, mule deer, bobcat.

INTERPRETATION: *Guided hikes* in summer, occasionally; notices posted.

Hiking, backpacking: 32 mi. of trails. Longest named trail is 7 mi. One trail camp with 6 sites. Reservations required, from HQ.

Park may be closed in midsummer if fire hazard is extreme.

PUBLICATION: Leaflet with map.

HEADQUARTERS: c/o Henry Cowell State Park, P.O. Box P-1, Highway 9, Felton, CA 95018; (408) 335-4598.

TURLOCK LAKE STATE RECREATION AREA
California Department of Parks and Recreation
228 acres.

21 mi. E of Modesto, off SR 132.

In foothill country, the Park lies between Turlock Lake, an irrigation reservoir, and the Tuolumne River, which originates in Yosemite National Park. The lake, 3,500 acres when full, is heavily used for water-based recreation. It is often drawn down to a surface area of 1,800 acres.

Were it not for the river, this site would not be an entry. Along the river, however, is a small fragment of the riparian habitat that once characterized all the rivers of the San Joaquin Valley. Over 190 plant species have been identified here, as well as 115 bird species. Site elevation is 250 ft. Warm summers, mild winters. A nature trail is near the river.

Camping: 65 sites. All year. Reservations Apr. 27–Sept. 30.

PUBLICATIONS
Leaflet with map.
Bird checklist.
Nature trail guide.

HEADQUARTERS: 22600 Lake Rd., Star Route, La Grange, CA 95329; (209) 874-2008.

WILDER RANCH STATE PARK
California Department of Parks and Recreation
4,528 acres.

Near Santa Cruz.

This State Park site was recently acquired. We heard about it, gathered data, and wrote an entry, expecting it would be open to the public by our publication date. It's an attractive place: 5 mi. of scenic coastline, fine forest and grassland, deep creek canyons.

When we submitted our entry for checking, we got the bad news. Budget problems have delayed the opening. The site may open in 1983. It's worth an inquiry.

ZONE 6

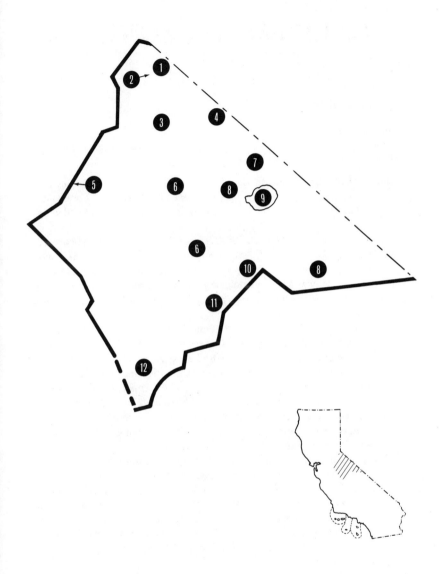

CALIFORNIA, ZONE 6

Includes these counties:

Alpine	Mono	Madera (E portion)
Tuolumne	Mariposa	

Due E of San Francisco, on the Nevada border, this zone straddles the Sierra Nevada, encompassing over 3.5 million acres of National Forest and National Park land. Yosemite National Park is at its center, surrounded by National Forests.

The Sierra, a gigantic fault block, rises gradually from chaparral-covered foothills to the Crest, a line of peaks, some over 13,000 ft. Snowfall is heavy in the high country, and the spring runoff brings to life countless waterfalls and cataracts, many of which dwindle or go dry in summer. The high country has many small lakes in glacial basins, deep canyons, flower-carpeted mountain meadows.

Few roads cross the Sierra, and all but one in this zone are closed in winter. Strangers to the West are often surprised to discover that "winter" here is a season that often extends to the Fourth of July. Much of the high country is closed by snow to foot or automobile travel until June or later.

The W slope is near San Francisco and other California cities. It sometimes seems that their entire populations head for the mountains on summer weekends. Resorts are crowded, as are most of the more accessible Park and Forest campgrounds. Quotas are in effect at most trailheads giving access to wilderness areas. But these areas are vast. Park and Forest Rangers will be happy to direct you to lightly-traveled trails and little-used destinations.

The High Sierra is unquestionably magnificent, but the snow-free season there is short. For those who do not choose to spend the other 10 months indoors, opportunities are great. We found Yosemite Valley uncrowded and at its best in April. Some outdoorsmen scorn the chaparral, but we were delighted by the hillsides and canyon trails we hiked in springtime, sunny and warm, alive with birds, brilliant with flowers. We met other hikers perhaps twice in a day.

Crossing the mountains from the W is difficult for those in the San Francisco area. From the Los Angeles area, it's a straight run up US 395 to the Owens Valley. The E side of the Sierra is steep, somewhat drier than the W but with enough snow to support a few ski areas. Here, too, are popular resorts, notably at Mammoth Lakes. Wilderness areas are more readily reached from the W side. In many cases, paved roads come to parking areas at or very near their boundaries. Here, too, trailhead quotas have become necessary to limit environmental damage in the more popular places. But here, too, the hiker who seeks isolation can find it.

Although the Sierra is the main attraction, the other side of the valley is well worth exploring. The White Mountains, for example, in the Inyo National Forest, have much of interest. So do parts of the Toiyabe National Forest on the NV border.

BODIE HILLS
U.S. Bureau of Land Management
85,000 acres.

From Bridgeport on US 395, E on Aurora Canyon Rd., SE on Bodie-Masonic Rd.

Rounded, pinyon-covered hills surround the ghost town of Bodie, now a State Historical Park. Most of the land between US 395 and the NV border, N of Mono Lake, is managed by the BLM, although there are scattered privately owned tracts. To the N is the Toiyabe National Forest. Terrain varies from rolling to steep. Hilltop elevations from 7,500 ft. to Potato Mountain and Bodie Peak, both over 10,000 ft. Lower slopes have sagebrush, mixed shrubs, annual grasses. Pinyon pine and juniper on higher slopes. Quaking aspen in drainages, turning bright yellow and gold in the fall. The area has many enclosed canyons, interior valleys, several springs.

Several features indicate past volcanic activity. Beauty Peak, NE of Bodie, is a volcanic cone. Alkali Meadows hot springs are N of Clearwater Canyon. The Alkali Meadows bowl is thought to be an old caldera. Other hot springs are in the area.

Several roads, mostly unpaved, enter the Bodie Hills through narrow canyons such as Aurora, Clearwater, Cottonwood, and Bridgeport, climbing to points with fine views of Mono Lake and the Sierra.

Wildlife includes deer, rabbit, coyote, sage grouse, a small population of pronghorn.

HEADQUARTERS: BLM, Bakersfield District Office, 800 Truxton, Room 302, Bakersfield, CA 93301; (805) 861-4191.

CALAVERAS BIGTREES NATIONAL FOREST
Our smallest (380-acre) National Forest, described in the entry for Stanislaus National Forest.

DEVILS POSTPILE NATIONAL MONUMENT
U.S. National Park Service
800 acres.

Near Mammoth Lakes Village, off US 395 39 mi. NW of junction with US 6.
Closed in winter; season determined by snow.

Within the Inyo National Forest; one of the attractions of the popular Mammoth Lakes resort area (see Inyo National Forest entry, zone 7). The Monument is about 7 mi. from the Village. Congestion in the Reds Meadow-Devils Postpile area has become so great that a shuttle bus may be provided to carry visitors to the National Monument and backpackers going beyond it

The Monument is at 7,600 ft elevation on the W slope of the Sierra Nevada, on the Middle Fork of the San Joaquin River. Its central feature is an impressive columnar basalt formation, individual columns 60 ft. high. Glacial action has sheared and polished the tops of the polygonal columns so that they resemble a tiled floor. At Rainbow Falls, the Middle Fork drops 101 ft. The area is within the Sierra lodgepole pine-red fir zone.

ACTIVITIES
Camping: 23 sites. Approximate season: June 20–Oct. 1.
Hiking: Trails to top of the basalt cliffs, Rainbow Falls. Trails into the surrounding National Forest.

PUBLICATION: Leaflet with map.

REFERENCES
Felzer, Ron. *Devil's Postpile.* 2nd ed. Berkeley: Wilderness Press, 1976.
The Devil's Postpile, Sequoia Natural History Association, Three Rivers, CA 93271. 75¢.

HEADQUARTERS: c/o Sequoia and Kings Canyon National Parks, Three Rivers, CA 93271; (209) 565-3341.

GROVER HOT SPRINGS STATE PARK
California Department of Parks and Recreation
519 acres.

From Markleeville on SR 89, W 4 mi. on Hot Springs Rd.

The hot springs once made this a health resort. Today it's a scenic camping and hiking base, a park surrounded by the Toiyabe National Forest. Elevation is about 5,800 ft. Terrain is gently sloping. About half of the Park is high mountain meadow, surrounded by forest, with 10,000-ft. mountains rising abruptly on three sides. Water flows from springs at 148°F and is regulated to about 102° in a small concrete pool. Most of those using the pool today seem more entertained by the phenomenon than persuaded the water has curative powers. Normal summer temperatures here range between 50°F at night, 80° by day, although June frosts are not uncommon. Autumn frost brings a blaze of colors. Annual precipitation is about 25 in. The Park is open all year; the campground is not.

Plants: About 50% forested: Jeffrey pine, white fir, ponderosa pine. California sage and bitterbrush in the understory. Meadow grasslands. Flowering species include asters, lilies.

Birds: No checklist. 75 species recorded, which seems low. No details.

Mammals: Often seen: coyote, squirrels, deer, chipmunk, raccoon, cottontail. Present, seldom seen: black bear, bobcat, long-tailed weasel.

Reptiles and amphibians: Species reported include western fence and alligator lizards, garter snake, western rattlesnake. Less often seen: rubber boa, western racer.

INTERPRETATION
Campfire programs and *guided hikes,* July–Aug. *Ranger-naturalist* present all year.

Self-guiding *nature trail,* 1 mi.

ACTIVITIES
Camping: 76 sites. May 15–Oct. 15, depending on snow. Reservations May 19–Sept. 17.

Hiking: Trails into the National Forest. One popular trail rises 2,000 ft. in less than 4 mi., on the way to Burnside Lake.

Fishing: Cutthroat and rainbow trout.

Ski touring: 3-mi. trail section of a longer trail within the Park. Trails into the Forest.

PUBLICATIONS
Leaflet with map.
Nature trail guide.

HEADQUARTERS: P.O. Box 188, Markleeville, CA 96120; (916) 694-2380.

HIDDEN DAM AND HENSLEY LAKE
U.S. Army Corps of Engineers
500 acres.

From Madera on SR 99, N on Yosemite Ave. (SR 145) and Road 400. Dam is 17 mi. from Madera.

The 500 acres refers to a wildlife area at the head of this lake, built for irrigation and flood control. The wildlife area is open to foot access only. The lake is about 4 mi. long at full pool, the dam over a mile long. In the gently rolling foothills of the Sierra Nevada. Like most such lakes, it is heavily used for water-based recreation. Site boundaries are generally less than 1/2 mile from the lakeshore. Natural vegetation is reclaiming the shoreline.

INTERPRETATION

Visitor information center at HQ. The site has a monument to Major James D. Savage, discoverer of Yosemite Valley, and the center presents somewhat sanitized information about his colorful activities

Campfire programs in summer.

Camping: 51 sites. All year.

PUBLICATION: Leaflet with map.

HEADQUARTERS: P.O. Box 85, Raymond, CA 93653; (209) 673-5151.

INDIAN CREEK RESERVOIR RECREATION SITE
U.S. Bureau of Land Management
7,008 acres.

From Markleeville, 2 1/2 mi. N on SR 89 and follow signs.

On the E slope of the Sierra Nevada. A small reservoir, 160 acres. In the N half of the area, land in the W and central portions is rolling, elevations 4,900 to 5,400 ft., several small peaks toward the center rising to over 5,600 ft. E portion is rough to mountainous, land rising from 5,400 ft. to 6,000 ft. steeply. In the S half of the area, elevations are from 5,600 ft. to 6,000 ft. in the W and central portions, rising to 7,600 ft. near the E boundary. The site is crossed by the E and W forks of the Carson River. Indian Creek rises on the site. Several other streams. Moderate flow all year. Annual precipitation is about 21 in. Winter storms are often severe. The camping season is normally May–Oct.

Plants: Principal tree species are ponderosa, Jeffrey, and pinyon pines;

white fir, incense cedar, Utah juniper, aspen, willow. On the lower slopes, big sagebrush, bitterbrush, rabbitbrush, low sagebrush, manzanita, snowberry, mountain mahogany, squaw carpet. Small marshy areas with cattail, sedges, rushes. Wildflowers include Sierra thistle, paintbrush, lupine, California poppy.

Birds: Species reported include mallard, Canada goose, pintail, cinnamon teal, ruddy duck, golden and bald eagles, mourning dove, American coot, California gull, California quail, common nighthawk, kestrel, white-headed woodpecker, Williamson's sapsucker, Steller's jay, cliff swallow, magpie, mountain chickadee, brown creeper, dipper.

Mammals: Include black-tailed jackrabbit, cottontail, California and golden-mantled ground squirrels, chipmunk, kangaroo rat, porcupine, coyote, striped skunk, mule deer.

INTERPRETATION: *Curtz Lake Environmental Study Area* is on Airport Rd., midway between Woodfords and Markleeville. It features three nature trails, each with a different theme, with trail markers. A full tour requires about one hour.

ACTIVITIES
Camping: 19 sites, plus a nearby tenting area with 10 sites.
Hiking: Trails into the Toiyabe National Forest. (See map of the Forest's South Sierra Division.)
Fishing: Mountain whitefish; brown, cutthroat, rainbow, and eastern brook trout; Lahontan redside, brown bullhead.

ADJACENT: Toiyabe National Forest.

PUBLICATIONS
Leaflet with map.
Curtz Lake Environmental Study Area leaflet.

HEADQUARTERS: BLM, Carson City District, 1050 E. William St., Carson City, NV 89820; (702) 882-1631.

INYO NATIONAL FOREST
U.S. Forest Service

Of this 1,900,000-acre National Forest, about 52% is in zone 7, 45% in zone 6, the remainder in Nevada. The zone 6 portion begins between Yosemite National Park and Mono Lake and extends S to the Inyo County line just N of Bishop. Some of the Forest's principal features are in zone 6, including the Hoover Wilderness, the Tioga Lakes area, the Minarets Wilderness, the Mammoth Lakes area, the John Muir Wilderness, the White Mountain area, and the Ancient Bristlecone Pine Forest. Also included: Devils Postpile National Monument (see entry). The Forest is best described as an entity. The entry is in zone 7.

MONO LAKE
U.S. Bureau of Land Management and others
About 100 sq. mi.

E of US 395 at Lee Vining, E entrance to Yosemite.

The lake, remnant of an ancient inland sea, has no natural outlet. The deep blue lake, islands, with the Sierra Crest as backdrop, is scenic. Surface evaporation is 4 ft. per year. The water is saline and alkaline. In 1941, Los Angeles began diverting water from the creeks feeding the lake. Since then the lake has dropped 40 ft.

The lake has produced vast quantities of brine shrimp and brine flies, food for the gulls, grebes, and phalaropes that gather here in great numbers in migrations. The nesting gull population is the largest in CA. Conservationists fear the lake will be lost as a valuable natural resource. Lowered lake level opened a land bridge to Negit Island, principal gull nesting area, allowing predators to cross.

The receding water has uncovered pinnacle-shaped tufa towers, formed at the lake bottom from the interaction of springs and lake water. A large grove of these tufa towers is on the S shore, a short walk from a BLM parking area on a dirt road N of SR 120.

Most of the land surrounding the lake is managed by the BLM. Some is owned by the City of Los Angeles. The Inyo National Forest is near the W shore. A few tracts are privately owned. The legal ownership of the land exposed by receding water has not been finally resolved. Presumably it will be either state or federal property. The BLM and the state are working together to preserve the tufa formations. The state legislature is considering a bill to make the tufa grove a State Reserve.

The "beaches" around the lake are eroded pumice. Paoha Island has several small fumaroles. Negit Island is black, somewhat conical, volcanic in origin. Panum Crater, near the SW shore, is a northern extension of nearby Mono Craters.

HEADQUARTERS: BLM, Bakersfield District, 800 Truxtun, Room 302, Bakersfield, CA 93301; (805) 861-4191.

SIERRA NATIONAL FOREST
U.S. Forest Service
1,303,120 acres.

Between Yosemite and Kings Canyon National Parks. SR 168 from Fresno penetrates the Forest. SR 41 crosses the NW portion en route to Yosemite's South Entrance Station.

The Forest lies W of the Sierra Crest, where it adjoins the Inyo National Forest and Kings Canyon National Park (see entries, zone 7). The Sequoia National Forest is on its S boundary (see entry, zone 7). Road entry to the Forest is somewhat limited. No paved roads enter from the E or S. SR 41, from the N, crosses only a neck of Forest land. The Forest has 1,970 mi. of roads in its internal system, most unpaved, many maintained only as Forest operations require.

Elevations range from 900 ft. to 13,986-ft. Mt. Humphreys. In the western portion, at low elevations, steeply rolling chaparral and grass- and woodland-covered foothills. Mid-elevations have steep-walled river canyons as well as moderately sloping, heavily forested areas and steep-walled basins. In the basins below the peaks are more than 1,000 lakes and ponds, most of them in the John Muir Wilderness. Above are knife-edged ridges and sharp peaks, barren wind-swept crags along the Sierra Crest.

Annual precipitation ranges from 20 in. at lower elevations to over 80 in. in the high country, where most of it falls as snow. Summers are dry, but thunderstorms are common in the higher elevations. Highest summer temperatures range from 100°F below 4,000 ft. to 80° at 7,000 ft. and above. Most of the recreational areas are above 4,000 ft. and snow-covered from late Oct. to late May. In most years, travel above 8,000 ft. is hazardous before June 1. Many high passes and streams are unsafe to cross with horses before July 1. Most Forest visitors come in July and Aug.

Runoff gathers in more than 1,200 mi. of streams that flow to rivers, including the San Joaquin, Merced, and Kings. Ten reservoirs in the Forest store water for irrigation and power generation. The reservoirs are used for boating, swimming, and fishing.

The Forest records more than 4 million visitor-days per year. The most heavily used areas are those along the better roads, especially the recreation areas beside the larger lakes. These are often crowded in summer, the lakeside campgrounds full. Some of the wilderness trails have become so popular that quotas have been applied to limit environmental damage. However, the Forest area is vast, and the hiker who wants solitude can find it. Ask at any Ranger Station for information on lightly-traveled areas.

More than one-quarter of the Forest is classed as wilderness, and other roadless areas have been proposed for additions to the wilderness system.

Plants: The several vegetation zones begin at low elevations with valley grassland, foothill woodland, and chaparral. The ponderosa pine forest extends from about 2,000 ft. to 6,500 ft. elevation, other tree species here including sugar pine, Douglas-fir, white fir, incense cedar, black cottonwood, black oak, bigleaf maple, California dogwood. Understory includes greenleaf manzanita, buckbrush, deer brush, birchleaf mountain mahogany, bitter cherry, serviceberry, kit-kit-dizze.

Somewhat higher, from about 6,500 ft. to 9,000 ft., is the lodgepole pine-red fir forest, including such tree species as silver and Jeffrey pines, Sierra juniper, and aspen; understory with bush chinquapin, snowbrush, huckleberry oak, green manzanita. Higher, somewhat overlapping, from about 7,500 ft. to 10,000 ft., is the subalpine belt, where stands are sparse rather than dense, species including whitebark, foxtail, and lodgepole pines, mountain hemlock, with shrubs, including red and white heathers. Above timberline are low-growing plants; grasses, sedges, various wildflowers, among them alpine buttercup, shooting star, elephant's head, rosy stonecrop, alpine paintbrush, alpine aster, alpine goldenrod.

The Forest has two notable groves of giant sequoias. Nelder Grove is in the NW sector, E of SR 41. The McKinley Grove is in the SE sector W of Wishon Reservoir.

Birds: Checklist available. Waterfowl are not numerous, but water-associated species are seen at the many lakes, among them mallard, ring-necked duck, lesser scaup, ruddy duck, common merganser. Common species of the Forest include red-tailed hawk, California and mountain quail, mourning dove, great horned owl, white-throated swift; black-chinned, Anna's, rufous, and calliope hummingbirds; Bullock's oriole, western tanager, black-headed and evening grosbeaks, lazuli bunting; purple, Cassin's, house, and gray-crowned rosy finches; American and lesser goldfinches, pine siskin, green-tailed and brown towhees; savannah, lark, chipping, white-crown, golden-crowned, fox, and song sparrows; Oregon junco; house, Bewick's, canyon, and rock wrens; California thrasher, robin, hermit thrush, western and mountain bluebirds, Townsend's solitaire, ruby-crowned kinglet; Hutton's, warbling, and solitary vireos; Nashville, yellow, yellow-rumped, black-throated gray, Townsend's, hermit, MacGillivray's, and Wilson's warblers; common flicker, acorn and white-headed woodpeckers, red-breasted sapsucker, western kingbird; ash-throated, Hammond's, dusky, Traill's, western, and olive-sided flycatchers; violet-green, rough-winged, and cliff swallows; Steller's and scrub jays, common raven, Clark's nutcracker, mountain chickadee, plain titmouse, bushtit, white-breasted and red-breasted nuthatches, brown creeper, wrentit, dipper.

Mammals: Common species include Trowbridge and dusky shrews, broad-handed mole, pallid bat, western pipistrelle, Yuma and California myotis, black bear, ringtail, coyote, gray fox, bobcat, raccoon, mountain beaver, beaver, yellow-bellied marmot; California, Belding, and golden-mantled ground squirrels; chickaree, gray and northern flying squirrels, lodgepole and alpine chipmunks, Botta pocket gopher, San Joaquin pocket mouse, Heermann kangaroo rat, white-footed deer mouse, dusky-footed and bushy-tailed wood rats, California and long-tailed meadow mice, pika, cottontail, brush rabbit, California mule deer.

FEATURES

John Muir Wilderness, 499, 675 acres plus 120,000 acres of proposed additions. About 55% in the Sierra National Forest, the rest in the Inyo National Forest. Extends along the Sierra Crest from the Mammoth Lakes area to near Mt. Whitney. The Wilderness is more readily accessible from the Inyo National Forest, auto roads leading to trailheads at or close to the boundary. Most visitors enter from the E side, and quotas are in effect at principal trailheads on both sides. Sectors reached by trails from the Sierra National Forest are less heavily used. This is California's largest wilderness, a region of high snow-capped peaks, steep slopes, knife-edge ridges, countless streams, several hundred lakes and ponds, dense forests.

Minarets Wilderness, 107,380 acres plus 48,500 acres of proposed additions. About 45% in the Sierra National Forest, the rest in the Inyo National Forest. Straddles the Sierra Crest on the SE border of Yosemite National Park. Elevations from 7,000 ft. to 14,000 ft. Sharp, rugged peaks. Remnants of glaciers are on several of the high mountains. The Minarets, thought to resemble mosque towers, are on the central portion of the divide, in the Ritter Range. This range divides the area and severely restricts travel from E to W. As in the case of the John Muir Wilderness, the E portion is more accessible and more heavily used. However, several trailheads in the Sierra National Forest, on the SW boundary of the Wilderness, can be reached by car with little difficulty. Most of this area is above timberline. The Trail Guide, listed at the end of this entry, identifies the least-used destinations.

Kaiser Wilderness, 22,500 acres, is just N of Huntington Lake, with trailheads reached by SR 168. The area is divided by the E–W Kaiser Ridge, on which the highest point is 10,320-ft. Kaiser Peak. The S part rises from the Huntington Lake resort area. The N part, considered the more attractive, contains all but 2 of the 20 small lakes, the largest about 40 acres. Travel into the N sector is usually over Potter Pass. Upper Twin Lake is the most popular, so overused that camping is now banned within 100 ft. of the lakeshore. Most lakes are reached by off-trail, cross-country hiking. Snow remains until early June.

South Fork, Merced River, area. On the S boundary of Yosemite National Park, in the Bass Lake Ranger District. Reached by Mt. Raymond Rd. and Sky Ranch Rd. from SR 41. Elevations from 5,000 ft. at the river to 9,165 ft. atop Iron Mountain. All below timberline. About 30 mi. of foot and horse trails lead to several attractive lakes, streams, and the river canyon. Several pleasant campsites are within easy hiking distance of trailheads. The area has a number of roads requiring 4-wheel-drive vehicles.

Bass Lake area. At 3,400 ft. elevation, E of SR 41 at Oakhurst. The lake, 4 mi. long, 1/2 mi. wide, is a popular resort, with some inholdings along the shore. It is accessible all year. Forest Service campgrounds are likely to be crowded Memorial Day weekend and July–Aug. Ten backcountry campgrounds, most of them on quiet fishing streams, are reached by unpaved roads. Trails lead through the South Fork Merced River area into the National Park. Points of interest in the area include the Nelder Grove of giant sequoias; the Yosemite Mountain Railroad, now operated by a concessioner; Fresno Dome, a viewpoint; Goat Mountain Lookout; Mile High Vista. Water level is usually maintained near full pool in summer, drops rapidly in the fall, fills in spring.

Huntington Lake area. At 7,000 ft. elevation, on SR 168. Also a popular resort. The lake is 4 mi. long, 1/2 mi. wide. The usual season is Memorial Day–Labor Day, but some Forest Service campgrounds remain open until closed by snow in late Oct. Summer daytime temperatures range from 60° to 85°F, dropping to 40° or below at night. The Kaiser Wilderness is a short distance N. The chair lift at the China Peak Ski Area operates in summer, taking visitors to the top. Black Point offers fine views to those climbing the steep 1/2-mi. trail from trailhead. Many unpaved Forest roads, some suitable for cars, others requiring 4-wheel drive, penetrate the lightly used backcountry. The road from the Eastwood Visitor Station toward Florence Lake leads to 9 High Sierra campgrounds at about 7,500 ft. elevation; lakes, streams, fine views.

Dinkey Lakes area is S of Huntington Lake. A large area at 8,000 ft. elevation reached only on foot or horse, or by 4-wheel-drive vehicle on primitive roads. Forest, meadow, many small lakes. No developed sites. Camp anywhere—but 100 ft. from the nearest lake or stream bank.

Redinger Lake area is near the W boundary, reached by road N from SR 168 through Auberry. At 1,400 ft. elevation, in the brushy front country, in a steep, narrow valley of the San Joaquin River, hills rising 1,000 ft. on either side. The lake is 3 mi. long, 1/4 mi. wide. Because of extreme fire hazard in this chaparral area, camping is restricted to designated sites and campfire permits are required.

Shaver Lake area, at 5,600 ft. elevation, on SR 168. Most of the land on and near the lake is privately owned. The Forest Service has one campground within walking distance of a swimming area.

Pine Flat Reservoir is at the SW corner of the Forest, on the Kings River, N of SR 180. National Forest land is on the N shore. Forest campgrounds here and on the N shore of the river, upstream. Trails and Forest roads N to primitive campsites on Big Creek and NE toward Dinkey Creek.

Other lakes, less developed, accessible by Forest road, include Mammoth

Pool, Lake Thomas A. Edison, Florence Lake, Courtright Reservoir, Wishon Reservoir. Edison and Florence lakes have commercial ferry service to reach trailheads into the John Muir Wilderness, usually early June–Sept.

INTERPRETATION

Visitor Information and Ranger Stations are located on most of the principal routes to recreation areas.

Campfire programs are offered from mid-June to Labor Day in the larger camping areas. Schedules available at Information and Ranger Stations and campground bulletin boards.

Nature trails include those at Nelder Grove and McKinley Grove. *Way-of-the-Mono Trail* is on County Road 222 near Bass Lake.

ACTIVITIES

Camping: 61 campgrounds. 1,357 sites. A few are open all year. Most are closed in winter, openings beginning mid-Apr., the latest opening mid-June. Closings from Sept. 10 to mid-Nov. Bass Lake campgrounds require reservations by Ticketron in summer.

Hiking, backpacking: 1,100 mi. of trails, ranging from short, easy day hikes to strenuous wilderness journeys. Permits required for wilderness areas, campfire permits for all other areas, except campgrounds. The John Muir Trail is a segment of the Pacific Crest Trail and is one of the most heavily used Wilderness trails. High-country trails can often be hiked by mid-June, but some passes and stream crossings may be difficult or hazardous into July.

Hunting: Deer, black bear, rabbit, dove, pigeon, quail.

Fishing: The 1,200 mi. of streams and over 1,000 lakes have 30-odd fish species, including rainbow, brown, golden, and brook trout; kokanee salmon, large- and smallmouth bass, bluegill, crappie, sunfish, catfish.

Swimming: Swimming areas at the resort lakes. Elsewhere as you choose.

Boating: Ramps on the larger lakes reachable by car. Sailing is popular on Huntington Lake, water skiing on Shaver and Bass Lakes. Speed limits and zones apply on some lakes.

Rafting: On the Merced and Kings rivers. Detailed information needed.

Horse riding: Packers at the principal resort areas and other main access points. HQ will supply a list.

Skiing: China Peak Ski Area.

Ski touring, snowshoeing: Favorite areas are Tamarack Ridge near Shaver Lake, Fish Camp area along SR 41. However, many trails and unplowed roads above 5,000 ft. offer good opportunities.

Snowmobiling: Whisky Trail (9 mi.); Tamarack Ridge Trail (3 mi.); Red Mountain Trail (9 mi.). Snowmobiles prohibited in Wilderness Areas.

PUBLICATIONS

Forest map. $1.00.
Recreation Guide.
John Muir Wilderness leaflet.

Minarets Wilderness information page.
Minarets Wilderness Trail Guide.
Minarets Wilderness Map. $1.00.
Kaiser Wilderness leaflet.
Bird checklist.
Mammal checklist.
Bass Lake Recreation Guide.
South Fork, Merced River trail guide.
Huntington Lake Recreation Guide.
Redinger Lake Recreation Guide.
Shaver Lake Recreation Guide.
Pacific Crest Trail information.
High Sierra Campgrounds information.
Whisky Snowmobile Trail leaflet.
Off-Road Travel Plan (for ORV's).

HEADQUARTERS: 1130 O St., Fresno, CA 93721; (209) 487-5155.

RANGER DISTRICTS: Mariposa R.D., Mariposa, CA 95338; (209) 966-3638. Bass Lake R.D., Oakhurst, CA 93644; (209) 683-4665. Minarets R.D., North Fork, CA 93643; (209) 877-2218. Pineridge R.D., Shaver Lake, CA 93664; (209) 841-3311. Kings River R.D., Trimmer Route, Sanger, CA 93657; (209) 855-8321.

STANISLAUS NATIONAL FOREST

U.S. Forest Service
899,894 acres of Forest land; 1,089,967 acres within boundaries.

Bounded by Eldorado National Forest on the N, Toiyabe National Forest and Yosemite National Park on the E, Sierra National Forest on the S. Crossed by SR 4, SR 108, SR 120. SR 140 and the Merced River are the boundary with the Sierra National Forest.

On the W slopes of the Sierra Nevada, a rugged, mountainous region deeply cut by the canyons of the Merced, Tuolumne, Stanislaus, and Mokelumne rivers. Elevations from 1,100 ft. to 11,570 ft. at Leavitt Peak. The Forest is the nearest high country to San Francisco. This, together with the crossing roads, makes it one of the most heavily used National Forests. The heaviest use occurs in summer, in recreation areas on and near these paved roads.

The most heavily used area is at Pinecrest and Strawberry, communities within the Forest on SR 108. Several resorts are here. The Forest Service has two campgrounds with a total of 300 sites. A lake about 1 mi. long offers swimming and boating. Winter sports centers are nearby. SR 108 E of here is closed in winter.

A somewhat similar development is at Lake Alpine on SR 4: a lake about 1 mi. long, Forest campgrounds, resorts, winter sports areas.

Cherry Lake, about 4 mi. long, largest in the Forest, has much less development. Only 11 airline mi. N of SR 120; the road distance is about double that. Boats can be launched at the S end. A Forest campground has 48 sites. Most of the lakeshore is roadless.

The Sierra Crest includes a succession of peaks over 9,000 ft. elevation, several of them over 11,000 ft. The slopes are drained by 810 mi. of streams. Many small lakes are in glacial bowls above 8,000 ft. elevation. From Sonora Pass S to Cherry Lake, the Crest is the boundary of the Emigrant Wilderness. The largest concentration of small lakes is in this Emigrant Basin area.

N of Sonora Pass, the NE sector of the Forest is mountainous and largely roadless. The area has fewer lakes, but hikers can find a number of attractive ones, notably the Highland Lakes cluster. Good trails follow several stream valleys. Hikers should be aware that several of these are open to trail bikes.

Annual precipitation ranges from 30 in. in the foothills to 50 in. in the high country. Most of the latter falls as snow. Summers are dry. Although summer thunderstorms are common in the high country, the alpine zone receives little or no moisture in the summer months.

Plants: Vegetation ranges from valley oak woodland to the alpine zone. Forested areas are mostly between 3,000 ft. and 8,000 ft. elevation. Principal tree species are ponderosa, Jeffrey, lodgepole, and sugar pines; red and white firs, incense cedar. Broadleaf species include black oak and canyon live oak in suitable habitats. Streamside species include bigleaf maple, white alder, willows, mountain dogwood, black cottonwood. Understory species include greenleaf manzanita, deer brush, buckbrush, kit-kit-dizze, birchleaf mountain mahogany, gooseberry, small-leaved ceanothus, snowberry. Wildflowers include striped coralroot, false Solomon's seal, prince's pine, rattlesnake orchid, California harebell, heartleaf arnica, California Indian pink, wild peony, eriogonums, waterleaf phacelia, fireweed, beargrass.

Wildflowers of the mountain meadows include monkeyflower, shooting star, geraniums, penstemon, sneezeweed, camas, lupine, elephant's head, starworts, marsh marigold, blue-eyed Mary, aster. Plant growth in the alpine zone is limited not only by harsh winter conditions but by lack of moisture in summer. Species adapted to such severe conditions include alpine fescue, alpine paintbrush, Sierra primrose, mountain sorrel, Colville's phlox, dense-leaved draba, alpine lupine, alpine columbine, dwarf daisy.

Birds: Checklist available. Common or abundant species include turkey vulture, sharp-shinned and Cooper's hawks, American kestrel, blue grouse,

California and mountain quail, California gull, band-tailed pigeon, mourning dove, white-throated swift; black-chinned, Anna's, and rufous hummingbirds; belted kingfisher, common flicker, acorn and hairy woodpeckers, black phoebe, western wood pewee, violet-green and cliff swallows, Steller's and scrub jays, Clark's nutcracker, mountain chickadee, plain titmouse, common bushtit, white-breasted and pygmy nuthatches, dipper, robin, varied and hermit thrushes, western bluebird, Townsend's solitaire, ruby-crowned kinglet. Warblers include Nashville, yellow, yellow-rumped, Wilson's. Also western tanager; Cassin's, house, and gray-crowned rosy finches; pine siskin, green-tailed and rufous-sided towhees; white-crowned and golden-crowned sparrows.

Mammals: Checklist available. Common species include various shrews and bats, pika, black-tailed and white-tailed jackrabbits, snowshoe hare, cottontail, yellow-bellied marmot, golden-mantled and California ground squirrels; alpine, lodgepole, Townsend, and long-eared chipmunks; western gray squirrel, chickaree, northern flying squirrel, mountain pocket gopher, Heermann kangaroo rat, western harvest mouse, deer mouse, bushy-tailed and dusky-footed wood rats, porcupine, gray fox, coyote, black bear, raccoon, long-tailed weasel, striped skunk, bobcat, mule deer.

Reptiles and amphibians: Checklist available. Common and abundant species include California newt, ensatina, California slender and arboreal salamanders, western and Yosemite toads, Pacific treefrog, bullfrog; western fence, sagebrush, Coast horned, western whiptail, southern alligator, and northern alligator lizards; common and western garter snakes, western ringnecked snake, racer, gopher snake, common and California mountain kingsnakes, western rattlesnake.

FEATURES

Emigrant Wilderness, 106,091 acres. 6,100-acre addition proposed. Trailheads near SR 108 on the N, Cherry Lake on the S, various Forest roads on the W. Elevations from 5,200 ft. at Cherry Creek to 11,570-ft. Leavitt Peak. Most trails are closed by snow until July. Winter snows often begin in Oct. A scenic area: rocky domes, deep granite-walled canyons, many high lakes, miles of rushing streams. Deer Lake, Wood Lake, and Emigrant Lake are popular destinations, heavily used. Less heavily used are trails from the Hells Mountain-Bourland Mountain area N of Cherry Lake to destinations such as Chain of Lakes in the SW sector. Wilderness permits are required for all-day or overnight trips.

Mokelumne Wilderness, 49,561 acres, of which 9,097 acres are in the Stanislaus, the larger part in the Eldorado National Forest. N of SR 4. Trails N from Lake Alpine and other points. The area is dominated by 9,332-ft. Mokelumne Peak, is bisected by the canyon of the SW-flowing Mokelumne River. Many small lakes are in the shallow valleys N of the Peak. Area use is light to moderate, heaviest on trails from Lake Alpine and at such destinations as

Camp Irene and Fourth of July Lake. Consult Ranger Station. Portable stove needed. Stock feed must be carried in. Wilderness permit required for all-day or overnight hikes.

Carson-Iceberg roadless area, 182,000 acres in the Stanislaus and Toiyabe National Forests, proposed for wilderness status. In the NE sector, between SR 4 and SR 108, straddling the Sierra Crest. Topography ranges from flat streams to steep, jagged cliffs. Elevations from about 6,000 ft. to over 12,000 ft. At least 12 peaks over 12,000 ft. Steep ridges, narrow valleys, granite peaks and boulders. Striking volcanic formations. The East Fork of the Carson River, Clark fork of the Stanislaus, and the Mokelumne River have their headwaters here. Carson Falls, with an 80-ft. drop, is a landmark. Long valleys with meadows are found in several places. Mixed conifer forest up to the timber line. About one-fourth of the area is alpine, with little vegetation. Wilderness status would exclude trail bikes from the area. Portions of this area, at 6,000 to 7,000 ft. elevation, become snow-free sooner than trails in the Emigrant Wilderness, permitting access as early as May 15.

The Tuolumne River has been proposed for inclusion in the Wild and Scenic Rivers system. The river flows from Yosemite National Park, entering the Stanislaus National Forest just N of the road to the Hetch Hetchy Reservoir. It flows generally westward through the Forest, exiting between the towns of Tuolumne and Groveland. Two Forest campgrounds, Lumsden and Lumsden Bridge, are on the river, on a steep unimproved road.

Calaveras Bigtree National Forest, 380 acres. We won't try to explain why this tiny tract is a National Forest. It is a fine grove of giant sequoias, within the Stanislaus National Forest. You reach it through the Calaveras Big Trees State Park (see entry, zone 4), which is also within the Stanislaus. Many visitors stop at the State Park, especially when the road beyond is wet and muddy.

Dardanelles Cone and *Columns of the Giants* are impressive volcanic formations seen from SR 108.

INTERPRETATION

Interpretive programs are limited to the Summit Ranger District, crossed by SR 108.

Campfire programs are offered July 2–Sept. 6, Mon., Wed., and Fri., at the Pinecrest Amphitheater. Programs are offered on Tues. and Sat. evenings at the Sand Flat amphitheater.

Guided tours are offered in the same season, daily except Sun., departing mornings from the Summit Ranger Station.

Nature trails are at 7 locations in the District: Beardsley Lake, Eagle Meadow Rd., Donnell Vista, Pinecrest School, Pigeon Flat Campground, Herring Creek, and Pinecrest Ranger Station.

ACTIVITIES

Camping: 27 campgrounds, 943 sites. Earliest season opening: Apr. 1.

Latest: July 1. Most close Oct. 1 or 15; latest closing: Nov. 15. Pinecrest, with 200 sites, requires reservations by Ticketron May 24–Sept. 10.

Hiking, backpacking: 750 mi. of trails. Linked with the trail systems of Eldorado, Toiyabe, and Sierra National Forests, Yosemite National Park.

Hunting: Bear, deer, grouse, quail, rabbit.

Fishing: Golden, rainbow, brook trout in many high lakes. Rivers and lakes stocked with Kamloops rainbow, kokanee, brown trout. Some lakes and streams lightly fished.

Swimming: Supervised only at Pinecrest. Elsewhere as you choose.

Boating: Ramps on Lake Alpine, Beardsley Reservoir, Pinecrest, Cherry Lake. 20-mph limit at Pinecrest and Alpine. Rentals at Pinecrest.

Canoeing, kayaking: White water on Stanislaus and Tuolumne Rivers. Rapids to class 4 and 5 seasonally. Get information.

Horse riding: Forest HQ will supply list of packers. Many trails are suitable for horse travel. In some areas it is necessary to carry feed.

Skiing: Ski areas at Dodge Ridge, near Pinecrest, and Mt. Reba, near Lake Alpine.

Ski touring: Winter sports areas near Pinecrest. Ski touring and snowshoeing on many trails. Map available.

Snowmobiling: Map of recommended trails available.

PUBLICATIONS

Forest map. $1.00.
Fish and wildlife checklist.
Mokelumne Wilderness leaflet.
Emigrant Wilderness leaflet.
Summit Ranger District information.
Mi-Wok Ranger District information.
Lake Alpine Recreation Area leaflet.
Groveland Ranger District information.
Off-Road Vehicle Plan.
Restricted Use and Fire Closure Plan.
Snow Mobile and Ski Trails. (map.)

HEADQUARTERS: 19777 Greenley Rd., Sonora, CA 95370; (209) 532-3671.

RANGER DISTRICTS: Mi-Wok R.D., P.O. Box 100, Mi-Wuk Village, CA 95346; (209) 586-3234. Calaveras R.D., P.O. Box 500, Hathaway Pines, CA 95232; (209) 795-1381. Summit R.D., Star Route, Box 1295, Sonora, CA 95370; (209) 965-3434. Groveland R.D., P.O. Box 709, Groveland, CA 95321; (209) 962-7825.

STANISLAUS RIVER RECREATION AREA

U.S. Bureau of Land Management
9 river miles.

Put-in at Camp Nine, reached by narrow paved road that leaves the Parrott's Ferry Rd. 1/2 mi. E of Vallecito. Takeout at Parrott's Ferry Bridge, S of Vallecito.

Downstream from the Stanislaus National Forest, the river here flows through BLM land. This 9-mi. segment is a popular whitewater run, with more than 50,000 visitor-use days per year. The route is past striking geological formations, open meadows, rocky chutes, wildflowers, some timbered slopes. Between put-in and takeout is a single exit route from the canyon, a foot trail at Duck Bar.

Season is mid-Apr. to mid-Oct. Rapids range from class 5 in normal spring runoff to medium class 3 in summer. About two-thirds of the traffic is by commercial outfitters operating under BLM permits. Weekends are always crowded; the BLM urges visitors to come in mid-week. Actual river mileage varies with reservoir level.

PUBLICATION: Leaflet.

HEADQUARTERS: BLM, Folsom District, 63 Natoma St., Folsom, CA 95630; (916) 985-4474.

TOIYABE NATIONAL FOREST; SIERRA FRONT DIVISION
U.S. Forest Service
600,923 acres.

On the CA-NV border between Reno and Mono Lake. Crossed by I-80, US 395, US 50, various CA and NV routes.

Largest National Forest in the lower 48, the Toiyabe is one of the most scattered and diverse. In CA, a small block N of Lake Tahoe is described in the entry for Tahoe National Forest. This entry describes a block lying between Lake Tahoe and Mono Lake, most of the acreage in CA but with significant pieces in NV on the E side of Lake Tahoe and further S. It also describes a block entirely in NV, in the Excelsior Mountains, on the CA border S of Walker Lake.

The Sierra Front is the E slope of the Sierra Nevada, which drops abruptly about 4,000 ft. from the Crest to the floor of the Great Basin. Along the Crest, this Division is bounded on the W by the Eldorado, Stanislaus, and Tahoe National Forests. It is bounded on the S by Yosemite National Park and the Inyo National Forest.

US 395 is the main travel route, roughly paralleling the base of the Sierra for 420 mi., from the Walker Pass turnoff near Freeman Junction N to Susanville. From US 395 the motorist has spectacular views of snow-capped peaks. About 165 mi. of the route are within this portion of the Toiyabe National Forest. From US 395 are the routes to the seven historic mountain passes into California. Five of these routes are within the Toiyabe: Donner Summit (I-80), Lake Tahoe-Echo Summit (US 50), Carson Pass (CA 88), Ebbetts Pass (CA 4), and Sonora Pass (CA 108).

The area just N of Donner Summit, extending to Beckwourth Pass, locally known as the Dog Valley area, is the portion described in the Tahoe National Forest entry. From I-80 S to Carson City, the site is entirely in NV, along the Carson Front, where the Carson Range forms the barrier containing Lake Tahoe. Mt. Rose is the only peak higher than 10,000 ft. The Mt. Rose Highway (NV 27) is a short, winding, cross-mountain road providing access to two ski areas and spectacular views.

Moving S, the next 70 mi. of the Sierra Front is in CA, about half in Alpine County, half in Mono County, extending to Yosemite National Park. Toiyabe National Forest land extends E of US 395 into NV around the Sweetwater Mountains, which have several peaks over 11,000 ft. elevation.

The Sierra Front is a popular recreation area. It has 30 peaks over 10,000 ft. elevation, 4 of them over 11,000 ft. The peaks are separated by deep canyons and valleys, sometimes green and lush, sometimes barren and rocky, nearly always with perennial streams. In the course of a planning study, the Forest Service rated the scenic qualities of various settings. An exceptional number here received the highest (A) rating. Included were all the present or proposed wilderness areas, described in this section. Also the areas around Ebbetts Pass, the Raymond-Reynolds Peak, the Markleeville-Hawkins Peak high country, the lake country at the head of Pleasant Valley, and the Crest from the Nipple N to the Freel-Jobs Peak complex. The A rank was also given to a number of valleys and canyons: the East and West forks of the Carson River; Silver King, Wolf, Pleasant Valley, Sawmill, Hot Springs, and Red Lake Creeks; and Horsethief Canyon.

Annual precipitation varies from less than 10 in. at low elevations to as high as 70 in. in the upper regions, where about 80% falls as snow. CA 4 and CA 108 are closed by snow each winter.

Although few roads cross the Crest, dead-end roads penetrate at least part-way into a number of the canyons, and recreation sites are clustered along these.

Plants: As in many other parts of the Sierra, the high alpine meadows and sparsely vegetated rocky areas are the least altered. Most of the timbered land was logged by 1900. Many areas have burned. Heavy grazing checked the regrowth of trees. Areas of sagebrush and chaparral expanded. Under Forest Service management, trees have reestablished.

Vegetation zones are exceptionally well marked on the Sierra Front, starting from sagebrush and grasses dominating the foothills, pinyon pine and juniper in the montane zone. Above this zone are ponderosa, Jeffrey, and lodgepole pines, Douglas-fir, incense cedar, mountain hemlock, red fir, some western white pine. Shrubs include waxberry, pinemat manzanita, mountain big sagebrush, antelope bitterbrush. Alpine vegetation occurs above 10,000 ft. elevation.

Birds: Information was available here associating bird species with habitats. Examples: *Riparian:* Common nighthawk, yellow-bellied sapsucker, hairy woodpecker, belted kingfisher, violet-green swallow, western wood pewee, robin, Swainson's thrush, dipper, solitary and warbling vireos; Mac-Gillivray's, Wilson's, and yellow warblers. *Rock and cliff:* Golden eagle, red-tailed hawk, cliff swallow, rock wren, rosy finch. *Mountain meadow:* Western bluebird, alder flycatcher, American goldfinch, western meadowlark, poor-will, spotted sandpiper, yellow-throated warbler, Lincoln's sparrow. *Alpine meadow:* Mountain bluebird, rosy finch, dark-eyed junco, horned lark, Clark's nutcracker, golden-crowned sparrow, rock wren. *Mountain chaparral:* Red-tailed hawk, mountain quail, calliope hummingbird, dark-eyed junco, rufous-sided towhee, western bluebird, lazuli bunting, MacGillivray's warbler, fox and lark sparrows. *Pinyon-juniper:* Pinyon and scrub jays, magpie, mourning dove, raven. *Jeffrey pine-white fir:* Golden eagle, mountain quail, Williamson's sapsucker; hairy, pileated, and white-headed woodpeckers; common flicker; Hammond's, olive-sided, and dusky flycatchers; Townsend's solitaire, pine siskin, western tanager; pygmy, red-breasted, and white-breasted nuthatches; Steller's jay, mountain chickadee, dark-eyed junco, golden-crowned and ruby-crowned kinglets; black-headed, evening, and pine grosbeaks; hermit and yellow-rumped warblers, fox sparrow.

Mammals: Include deer, meadow, long-tailed meadow, canyon, pinyon, white-footed, and western harvest mice; dusky shrew, northern and mountain pocket gophers; long-eared, least, Townsend, Belding, and golden-mantled ground squirrels; marmot, raccoon, beaver, muskrat, pine marten, pika, spotted skunk, short-tailed weasel, porcupine, black bear, coyote, bobcat, mountain lion, mule deer.

FEATURES

Carson-Iceberg proposed wilderness, 182,000 acres in the Toiyabe and Stanislaus National Forests, proposed for wilderness status. Elevations from 6,000 ft. to over 12,000 ft. Steep ridges, narrow valleys, granite peaks and boulders, jagged cliffs. Striking volcanic formations. The East Fork of the Carson River has its headwaters in the wilderness. Carson Falls, 80-ft. drop, is a landmark. Seven small lakes. Springs of carbonated, mineralized water in the Silver King drainage and lower reaches of Poison Creek. Heavy use by backpackers, horsepackers, and fishermen in summer, concentrated along streams, especially Silver King and Wolf Creeks. 45 mi. of the Pacific Crest Trail. SR 4 is the N boundary.

Carson River has been suggested for protection under the National Wild and Scenic Rivers Act. The West Fork flows into Nevada past Woodfords, the East Fork past Markleeville. Canoeing and rafting on the East Fork are popular.

The *Indian Creek Reservoir area* (see entry, zone 6) is a little N of Markleeville, within the boundaries of this Division.

Hoover Wilderness, 47,937 acres, of which 9,000 acres are within the Inyo National Forest. A pending proposal would more than double its total acreage. The Hoover is on the N boundary of Yosemite National Park, and many who enter it from the N and E cross into Yosemite's high country. The Wilderness is a narrow border for the Park, nowhere more than 5 mi. wide, not much over one mi. at its narrowest point. Elevations range from 7,700 ft. to 12,596 ft. The Sawtooth Ridge forms a portion of its E boundary. Prominent peaks include Matterhorn, Twin, Crown Point, Eagle, Dunderberg, Excelsior, Hawksbeak, and Black. The Matterhorn area has five remnant glaciers. The area is characterized by U-shaped canyons. Canyon bottoms commonly have extensive flats with shallow streams and grassy meadows. The six major drainages are Little Walker River, Molybdenite Creek, Buckeye Creek, Robinson Creek, Green Creek, and Virginia Creek. The original wilderness area has 34 lakes; almost as many are in the proposed addition.

Trails generally cross the Wilderness, rather than running its length. More extensive hiking is available in the proposed addition, along the West Walker River and several canyons. Trailheads and pack stations are mostly on the E side, at Twin and Virginia Lakes, Green Creek, and Leavitt Meadows.

Vegetation zones are similar to those of the NW sector, but most of the Hoover Wilderness is high country, much above timberline. Scattered stands of timber grow on little more than 10% of the area. Mixed conifers with Jeffrey pine and white fir predominate in the lower elevation stands. Higher up: lodgepole pine with red fir, limber pine, western hemlock, western white pine, western juniper. Small subalpine meadows are associated with some lakes and larger streams. Unfortunately, these are attractive to visitors as campsites and are also extremely fragile.

Average annual precipitation in the Wilderness is 25 to 30 in., most of it as snow. Some high country trails are closed by snow into June or early July. The recreation season is usually June 15–Oct. 1.

Many visitors camp at one of the several campgrounds just outside the Wilderness boundary, entering only for day hikes. Of those who stay overnight, backpackers outnumber horsepackers 20 to 1. Heavy use has become a matter of concern, and studies are being made of ways to limit damage to the environment.

Lake Tahoe area. The Forest map shows a few scattered bits of land on and near the E side of Lake Tahoe, in NV. The map of Lake Tahoe Nevada State Park, which adjoins Forest land, shows additional tracts. We were told these are additions to the National Forest. We could find no current map.

Several tracts are on or near NV 431, which crosses the Carson Range, from the NE edge of Lake Tahoe to Mt. Rose Junction on US 395. Mt. Rose, 10,778 ft., is the highest point. A number of ski areas are on this route. The 24-site Mt. Rose campground opens about June 15. Hiking trails on the mountain.

US 50 turns inland from the lake at Glenbrook, crossing a block of Forest land. Kings Canyon Rd., SW from Carson City, also enters this area. The Clear Creek campground has 14 units, opens about June 1.

Nevada Beach is a small fragment of Forest land on the lakeshore about 1 mi. N of the CA line. 1/2-mi. beach. 60-site campground.

Excelsior Mountains. On the CA–NV border, crossed by NV 359. This irregularly shaped area is about 25 mi. N–S, 18 mi. W–E, adjoining a block of Inyo National Forest land in CA. Almost all of the area S and E of NV 359, plus adjoining Inyo National Forest land, is a 160,000-acre roadless area proposed for wilderness status. Elevations from about 6,000 ft. to several peaks over 9,000 ft. Annual precipitation is less than 12 in. Thunderstorms often cause flash floods. Rugged hills, including the SW portion of the Excelsior Mountains. Steep cliffs, ridges, slopes, canyons, dry lake beds. Vegetation is mostly pinyon-juniper; sagebrush-bitterbrush flats. Scattered dry and wet meadows, the latter dependent on springs. Wildlife includes sage grouse, mule deer, pronghorn, wild horse.

Portions of the area are much used for ORV activity. The proposed wilderness area is lightly used, and wilderness status would exclude all motorized equipment.

ACTIVITIES

Camping: 20 campgrounds. 549 sites. Most are May–Oct., several not open until June.

Hiking, backpacking: Extensive trail system. Wilderness permits required for Hoover Wilderness.

Hunting: Deer, upland game birds.

Fishing: Prior to settlement, the lakes were barren, and Lahontan cutthroat trout inhabited some streams. Extensive and varied stocking has since occurred, with mixed results. Several trout species are now common. Some lakes are overfished, a few underfished.

Boating: Twin Lakes, Trumbull Lake.

Canoeing, rafting: East Fork, Carson River.

Skiing: Three developed ski areas: Mt. Rose, Flag Mountain, Heavenly Valley.

Ski touring: No groomed trails, but some naturally fine areas.

PUBLICATIONS
Forest map, South Sierra Division. $1.00.
Hoover Wilderness map. $1.00.
Carson Ranger District map. $1.00.

HEADQUARTERS: III N. Virginia St., Reno, NV 89501; (702) 784-5331.

RANGER DISTRICTS: Bridgeport R.D., Bridgeport, CA 93517; (714) 932-7070.
Carson R.D., 136 S. Carson, Carson City, NV 89701; (702) 882-2766.

YOSEMITE NATIONAL PARK
U.S. National Park Service
760,917 acres.

From San Francisco and points N, SR 120. From the S, SR 41. Only access from the E is SR 120 over Tioga Pass, a steep, winding, 2-lane road, closed in winter.

One of the first and greatest U.S. National Parks, Yosemite has also been one of the first to experience the problems of overcrowding. The acute problems have been in Yosemite Valley. For many visitors, especially those from outside California, the Valley is Yosemite, although it occupies only 7 of the Park's 1,200 sq. mi. Over the years, far too much development was permitted in the Valley: more than 1,000 buildings, 30 mi. of roads, large parking areas, a golf course. In summer, over 1,500 employees live in the Valley, most of them employees of concessioners. More than a million vehicles a year travel on the Valley roads.

The situation became intolerable: traffic jams, campgrounds termed "outdoor slums," damage to vegetation, visitor misbehavior. Several years of study and public hearings yielded plans for change: 90% of the Park's area to become wilderness, free from development; removal of most staff housing, warehouses, offices, etc., from the Valley; more public transportation to limit use of private cars in the Valley; abandoning the golf course and other unwanted facilities; eliminating some parking lots. Commercial interests objected to some proposals. Conservationists argued for stronger measures. Successive versions of the plan have been modified, and the present outlook is uncertain. Some changes have been made. A reservation system eliminated long waiting lines at campgrounds. A few roads have been closed to autos, others made one-way.

To enjoy the Valley, don't come on summer weekends or holidays. We last visited in April and thought it the best time of year. Campgrounds were less than a quarter full. Waterfalls were at their best; many go dry in summer. Wildflowers were dazzling. Some trails had numerous hikers, but we found others untraveled. But April is not the time for the high country. The backpacking season often begins in June but in some years the trails are not snow-free until early or mid-July.

Yosemite as a whole is a land of scenic wonders. On the gentle western slope of the Sierra Nevada, the average grade is only 2.5%. Terrain is mountainous, with peaks, domes, and deep, glacier-carved canyons. Elevations range from 2,127 ft. to over 13,000 ft. Annual precipitation ranges from 36 in. in the Valley to about 50 in. at Snow Flat, elevation 8,700 ft. Summers are hot and dry, winters moist and cool.

The Park is entirely surrounded by National Forests: the Stanislaus, Toiyabe, Inyo, and Sierra. It is crossed by a single road, SR 120, from the Big Oak Flat entrance on the W to the Tioga Pass entrance on the E. This Tioga Road is closed in winter—a season that here can extend beyond June. Outside the Valley the only other roads are SR 41, entering from the S; a spur from SR 41 to Glacier Point, closed in winter beyond Summit Meadow; SR 140, entering on the W by way of Merced and Mariposa; and a spur road from SR 120 to the Hetch Hetchy Reservoir. Construction of the Hetch Hetchy Dam was bitterly opposed by conservationists in a fight they lost in 1913. The defeat did much to promote establishment of the National Park Service and the principle that National Parks should be inviolate—a principle once again being challenged.

Most of the high country is roadless. An area of 684,000 acres, 90% of the Park, has been proposed for wilderness status. Final decision is up to the Congress. This backcountry is accessible only by foot or horse in summer, by ski or snowshoe in winter. Overnight use is regulated by permit, and the number of permits is subject to trailhead quotas.

Plants: Plant communities include chaparral, mixed conifer, giant sequoia, red fir, lodgepole pine-subalpine, and alpine. Chaparral covers less than 20,-000 acres at the lowest elevations. The mixed conifer community extends to about 6,500 ft. elevation, covering about one-fifth of the Park. Prominent tree species of this zone are ponderosa and sugar pine, incense cedar, Douglas-fir, and white fir. At three locations are groves of giant sequoias, notably the Mariposa Grove near the S entrance. From about 6,500 ft. to 8,000 ft. is the red fir community, covering almost one-quarter of the Park. Pure stands of red fir are common, but most of this forest includes Jeffrey pine and lodgepole pine.

By far the largest plant community, covering two-fifths of the Park, is the lodgepole pine-subalpine association. Here, below timberline, are western white pine, western juniper, whitebark pine, mountain hemlock, with some pure lodgepole stands.

What makes the Yosemite forests so unique and impressive is their pristine quality. Almost none of the Park acreage has ever been logged, and few areas show marks of recent severe fires.

Between 7,000 ft. and 10,000 ft. elevation are mountain meadows with countless wildflowers. Spring in the high country comes in July and lasts only 7 to 9 weeks. During this time many species bloom simultaneously. Lemmon's paintbrush appears in vivid magenta patches in Tuolumne Meadows. Buttercup and bright pink pygmy shooting stars are early bloomers. In the higher meadows, large blue lupine, lavender asters, forget-me-nots, and yellow wallflowers are prominent.

No plant lists are provided by the Park, but the Yosemite Natural History Association offers several publications, noted in this section. About 1,500 plant species have been identified.

Birds: 223 species have been identified. Checklist available. Seasonally common or abundant species include band-tailed pigeon, black and white-throated swifts, rufous hummingbird, common flicker, acorn woodpecker; Hammond's, dusky, and olive-sided flycatchers; violet-green swallow, Steller's jay, western wood pewee, Clark's nutcracker, mountain chickadee, red-breasted nuthatch, brown creeper, American robin, golden-crowned kinglet. Warblers: orange-crowned, Nashville, yellow-rumped, black-throated gray, hermit. Also Brewer's blackbird, western tanager, black-headed grosbeak, Cassin's finch, pine grosbeak, gray-crowned rosy finch, Oregon junco; chipping, white-crowned, fox, Lincoln's, and song sparrows.

Mammals: No checklist available. 80 species have been recorded. Species often seen include raccoon, California mule deer, black bear, yellow-bellied marmot, California gray squirrel, Belding ground squirrel, coyote. Present but seldom seen: mountain lion, wolverine, fisher.

Reptiles and amphibians: No checklist available. About 12 amphibians, 16 reptiles recorded. Often seen: mountain yellow-legged frog, Yosemite toad, western fence and northern alligator lizards, western rattlesnake.

FEATURES

Yosemite Valley is so well known and publicized that description of its features would be redundant. They include Yosemite Falls, Bridalveil Fall, El Capitan, Half Dome, Sentinel Rock, Cathedral Rocks, Mirror Lake, The Three Brothers, Washington Column, the Merced River. The Happy Isles Trail Center, served by shuttle bus, is a high country trailhead and provides trail information.

Glacier Point overlooks the Valley. The road from Summit Meadow is closed in winter.

Tuolumne Meadows, at 8,600 ft., is the largest subalpine meadow in the High Sierra, bordering the Tioga Road, SR 120. The campground here is the one nearest to Tioga Pass. A popular base for day hikes and backcountry travel.

Tuolumne Grove, one of the three groves of giant sequoias, is near the Big Oak Flat entrance, on SR 120 W.

The Grand Canyon of the Tuolumne River is a mile-deep gorge. Waterwheel Falls, near the head of the canyon, is most spectacular in the days just after the hiking season opens. The falls and canyon are about a 6-mi. hike from the nearest trailhead on SR 120. The trail in the canyon is suitable for foot or horse travel.

The *Hetch Hetchy Valley* was spectacular before the dam was built. A road leads to the O'Shaughnessy Dam parking area, a good trailhead for backpacking into Yosemite's N country.

North of the Tuolumne River is some of the Park's most rugged, least traveled backcountry, almost a third of the Park's area. Terrain ranges from subalpine to alpine. Timberline is at about 9,500 ft. Above that, hikers find stark granite peaks, dwarfed vegetation, shallow meadows. Climatic extremes. Drainages are generally NE–SW, with such streams as Falls, Rancheria, and Return creeks. Upstream are numerous canyons: Jack Main, Stubblefield, Thompson, Kerrick, Matterhorn, Virginia. Most trails follow stream courses. The region has many small lakes. On its boundaries are the Stanislaus and Toiyabe National Forests, with trail links.

South of the Merced River the landscape is softened by giant sequoias, many species of broadleaf trees, shrubs, and flowered meadows, forms and colors changing with the seasons. Several of the most popular backcountry routes are in this area. One from the Happy Isles Trail Center in the Valley follows the Merced River to Merced and Washburn lakes, then loops S and SW to Wawona. Popular day hikes from Wawona include Chilnualna Falls and Wawona Point.

The *Wawona Basin*, 4,012 ft. elevation, a few mi. beyond the South Entrance and Mariposa Grove, is a developed area with store, campground, and other facilities. Trails to Crescent Lake and backcountry points.

INTERPRETATION

We know of no park with a more complex and comprehensive interpretive program. On entering the Park, obtain the latest issue of *Yosemite Guide,* a newspaper-style bulletin issued seasonally, which lists all current programs and describes new and changed facilities.

Three visitor centers and four museums have information, publications, exhibits, slide shows. Information is also available at entrance stations and Ranger Stations.

Bus and tram tours are offered daily. Valley and Mariposa all year; Mariposa Grove 6 months; Glacier Point from the Valley, 5 months.

Park naturalists are present all year, currently 55 of them in summer, 14 in winter.

Campfire programs are offered daily, at 8 locations in summer, in the Valley in winter. Notices posted throughout the Park.

Guided hikes are also offered daily, with notices posted. Some are brief and easy, others all day. Many have special themes: camera walks, snowshoe walks in winter.

Nature trails are at numerous locations, including Mariposa Grove, Cooks Meadow, Tuolumne Grove, Olmstead Point.

Many special programs are offered, including programs for handicapped people. Look for announcements.

The Yosemite Institute (P.O. Box 487, Yosemite, CA 95389) offers a variety of courses, seminars, and workshops, including weekend outdoor workshops on such subjects as winter ecology, winter survival, wildflowers and waterfalls, outdoor skills.

The Yosemite Natural History Association (P.O. Box 545, Yosemite, CA 95389) publishes literature and maps. It also offers college-level seminars, study classes, etc.

ACTIVITIES

Camping: 20 campgrounds. 2,161 sites. All year in Wawona and the Valley; summer and early fall elsewhere. Reservations required in the Valley, spring through early fall. Reservations can be made up to 8 weeks in advance by Ticketron or at the Park Campground Reservation Center in Camp Curry. 7 day limit in the Valley, 14 days elsewhere, June 1–Sept. 15.

Hiking, backpacking: More than 700 mi. of trails. Many short, easy trails for day hikes. Others, some strenuous, into the backcountry. Wilderness permits are required for overnight trips. Good trail guides are available for the principal trails.

Fishing: State regulations, plus special Park regulations. Trout are established in 880 mi. of permanent streams. Lakes have been stocked in the past, introducing species exotic to the area; the practice may be discontinued.

Swimming: Streams, unsupervised. Some backcountry lakes.

Canoeing, kayaking: Merced River, in the Valley. Tenaya Lake on the Tioga Road.

Horse riding: 635 mi. of suitable trails. 4 stables in the Park, 8 pack stations adjacent to the Park boundary. List of packers available.

Skiing: Ski area at Badger Pass. Usual season: Dec.–Apr. 15.

Ski touring: 500 mi. of trails. Season Dec. through May. Trees and limbs removed from trails; no snow grooming.

Snowmobiling is prohibited.

Pets must be restrained at all times. No pets in backcountry.

PUBLICATIONS

Leaflet with map.
Yosemite Guide (issued seasonally).
Bird checklist.
Information pages, mimeo:
Geology.
Giant sequoia.
Birds and mammals.
Black bears.

Fire management.
Campers' information.
Hiking in Yosemite.
Backcountry use control.
Fishing regulations.
List of packers.
Welcome to the Yosemite Backcountry (leaflet).

REFERENCES
The following are among the publications listed by the Yosemite Natural
History Association (P.O. Box 545, Yosemite, CA 95389). Publications
list is available.
Yosemite Nature Notes. 1977, $2.00. 1978, $3.00.
Yosemite Road Guide. $1.89.
Birds of Yosemite. $2.50.
Domes—Cliffs—Waterfalls. 95¢.
Yosemite Waterfalls. $1.25.
Yosemite Wildflower Trails. $3.50.
Trails of Yosemite Valley. 25¢.
Other sources:
Winnett, Thomas. *The Tahoe-Yosemite Trail.* Berkeley, CA: Wilderness
Press, 1979.
Winnett, Thomas. *Matterhorn Peak.* 2nd ed. Berkeley, CA: Wilderness
Press, 1975.
Winnett, Thomas. *Mono Craters.* Berkeley, CA: Wilderness Press, 1975.
Pierce, Bob and Margaret, and Winnett, Thomas. *Yosemite.* 3rd ed.
Berkeley, CA: Wilderness Press, 1974.
Pierce, Bob and Margaret. *Merced Peak.* Berkeley, CA: Wilderness
Press, 1973.
Schaffer, Jeffrey P. *Yosemite National Park.* Berkeley, CA: Wilderness
Press, 1978.
Schaffer, Jeffrey P., and Winnett, Thomas. *Tuolumne Meadows.* 2nd ed.
Berkeley, CA: Wilderness Press, 1977.
Felzer, Ron. *Hetch Hetchy.* Berkeley, CA: Wilderness Press, 1973.
Fawcett, Ken. *Tower Peak.* Berkeley, CA: Wilderness Press, 1975.

HEADQUARTERS: P.O. Box 577, Yosemite, CA 95389; (209) 372-4461.

FOR RECORDED INFORMATION ON ROAD CONDITIONS, WEATHER, CAMPING:
(209) 372-4605. In San Francisco: (415) 556-6030. In Los Angeles: (213)
688-2902.

ZONE 7

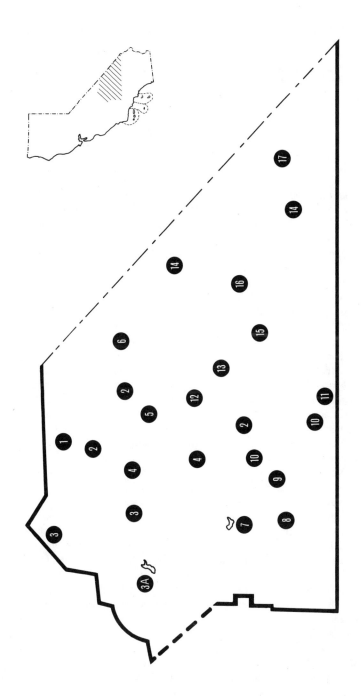

CALIFORNIA, ZONE 7

Includes these counties:

Fresno (E portion)   Inyo   Tulare

This zone includes well over a third of the Sierra Nevada Crest. It includes the W foothills and slopes, the E escarpment, Owens Valley, the Inyo Mountains, and, in Death Valley National Monument, the Panamint and Margosa ranges.

Kings Canyon and Sequoia National Parks are its centerpiece, almost entirely surrounded by the Sierra, Sequoia, and Inyo National Forests. Death Valley, with over a million acres, is by far the largest site.

Along the Crest, Mt. Whitney, highest peak in the Lower 48, is within this zone. Many points along the Crest are over 12,000 ft., an impressive number of them over 13,000 and 14,000 ft. In this zone, no all-year road crosses the Sierra Nevada. Most of the roads penetrating the Parks and Forests are closed by snow in winter above 7,000 ft. elevation. The hiking season in the high country usually begins in June, but sometimes not until July.

Most of the area within the National Parks is roadless and wilderness, as is most of Death Valley Monument. Large areas of wilderness are within the National Forests, also, and current studies will add more to the wilderness system in the Forests and in the public domain administered by the Bureau of Land Management. In the progression from N to S, this is the first California zone that includes large areas of public domain.

No section of the Sierra Nevada is more heavily impacted by visitors. The W slope is within easy driving distance of San Francisco, Sacramento, Stockton, and other cities. It is almost as easy for residents of the Los Angeles area to drive N into the Owens Valley on the E side of the great mountains. Many trails show signs of overuse, and vegetation around the edges of some mountain lakes has been trampled to death. Quotas are now in effect at many wilderness trailheads, and backpackers must now make camp at least 100 ft. away from the shores of affected lakes.

Mt. Whitney is the highest mountain. Giant Forest has the biggest trees. The John Muir Trail may well be the most scenic. Badwater, in Death Valley, is 280 ft. below sealevel. Such features attract people, and one who follows the crowds can't expect to find solitude. None the less, solitude is easily attained. We found many quiet places no less lovely than the famous ones and never spent a night in a crowded campground.

E of the Sierra, much of the zone is arid or semiarid. The brown tones used to show this area on many maps suggest a region of unrelieved heat and dryness. The landscapes beside many roads across the desert can seem monotonous and forbidding. But increasing numbers of visitors are becoming desert enthusiasts, finding here new kinds of variety in flora, fauna, and personal experience.

ALABAMA HILLS RECREATION LANDS
U.S. Bureau of Land Management
30,000 acres.

W of US 395 at Lone Pine.

Millions of people have seen this area, setting for many motion pictures and TV shows. Needless to say, it's scenic. The road from Lone Pine to Whitney Portal, trailhead for Mt. Whitney, passes through the area, which lies between the Owens Valley and the Inyo National Forest boundary.

The Alabama Hills are granitic, rounded, highly eroded, resembling giant boulder piles. Their appearance contrasts with the sculptured Sierra peaks, and they were once thought to be much older, although they were formed in the same period.

Vegetation is sparse, mostly scattered sagebrush and other desert shrubs. Lone Pine and Tuttle Creeks are perennial water sources. Wildlife includes small game and raptors. Deer and a herd of tule elk inhabit the valley areas.

Movie Flat is about 1 mi. N of the Whitney Portal road. Several graded dirt roads lead to colorful rock formations the moviegoer may find familiar. A BLM campground is in the Tuttle Creek area SW of Lone Pine.

The Independence Creek area, NW of Lone Pine on the Forest boundary, has been considered for wilderness status, chiefly because it adjoins a wilderness study area in the Forest. This area is part of the broad, rocky, alluvial apron of the Sierra Nevada, with dense stands of big sage and other shrubs.

The Winoga Peak area, S of Tuttle Creek, is similar, also considered for wilderness status, also adjoining a potential wilderness area in the Forest.

PUBLICATION: Leaflet.

HEADQUARTERS: BLM, Bakersfield District Office, 800 Truxtun, Room 302, Bakersfield, CA 93301; (805) 861-4191.

CERRO GORDO

U.S. Bureau of Land Management
40,000 acres.

E of Owens Lake. SR 136 is W boundary, SR 190 on the S. N boundary is an unpaved road from Keeler on SR 136 NE over Cerro Gordo Mountain.

Includes the S end of the Inyo Mountains, the Santa Rosa Hills, and the Santa Rosa Flats. Areas at the S end are flat, rising to low, rolling hills and to Malpais Mesa, a lava flow. The land rises steeply in the NE. Cerro Gordo Peak is 9,217 ft. Rugged valleys, deep canyons, sheer mountainsides, meadows, and mesas are in proximity on the E side. Vegetation ranges from saltbush-shadscale communities with scattered Joshua trees to pinyon-juniper on mountain slopes. Many historic mines and mine structures.

The E boundary is the Saline Valley Rd. (see entry), here at about 6,500 ft. elevation.

Caution: Very steep road. Use low gear and check brakes.

HEADQUARTERS: BLM, Bakersfield District Office, 800 Truxtun, Rm. 311, Bakersfield, CA 93301; (805) 861-4191.

CHIMNEY PEAK RECREATION AREA; OWENS PEAK AREA

U.S. Bureau of Land Management

This area adjoins the Dome Land Wilderness of Sequoia National Forest. It lies generally N of Walker Pass on SR 178. Most of the area is in zone 8, and the entry appears there.

DARWIN FALLS AND CANYON

U.S. Bureau of Land Management
22,400 acres.

From Olancha on US 395, 27 mi. E on SR 190. Area is S of SR 190, near the town of Darwin, extending to boundary of the Naval Weapons Center.

Waterfalls in the desert always seem dramatic, and this one stops many travelers driving to or from Death Valley. The stream flows all year, supporting thick green vegetation in striking contrast to the surrounding sparse desert shrubs.

There is more to the area than the falls. The Argus Range forms a long, narrow chain E of the area, rising to 8,839 ft. from the valley floor at 2,200 ft. W of the range, the Darwin Plateau is about 4,000 ft. elevation. The Plateau is cut by deep chasms, exposing volcanic rock faces. Spring-fed creeks within the canyons create cool, moist, shaded canyon floors. Darwin Falls and China Garden Spring are scenic places where falls and shaded pools are framed by mosses, ferns, and other riparian vegetation. The habitat is highly attractive to wildlife.

HEADQUARTERS: BLM, California Desert District Office, 1695 Spruce St., Riverside, CA 92507; (714) 787-1465.

DEATH VALLEY NATIONAL MONUMENT
U.S. National Park Service
2,048,851 acres.

On the NV border, W of Las Vegas. Principal E–W route is SR 190. SR 178 from the S joins SR 190, as does SR 374 from Beatty, NV, in the NE.

A common concept of Death Valley is a huge waterless desert, below sealevel, baking in the sun, where a flat tire or broken fan belt can become a fatal accident. The concept is partly right. People have died here, and it is not a place to become careless, especially off the main roads. But it is also a place of surprising variety and singular beauty.

Two places W of Badwater are 282 ft. below sealevel, the lowest dry-land points in the United States. The sand dunes near Stovepipe Wells cover 14 sq. mi., the saltflat further S more than 200 sq. mi. Death Valley itself is a relatively minor portion of the National Monument, a narrow N–S strip along the dry course of the Amargosa River, 6 mi. across at its widest point. To the E, the land rises steeply in the Amargosa Range, with several peaks over 1 mi. high. On the W, the Panamint Range is even higher, Telescope Peak reaching 11,049 ft. Enough snow and rain fall on the upper mountain slopes to support forests with juniper, mountain mahogany, pinyon and other pines. Snow accumulates on the high peaks, at times in deep drifts, and roads over high passes are sometimes closed.

The highest temperature of record was 134°F at Furnace Creek. The average

July maximum at this point is 116°. At this same point the lowest winter temperature on the Valley floor was recorded, 15° in January. The average minimum for that month is 39°. Small wonder most visitors to the Monument come in winter!

It's cooler upstairs, and the native Indians took to the mountains in summer. Normally temperature declines by 3 1/2 to 5 degrees for each 1,000 ft. of elevation. It's cooler at night, too, and many desert wildlife species remain underground by day, emerging only after the surface soil radiates away much of its store of daytime heat.

The Monument offers many opportunities for hiking and backpacking, but its size and the long distances between points of interest mean that most travel is by automobile. The Monument has several hundred miles of roads, including unpaved roads suitable for ordinary cars and about a hundred miles of jeep tracks. The first-time visitor should stay on the main routes. There's plenty to see and do along these routes. Backcountry touring is for those who understand the desert and their vehicles and know what to do when things go wrong. Even on the main routes precautions are essential. Gasoline is available at only three places in the Monument. Although any decent person will stop to aid a motorist in trouble, it could be hours before a summoned tow truck appears.

The principal centers in the Monument are around Scotty's Castle, Furnace Creek, and Stovepipe Wells, all N of the midpoint. A typical auto tour of the most popular park features covers about 200 mi., plus side trips and the entering and departing mileages. Some of these miles are on steep, winding roads where vehicles over 25 ft. long are not recommended.

Winter temperatures in the Valley are pleasant, usually in the 60's or 70's by day, in the 40's or 50's at night. Rainfall in the Valley is so slight that monthly averages have little meaning. The annual average is less than 2 in. The wettest year of record had about 4 1/2 in. Even so, as in other desert regions, flash floods are a hazard. A summer cloudburst can dump a sudden load of rain in a small area, most of which may run off through a single drainage, sending a wall of water down a dry channel to places where no rain has been seen or suspected. It's wise to be alert whenever a road dips down into such a dry channel.

Plants: With a range of elevations of more than 11,000 ft., the Monument has numerous plant communities. Botanists have identified some 20 plant species here that grow nowhere else. The saltflats are nearly barren. One would have to look closely to find any of the primitive, inconspicuous algae and fungi that live marginal existences here. On the perimeter, pickleweed and saltgrass grow, plants with a peculiar adaptation: they require much moisture, but they are salt tolerant.

Beyond the saltflats are zones of desert plants: creosote bush, mesquite, shadscale, arrowweed, rabbitbrush, sagebrush, burrobrush, desert tea, and various cacti, notably beavertail, cholla, and cottontop. On the mountain slopes are pinyon pine and juniper. Species occurring in scattered locations include Joshua tree and tamarisk.

The desert wildflower display is unpredictable. It may occur between Nov. and Mar., most often after early Jan. Temperature and moisture conditions must be just right for seeds to germinate. On one of our visits, conditions seemed right but the display was thin; botanists told us that conditions had been optimum for several previous years and the seeds required resting time. Even this thin display was rewarding, however, and in peak years great carpets of blooms, over 100 species, cover the desert floor.

Birds: Death Valley would not be our first choice for a birding expedition, but there are birds here. Indeed, the checklist has an astonishing 258 species, plus 74 others considered casual or accidental. The list even includes an assortment of waterfowl and shorebirds. Ruth Kirk (see References in this section) reports that 1,342 individuals of 44 species were once counted here in a single day. She does not say how or when, but we would guess the observer traveled from the salt creeks that attract snipe, sandpipers, and herons up through the life zones to the ridges, and that it was done in springtime. The checklist shows most entries in spring and fall, many fewer in summer and winter. The checklist compiler notes that some species were attracted by an irrigated golf course and date orchard.

Mammals: The checklist includes an array of species that have learned to take shelter from daytime heat, as well as species limited to the cooler upper slopes. They include various bats, ringtail, spotted skunk, badger, kit fox, coyote, bobcat, mountain lion, pronghorn, and round-tailed ground squirrels, pocket gophers, kangaroo rats, various mice and rats, porcupine, black-tailed jackrabbit, cottontail, mule deer, and bighorn sheep. Two unwanted species are the wild (feral) horse and burro. The burros, especially, have caused much environmental damage, threatening the existence of other species, but efforts to remove them have aroused controversy.

Reptiles and amphibians: Include red spotted toad, Pacific tree frog, bullfrog, desert tortoise, desert banded gecko, iguana, chuckwalla, other lizard species, western blind snake, desert rosy boa, striped whipsnake, gopher snake, California kingsnake, Panamint rattlesnake, Mojave Desert sidewinder.

FEATURES

Ubehebe Crater, near Grapevine, is about 500 ft. deep, 1/2 mi. in diameter. Smaller craters are nearby. Cinders from past steam and gas explosions cover the surrounding area.

Scotty's Castle is the Valley's most publicized feature, site of many legends. Near Grapevine.

Sand dunes, E of Stovepipe Wells, are a popular site for day hikes.

Mosaic Canyon, also near Stovepipe Wells, has water-polished marble walls in white, gray, and black.

Telescope Peak, S from Stovepipe Wells, is the highest point in the Monument, a stiff hike from trailhead. Ascending the peak in winter requires snow equipment and experience.

Golden Canyon is about 3 mi. S of Furnace Creek. A 1 1/2 mi. nature trail, with guide pamphlet, explains Death Valley geology. Nearby is *Zabriskie Point,* a viewpoint, and a loop dirt road through *Twenty Mule Team Canyon.*

Artists Drive is another loop, on a somewhat better road, through colorful badlands and canyon country.

Badwater, a bit further S, was once thought to be the lowest point in the United States. Then they found a nearby spot 2 ft. lower.

The backcountry offers at least as great variety, with many fewer people. Although some of the unpaved roads can be traveled by an ordinary car, one can visit more areas with greater security in a pickup truck or 4-wheel-drive vehicle. Some of the most fascinating trips are up canyons. The Phinney Canyon road tops out at 7,500 ft. elevation. Off-road vehicular travel is banned.

INTERPRETATION

A *visitor center, Death Valley Museum,* and *Borax Museum* are at Furnace Creek.

Guided walks and auto caravans are offered daily in winter. Schedules are posted.

Evening programs are presented daily in winter. Schedules are posted.

Walking tours are conducted regularly at Scotty's Castle.

Nature trails are at Salt Creek and Golden Canyon.

ACTIVITIES

Camping: 9 campgrounds. 1,601 sites. (The largest, Sunset, has 1,000 sites!) Several operate all year. Others, at low elevations, Nov.–Apr., those at high elevations Apr.–Oct. Campgrounds are crowded on any 3-day winter weekend, the 2nd weekend of Nov., Thanksgiving weekend, Christmas–New Year's week, Easter week. No reservations.

Hiking, backpacking: Monument guides describe many short hikes, plus longer trips. Backcountry travel is fascinating for those who know what they're doing. That means careful choice of season and routes, checking with rangers before departure, knowing how to use map and compass—and having both, carrying sufficient water, having the right gear, and knowing what to do if something goes wrong. The Monument has almost 1 1/2 million acres of backcountry, a part of it accessible by 4-wheel-drive vehicles, most only to those who travel on foot.

PUBLICATIONS

Leaflet with map.
Information pages, mimeo:
The burro problem.

Road grades leaving Death Valley.
General description.
Flora.
Endemic plants.
Average temperatures; precipitation.
Hiking Telescope Peak.
Mesquite Spring.
Ubehebe Crater.
Ghost towns.
Cacti of Death Valley.
How to Survive Your Summer Trip.
Picture-Taking in Death Valley.
Camping in Death Valley.
Dirt Road Travel and Backcountry Camping.

REFERENCES

Kirk, Ruth. *Exploring Death Valley.* Stanford, CA: Stanford University Press, 1976.
The following publications, of various publishers, are offered by the Death Valley Natural History Association, P.O. Box 188, Death Valley, CA 92328:
Badwater Self-Guiding Auto Tour. 25¢.
Common Sense in Desert Travel. $2.00.
Death Valley Geology, Ecology, Archaeology. $7.95.
Death Valley, Guidebook and Summary. 75¢.
Death Valley, the Story Behind the Scenery. $3.00.
Desert Survival. $3.95.
Getting Around in the Death Valley Backcountry. 25¢.
Golden Canyon Trail Guide. 25¢.
Inside Death Valley. $5.95.
A Naturalist's Death Valley. $2.95.
Death Valley Geology. $3.50.
Bird checklist. 15¢.
Checklist of fishes, amphibians, reptiles, mammals. 15¢.
Salt Creek nature trail guide. 25¢.
Death Valley Wildflowers. $3.25.

HEADQUARTERS: Death Valley, CA 92328; (714) 786-2331.

GREENWATER RANGE AND VALLEY
U.S. Bureau of Land Management
187,900 acres.

E of Death Valley National Monument. Bounded by SR 190, SR 127, SR 178, and the Monument.

One of the few very large, relatively pristine valleys in the desert region. Most of the area is in natural condition. The Valley lies between the Greenwater Range to the E and the Black Mountains, within the Monument, to the W. The Greenwater Range extends about 30 mi. NW–SE, its highest point 5,148 ft. The mountains are rough and irregular, with an eroded break at Deadman Pass, 3,263 ft., where a road once crossed. At Greenwater Canyon, waters have carved a narrow, steep-sided, twisting passage through volcanic rock.

The Valley also slopes NW–SE, dropping from about 4,500 ft. to 2,500 ft., much higher than the below-sealevel Death Valley. Valleys and canyons are well vegetated, hillsides sparsely. Creosote is the dominant plant species, with sagebrush, desert holly, prickly pear, bunchgrasses, annuals. Quail and chukar populations are good in the Valley. The Range is an important corridor for bighorn sheep.

The Valley adjoins a proposed wilderness area within the Monument.

HEADQUARTERS: BLM, California Desert District Office, 1695 Spruce St., Riverside, CA 92507; (714) 787-1465.

INYO NATIONAL FOREST
U.S. Forest Service
1,798,638 acres in CA; 60,576 acres in NV.

Lies both E and W of US 395 for over 175 mi. S of Mono Lake.

The Toiyabe National Forest is on the N. The W boundary adjoins Yosemite National Park, Sierra National Forest, Kings Canyon National Park, Sequoia National Park, and Sequoia National Forest. This boundary is the crest of the Sierra Nevada. In the entire 165-mi. distance N to S, only one road crosses the Sierra: SR 120, through Yosemite. It is closed in winter.

Between Mono Lake and Lake Crowley, the Forest includes 11,123-ft. Glass Mountain and the Banner Ridge. A separate, roughly parallel section of the Forest E of US 6 and 395, along the NV border, includes the White Mountains and part of the Inyo Mountains. The Forest sections are divided by the Owens Valley.

W of the Valley, the mountains rise in a steep, dominating escarpment up to 2 mi. above the valley floor, a continuous ridge with many peaks over 13,000 ft. Further N, toward Mono Lake, the peaks are not quite as high, and the valley floor is higher than to the S. The pattern of the mountains is more complex, spur ranges extending E.

Mt. Whitney, 14,495 ft., is the highest peak in the Lower 48. It is on the boundary of the Sequoia National Park, and the last bit of the trail from Whitney Portal is inside the Park.

Winter and summer, this is one of the most heavily used National Forests. US 395 leads directly here from Los Angeles. Backpacking became not only popular but fashionable. So many boots trampled fragile vegetation that a wilderness permit system had to be adopted, with access to certain trails and destinations rationed. The Pacific Crest Scenic Trail passes through the area. Best-known locally is the John Muir Trail, longest mountain wilderness trail in the Lower 48, 200 mi. without crossing a paved road. Californians told us that hikers on this trail even affect a certain style of dress and gear, displayed elsewhere to show "I was there." But the Forest has 1,150 mi. of trails, as well as many areas where off-trail hiking is feasible. Anyone who wants isolation can find it, especially with help from maps, trail guides, and a Ranger.

Much of the moisture blown in from the sea drops on the W side of the crest. Most of the annual precipitation falls in winter as snow in the higher altitudes, as much as 40 ft. of snow in some locations. Between 5,000 and 6,000 ft. elevation, annual precipitation is about 12 in. On the W-facing slopes in the E portion of the Forest, the average is 6–12 in. per year.

This is enough moisture to supply some 500 lakes in the Forest, however, and to feed about 100 streams. S of the Mono Basin, these streams join in the Owens River, and this water made the Owens Valley attractive to farmers. No longer. The water supply was acquired by the Los Angeles Department of Water and Power. The flow of the Owens River has been diverted into concrete ditches. Desert plant species are appearing on land that once was farmed.

To visit the Forest, one has little choice other than to take US 395. Along the way are many side roads, to E and W, some paved, some all-weather gravel roads, some that—at least at times—require 4-wheel drive. These side roads lead to busy resorts, lakes, canyon campgrounds, viewpoints, wilderness trailheads.

One effect of the steep escarpment is the quick transition visitors can make from one climate and life zone to another. In early June they can stand in snow beside a frozen lake, and only a few minutes later feel the blasting heat of summer sun in the valley below. In so doing, they will leave the zone of alpine vegetation, where flowers will soon poke up through melting snow, descend through several forest zones, and arrive in sagebrush desert. The ski areas are usually still operating at the end of May, sometimes even a month later. Long before then many trails at lower elevations are snow-free.

Most of the land around Mono Lake and along US 6 N of Bishop is public domain, administered by the Bureau of Land Management. The land surrounding Lake Crowley is BLM or City of Los Angeles land. The Owens Valley S of Bishop is also part BLM, part City of Los Angeles land. The BLM has a large recreation area W of Lone Pine (see entry, Alabama Hills).

Plants: A typical transect down from the high Sierra would pass through the alpine zone and subalpine forest, across mountain meadows, then down through forests of lodgepole pine, red fir, mixed conifers, and pinyon woodland to desert shrubs.

Common trees of the E slope of the Sierra include Jeffrey pine, white and red firs, western white pine, lodgepole pine, western juniper. In moister areas: quaking aspen, cottonwood. Because of the wide range of life zones, hundreds of species of flowering plants occur here. Among them: tiger lily, western wall flower, cinquefoil, yarrow, cow parsnip, corn lily, thistle poppy, evening primrose, pyrola, mariposa lily, monkeyflower, red columbine, mullein, Indian paintbrush, scarlet gilia, shooting star, larkspur, lupine, gentian, fireweed, red and white heathers, rein orchid. The W slopes of the White and Inyo Mountains, across the valley, are dry, with juniper, pinyon pine, limber pine, bristlecone pine, and areas of sagebrush-bitterbrush.

Birds: No checklist is available, although HQ states that 242 species have been recorded. Reported: golden eagle, sharp-shinned hawk, goshawk; pygmy, great horned, great gray, and saw-whet owls; Williamson's and yellow-bellied sapsuckers, pileated and white-headed woodpeckers, blue and sage grouse, chukar; pinyon, gray, and Steller's jays; raven, Clark's nutcracker, hermit thrush, mountain bluebird, olive-sided flycatcher, western wood pewee, pine siskin, pygmy nuthatch, brown creeper, mountain chickadee, hermit warbler, Oregon and gray juncos, fox sparrow.

Wetland species were far more abundant before the valley habitat was drastically altered. Mono Lake still supports large numbers of gulls, phalaropes, avocet, plover, sandpipers, and waterfowl, although this habitat is threatened. The remaining valley marshes and lakes offer good birding. Species of the sagebrush and pinyon-juniper areas include loggerhead shrike, horned lark, western kingbird, nighthawk, black-billed magpie, rufous-sided towhee, kestrel.

Mammals: Species differ from habitat to habitat: white-tailed antelope squirrel and black-tailed jackrabbit in the desert zone, pica on high talus slope, alpine chipmunk near timberline. Species of the area include California and golden-mantled ground squirrels, Panamint kangaroo rat, white-tailed jackrabbit, least chipmunk, chickaree, cottontail, weasel, marmot, beaver, badger, coyote, black bear, bobcat, mountain lion, mule deer, California and desert bighorn sheep. Tule elk range from Sequoia-Kings Canyon National Park to Owens Valley.

FEATURES

Hoover Wilderness, 48,601 acres, in the extreme N of the Forest, W of Mono Lake, bordering Yosemite National Park. About 9,500 acres is in the Inyo National Forest, the larger part in the Toiyabe. Extremely rugged terrain. Elevations from 8,000 ft. to 13,000 ft. Alpine zone, with little timber. Numerous lakes bordered by meadows. An occasional small stand of aspen or lodgepole pine. Recommended travel period is July–Aug., possibly Sept., but heavy rain, blizzards, extreme cold, and high winds are possible even then. Good trout fishing. The S part, access from the Inyo National Forest, is heavily used, the N part less so, except for the Pacific Crest Trail.

Minarets Wilderness, 107,380 acres, on the border of Yosemite National Park just S of SR 120, about 55% in the Inyo National Forest, the remainder in Sierra National Forest. High country E of the Sierra Crest. Elevations from 7,000 ft. to 14,000 ft. The Minarets are on the central portion of the divide, W of Mammoth Lakes, in the Ritter Range. The area has many lakes, the largest of them, in the central portion, over a mile long. Crossed by the John Muir Trail and Pacific Crest Trail. Because of its proximity to Mammoth Lakes, this area is heavily used, and quotas are in effect at principal trailheads.

John Muir Wilderness, 499,675 acres, is California's largest Wilderness, about 45% in the Inyo National Forest, the larger part in the Sierra National Forest. Extends from the Mammoth Lakes area S along the Sierra Crest, bordering Kings Canyon and Sequoia National Parks, to a point near Mt. Whitney. Snow-capped mountains, many lakes and streams. Its general shape is long and narrow, in places only 2 mi. wide. Areas accessible in an overnight trip are heavily used. Quotas are in effect at many trailheads.

Golden Trout Wilderness, 302,800 acres, about 55% in Inyo National Forest, the remainder in Sequoia National Forest. Adjoins the S boundary of John Muir Wilderness. On the SE boundary of Sequoia National Park. W portion is a large drainage basin surrounded by high, rugged mountains. E part is an extension of the Kern Plateau. Many mountain streams, flowing into the Kern River. Pacific Crest Trail crosses. Not as heavily used as the other Wilderness Areas. Quota for entry into the National Park.

Mammoth Lakes is a resort, the most popular place in the Forest. The village is on SR 203, at the gateway to many of the Forest's most scenic backcountry. Mammoth Mountain is a popular ski area. A commercial gondola gives summer visitors views of the high country. Nearby are the Devils Postpile National Monument (see entry in CA zone 6), Rainbow Falls, Minaret Vista, trails into the John Muir Wilderness. Above the village is 1 mi.-wide lakes basin. Many Forest campgrounds are nearby. These campgrounds begin opening in late Apr. or early May, some remaining open after Labor Day until ⁻ closed by snow.

Mt. Whitney is not the place to seek solitude. Because it is the highest point in the Lower 48 and has a trail to the top, many people make the trip. Trailhead is Whitney Portal. From there it's 10 1/2 mi., with a 6,000-ft. rise. Some physically fit hikers make the trip in one day, but two days is recommended. Altitude sickness affects many. Trail use is now limited to 75 people per day, by reservation.

Big Pine Canyon is another popular resort area, on a road W from Big Pine and US 395. The developed area has a lodge, campgrounds, trailheads for the John Muir Wilderness. Pack trains depart from here. *Palisade Glacier* is 7 mi. from the road's end. It is the most S glacier in the United States.

Rock Creek Canyon also has commercial resort facilities and Forest campgrounds. The road S from Toms Place on US 395 is in a corridor penetrating several miles into the John Muir Wilderness. Near its end, at Mosquito Flat, the road reaches an elevation of 10,250 ft., highest road point in the Sierra. The canyon area is popular for ski touring in winter.

Bishop Creek, still another resort area, is on a road SW from Bishop. The road divides, the N branch ending at Sabrina Lake, the S at South Lake, both on the John Muir Wilderness boundary.

The *White Mountain area* is on the drier E side of the Forest. A circuit auto tour begins at Big Pine, proceeds NW on SR 168, N on SR's 266 and 264, W and S on US 6, returning to US 395 at Bishop. The 160-mi. loop passes Deep Springs Valley, Fish Lake Valley, viewpoints at Montgomery Pass, and other points of interest.

Ancient Bristlecone Pine Forest, 28,000 acres, is reached by taking SR 168 from Big Pine, turning N at Cedar Flat S of Westgard Pass. These bristlecone pines are said to be the world's oldest living things. High on the rocky slopes of the White Mountains, elevations over 10,000 ft. Many wildflowers. Trails through the groves. No water, gas, or commercial facilities nearby.

INTERPRETATION

Visitor Center at Mammoth. *Entrance/information stations* at Bishop Creek, Rock Creek, and Ancient Bristlecone Pine Forest.

Evening programs at the Mammoth Visitor Center and at Schulman Grove in the Bristlecone Pine Forest. Occasionally elsewhere.

ACTIVITIES

Camping: 67 campgrounds. 2,009 sites. Most are closed in winter, Nov.–May. Some at lower elevations remain open.

Hiking, backpacking: 1,150 mi. of trails. Permit is required to enter any Wilderness Area, even for a day hike. Quotas are in effect at many trailheads. Ask about reservations. John Muir Trail, Pacific Crest Trail, Mt. Whitney Trail, and others are popular. Trail guides and Ranger advice can identify lightly traveled areas.

Hunting: Chiefly mule deer, black bear, sage hen, grouse, quail, chukar.

Fishing: Hundreds of lakes and streams, many of them stocked. Rainbow, brook, brown, golden trout.

Swimming: At lakeside campgrounds, or wherever you find suitable water.

Boating: Ramps at the larger road-access lakes. Rentals at several resorts.

Horse riding: Outfitters and liveries at several resorts.

Skiing: Mammoth and June mountains have ski areas. Mammoth's is the largest in CA.

Ski touring: Several popular areas.

Snowmobiling: Prohibited in Wilderness Areas. Restrictions apply elsewhere; inquire.

PUBLICATIONS

Forest map. $1.00.
Minaret Wilderness map. $1.00.
John Muir Wilderness maps. 2 sections (in production). $1.00 each.
Mammoth Guide.
Whitney Mountain Trail Guide.
Big Pine Creek Journal.
Rock Creek Journal.
Bishop Creek Journal.
Hill and Mountain Journal.
White Mountains Journal.
Ancient Bristlecone Pine Forest Guide.
Interagency Motor Vehicle Use map. (Shows areas closed to vehicles.)

REFERENCES

Smith, Genny Schumaker, ed. *Mammoth Lakes Sierra.* Palo Alto, CA: Genny Smith Books, 1976.

Smith, Genny Schumacher, ed. *Deepest Valley.* Palo Alto, CA: Genny Smith Books, 1969. (Available from Southern Mono Hospital Auxiliary, P.O. Box 1399, Mammoth Lakes, CA 93456.)

Winnett, Thomas. *Mount Whitney.* 3rd ed. Berkeley, CA: Wilderness Press, 1978.

Jenkins, J. C., and Robinson, John W. *Kern Peak—Olancha.* 2nd ed. Berkeley, CA: Wilderness Press, 1979.

HEADQUARTERS: 873 N. Main St., Bishop, CA 93514; (714) 873-5841.

RANGER DISTRICTS: Mt. Whitney R.D., P.O. Box 8, Lone Pine, CA 93545; (714) 876-5542. White Mountain R.D., 798 N. Main St., Bishop, CA 93514; (714) 873-4207. Mammoth R.D., P.O. Box 148, Mammoth Lakes, CA 93546; (714) 934-2505. Mono Lake R.D., P.O. Box 10, Tioga Pass Highway, Lee Vining, CA 93542; (714) 647-6525.

KINGS CANYON NATIONAL PARK
See Sequoia and Kings Canyon National Parks.

LAKE KAWEAH
U.S. Army Corps of Engineers
1,945 acres of water.

From Visalia, 20 mi. E on SR 198.

A flood control project on the Kaweah River. The lake is 5 mi. long and much used for water-based recreation. In the foothills area, chaparral-covered slopes on both sides of the inundated valley. The N side of the lake appears to be roadless. However, the government-owned land is only a narrow strip around the lake shore. SR 198 is a loop route passing through Sequoia National Park and meeting the Kings Canyon National Park access road.

Camping: 80 sites. All year.

PUBLICATION: Leaflet.

HEADQUARTERS: P.O. Box 346, Lemoncove, CA 93244; (209) 597-2301.

MOUNTAIN HOME STATE FOREST
California Department of Forestry
4,590 acres.

From Porterville, NE on SR 137.

A State Forest within the Sequoia National Forest, on the boundary of and trailhead for the Golden Trout Wilderness. The site has many old-growth giant sequoias, including one specimen 31 1/3 ft. in diameter, 247 ft. tall. Elevations from 5,100 ft. to 7,200 ft. Annual precipitation about 45 in. A curiosity of the site are its "Indian bathtubs," depressions in granite outcrops 3–5 ft. across, 2–5 ft. deep, their origin unexplained.

Plants: Although the sequoias are protected, this is a working forest: other species are harvested and planted. Generally a mixed conifer forest with a mixture of black oak. Understory of littleleaf, whitethorn, deerbrush, Pacific dogwood, wild gooseberry, elderberry, western raspberry.

Birds: No checklist, but checklist for the Sequoia National Forest should be applicable. Mentioned by local staff: blue jay, red-tailed hawk, band-tailed pigeon, woodpeckers, nuthatches, raven, junco, robin, warblers. Condor have been seen overhead.

Mammals: Generally those found in the Sequoia National Forest. Bear have been a campground nuisance at times.

INTERPRETATION: *Forest Information Trail* is a self-guiding nature trail jointly maintained by the Department of Forestry and the Tulare County Parks Department.

ACTIVITIES

Camping: 7 campgrounds. 100 sites. May 15–Oct. 15.

Hiking, backpacking: Permits can be obtained here for entry into the Golden Trout Wilderness of the Sequoia National Forest. 19 mi. of trails within the State Forest.

Hunting: Mule deer, bear, tree squirrel.

Fishing: Wishon Fork of the Tule River is the largest of several streams. Rainbow and brown trout.

Horse riding: Balch Park Pack Station, on the site, has horses for local or wilderness travel.

Ski touring: No maintained trails. Usual season Jan.–Apr.

Snowmobiling: On roads only. Not in the Wilderness Area.

PUBLICATIONS

Leaflet with map.

Nature trail guide.

National Forest wilderness information is available.

HEADQUARTERS: P.O. Box 517, Springville, CA 93265; summer: (209) 539-2321; winter: (209) 539-2855.

OWENS VALLEY

U.S. Bureau of Land Management and others

On US 395 from Owens Lake N to Bishop.

The Valley runs between the Sierra Nevada on the W and the Inyo Mountains on the E. In the past, the Owens River flowed through the Valley. Now, from Mono Lake S, the water is in an aqueduct, and the City of Los Angeles, which takes the water, owns a corridor of land 1–8 mi. wide down the center of the Valley. Diversion of the water has caused disappearance of the green riparian vegetation along the river banks, as well as of the associated wildlife.

The Inyo National Forest occupies the E slope of the Sierra, as well as the Inyo Mountains N from a point about 10 mi. N of Lone Pine. Between the Forest boundaries on each side and the City of Los Angeles land at the

Valley's center are two strips of BLM-managed public land, in width from less than a mi. to as much as 8 mi.

The BLM land is at the base of the Sierra escarpment, including alluvial aprons, rugged lava flows, canyons, low granitic hills, and benchlands. Much the same kind of terrain, on a somewhat reduced scale, is on the E side of the Valley. A striking feature of the Valley is its depth in relation to the Sierra on the W, Inyo and White Mountains on the E. Countless dramatic views of the snowy crests. Vegetation ranges from big sage on the alluvial lands to mixed shrubs and annual grasses, with pinyon-juniper at higher elevations.

Much of the BLM land has been recommended for wilderness study; because roads, structures, and other artifacts are disqualifying, the proposed wilderness areas are a number of tracts separated by such development. In most cases, a primary factor favoring wilderness designation is that a tract adjoins acreage within the National Forest selected for wilderness consideration.

REFERENCE: Smith, Genny Schumaker, ed. *Deepest Valley.* Palo Alto, CA: Genny Smith Books, 1969. (Available from Southern Mono Hospital Auxiliary, P.O. Box 1399, Mammoth Lakes, CA 93456.)

HEADQUARTERS: BLM, Bakersfield District Office, 800 Truxtun, Rm. 311, Bakersfield, CA 93301; (805) 861-4191.

PANAMINT MOUNTAINS AND VALLEY
U.S. Bureau of Land Management
210,000 acres.

On the W boundary of Death Valley National Monument, N and S of SR 190.

Several good roads make this area somewhat more accessible than the lands described in the Saline Valley entry. Included are 4 BLM Wilderness Study Areas:

Hunter Mountain, 23,844 acres, between the Monument boundary and the Saline Valley road, with the road over Hunter Mountain to the S. At the junction of Panamint, Saline, and Death valleys. Hunter Mountain, 7,454 ft., is at the Monument boundary. The road, unpaved, hazardous in inclement weather, originates at SR 190, crosses into the Monument, and continues N to Ubehebe Crater and Grapevine.

Terrain varies from flat valley floor to bajada, sheer smooth walls, jagged

rock outcrops, deeply eroded canyons and valleys, plateaus, and coarse moun-
taintops. Grapevine Canyon, paralleling the Hunter Mountain road, has an
abundance of water, supplied by springs high up the slopes. Vegetation is lush
in the canyon, the riparian habitat continuing to a thick stand of pinyon pine
and juniper on the high slopes. Valley vegetation is mainly creosote and low
desert shrubs. Wildlife includes bighorn sheep, mule deer, various small
mammals. Birding is said to be good in the N portion.

Scenically the Wilderness Study Area is highly rated. The mountain offers
fine views of Mt. Whitney and the Death Valley area. The BLM ranked the
site second among the 137 CA Wilderness Study Areas.

Panamint Dunes, 93,220 acres, has SR 190 as its S boundary, Death Valley
National Monument on the E and NE. A maintained road N from SR 190
is its W boundary. The area includes the N portion of Panamint Valley,
elevations ranging from 1,500 ft. at the valley floor to 6,000 ft. in the Panamint
Mountains. In the S, the valley includes a flat, dry lakebed. Land slopes
upward toward the N, where a dune system is developing. The dunes, covering about 6 sq. mi., are isolated, peaked sand hills known as "star dunes,"
rising as much as 250 ft. above the floor. Rainbow Canyon, on the W side of
the valley, N of Panamint Springs on SR 190, is a steep-sided, brightly colorful
area.

Vegetation varies from virtually nil on the dry lake bottom to exceptionally
lush pinyon-juniper growth on the peaks. Intermediate areas include creosote,
bunchgrasses, desert holly, Joshua trees, many annuals. Notable wildlife
includes desert bighorn sheep, mule deer, Panamint chipmunk, prairie falcon,
golden eagle.

The *Wildrose Canyon* area, 38,900 acres, is just to the S, across SR 190,
Panamint Valley Rd. on the W, Wildrose Canyon Rd. on the S. Elevations
from 1,600 ft. on the Panamint Valley floor to 6,200 ft. in the Panamint
Mountains. The mountains are cut by deep canyons from which gently sloping alluvial fans emerge. In the SE, broken and eroded hills have a badlands
appearance. The W half consists of low rolling hills.

Creosote bush and desert holly are the principal vegetation on the fans.
Creosote in the canyons is sparse but tall. The slopes have a thin cover of low
shrubs.

Surprise Canyon, 54,400 acres, exceptionally scenic, has been designated an
Area of Critical Environmental Concern. It adjoins the National Monument
on the SW, S of Wildrose Canyon Rd. The county-maintained Indian Ranch
Rd. is the W boundary. The heights of the Panamint Range are well inside
the Monument, the highest point being Telescope Peak, 11,045 ft. Elevations
at the boundary are roughly 5,000–6,500 ft. Terrain is mostly rugged mountains and deep canyons, with small, steep alluvial fans emerging from the
canyons. A small badlands area is in the NW.

From the county road, a number of stub roads penetrate the canyons, reflecting the history of mining here. At least four of the canyons have flowing springs. The flow maintains riparian vegetation, including several unusual species, among them the Panamint daisy. Birding is good, as is deer hunting. The alluvial fans have bright seasonal flower displays. The adjacent area within the Monument has been proposed for wilderness status. A pickup truck or 4-wheel-drive vehicle is needed on the canyon roads.

HEADQUARTERS: California Desert District Office, 1695 Spruce St., Riverside, CA 92507; (714) 787-1465.

PINE FLAT LAKE
U.S. Army Corps of Engineers
4,000 acres of water (average recreation pool).

From Fresno, about 19 mi. E on SR 180, then NE on Trimmer Springs Rd.

Flood control project on the Kings River. The Kings River Canyon is the boundary between the Sierra and Sequoia National Forests, which surround 2/3 of the project area. The lake, much used for water-based recreation, is 20 mi. long, irregular in shape. Boat camping is popular. A Forest Service campground is at the upper end of the lake.

Camping: 2 campgrounds. 80 sites. All year.

PUBLICATION: Leaflet.

HEADQUARTERS: P.O. Box 117, Piedra, CA 93649; (209) 787-2589.

SALINE VALLEY AREA
U.S. Bureau of Land Management
700,000 acres.

NV border and Death Valley National Monument are the E boundary, SR 168 the N. Extends W to the Inyo National Forest. Access by unpaved roads: Eureka Valley Rd., Cucamonga Rd., Saline Valley Rd., Death Valley Rd.

This area is not one to be explored on a Sunday drive. One needs a 4-wheel-drive vehicle, good maps, water, and emergency supplies. Even on one of the named roads, it might be more than a day or two before another vehicle appeared. The large central part of the area is roadless. If wilderness status is approved, ORV's will be banned, so the only entry will be on foot or horseback.

The area has great diversity and many attractive features. Its valleys are 1/4 mi. higher than the below-sealevel Death Valley. It includes portions of several mountain ranges, with several peaks over 8,000 ft. With advice and a topo map, a hiker can find his or her way to a canyon with a flowing spring and lush vegetation, where he or she can be sure of solitude.

The central portion of this region is the Saline Valley Wilderness Study Area, 418,015 acres, adjacent to the Monument. The BLM ranked it first among the 137 such areas in CA. It includes the Saline Valley and the S half of Eureka Valley. Terrain varies from flat to rolling in the N and NE, sloping to the SE toward playas near the Eureka Sand Dunes. The remainder of the area is rolling to steep and mountainous. Elevations range from 1,150 ft. in the SW to 8,674 ft. atop Dry Mountain near the Monument boundary. Land forms include flat, white, dry lake; heavily vegetated salt marsh; low rolling hills; sand dunes; rugged mountain ranges; colorful badlands.

This is desert country, where availability of water creates oases with rich plant and animal life. Springs flow in several canyons, notably eight springs in the canyon separating Eureka and Saline Valleys. The Saline Valley also has three mineral hot springs, two of them popular recreation sites.

Plants: Vegetation includes Joshua tree-creosote-burrobrush scrub at low elevations to pinyon-juniper woodlands on the upper slopes. The Eureka Valley Joshua tree forest is the northernmost large stand of this species. Riparian vegetation, sometimes lush, occurs in canyons. In the marsh, tall cattails and other reedy plants, and a dense growth of catclaw. Spring wildflower displays are often colorful in both Saline and Eureka Valleys.

Wildlife: Includes large numbers of migratory waterfowl. Resident bird species range from those found in Death Valley to those of the Inyo Mountains. Foraging range for golden eagle and prairie falcon, with several eyries. Much of the area is used by bighorn sheep. Large mule deer population. Among the rare species in the valley: pale kangaroo mouse.

ADJACENT BLM AREAS

Sylvania Mountains, 15,450 acres, between Eureka Valley Rd. and the NV border, S of Sylvania Canyon Rd. Rugged mountains dissected by several large washes. Elevations to 7,998 ft. Vegetation mostly shadscale and blackbrush types, with Joshua tree; pinyon-juniper at higher elevations. Canyons have colorful strata. Good deer and chukar hunting in SW.

Eureka Sand Dunes Natural Area can be reached by Eureka Valley Rd.,

which runs S from SR 168, about 32 mi. NE of Big Pine on US 395. The area
has the largest dunes in CA. The system is about 3 mi. long, 1 mi. wide, rising
to 680 ft. The Eureka Valley lies between the White Mountains and the Last
Chance Range, at about 3,000 ft. elevation. The area has had considerable
scientific study, in which a number of rare plants were identified. ORV use
of the area has been heavy, with severe impact on dune vegetation. The BLM
has adopted some protective rules, including vehicle closures, but found them
difficult to enforce.

Last Chance Mountains, 38,200 acres, just S of Sylvania Mountains area,
between Eureka Valley Rd. and NV border. Mountainous, elevations to 8,456
ft. Many deep canyons. A few springs. An extremely scenic area. Eroding
rock formations in Cucamonga Canyon expose strata with bands in many
shades of red, yellow, blue, purple. Seasonal range for desert bighorn. Cucamonga Canyon attracts the most visitors, 745 visitor-days in the most recent
reported year.

Piper Mountain, 72,930 acres, W of Eureka Valley Rd. and the two preceding areas, N of Saline Valley area. Includes the N end of Eureka Valley and
the surrounding mountains, the Inyo Mountains to the N and W. Terrain in
SE portion rolling to gently sloping, the remainder rough and mountainous.
Highest point is 9,792 ft.

Brushy valley floor. Joshua tree woodland near the base of the Inyo Mountains. Cottonwood and willow dominant in the canyons.

Includes desert bighorn range. Mule deer, pale kangaroo mouse, western
pipistrel bat.

Little Sand Spring, 33,500 acres, on Death Valley Rd., on the N boundary
of the Monument and the NV border. Contains the W foothills of the Gold
Mountain Range, sloping gradually to Death Valley, the foothills rounded,
with many canyons draining to the Valley. Big Sand Springs and Little Sand
Springs are in the Valley. The BLM rates the scenic values "medium."

Waucoba Wash, 11,700 acres, W of the Saline Valley, adjoining a part of
the Inyo National Forest proposed for wilderness designation. Flat to rolling
in the E; rough and mountainous in the W, with deeply cut canyons. Elevations to 7,600 ft. Numerous springs and intermittent streams.

Saline Dunes, 5,800 acres, in the heart of the Saline Valley, treated separately because it is surrounded by dirt roads, including Saline Valley Rd. Sand
dunes surrounded by relatively flat land. Groundwater and runoff from the
Inyo Mountains support dense vegetation, in sharp contrast to the surrounding area. Tall stands of catclaw. Also arrowweed, mesquite, and marsh
grasses.

Inyo Mountains, 87,945 acres, on the W side of Saline Valley, between
Saline Valley Rd. and the Inyo National Forest. From the S, the Saline Valley
Rd. drops sharply through Grapevine Canyon to the valley floor at about
1,000 ft. elevation. Beyond the Valley, the Inyo Mountains rise to about 9,000

ft. Vegetation on the valley floor is chiefly creosote, catclaw, annual grasses, low desert shrubs. On the lower slopes, Joshua tree is prominent, with yucca, cacti, and shrubs. Higher, dense stands of pinyon and juniper. Grapevine Canyon is fed by numerous springs on the side of Hunter Mountain, forming a stream with a lush riparian vegetation. On the high slopes of the Inyo Mountains is a stand of bristlecone pine. The area was rated high on scenic quality. Abundant wildlife.

INCLUDES: Saline Valley Ecological Reserve, 200 acres, Department of Fish and Game. Salt Lake, shown on most highway maps, is in the SW sector of the valley. The Reserve, on the E side of the lake, includes a number of freshwater springs. The dry lakebed has been used by ORV's. One purpose of the Reserve is to protect this special habitat from ORV and other damage.

HEADQUARTERS: BLM, California Desert District Office, 1695 Spruce St., Riverside, CA 92507; (714) 787-1465.

SEQUOIA AND KINGS CANYON NATIONAL PARKS
U.S. National Park Service
402,108 acres and 459,995 acres.

To Kings Canyon: SR 180 E from Fresno. For Sequoia, turn S from SR 180 in Grant Grove area onto Generals Highway. Or SR 198 E from Visalia.

These adjoining Parks are part of the enormous area of public land that occupies most of the Sierra Nevada. They are almost completely surrounded by National Forests: the Sierra on the W and N, Inyo on the E, Sequoia on the W and S. Within the Parks is a great range of elevations, from about 1,500 ft. to Mt. Whitney, at 14,495 ft. the highest peak in the Lower 48. Here is some of the most magnificent scenery of the Sierra: towering granite mountains, sharp ridges, deep canyons, waterfalls and cascades, high mountain lakes, forests of great trees, including the greatest of all, the giant sequoia.

Most of the Parks' area is roadless and undisturbed, with many stands of virgin timber. No road crosses the Sierra here. Roads enter the Parks only from the W.

For visitors who see the Parks from their cars, the primary route is SR 180 to Grant Grove, a detached bit of Kings Canyon National Park, then by the Generals Highway through the Giant Forest area of Sequoia National Park, continuing SW to SR 198.

A single road penetrates the main portion of Kings Canyon National Park: SR 180, N and W from Grants Grove to a developed area at Cedar Grove. This road is open in summer only. Generals Highway, from Grant Grove through Sequoia National Park, is also closed by snow in winter, generally from mid-Nov. through Apr. The road from the SW, SR 198, is kept open as far as the Giant Forest. From SR 198, two roads enter the S part of Sequoia National Park: the Mineral King road, open in summer only, and a road along the South Fork of the Kaweah River that ends just inside the Park boundary.

Thus except in summer the motorist visitor is limited to Grant Grove and the Giant Forest. In Apr., we found great masses of wildflowers blooming at about 3,500 ft. elevation. Patches of snow were just above. From Park HQ at Ash Mountain, near the entrance, the road rises 5,700 ft. in 16 mi., with 230 curves and 24 major switchbacks. The views are splendid, and the road has many turnouts.

Above 5,000 ft. we were in snow. At Lodgepole Visitor Center, the elevation is 6,720 ft. Here the snow had been cleared only from the road, a few parking places, and a few walkways. One could camp only by pitching a tent in the snow.

We were not disappointed. Photographs can't portray the awesome size of the great sequoias, and hundreds of them are near the road. Indeed, the ponderosa and Jeffrey pines are also magnificent here. Rangers told us the backpacking season usually begins in June, but deep snow in 1980 would delay it until July. We asked about hiking at lower elevations and were told few people do it. We camped at a campground just above 2,000 ft. elevation and hiked all the next day, usually near a rushing stream, on chaparral hillsides, bright with sun and flowers. The Marble Fork Trail climbed 2,000 ft. in the first 3 1/2 mi.

At Ash Mountain, 1,700 ft. elevation, winter temperatures range between 32° and 57°F, rarely dropping below 25°. At 6,400 ft. the winter average range is 21° to 40°F, with extreme lows below 10°. In the high country, summer days are generally mild and sunny, but afternoon thundershowers are common and night temperatures below freezing are not unusual.

Many visitors never stray far from their cars. From the developed areas, many trails offer opportunities for short or all-day hikes or one-night backcountry trips. Most of the Park area, however, is beyond this range. The long-distance hiker, unlike the motorist, can enter the Park from the N, E, or S. Many do enter from the Inyo National Forest, along the John Muir Trail and by other routes. The Park has a dozen backcountry Ranger Stations, most of them near points of entry, operated mid-June to Labor Day.

Sequoia became a National Park in 1890, the same year as Yosemite. General Grant National Park was also established that year, a small area around Grant Grove. In 1940 Kings Canyon National Park was established, incorporating General Grant National Park.

Plants: At elevations below 4,000 ft., chaparral on the lower slopes, blue oak and California buckeye in the valleys and on the higher slopes. In this zone: manzanita, ceanothus, mountain mahogany, live oak, poison oak. Flowering species include lupine, yucca, monkeyflower, bush poppy, blazing star, paintbrush, fiddleneck, miner's lettuce, popcorn flower, brodiaea, California poppy, wild iris, fiesta flowers, baby blue eyes.

From 4,000 to 9,000 ft., forests of red and white firs; sugar, Jeffrey, and ponderosa pines; incense cedar, and the giant sequoias. Understory species include rabbitbrush, kit-kit-dizze, bitter cherry, birchleaf mountain mahogany, greenleaf manzanita, serviceberry, wallflower. The giant sequoia occurs only on the W slopes of the Sierra Nevada, in scattered sites or groves. The 75 groves each contain from less than a dozen to many thousands of individual trees. 92% of the sequoia lands are in public ownership, more than 2/3 in National Parks. The largest specimen, the General Sherman tree, is in Sequoia National Park. It is 2,500–3,000 years old, 275 ft. tall, 36 1/2 ft. in diameter.

Above 9,000 ft. is the high country, an area of lakes and meadows, some open forest, and bare rock. Trees of this zone include whitebark and lodgepole pines, mountain hemlock, foxtail pine. Wildflowers of the mountain meadows include gentians, geraniums, buttercups, shooting star, blue-eyed Mary, elephant's head, alpine aster, camas, penstemons, paintbrush, lupines, heathers.

Birds: Checklist published by Sequoia Natural History Association. Species in the foothills include California quail, scrub jay, house finch, lesser goldfinch, Bewick's wren, wrentit, woodpecker, brown towhee, ash-throated and dusky flycatchers, Say's phoebe, California thrasher, western bluebird; sage, white-crowned, golden-crowned, fox, and black-chinned sparrows. In the forest zone: great horned, flammulated, and spotted owls; goshawk, Cooper's and red-shouldered hawks, common flicker; pileated, hairy, and white-headed woodpeckers; yellow-bellied sapsucker, Hammond's and olive-sided flycatchers, wood pewee, Steller's jay, raven, white-breasted and red-breasted nuthatches, winter wren, American robin, hermit thrush, Townsend's solitaire, golden-crowned kinglet, warbling and solitary vireos. Warblers include: Nashville, yellow, yellow-rumped, black-throated gray, hermit, MacGillivray's. Also western tanager, black-headed and evening grosbeaks, purple and Cassin's finches, dark-eyed junco, chipping and Lincoln's sparrows, mountain quail, blue grouse.

Mammals: Species frequently seen include cottontail, California ground squirrel, California gray squirrel, yellow-bellied marmot, black bear, California mule deer. Also resident: mountain beaver, mountain lion, bobcat, coyote, several chipmunk species, pocket gophers, Heermann kangaroo rat, beaver, pika, jackrabbits, porcupine, shrews, bats, ringtail, raccoon, marten, fisher, long-tailed weasel, wolverine, badger, spotted and striped skunks. A few mountain bighorn in high country.

Reptiles and amphibians: Include California newt, ensatina, slender sala-manders, western and Yosemite toads, Pacific tree frog, yellow-legged frogs, western fence and sagebrush lizards, western whiptail, alligator lizards, rubber boa, ring-necked snake, sharp-tailed snake, racers, gopher snake, common and California mountain kingsnakes, garter snakes, western rattlesnake.

FEATURES

The backcountry is high, with many peaks over 12,000 ft., several over 14,000 ft. Trails often cross high passes, some higher than 12,000 ft. The region has about 1,000 lakes, none large, and many mountain streams. Some of the less difficult trails follow stream valleys. Trailheads are on and at the ends of all access roads. Cedar Grove is a principal trail center. However, many hikers enter the Parks on foot from adjacent National Forests.

Cedar Grove is the center of summer activity in Kings Canyon National Park. The access road follows the Canyon, on the South Fork of the Kings River. Several campgrounds are on the S side of the Canyon. A motor nature trail is on the N side. Hiking trails and overlooks are along the Canyon rim. Features such as Zumwalt Meadow and Roaring River Falls are easily reached on foot. The Mist Falls trail is a strenuous all-day hike.

Grant Grove is on SR 180, about 40 road mi. W of the main body of the Kings Canyon National Park. Several famous trees are here, the Centennial Stump, and the basin where giant trees were cut in the early logging era. Several short trails offer easy day hikes. Somewhat longer is the 10-mi. loop to Redwood Canyon, site of one of the finest sequoia groves.

Giant Forest is the activity center in Sequoia National Park. The largest of all the trees is here, but so are many other giants. The area has campgrounds, a variety of visitor facilities, many trailheads. Many day-hiking opportunities include such features as Moro Rock, a viewpoint, Crescent Meadow, and Sunset Rock, another viewpoint. *Crystal Cave* has conducted tours in season.

Mineral King was added to Sequoia National Park in 1978. It is reached by a narrow, winding road that climbs close to 5,000 ft. in 25 mi. The road has almost 700 curves. Trailers are prohibited. Ranger station is operated Memorial Day–Labor Day. Campground. Many backcountry hikes begin or end here.

INTERPRETATION

Visitor centers are at Grant Grove, Ash Mountain, and Lodgepole. Information, exhibits, publications.

Evening programs are offered at Lodgepole, Grant Grove, Dorst, Mineral King, and Cedar Grove. Notices posted.

Guided walks are scheduled all year in the big-tree areas, in summer at Mineral King and Cedar Grove.

Nature trails are at several points in the main activity areas.

ACTIVITIES

Camping: 13 campgrounds. 1,375 sites. Most are open from Memorial Day until closed by snow in Oct. Potwisha, near the Ash Mountain entrance to Sequoia, Lodgepole, and Azalea campgrounds are open all year. Reservations at Lodgepole only, by Ticketron, Memorial Day–Labor Day.

Hiking, backpacking: About 900 mi. of trails. Wilderness permits required for backcountry travel. Backpackers should have topographic maps, gear suitable for the variety of weather that may be encountered. Trailhead quotas Memorial Day–Labor Day.

Fishing: Many lakes and streams have brook, brown, rainbow, and golden trout.

Horse riding: Saddle horses and pack animals at Giant Forest, Grant Grove, Cedar Grove. Many pack trips originate on the E side, in the Owens Valley, from the Inyo National Forest.

Skiing: At Wolverton, in the Giant Forest area.

Ski touring: Marked trails connect the Giant Forest, Wolverton, and Lodgepole areas with scenic points. Trail guide available. Giant Forest has a ski touring center with instructors, rentals. Backcountry touring is increasingly popular; check with Park Rangers before departure.

PUBLICATIONS

Leaflet with map.

Information pages, mimeo:

The Giant Sequoia and the Coast Redwood.
General Sherman and General Grant—Giant Sequoias.
A Brief History of Sequoia and Kings Canyon National Parks.
Average Temperatures.
A Brief Geologic Story.
A Brief Account of the Wildlife.
Bird checklist.
Mammals checklist.
Reptile and amphibian checklist.
Suggested Hikes.
Suggested backpack trip: Mt. Whitney.
Bearpaw Meadow Sierra Camp and Spur Trips.
Trails of Redwood Canyon.
Campground Information.
Crystal Cave.
How to Survive Your Winter Weekend.

REFERENCES

A list of books, pamphlets, and maps, with prices, is available from the Sequoia Natural History Association, Ash Mountain, Three Rivers, CA

93271. Included are U.S. Geological Survey topographic maps and publications of various publishers. The list includes:

Sequoia-Kings Canyon: The Story Behind the Scenery. $3.50.
Family Fun in Sequoia & Kings Canyon National Parks. $1.95.
Wildflowers of Sequoia-Kings Canyon National Parks. $1.95.
Trails of the Giant Forest Area. 25¢.
Big Stump Trail Guide. 15¢.
Cedar Grove Motor Nature Trail. 25¢.
Trails of Cedar Grove. 25¢.
Congress Trail Guide. 25¢.
Moro Rock. 35¢.
Cascade Creek Trail Guide. 15¢.
Winter Trails of Giant Forest. 25¢.
Crystal Cave. $1.95
Bird checklist. 15¢.

Other references:

Felzer, Ron. *Mineral King.* Berkeley, CA: Wilderness Press, 1972. With 1977 supplement.

Pierce, Bob and Margaret. *Marion Peak.* Berkeley, CA: Wilderness Press, 1972.

Robinson, John W. *Mt. Goddard.* Berkeley, CA: Wilderness Press, 1973.

Robinson, John W. *Mt. Pinchot.* 2nd ed. Berkeley, CA: Wilderness Press, 1978.

Winnett, Thomas. *Mt. Whitney.* 3rd ed. Berkeley, CA: Wilderness Press, 1978.

HEADQUARTERS: Three Rivers, CA 93271; (209) 565-3341. For recorded weather and road information: (209) 565-3351. For backpacking information: (209) 565-3306.

SEQUOIA NATIONAL FOREST
U.S. Forest Service
1,115,375 acres.

E of the San Joaquin Valley between Visalia and Bakersfield. Access routes include SR 190 E from Porterville, SR 155 E from Delano, SR 178 NE from Bakersfield.

At the S end of the Sierra Nevada. From the Kings River on the N to the Kern River and Piute Mountains, near its S boundary. Elevations from 1,000 ft. to 12,000 ft.

The Forest land is in several large units. In the N, a unit adjoins the Sierra National Forest, the Kings River serving as boundary; this unit adjoins Kings Canyon National Park on the E and S.

The largest unit extends from the S boundary of Sequoia National Park beyond Lake Isabella almost to Bakersfield. Its SW corner is crossed by the Kern River. Two smaller units, the Piute and Scodic mountains, are S and E of Lake Isabella. Together the three almost completely surround the lake, although the Forest has no lake frontage and its boundary is generally 3 or more mi. from the lakeshore.

This region is drier than the mountains to the N. Most of the San Joaquin Valley receives less than 8 in. of precipitation annually; Bakersfield has less than 6 in. More moisture is received at higher elevations, but most of the mountain slopes receive no more than 40 in., and desert to semiarid conditions prevail in the Domeland Wilderness on the E side of the Forest, even at relatively high elevations. High roads and trails are blocked by snow in winter, but the hiking season begins a few weeks earlier here than in the Sierra to the N. Several of the Forest campgrounds at low elevations are open all year, and most others open in Apr. or May.

This is the part of the Sierra nearest to the Los Angeles area, and heavy public use is concentrated in the several resort areas, among them Hume Lake and Kern Canyon. The largest of the Forest campgrounds, on good roads in attractive settings, are in demand. Some of the trails, including wilderness trails, show the marks of too many boots. One can find quiet trails, and Rangers can point the way. The choice is more limited, of course, on holiday weekends, greatest out of season.

The Forest is best known for its giant sequoias. Of the 30-odd groves, some have a hundred trees or less, but several have thousands of them. The Boole Tree on Converse Mountain, NW of Hume Lake, is the largest tree in any National Forest, 90 ft. around at the base, 269 ft. tall.

The Forest has over 800 mi. of fishing streams, some of them with fine cascades and waterfalls. Some three dozen small lakes are in the high country. 87-acre Hume Lake is the largest wholly within the Forest. Pine Flat Lake (see entry) is partly within the N sector, but the shoreline and recreation facilities are managed by the U.S. Army Corps of Engineers.

Only the Wilderness Areas and High Sierra Primitive Area are closed to all motorized vehicles. In certain other zones, ORV's may use roads and trails but may not travel crosscountry. A majority of the Forest area, however, is open to ORV's on or off trail, except in special locations.

Many visitors come for sightseeing by car. One popular scenic route is SR 180 E from Fresno, which passes the General Grant Grove, continues through the Forest, and enters Kings Canyon National Park along the South Fork of the Kings River. Another is SR 190 E from Porterville. On a long loop, one can turn S, follow the Kern River to Lake Isabella, then drive to Bakersfield on SR 178. Or, with a Forest map, one can explore the several hundred mi. of Forest roads.

Outstanding waterfalls include Grizzly Falls, N of SR 180 in Kings Canyon; Salmon Creek Falls, E of Sierra Way (Fairview Campground in Kern Canyon); South Creek Falls, W of the Kern River on Forest Highway, from the end of Sierra Way in Kern Canyon.

Plants: More than 2/3 of the Forest is conifer forest. Below 4,000 ft., chaparral and oak woodland. Chaparral species include chamise, white-leaf manzanita, redbud, buckbrush, chaparral whitethorn, silk-tassel, flannelbush. Areas of annual grasses with blue oak. The ponderosa and Jeffrey pine forests are between 4,000 and 7,500 ft., though predominant between 4,500 and 6,500 ft. elevation. Tree species include ponderosa, Jeffrey, and sugar pines, white fir, incense cedar, black oak. Somewhat higher is the fir forest, to 8,500 ft., with red and white firs, lodgepole pine, chinquapin oak. Lodgepole pine and numerous mountain meadows are just below the subalpine forest, where the principal tree species is foxtail pine, related to the bristlecones. Understory species above 5,000 ft. include bitter cherry, bear clover, mountain whitethorn, Sierra gooseberry, squaw currant, green-leaf manzanita, willows, chinquapin oak.

The Forest is the most southern habitat for the giant sequoia and foxtail pine. Numerous old-growth stands of these and red fir. Virgin stands of all of the principal conifers of the Forest can be observed.

No plant checklist is available, but over 2,500 species are known to occur in the southern Sierra. Principal display species here include buckeye, redbud, quaking aspen, flannel bush, California lilac, dogwood, many wildflowers. Best flowering season is usually Mar.–Apr. in the foothills, May–June from 4,500 to 6,500 ft., July in the next higher region, to 8,500 ft., Aug. in the subalpine zone.

Birds: Checklist available. Seasonally common and abundant species include turkey vulture; sharp-shinned, Cooper's, and red-tailed hawks; kestrel, blue grouse, band-tailed pigeon, mourning dove, great horned owl, poor-will, common nighthawk, white-throated swift; Anna's, rufous, and calliope hummingbirds, common flicker; acorn, Nuttall's, and white-headed woodpeckers; ash-throated flycatcher, western wood pewee, horned lark, violet-green swallow, Steller's and scrub jays, common crow, Clark's nutcracker, mountain chickadee, plain titmouse, common bushtit, white-breasted and red-breasted nuthatches, wrentit, dipper; house, Bewick's, and rock wrens; mockingbird, American robin, hermit thrush, western and mountain bluebirds, golden-crowned and ruby-crowned kinglets, warbling vireo. Warblers include Nashville, yellow, yellow-rumped, MacGillivray's, Wilson's. Also western meadowlark, red-winged blackbird, northern oriole, western tanager, blackheaded grosbeak; purple, Cassin's, and house finches; pine siskin, lesser goldfinch, green-tailed towhee, dark-eyed junco; chipping, white-crowned, golden-crowned, fox, and song sparrows. Around water: pied-billed grebe, great blue heron, mallard, pintail, redhead, ring-necked duck, ruddy duck, coot.

Mammals: Regional checklist available. Species include opossum; various bats, shrews, mice; snowshoe hare, white-tailed jackrabbit, cottontail, Belding and golden-mantled ground squirrels, pika, California gray squirrel, northern flying squirrel, porcupine, striped and spotted skunks, raccoon, ringtail, black bear, badger, coyote, bobcat, mountain lion, California mule deer. Present but seldom seen: wolverine, fisher, marten, red fox.

Reptiles and amphibians: Include California newt, ensatina, California slender salamander, Sierra Nevada salamander, western toad, Pacific treefrog, mountain yellow-legged frog, western fence and sagebrush lizards, southern and northern alligator lizards, western whiptail lizard, rubber boa, striped racer, gopher snake, California mountain kingsnake, garter snakes, western rattlesnake.

FEATURES

Golden Trout Wilderness, 305,484 acres, 36% in the Sequoia National Forest. It adjoins the S boundary of the John Muir Wilderness. Further W, the Wilderness adjoins the S boundary of Sequoia National Park. W part is a large drainage basin surrounded by high, rugged mountains, E part is an extension of the Kern Plateau. Elevations from 4,800 ft. at the Forks of Kern to 12,432 ft. at Mt. Florence, at the borderline of the Mineral King area, and 12,900 ft. at Cirque Peak in the Inyo National Forest, at the John Muir Wilderness boundary. Many mountain streams, flowing to the Kern River and its South Fork. Portions of the area are above timberline. The Pacific Crest Trail crosses. For season and trail information, consult the Tule River or Cannell Meadow Ranger District (see following descriptions) or the Mt. Whitney Ranger District in Inyo National Forest. Wilderness permit required.

Dome Land Wilderness, 62,695 acres, is the southernmost Wilderness Area in the Sierra. At the S end of the Kern Plateau, the area is on the E boundary of the Forest, N of SR 178. The Forest map shows no trail entering from the S. Trailheads are at Big Meadow and Taylor Meadow on the W, both accessible from Kernville via the Sierra Highway and Cherry Hill Rd., and at Long Canyon in the E. Elevations from 3,000 ft. to 9,730 ft. Climate is desert to semiarid, but several perennial streams flow through the area. Vegetation is mostly mixed conifer and pinyon. The name derives from the many granite domes in the area. Wilderness permit required.

Note that Owens Peak and Chimney Creek Recreation Areas (BLM) are adjacent. (See entry in CA zone 8.)

High Sierra Primitive Area, 11,656 acres, is part of a proposed Monarch Wilderness. At the NE corner of the northern unit of the Forest, just N of the Kings River, with the Kings Canyon National Park backcountry on its N and E boundaries. The area is dramatically scenic, rising from 4,300 ft. at the river to 11,077 ft. at Hogback Peak. Terrain is so steep and rugged that trail access is limited. From SR 180, the Deer Cove Trail climbs over 3,000 ft. in 4 mi., on a S-facing slope. This trail gives access to Wildman Meadow, Grizzly Lakes, and the National Park. The lakes are small, shallow, have no fish. Grizzly Creek and Silver Creek are the principal drainages. Wilderness permit and trail information: Hume Lake Ranger District (see following description).

Kern Canyon is a popular resort area. SR 178 from Bakersfield follows the Kern River to Isabella Lake. Three Forest campgrounds are on this part of the river, as well as private resorts. The U S Army Corps of Engineers manages the lake and has 9 campgrounds around it. N of the lake, the Sierra Highway follows the Canyon. The Kern Canyon Information Station is 2 mi. N of Kernville, at the entrance of the Upper Kern Canyon Recreation Area, which includes 15 Forest campgrounds as well as private resorts.

The Hume Lake area is also popular, accessible all year. The access road, SR 180, passes through the Grant Grove section of Kings Canyon National Park. The lake, only 87 acres in size, is the center of an area with numerous attractions, notably the giant sequoias. Kings Canyon is more than 7,000 ft. deep at its deepest point. Buck Rock Lookout offers splendid views. SR 180 continues into the main portion of Kings Canyon National Park. At Grant Grove, Generals Highway turns S into Sequoia National Park.

Includes: Mountain Home State Forest (see entry).

Dome Rock, 7,221 ft. high, is 4 mi. S of Quaking Aspen. The Rock is a massive granite monolith. Splendid vistas from the top.

ACTIVITIES

Camping: 55 campgrounds. 1,189 sites. Several open all year; others open Apr. or May. No reservations.

Hiking, backpacking: Over 1,300 mi. of trails, in all parts of the Forest. The Forest map shows numbered and maintained trails, but it is advisable to consult Ranger Districts for current conditions, routes, destinations. The Pacific Crest Trail crosses the Forest for about 78 mi.; portions are under construction, but temporary routes are available.

Summit, a National Recreation Trail, is about 12 mi. long. It crosses SR 190 about 1/2 mi. W of Quaking Aspen campground. Cornell Meadow, a 9-mi. trail, begins on Sierra Way 1 mi. N of Kernville. Jackass Creek Trail, 3 mi., begins 1 mi. N of Fish Creek Campground. The latter two are also National Recreation Trails.

Hunting: Deer, bear, small game.

Fishing: Most streams and lakes. Golden trout in some high-country streams.

Kayaking, rafting: Commercial raft trips on Kings River begin 3 1/2 mi. above Mill Flat Campground. This section considered suitable for kayaks, not open canoes. Rafting above this stretch should not be attempted. Whitewater trips also available on most of the Kern River.

Horse riding: Packers and stables at several points adjoining the Forest. HQ and Ranger Districts can provide current list.

Skiing: Ski area at Shirley Meadow. Dec.–Mar., weekends and holidays only, if snow is sufficient.

Ski touring: Stony Creek-Big Meadows and Quaking Aspen areas.

PUBLICATIONS

Forest map. $1.00.

Recreation facilities booklet.

Species checklists.

Fact sheets:

Golden Trout Wilderness.

Domeland Wilderness.

High Sierra Primitive Area.

Recreation information:

Kern Canyon area.

Hume Lake area.

Off-road vehicle map.

HEADQUARTERS: 900 W. Grand Ave., Porterville, CA 93257; (209) 784-1500.

RANGER DISTRICTS: Hume Lake R.D., 36273 E. Kings Canyon Rd., Dunlap, CA 93621; (209) 338-2251. Tule River R.D., 32588 Highway 190, Porterville, CA 93257; (209) 539-2607. Hot Springs R.D., Rt. 4, Box 548, California Hot Springs, CA 93207; (805) 548-6503. Greenhorn R.D., Rm. 322 Federal Building, 800 Truxtun Ave., Bakersfield, CA 93301; (805) 861-4212. Cannell Meadow R.D., P.O. Box 6, Kernville, CA 93238; (714) 376-2294; recreation information May 15–Oct. 15: (714) 376-6261.

SIERRA NATIONAL FOREST

U.S. Forest Service

See entry, Zone 6.

SUCCESS LAKE

U.S. Army Corps of Engineers

2,450 water acres.

From SR 99 at Tipton, E 5 mi. beyond Porterville on SR 190.

A flood control project on the Tule River, about 7 mi. W of the Sequoia National Forest. In the foothills of the Sierra Nevada, with fine views of the mountains. Elevation is about 650 ft. Low hills surround the lake covered with annual grasses, shrubs, many wildflowers. The lake is 3 1/2 mi. long, has 30 mi. of shoreline. The site is heavily used for camping and water-based recreation. However, around two arms of the lake in the NW, the Corps has set aside 1,400 acres as a roadless wildlife management area. The Corps reports that many sightings of California condor have occurred above the hills in the NW.

Camping: 104 sites. All year. Also a primitive camping area.

HEADQUARTERS: Porterville, CA 93257, (209) 784-0215.

VOLCANIC TABLELANDS
U.S. Bureau of Land Management
36,000 acres.

N of Bishop, on US 395.

From about 3 mi. N of Bishop to Mono Lake, most of the area between the E and W portions of the Inyo National Forest is BLM land. This entry concerns the S portion. An improved road along the Owens River is part of the S boundary. An unpaved road from Bishop NW to Casa Diablo Mountain crosses the area.

A series of lava flows built the tablelands above the valley floor. They appear as a wall standing N of Bishop, the river at its base. The road to Casa Diablo Mountain has a series of drops over the edges of terraces, then climbing over the lip of the next terrace. Numerous canyons and drainages dissect the E portion.

The land becomes steeper and more rugged in the NW, rising to 7,912-ft. Casa Diablo Mountain, just across the National Forest boundary.

Fish Slough has a perennial water source. It is noted for its populations of Owens Valley pupfish, an endangered species. Other features include Chidago and Red Rock Canyons. A road passes through Red Rock Canyon, a narrow cut with some nearly vertical walls, often colorful.

Vegetation is sparse, low shrubs, cholla, and annual plants at the lower elevations, some juniper on higher slopes. The open terrain provides splendid, sweeping views of the Sierra Nevada to the W and White Mountains to the E. Striking visual effects are provided by the low sun angle morning and evening.

HEADQUARTERS: BLM, Bakersfield District Office, 800 Truxtun, Rm. 302, Bakersfield, CA 93301; (805) 861-4191.

ZONE 8

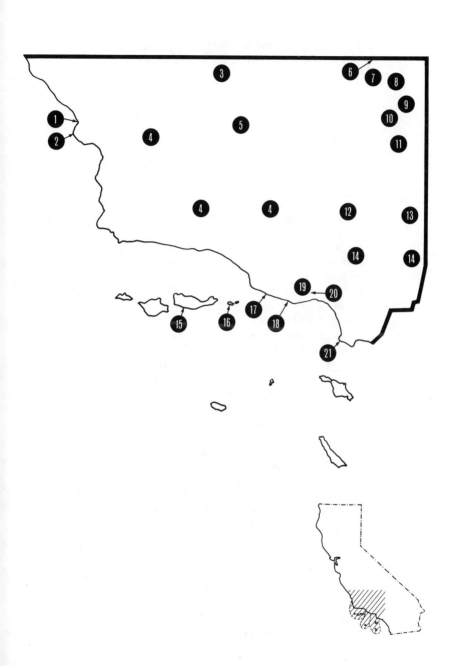

CALIFORNIA, ZONE 8

Includes these counties:

San Luis Obispo	Santa Barbara	Los Angeles
Kern	Ventura	

Zone 8 extends from the ocean to the Mojave Desert, from San Simeon to Long Beach. A population of 8.5 million lives here, and the pressure on most outdoor recreation sites is intense.

The S end of the Sierra Nevada is in the NE corner of the zone. Several large blocks of the Sequoia National Forest surround Isabella Lake; because most of this Forest is in zone 7, the entry appears there.

The largest public land areas in the zone are the Los Padres and Angeles National Forests. Both are heavily used, but one need not follow the crowds. Each has extensive backcountry. Backpacking is popular, but with a bit of advice from the Rangers one can find times and places to enjoy the hills without too much company.

US 101 and SR 1 take turns serving as the Coast Highway, although in several places neither is near the beach. Weekend and holiday traffic is likely to be heavy, and beaches near the city are crowded whenever the sun shines. We have not written entries for beach sites as such. It is enough to say that on weekdays, out of season, driving the Coast Highway can be pleasant, and one may have a choice of beaches for easy hiking. We have included several coastal sites that extend back into the hills.

S and E of the Sierra Nevada is desert. Although the largest areas of California desert are in zones 7 and 9, a number of interesting sites are here. Many motion pictures have been made in the colorful Red Rock Canyon area. At Saddleback Butte, one can see many Joshua trees and, perhaps, a desert tortoise.

ABALONE COVE ECOLOGICAL RESERVE
California Department of Fish and Game
124 acres.

Coast of Rancho Palos Verdes, S of Los Angeles. Seaward of Palos Verdes Drive South, E of Sea Cove Drive.

Concentration of geological, biological, historical, and archeological resources unique to this peninsula. Beach and offshore area set aside for preservation and public observation of natural marine environment. The cove, protected from most storms, had the last naturally occurring giant kelp; the species is now restored.

ANACAPA ISLAND ECOLOGICAL RESERVE
California Department of Fish and Game
9,114 acres.

Ocean waters adjacent to Anacapa Island, 10.6 nautical mi. SW of Port Hueneme.

See entry for Channel Islands National Monument. These waters were part of the Monument until a U.S. Supreme Court decision held that submerged lands and waters within 1 nautical mi. of the island are state property. The Monument entry describes the complex.

ANGELES NATIONAL FOREST
U.S. Forest Service
652,704 acres of Forest land; 693,452 acres within boundaries.

Northern Los Angeles County. Numerous access routes, including roads N from Foothill Blvd. and I-210.

Two large blocks. The Saugus Unit is N of Saugus, W of Palmdale. The Main Unit includes the San Gabriel Mountains from the San Fernando Valley E to San Bernardino County and the San Bernardino National Forest. Mountainous. The highest point is 10,064-ft. Mt. Baldy. The Forest adjoins a huge metropolitan area and receives over 15,000,000 visitors a year, yet it includes roadless areas, secluded canyons, peaks reached only by energetic hikers. The Forest includes the watersheds of four rivers: Los Angeles, San Gabriel, Santa Clara, and Mojave. It has 189 mi. of fishing streams and eight lakes, four of them natural.

Two-fifths of the many visitors have just come for the ride, sightseeing along one of the Forest's scenic drives. Second in popularity is picnicking, while third, somewhat surprisingly, is winter sports. The Forest has nine winter sports areas. Hikers and backpackers from the Los Angeles area are attracted because the Forest is nearby and many trails are open in the spring, when the high country of the Sierra Nevada is still deep in snow.

Annual precipitation ranges from more than 30 in. on the high ridges to less than 15 in. on the lower N slopes. Summers are hot and dry. The fire season usually begins about May 1, after which fire permits are required. Restrictions become tighter as the fire hazard increases. In extreme circumstances, parts of the Forest may be closed.

Plants: Diverse terrain, together with a range of soil and moisture conditions, produces a variety of plant communities, marked changes occurring as one rounds a bluff or crosses a ridge line. In general, the lower slopes, including most of the Forest acreage, have thickets of chaparral: chamise, toyon, buckthorn, scrub oak, mountain mahogany, yucca, wild lilac, ceanothus, manzanita. Higher, generally above 5,500 ft., slopes are forested, tree species including incense cedar, Douglas-fir; ponderosa, sugar, Jeffrey, and limber pines; white fir, golden cup oak, interior live oak, white alder. Understory includes yerba santa, yucca, coffeeberry, rabbitbrush, willow, elderberry, ironwood, mountain mahogany, bush penstemon, manzanita, poison oak. The numerous wildflowers include California goldenrod, blue-eyed grass, Indian paintbrush, prickly phlox, prickly poppy, beards tongue, wild orchid, snakeweed, scarlet bugler, snow plant, Indian tobacco.

Ancient limber pines, over 2,000 years old, occur near timberline, above 8,000 ft. elevation, on Mt. Baden-Powell to Mt. Burnham and Throop Peak.

Birds: Checklist available. Around lakes and reservoirs: great blue heron, mallard, green-winged teal, canvasback, ring-necked duck, American merganser, baldpate, American coot, killdeer, spotted sandpiper, black phoebe. Common species of forested and brush areas include Cooper's, red-tailed, and sharp-shinned hawks; mountain and California quail, band-tailed pigeon, screech and great horned owls, poor-will, white-throated swift, black-chinned and Anna's hummingbirds, common flicker, hairy and Nuttall's woodpeckers, ash-throated and western flycatchers, wood pewee; violet-green, rough-winged, and cliff swallows; Steller's and scrub jays, mountain chickadee, plain titmouse, bushtit, wrentit, Bewick's and canyon wrens, mockingbird, California thrasher, western bluebird, yellow warbler, Bullock's oriole, western tanager, black-headed grosbeak, lesser and Lawrence's goldfinches, spotted and brown towhees, dark-eyed junco, white-crowned and song sparrows.

Mammals: Include ground squirrel, gray squirrel, cottontail, raccoon, striped skunk, coyote, bobcat, gray fox, black bear, mule deer.

Reptiles and amphibians: Include California newt, alligator and whiptailed lizards, horned toad, coral kingsnake, gopher snake, Pacific rattlesnake.

FEATURES

San Gabriel Wilderness, 36,118 acres, on the S slope of the San Gabriel Mountains, from the Angeles Crest down to the West Fork of the San Gabriel River, between SR 2 and SR 39. Scenic, rugged terrain; elevations from 1,600 ft. to 8,200 ft. Much of the area is covered with chaparral, often in dense thickets. Mixed pine and fir along the ridgetops. Several trails, moderate to strenuous, lead to the interior, where off-trail hiking is feasible in some places. Fishing is said to be good in several streams. Wilderness permit is required.

Sheep Mountain roadless area, 30,100 acres. E of the San Gabriel Wilderness, separated from it by the Crystal Lake Recreation Area. Wilderness status proposed. Includes Mt. Baldy, 10,064 ft., and Mt. Baden-Powell, 9,399 ft. Numerous streams, including the East Fork, San Gabriel River. Chaparral, montane forest, and southern mixed evergreen forest. Stands of ancient limber pine. Wildlife includes a herd of Nelson bighorn sheep.

Fish Canyon roadless area, 32,900 acres, in the N central portion of the Saugus Unit. Wilderness status is proposed. Rugged. Steep-walled canyons. Dense chaparral thickets. Large stand of black oak. Fish Canyon is a flight area for the California condor. According to the Forest map dated 1977, this is part of a larger area that has been open to ORV travel. Several roads penetrate the area to campgrounds; these corridors are excluded from the wilderness proposal.

Cucamonga roadless area, 4,400 acres. This is a proposed addition to the Cucamonga Wilderness in the adjacent San Bernardino National Forest (see entry). It lies immediately E of Mt. Baldy, S of Thunder Mountain.

Pyramid Lake, about 3 mi. long, lies between the W boundary of the Saugus Unit and the Los Padres National Forest, beside I-5. It is heavily used for boating, fishing, and swimming. Boats must conform to a one-way traffic pattern. Day use only.

Crystal Lake is the principal center in the Main Unit, on SR 39. The lake is only a pond. The main campground has 233 sites and others are nearby. The complex includes Ranger Station, store, visitor center, nature trails, amphitheater, hiking trails. The area lies between the San Gabriel Wilderness and the proposed Sheep Mountain wilderness; trails into both.

Charlton-Cilao Recreation Area is just W of the San Gabriel Wilderness, on the Angeles Crest Highway, SR 2. It has a large campground, Ranger Station, inn, amphitheater, trails.

The Angeles Crest Highway, SR 2, is the principal scenic route in the Forest, from La Canada on I-210 NE to Big Pines. The Angeles Forest Highway, N-3, branches off to the N 9 mi. from La Canada.

INTERPRETATION

Visitor centers are at Red Box (on SR 2), San Gabriel Canyon entrance station on SR 39, Pyramid Lake, and San Fernando.

Naturalist programs, in summer at the major recreation centers, include *campfire programs, guided walks.*

An *auto tour* begins at the Big Pines Area on Sunday mornings in summer.

Nature trails are at several recreation areas.

Interpretive signs are fixed along SR 2 and SR 39.

ACTIVITIES

Camping: 64 campgrounds. 1,173 sites. Most open all year.

Hiking, backpacking: 556 mi. of trails. 28-mi. Gabrielino Trail links 7 campgrounds, crosses diverse habitats from canyon bottoms to forested ridgetops. Pacific Crest Trail from the N runs close to N boundary of Saugus Unit, enters Main Unit, continues into San Bernardino NF.

Hunting: Deer, quail. Discharge of firearms prohibited near roads, recreation areas, etc.

Fishing: Lakes and streams. Some water stocked with rainbow trout.

Swimming: Facilities at three lakes. Usual season May 1–Oct. 1.

Boating: Pyramid Lake and Castaic Lake. On Elizabeth Lake, motors of 10 hp or less.

Horseback riding: On most trails.

Skiing: 9 winter sports areas.

Ski touring: Trails and unplowed Forest roads.

Smoking is prohibited except in camp and picnic areas, other approved locations.

Roads are sometimes closed by snow, rainstorm, mudslides.

ADJACENT: Los Padres and San Bernardino National Forests.

PUBLICATIONS

Forest map.

Forest facts.

Trees of the Angeles National Forest.

Bird checklist.

Flora-Fauna of Crystal Lake.

Pyramid Lake leaflet.

Recreation Area Information—Saugus Ranger District.

Self-Guided Hiking Tour of Historic Mt. Lowe.

San Gabriel Wilderness information.

Gabrielino Trail information.

REFERENCE: Robinson, John W. *Trails of the Angeles.* Berkeley, CA: Wilderness Press, 1979.

HEADQUARTERS: 150 S. Los Robles, Pasadena, CA 91101; (213) 577-0050; from Los Angeles (213) 684-0350.

RANGER DISTRICTS: Arroyo Seco R.D., Oak Grove Park, Flintridge, CA 91011; (213) 790-1151. Mt. Baldy R.D., 110 N. Wabash Ave., Glendora, CA 91740; (213) 335-1251. Saugus R.D., 23759 W. Valencia Blvd., Rm. 20, Valencia, CA 91355; (805) 259-2790. Tujunga R.D., 12328 Gladstone Ave., San Fernando, CA 91342; (213) 365-9107. Valyermo R.D., 34146 Longview Rd., Pearblossom, CA 93553; (805) 944-2187.

ANTELOPE VALLEY CALIFORNIA POPPY PRESERVE
California Department of Parks and Recreation
1,630 acres.

From Lancaster on SR 14 (N of Pasadena), 15 mi. W on Ave. I.

An extraordinary floral display, poppies and other species, in mid-spring. Small, rolling hills; area of disturbed grassland.

CHANNEL ISLANDS NATIONAL PARK
U.S. National Park Service
1,120 land acres.

By commercial boat from Ventura or private boat.

Of the eight Channel Islands off the southern CA coast, five are included in the National Park. *San Miguel,* the one furthest W of Ventura, is owned by the U.S. Navy, but administered by the Park Service. Landing by special permit. No regularly scheduled public transportation. Some of the surrounding waters are part of an ecological reserve and are closed to boats.

Anacapa is a chain of three islands, about 5 mi. long, S of Ventura. West Anacapa, the largest, rises abruptly from the sea to two peaks, the higher 930 ft. elevation.* East and Middle Anacapa have rolling plateaus almost entirely

---

*The illustration in the Monument leaflet makes East Anacapa appear many times larger than West Anacapa. The reason, we learned, is that it was taken from an aerial photo showing East Anacapa in the foreground, West in the far distance.

surrounded by cliffs 90–300 ft. high. Travel from one island to another is by boat only. The commercial boat lands only at East Anacapa and Frenchy's Cove on West Anacapa. A nature trail and campground are on East Anacapa.

Island vegetation is short and scrubby, appearing brown and lifeless until the winter rains come. Past farming, grazing, and burning almost eliminated most native plant species, but there is now a slow recovery.

The boat from Ventura, weather permitting, allows day visitors 2 1/2–3 hrs. ashore. This is ample time to explore East Anacapa, because there are only 2 mi. of trails and visitors must stay on the trails. The islands have no beaches, and the cliffs at East Anacapa prevent any approach to the shore by land except at the landing. A nature trail covers most of the island, noting points of interest, from the giant kelp in Cathedral Cove to the giant coreopsis, or tree sunflower, which grows only here and in isolated stands along the mainland Coast.

The islands are rookeries for seabirds, including a large brown pelican nesting site. Sea lions and harbor seals are often seen around Anacapa, although they are more abundant around Santa Barbara Island. In Dec.–Mar. the annual gray whale migration passes close to Anacapa.

Visitors who come by private boat can anchor at Frenchy's Cove on Middle Anacapa, picnic ashore, and enjoy the activity in nearby tidepools. Scuba diving off West Anacapa is popular. Several caves can be explored by skiff when waters are calm.

Camping is permitted on East Anacapa, in a small campground limited to 30 people. Everything, including water, must be carried up 152 steps and 3/8 mi. uphill by trail. Extra food should be brought in the event that weather delays the boat. Gear should be adequate for strong winds, wet fog, unshaded sun. A free camping permit must be obtained from HQ in advance of visit.

Santa Barbara Island, about 640 acres, is SW of Los Angeles. There is no regularly scheduled boat service. Groups often arrange charter trips, and individuals can often arrange to join one. Like Anacapa, Santa Barbara is almost entirely surrounded by cliffs, some more than 500 ft. high. The island has two hills, the highest 635 ft. elevation. Caves, coves, offshore pillars, blowholes.

Here, too, native plants were almost eliminated by past abuse. Introduced species, notably grasses and iceplant, are prominent. The giant coreopsis is here in small stands. Native vegetation is slowly recovering.

Sea mammals are abundant, mostly California sea lions and harbor seals. A few elephant seals appear in late summer and fall. Whales in migration are often seen. Western gulls nest in large numbers. Birds include brown pelican, burrowing owl, horned lark, scoter, black oystercatcher. Early summer is best birding season.

Santa Barbara has about 5 mi. of trails, and visitors must stay on them. Access to the shore is at the landing cove only, and swimming from shore is possible only here; the beach is stony. Some tidepools can be explored from the land side.

A primitive campground is available, occupancy limited to 30. Everything, including water, must be carried in up a steep trail. A free camping permit must be obtained from HQ in advance of visit.

INTERPRETATION

Visitor center is on the mainland, at Ventura. Information, exhibits, publications, interpretive slide program, and films are available.

Park rangers are stationed on Anacapa, San Miguel, and Santa Barbara islands. *Campfire programs* when enough people are camping and weather permits. *Guided hikes* can also be arranged.

ACTIVITIES

Camping: See preceding descriptions.

Fishing: From boats. The surrounding waters are a state ecological reserve, and special regulations govern fishing and diving for invertebrates. Inquire.

Swimming: Chiefly from boats. Popular scuba area.

Boating: Visiting the islands by private boat should be undertaken only by people with experience in these waters. Islands have anchorages but no docks. Skiff needed to go ashore.

Pets are not permitted.

PUBLICATIONS

Leaflet.

Camping information.

Excursion information.

HEADQUARTERS: 1901 Spinnaker Dr., Ventura, CA 93001; (805) 644-8157 or 485-4525.

FOR BOAT EXCURSION INFORMATION: Island Packers Co., 1695 Anchors Way, Ventura, CA 93003; (805) 642-1393 or 642-3370.

CHIMNEY PEAK RECREATION AREA; OWENS PEAK AREA

U.S. Bureau of Land Management
About 75,000 acres.

SR 178 is the S boundary, from about 15 mi. E of Isabella Lake to Walker Pass. N boundary is Nine Mile Canyon Rd., W of US 395 about 12 1/2 mi. N of Inyokern. On the W the area adjoins the Sequoia National Forest.

This area straddles the Sierra Crest. Part of it is in zone 7. Easiest access to the Chimney Peak area is in zone 7: Nine Mile Canyon Rd. W to 1/4 mi. beyond the BLM fire station, then S and follow signs. The Owens Peak area is roadless, recommended for wilderness designation. The 8,475-ft. peak is about 8 mi. N of Walker Pass. The Owens Peak area is E of the Sierra Crest and has desert-type qualities. The Chimney Peak area is generally W of the crest.

Elevations range from about 3,000 ft. to the highest point, Owens Peak. Chimney Peak, in the N part of the area, is 7,990 ft. Several other peaks along this section of the crest are above 7,500 ft. The Pacific Crest Trail follows the crest through much of this area.

The ridge rises abruptly from sagebrush meadows to rocky peaks. Numerous canyons. Some valleys are relatively open and flat, others enclosed by steep slopes.

The climate is semiarid. Winters are cold, and snow covers the area, but not for long. Snow is neither as deep nor as long-lived as in more N parts of the Sierra. Summer daytime temperatures are in the 80's, summer nights cool.

The Chimney Peak area adjoins the Dome Land Wilderness of Sequoia National Forest. Its campgrounds and parking areas serve as bases for hikers and equestrians entering the wilderness.

Plants: Creosote and associated desert shrubs with scattered yucca in the valleys and bajadas. Further up the canyons: yucca, cacti, desert shrubs, annuals, cottonwood. Much of the Chimney Peak area is in the pinyon-juniper woodland community. Some ponderosa pine occurs on N slopes at high elevations. Digger pine and canyon oak occur in many places. Common shrubs include big sage, Mormon tea, silktassle, flannelbush, buckwheat. Near Walker Pass is a Joshua tree woodland.

ACTIVITIES

Camping: Three BLM campgrounds. Over 50 sites. Water available mid-May to Oct.

Hiking, backpacking: From the Chimney Peak area, one can take the Pacific Crest Trail into the National Forest. Wilderness permit is required. In the Owens Peak area, the Pacific Crest Trail has a 7-mi. gap in the Spanish Needles section, and the terrain makes passage impossible. Because of incomplete sections N and S of this site, this portion of the Trail is not yet tied in with the Pacific Crest Trail system. Off-trail hiking is feasible in a number of the valleys and canyons.

Hunting: Deer, quail, dove, rabbit.

PUBLICATION: Chimney Peak Recreation Area leaflet.

HEADQUARTERS: BLM, Bakersfield District, 800 Truxtun, Bakersfield, CA 93301; (805) 861-4191.

DESERT TORTOISE RESEARCH NATURAL AREA

U.S. Bureau of Land Management
14,980 acres + 9,200 acres of nonfederal land.

From Mojave, NE 4 mi. on SR 14. E 10 mi. on California City Blvd. NE
5 1/2 mi. on Randsburg-Mojave Rd.

On the W edge of the Mojave Desert. Elevations from 2,100 ft. to 3,100 ft. A
unique habitat with the densest known population of the desert tortoise, a
burrowing species that often digs long tunnels, winters in a communal den.
Parts of the area have more than 200 tortoises per sq. mi. Because of threats
to the species, the BLM closed the public land to vehicles in 1973. Fence was
erected to exclude livestock. A Desert Tortoise Preserve Committee has
assisted by raising money to buy private land and by providing guided tours
to school and conservation groups.

Plants: Tortoises feed on annual wildflowers and grasses in the spring and
sometimes again in the fall; summers and winters are generally spent underground. Wildflowers are a major attraction of the area. Species include Bigelow coreopsis, goldfields, desert dandelion, Mojave aster, blazing star, phacelia, forget-me-not, lupine, primrose, desert candle, desert trumpet, gilia.

Birds: Species include turkey vulture, red-tailed and marsh hawks, golden
eagle, prairie falcon, kestrel, chukar, roadrunner, burrowing owl, lesser nighthawk, ash-throated flycatcher, Say's phoebe, horned lark, sage sparrow.

Mammals: Include the rare Mojave ground squirrel. Also black-tailed
jackrabbit, cottontail, antelope ground squirrel, desert wood rat, kit fox,
coyote, badger, bobcat.

Reptiles: In addition to the tortoise: desert iguana, chuckwalla; zebra-tailed,
leopard, side-blotched, and desert horned lizards; western whiptail, gopher
snake, red racer, glossy snake, sidewinder, Mojave rattlesnake. The tortoises
are best seen mid-Mar. to mid-June, morning and late afternoon.

INTERPRETATION: *Interpretive center* is near entrance. Signs; exhibits; species
checklists.

*Visitors should stay on marked trails. Tortoises must not be touched or
approached closely. Pets must be leashed, and not taken beyond the parking
lot. Bring water; none is available.*

PUBLICATION: Leaflet.

HEADQUARTERS: California Desert District Office, 1695 Spruce St., Riverside,
CA 92507; (714) 787-1465.

EL PASO MOUNTAINS
U.S. Bureau of Land Management
19,600 acres.

E of SR 14; N of the Red Rock-Randsburg-Garlock Rd.

From 2,000 ft. elevation on the S boundary in Fremont Valley, terrain rises sharply. Numerous reddish-colored buttes and dark, uplifted volcanic mesas. At times the intervening slopes appear golden because of masses of annuals. Highest point is 5,244-ft. Black Mountain. Ridges are generally SW–NE. The terrain descends more gradually in the N to a broad wash at about 3,000 ft. elevation. Slopes are dissected by narrow canyons, creating a badlands appearance. Last Chance Canyon, originating near Saltdale, is deep and winding, with an intermittent stream draining from Black Mountain. Scenic value of the area was rated high.

Vegetation is mostly creosote bush scrub, with a notable array of conspicuous flowering annuals. 22 sq. mi. of the El Paso Raptor Management Area is within the site, one of the principal breeding areas for golden eagle, prairie falcon, and other raptors. Hunting for dove, quail, chukar, and rabbit is said to be good.

The BLM has recommended a roadless area of 19,600 acres for wilderness status. A bordering area of roughly equal size was deemed unsuitable because of access roads and recreational activities, including hunting, rockhounding, camping, and ORV action. The most popular areas are near the lower ends of Last Chance and other canyons.

HEADQUARTERS: BLM, California Desert District Office, 1695 Spruce St., Riverside, CA 92507; (714) 787-1465.

KERN NATIONAL WILDLIFE REFUGE
U.S. Fish and Wildlife Service
10,616 acres.

From Delano on SR 99, 19 mi. W on Garces Highway.
Open: Daylight hours.

Much of the lower San Joaquin Valley was once a large, shallow lake and marsh. When it was drained in the late 1800s, millions of waterfowl and other fauna lost their habitat. The Kern and other federal and state refuges in the Valley were established to restore a small fraction of that habitat. However, the region is dry, receiving only about 7 in. of precipitation yearly, and the refuge has no claim on the water brought to the region for irrigation. Thus the number of waterfowl remaining to nest on the refuge depends on moisture conditions that change from year to year.

Much of the refuge is flat alkali grassland; about 2,500 acres is marsh. A Research Natural Area set aside for study of the grassland community is closed to the public.

The best time to visit the refuge is Oct.–Mar. Summers are hot, dry, and dusty, and in many years summer birding is not impressive. In winter, many waterfowl, shorebirds, and upland species are present.

Birds: Checklist of 199 species available. Seasonally common and abundant species include eared and pied-billed grebes, great blue heron, snowy egret, black-crowned night heron, American bittern, mallard, gadwall, pintail, green-winged and cinnamon teals, American wigeon, northern shoveler, ruddy duck; red-tailed, Swainson's, and marsh hawks; American kestrel, ring-necked pheasant, Virginia rail, sora, common gallinule, American coot, killdeer, common snipe, long-billed curlew, greater and lesser yellowlegs, least and western sandpipers, dowitcher, avocet, black-necked stilt, California and ring-billed gulls, mourning dove, roadrunner; barn, burrowing, and short-eared owls; horned lark; rough-winged, barn, and cliff swallows; common raven, common crow, long-billed marsh wren, loggerhead shrike, yellow-rumped warbler, house sparrow, western meadowlark; yellow-headed, red-winged, and tri-colored blackbirds; western tanager; vesper, lark, white-crowned, and song sparrows.

Hunting: Ducks, geese, coots. Special regulations posted.

NEARBY: Pixley National Wildlife Refuge, 4,131 acres, managed by Kern, is about 20 mi. N. Similar habitat. Open by permit only. Inquire at Kern.

PUBLICATIONS
Site map.
Bird checklist.

HEADQUARTERS: P.O. Box 219, Delano, CA 93216; (805) 725-2767.

LEO CARILLO STATE BEACH
California Department of Parks and Recreation
1,578 acres.

On SR 1, 28 mi. W of Santa Monica.

Rocky Sequit Point divides 1 1/4 mi. of broad sand beach. Close to Los Angeles, the beach is often crowded, and the campground across SR 1 is often at capacity. Mulholland Highway, running inland from SR 1, divides the camping area from the largest section of the park, undeveloped except for a trail. At the foot of the Santa Monica Mountains, this is about 1,000 acres of upland, elevations to 1,500 ft., heavily wooded with Coast live oak, California sycamore, willow, sumac, poison oak. Wildlife includes gray fox, coyote, mule deer, raccoon, skunk, bobcat, various rodents.

Camping: 138 sites. All year. Reservations May 18–Oct. 1.

PUBLICATION: Leaflet.

HEADQUARTERS: Santa Monica Mountains Area, P.O. Box 2678, Oxnard, CA 93034; (213) 457-5538; (805) 488-4111.

LOS PADRES NATIONAL FOREST
U.S. Forest Service
1,751,698 acres; 1,963,249 acres within boundaries.

Mountains of the central CA Coast. The smaller of two sections is on or near the Coast and SR 1 between Point Sur and San Simeon. This section is in zone 5. The larger is N and E of Santa Barbara, crossed by SR 166, SR 33, and SR 154.

Most of the mountainous land near the central Coast of California is within this National Forest. The smaller unit includes the Santa Lucia Mountains. The larger includes the La Panza, Santa Ynez, San Rafael, and Sierra Madre mountains. Elevations from sealevel to 8,831-ft. Mt. Pinos. On the E, the Forest adjoins the Angeles National Forest. Close to the Los Angeles area, the Forest receives great numbers of visitors.

Although about 1/3 of the area is forested, this is not a timber-producing forest. Trees are cut only to maintain or improve the stand. Steep slopes, thin soils, and a generally dry climate are unfavorable for tree growth. The Forest's chief economic value is as a supplier of water to the towns and cities of the Coast and valleys. The Big Sur, Carmel, Salinas, Santa Maria, Santa Ynez, Santa Clara, and Ventura rivers originate in the Forest. 35 lakes and reservoirs larger than 5 acres are on or adjacent to Forest land.

This Forest is highly vulnerable to fire. Seldom does a summer pass without a fire in this region making news across the country. Firefighting is highly organized and effective. Two large areas, shown on the Forest map, are closed to visitors every year during the fire season, July 1 (or earlier) to about Nov. 15.

Smoking is forbidden throughout the Forest, at all times, except in designated places. Permits are required for fires or camp stoves except at established camp and picnic grounds accessible by road.

Pleasure driving is the chief recreation use of the Forest. The number of motorists cited—5,000,000 per year—is so high because the Coast Highway, SR 1, passes through. 18 mi. of it are within the Forest. But the Forest has 1,611 mi. of roads in its internal system, and it is not difficult to escape traffic.

On fine weekends and holidays, the larger campgrounds, picnic areas, and other developed sites are overloaded. Sites on water are especially in demand. A car camper may be able to find an isolated spot that's uncrowded, but only if he knows the Forest well or takes time for some back-road exploring. It's not quite so bad on foot. Backcountry visitors are less than 3% as numerous as car campers. Some trails and destinations are popular. Rangers can advise where trail use is lightest.

Climate varies greatly with elevation and terrain. At and near the Coast, annual precipitation is about 16 in. per year. On only a very few days a year does the temperature dip below 32°F, and it is equally unusual for it to rise above 90°. Along the ridges, precipitation is as high as 120 in. per year, and several feet of snow may remain on N-facing slopes in the winter months. The dry season is May–Oct. Across the ridges, in the E part of the Forest, semiarid conditions prevail. Many of the campgrounds are open and accessible all year.

Plants: Only about 30% of the area is forested. Lower slopes are generally chaparral, with such shrubs as scrub oak, poison oak, chamise, and manzanita. Flowering species include dodder vine, Indian paintbrush, owl's clover, monkeyflower, many more. Coast redwood is commonly found along the Coast, except in the extreme S of the Forest. Southern slopes and poorer soils normally support stands of annual grasses, chamise, and sagebrush. Mixed coniferous forests occur at the higher elevations. These stands are described as "esthetic" rather than "commercial productive." Species include Monterey, sugar, Coulter, and ponderosa pines; and white firs. The area has great botanical diversity. Plants identified in the Monterey Ranger District represent more than 3/4 of the vascular plant families found in the entire state. The bristlecone fir, rarest and most unusual North American fir, was discovered on Cone Peak. The Cuesta Ridge Botanical Area, located N of San Luis Obispo, contains one of the larger groves of the Gowan cypress.

Birds: Checklist available, classifying species by abundance, location, and habitat. The Forest is best known for its population of California condor, largest North American land bird, only a few of which remain. Two condor sanctuaries have been established within the Forest. From June through Oct., condors are often seen from the Condor Observation Site on Mt. Pinos and the Squaw Flat Condor Observation Site along the Squaw Flat road corridor in the Sespe Condor Sanctuary. Condors are occasionally seen in flight from other points in the Ojai and Mt. Pinos Ranger Districts.

Species of the grassland and chaparral include white-tailed kite; sharp-shinned, Cooper's, red-tailed, and Swainson's hawks; golden eagle, mountain quail, killdeer, poor-will, white-throated swift; Anna's, rufous, and Allen's hummingbirds; common flicker, dusky flycatcher, scrub jay, house and Bewick's wrens, cedar waxwing, loggerhead shrike, Hutton's and solitary vireos; orange-crowned, yellow, yellow-rumped, black-throated gray, and Wilson's warblers; purple and house finches; chipping, white-crowned, golden-crowned, and song sparrows. Coniferous forest species include band-tailed pigeon, great horned owl, calliope hummingbird; Lewis's, hairy, downy, and white-headed woodpeckers; western and olive-sided flycatchers, western wood pewee, Steller's jay, mountain and chestnut-backed chickadees; white-breasted, red-breasted, and pygmy nuthatches; varied and hermit thrushes; black-throated gray, Townsend's, and hermit warblers; purple and Cassin's finches, dark-eyed junco, chipping sparrow. Many seabirds can be seen on the bays and ocean, within binocular range of the Monterey Ranger District coastline.

Mammals: Include numerous bat species, opossum, various shrews and moles, California ground squirrel, Merriam chipmunk, Valley pocket gopher, California pocket mouse, western harvest mouse, black-tailed jackrabbit, brush rabbit, raccoon, ringtail, badger, coyote, gray fox, wild pig, spotted skunk, black bear, bobcat, mountain lion, California mule deer, Columbian black-tailed deer. Several species escaped from the Hearst Ranch are occasionally seen, including Rocky Mountain elk, tahr, Barbary sheep.

Reptiles and amphibians: Include California tiger salamander, Monterey and yellow-eyed salamanders, California toad, California tree frog; Great Basin, northwestern fence, and blunt-nosed leopard lizards; western skink, alligator lizards, red racer, Coast patch-nosed snake, gopher snakes, California and Coast mountain kingsnakes, garter snakes, Pacific rattlesnake.

FEATURES

San Rafael Wilderness, 149,170 acres, in the San Rafael Mountains N of Santa Barbara. The first primitive area brought into the National Wilderness System, in 1968. Elevations from 1,166 ft. near the junction of Manzana Creek and the Sisquoc River to 6,828 ft. on Big Pine Mountain. Chaparral slopes; pine forest on the highest ridges. The relatively low elevations make this area attractive in winter and spring, when higher mountains are snow-covered. Portions are closed summer and fall because of fire hazard. Deer are plentiful, but fire danger usually prevents entry in hunting season. The 1,200-acre condor sanctuary is closed at all times. Visitor permit is required.

Ventana Wilderness, 161,005 acres, in the Santa Lucia Mountains, inland from the Monterey Coast. Rugged terrain. Elevations from 1,200 ft. on Little

Sur River to 4,833 ft. on Ventana Peak. Lower slopes are chaparral covered. Woodland and timber along many miles of perennial streams. One of the most popular hiking areas. Because of high fire hazard, use of fire and stoves is limited to trail camps. Visitor permit required.

Santa Lucia Wilderness, 21,678 acres, in a narrow arm of the Forest E of San Luis Obispo. Streamside vegetation and chaparral-covered slopes of Lopez Canyon. Perennial stream flows through the canyon to Lopez Reservoir, outside the area. Elevations from 800 ft. along the creek to 3,000 ft. at Hi Mountain Lookout. Canyon trail. Spring and fall months are the most scenic. Visitor permit is required.

Pfeiffer Beach and Sand Dollar Beach are the two principal ocean recreation areas. Swimming is unsafe. Sand Dollar is a popular day-use area. Pfeiffer is a fragment of Forest land near Pfeiffer-Big Sur State Park (see entry).

Santa Ynez River, 6 mi. N of Santa Barbara, E of SR 154. The Paradise-Santa Ynez road follows the river for 5 miles. River hiking trails.

Big and Little Caliente Hot Springs, by dirt road, 25 mi. N of Santa Barbara, off East Camino Cielo Road. Hot springs are 2 1/2 mi. from Pendola Station. Water as hot as 118°F.

East and West Camino Cielo Scenic Drive, 14 mi. N of Santa Barbara. Views of the ocean and front country on one side, backcountry on the other.

INTERPRETATION: According to Forest HQ, "Present programs have been confined to information displays, nature trails, vista points, wildlife observation stations, and occasional evening campfire programs. . . ." No specifics were provided, but new programs were being developed. Best advice is to check at Ranger Districts, campground bulletin boards.

ACTIVITIES

Camping: 88 campgrounds. 986 sites. Many all year, others May 13–Oct. 31. The largest campground has 68 sites. Many have 5 or less.

Hiking, backpacking: 1,762 mi. of trails. 265 trail camps, the only backcountry places where chemical fuel stoves can be used, or fires in the provided stoves. A visitor permit is required to camp anywhere except in one of these trail camps.

Hunting: Deer, outside the fire closure area. Some black bear. Chiefly rabbit, turkey, quail, pigeon, dove, wild pig.

Fishing: 485 mi. of streams. Some native trout, some stocked. Many streams have water only in the wet season.

Swimming: About 14 of the campgrounds have swimming opportunities. Elsewhere, find a pool large enough, swim at your own risk. The ocean is not safe.

Horse riding: Although most visitors hike, some use pack and saddle stock in the wilderness areas. A visitor permit is required.

Ski touring: Mt. Pinos is the most popular area for snow play. A 6-mi. flagged Nordic ski trail begins at the top parking lot. The Mt. Pinos road is sometimes closed, either because new snow has not yet been plowed or because the area is full. People are often turned away on weekends. No winter camping is allowed on the mountain.

Snowmobiling: Prohibited in wilderness areas. Snowmobiles are restricted to unplowed roads.

PUBLICATIONS

Forest map. $1.00.

Recreation information, maps and publications for each Ranger District.

Campground information, for each Ranger District.

Bird checklist.

Campfire restrictions.

California Condor. (Published by National Audubon Society.)

Deer season information.

REFERENCES

Trail Guide to the Los Padres National Forest. Ventana Chapter, Sierra Club, Box 5667, Carmel, CA 93921. U.S. Geological Survey topographic maps and books with information about the area are sold by the Los Padres Interpretive Association, P.O. Box 3502, Santa Barbara, CA 93105. These items are also available for purchase at HQ and at Ranger District Offices (except Monterey).

HEADQUARTERS: 42 Aero Camino St., Goleta, CA 93017; (805) 968-1578.

RANGER DISTRICTS: Monterey R.D., 406 S. Mildred, King City, CA 93930; (408) 385-5434. San Lucia R.D., 1616 N. Carlotti Dr., Santa Maria, CA 93454; (805) 925-9538. Santa Barbara R.D., Star Route, Los Prietos, Santa Barbara, CA 93105; (805) 967-3481. Ojai R.D., 1190 E. Ojai Ave., Ojai, CA 93023; (805) 646-4348. Mt. Pinos R.D., Frazier Park, CA 93225; (805) 245-3731.

MALIBU CREEK STATE PARK
California Department of Parks and Recreation
Over 4,000 acres.

From US 101 about 14 mi. W of I-405, S 4 mi. on Las Virgenes/Malibu Canyon Rd.

Rugged, mainly virgin land in the middle of the Santa Monica Mountains, a site with little development thus far. Mulholland Highway crosses the site, and internal roads open to hikers, but closed to vehicles, follow Malibu Creek, which meanders W to E, dropping from 700 to 500 ft. Numerous small streams join the creek in winter and spring. The creek was dammed years ago to form Century Lake, now about 4 acres. Rainfall averages 20–25 in. a year, most of it in winter. No trails reach the highest and most rugged sector, in the S, with peaks over 2,000 ft.

Plants: From the creek to the N border, mostly sloping grassland with scattered valley oak; some chaparral-covered slopes. Patches of Coast live oak include some over 6 ft. in diameter, with poison oak and some bay laurel trees. Other vegetation includes coffeeberry, ceanothus, currant, snowberry, ferns. Along the creek: willow, sycamore, leatherleaf ash, cottonwood. Some more remote canyons have bigleaf maple. Blackberry, wild rose, and mugwort are also common. Several fine wildflower areas. Late Mar. to early May: California poppy, wild pansy, lupine, goldfield, larkspur, Chinese houses, creamcups, golden currant, gooseberry. Mid-May through June: clarkia, golden yarrow, penstemon, Mariposa lily, Humboldt lily, yucca, ceanothus, bush monkey-flower.

Birds: Checklist on display at Gatehouse. Species reported include some ducks, coot, and great blue heron along the creek and at the lake. Cooper's, red-shouldered, and red-tailed hawks; occasional golden eagle; scrub jay, acorn woodpecker, violet-green swallow, roadrunner. Many migratory species.

Mammals: Include ground squirrels, brush rabbit, coyote, gray fox, mule deer, bobcat, raccoon, skunk, occasional mountain lion.

INTERPRETATION: *Interpretive walks* are led by volunteer guides on weekends and most holidays, weekdays by appointment.

ACTIVITIES
Hiking: 15 mi. of trails. No overnighting.
Horse riding: Combination trails. No facilities.

PUBLICATION: Leaflet with map.

HEADQUARTERS: 28754 Mulholland Highway, Agoura, CA 91301; (213) 991-1827.

MONTANA DE ORO STATE PARK
California Department of Parks and Recreation
Over 10,000 acres.

From San Luis Obispo, 12 mi. NW on Los Osos Valley Rd. to Los Osos, then S 3 mi. on Pecho Rd.

On the ocean, 5 mi. of coastline, most of the upland area undeveloped. The coast has coves, sand beaches, bluffs, tidepools, scenic rock formations. From primary dunes the land rises to flat marine terraces, from which the coastal hills rise to almost 1,700 ft. Between the ridges are wooded valleys, some with streams. A sand spit extending 3 mi. N along the Coast was recently added to the Park and is maintained as a natural area.

The access road enters from the N, runs above and parallel to the beach, with numerous parking areas, from which trails lead down to the shore. This is the only internal road. From several parking areas trails go back into the hills, the longest about 4 1/2 mi. to 1,649-ft. Alan Peak. Trails along Hazard Canyon, Coon Creek, and Islay Creek; Islay has a small waterfall.

Plants: Steep hills are covered primarily with chaparral intermixed with grassland. Few trees, except along creeks: black cottonwood, box elder, creek dogwood, wax myrtle. A few California live oak, interior live oak. In the S, a stand of Bishop pine, unusual in this region. Riparian community includes hemlock, monkeyflower, watercress, horsetail. Chaparral includes black sage, lotus, chamise, California sage.

Some 260 species of flowering plants have been identified, among them California poppy, fiddleneck, mustard, paintbrush, morning glory, brass buttons, red maids, tidy tips, mariposa lily, farewell to spring, hummingbird sage.

Beach plants on the sand spit include sea rocket, sand verbena, beach primrose, silver beach weed, sea fig, hottentot fig, yarrow, beach lupine, and sea thrift.

Birds: Checklist available, includes double-crested, Brandt's, and pelagic cormorants; brown pelican, oystercatcher, surfbird; western, eared, and horned grebes; plovers, curlew, whimbrel, willet, black turnstone, black-necked stilt, avocet, pigeon guillemot. Upland species include barn, screech, and great horned owls; Anna's, Allen's, and rufous hummingbirds; American kestrel, merlin, common flicker, acorn woodpecker, western kingbird, plain titmouse, wrentit; house, rock, and Bewick's wrens; barn and bank swallows, yellow-rumped warbler, white-crowned sparrow.

Mammals: California and Steller sea lion, harbor seal, and sea otter often seen. On land: badger, striped skunk, bobcat, mule deer, opossum, broad-handed mole, black-tailed jackrabbit, pocket gopher, Morro Bay kangaroo rat, coyote, long-tailed weasel, gray fox. Mountain lion has been seen.

FEATURES
Valencia Peak, 1,345 ft. elevation, offers a view of 90 mi. of coastline. *Corallina Cove* has fine tidepools.

INTERPRETATION: *Campfire programs* in summer. Schedule posted. *Guided hikes* are offered occasionally all year, depending on interest. Ask at HQ. A small *museum* is open in summer. Junior Ranger program daily in summer for young people.

ACTIVITIES
Camping: 50 primitive sites. All year. Reservations Memorial Day weekend to Labor Day weekend.
Hiking: 35 mi. of trails.
Fishing: Surf. Perch, rockfish.
Swimming: Unsupervised.
Horse riding: Horses are allowed on some hiking trails. A horse camp is available on request.

NEARBY: Morro Bay State Park (see entry).

PUBLICATION: Leaflet with map.

REFERENCES: From Morro Coast Audubon Society, P.O. Box 160, Morro Bay, CA 93442: Bird checklist for western San Luis Obispo County; map of Morro Bay area with locations of good birding spots, illustrated list of common species.

HEADQUARTERS: c/o San Luis Obispo Coast Area, Dept. of Parks and Recreation, 20-A Higuera St., San Luis Obispo, CA 93401; (805) 543-2161.

MORRO BAY AREA
California Department of Parks and Recreation
About 1,500 acres.

On and near Morro Bay, N of San Luis Obispo, off SR 1.

Morro Bay is enclosed by a long sand spit, now part of Montana de Oro State Park (see entry).
Morro Rock Ecological Reserve, 30 acres, is at the N of the harbor entrance. The rock was once about 1,000 ft. offshore, was then linked with the mainland

by a revetment. It is an important nesting area for marine and pelagic birds. Peregrine falcon have nested recently. A parking lot adjoins the site. Some of the best birding is on the causeway.

Morro Strand State Beach, 34 acres, is about 6 mi. N of Morro Rock, on the ocean. A sandy beach. Day use only.

Atascadero State Beach, 75 acres, lies between the two sites just named. Several miles of beach are accessible for hiking.

Morro Bay State Park has several developed sectors, with a golf course, clubhouse, small boat harbor, snack bar, etc. At the mouth of Los Osos Creek, an extensive salt marsh opens onto Morro Bay, one of the largest natural marshes remaining on the Coast.

Los Osos Oaks State Reserve, 90 acres, is SE of the bay on Los Osos Valley Rd. Acquired in 1972 to preserve an old oak forest, one of the few remaining stands of Coast oak in this area. The old oaks, Coast live oak, scrub oak, and hybrids, have grown into bizarre, gnarled shapes. Understory is mostly poison oak. The site is open but not well marked. A nature trail is planned.

Birds: Checklist available from Morro Coast Audubon Society (see References, following). As many as 173 species have been seen in the area on a single day, over 250 recorded. Included are pelagic species, waterfowl, wading and shore birds, upland species.

Camping: 135 sites at Morro Bay State Park. Reservations all year. 103 sites at Atascadero; reservations Memorial Day–Labor Day.

PUBLICATION: Leaflet.

REFERENCES: From Morro Coast Audubon Society, P.O. Box 160, Morro Bay, CA 93442: bird checklist; map of area with locations of best birding spots, illustrated list of common species.

HEADQUARTERS: San Luis Obispo Coast Area, Dept. of Parks and Recreation, 20-A Higuera St., San Luis Obispo, CA 93401; (805) 543-2161.

POINT MUGU STATE PARK
California Department of Parks and Recreation
14,979 acres.

From Oxnard, S 15 mi. on SR 1.

The park has 3 1/2 mi. of ocean beach, extending SW from Pt. Mugu. The

Coast Highway is just back of the beach, and the two campgrounds are just off the highway. In summer, the beach is often crowded, the campgrounds full. Most visitors are unaware that the park extends more than 6 mi. inland, a large area open to foot and horse travel only.

The beach is generally broad and sandy, offering good swimming, body surfing, fishing, and skin diving. It has one exceptionally large dune, several rocky bluffs.

The site is at the W end of the Santa Monica Mountains, a rugged, hilly area. Near Pt. Mugu, the land rises steeply to the top of Mugu Peak, 1,266 ft., in less than 1/2 mi. The campgrounds are at the mouths of La Jolla and Big Sycamore canyons, each with trails leading into the hills. Highest point is Tri-Peaks, 3,010 ft.

The park is within the planned Santa Monica Mountains National Recreation Area. Proposed land acquisitions would link the several state and federal sites in the hills and along the Coast. In 1981 the Reagan Administration called a halt to all such acquisitions, and Administration spokesmen said this project should be scrapped.

Plants: Most open slopes are covered with chaparral, prominent species including black and California sage, chamise, lotus, toyon, ceanothus, coffeeberry. The steep, irregular contours and interior springs combine to create cool, damp areas along stream valleys, with tall oaks, sycamore, cottonwood, ferns in the understory, grassy areas on the adjoining slopes.

Birds: No checklist.

Mammals: Species reported include mule deer, ground squirrel, gray fox, striped and spotted skunks, badger, coyote, bobcat. Mountain lion have been seen. Seal and sea lion visit the Coast. Gray whale seen offshore in migration.

INTERPRETATION: *Guided hikes* are offered in summer. Notices posted.

ACTIVITIES
Camping: 2 campgrounds, 155 sites. All year. Reservations Mar. 1–Oct. 1.
Hiking, backpacking: More than 70 mi. of trails, through the several backcountry habitats. Overlook Trail has viewpoints. One hike-in campground 2 mi. from La Jolla trailhead. Register at the family campgrounds.
Swimming: Supervised areas in summer.

PUBLICATIONS: Leaflet with map.

HEADQUARTERS: P.O. Box 2678, Oxnard, CA 93034; (213) 457-5538.

RED ROCK CANYON STATE PARK
California Department of Parks and Recreation
4,000 acres.

25 mi. NE of Mojave on SR 14.

The canyon is a long-established travel route between the E edge of the El Paso Mountains and the S tip of the Sierra Nevada. The canyon and surrounding desert mountains are colorfully scenic, each tributary canyon distinctive, sedimentary layers showing color contrasts from white to vivid reds and chocolate brown. The site and surrounding area have been used as locations in many films. Much of the surrounding area is BLM land, crossed by primitive roads, some parts much used by ORV's.

SR 14 traverses the canyon, crossing the site. On the W is the Hagen Canyon Natural Preserve, on the E the Red Cliffs Natural Preserve, both open to foot travel only. Terrain is generally hilly, with cliffs, palisades, rimrock. Highest point is 3,310 ft. The park includes natural springs and seeps.

Climate is arid. Spring is the best time for a visit. Winters are cool, summers hot and dry.

Plants: Desert vegetation. Joshua tree, creosote bush, desert holly. Several rare species occur. The area is known for spectacular spring wildflower displays when winter rain has been sufficient.

Birds: Checklist can be seen at Ranger Station. Reported: hawks, vultures, owls, cactus wren, Say's phoebe, roadrunner, common raven, horned lark, Le Conte's and crissal thrashers, loggerhead shrike, quail, chukar, canyon and rock wrens, mourning dove.

Mammals: Checklist can be seen at Ranger Station. Mentioned: bats, mice, rabbits, squirrels, occasional coyote, kit fox.

ACTIVITIES

Camping: 50 primitive sites. All year.

Hiking: No formal trails, but none are needed. Several primitive roads cross the area, open to ORV's.

PUBLICATION: Leaflet with map.

HEADQUARTERS: RRC Box 26, Cantil, CA 93519. Or High Desert Area HQ, Gen. William J. Fox Airfield, 4555 West Ave. G, Lancaster, CA 93534; (805) 942-0622.

SADDLEBACK BUTTE STATE PARK
California Department of Parks and Recreation
2,875 acres.

17 mi. E of Lancaster on Ave. J E.

In the Antelope Valley on the W edge of the Mojave Desert. A desert park near the Los Angeles metropolitan area. The park acreage is a bit misleading, because the surrounding landscape has much the same appearance as the park, with only a few signs of development. Elevation is 2,600 ft. at the campground. To the E, the land rises steeply to Saddleback Butte Peak, 3,651 ft., a jagged mound of granite above the alluvial bottomland.

The park and surrounding area have numerous Joshua trees. Spring is the best time to visit, both because of the weather and the chance that the desert may then be in bloom. When we visited in early April, there were masses of coreopsis. Few animals will be seen by day, except perhaps a desert tortoise.

Camping: 50 sites. All year.

PUBLICATION: Leaflet with map. 25¢.

HEADQUARTERS: c/o High Desert Area HQ, Department of Parks and Recreation, 4555 West Ave. G, Lancaster, CA 93534; (805) 942-0662.

SANTA MONICA MOUNTAINS NATIONAL RECREATION AREA
U.S. National Park Service

In the Santa Monica Mountains, between US 101 and the Pacific Coast Highway (SR 1), including the beaches between Pt. Mugu and Santa Monica.

Over 35,000 acres of city, county, state, and federal park lands are located along the Coast and in the mountains within the 150,000 acres lying inside the authorized boundary. In November 1978 the U.S. Congress authorized the National Recreation Area, directing the National Park Service to head the planning process and to acquire certain lands within the boundary. Since then local, state, and federal agencies have been meeting to work out cooperative and coordinated planning, acquisition, and recreation programs. To date the National Park Service has acquired an additional 3,500 acres to preserve coastal uplands, stream drainage basins, and beaches; connect existing parks; protect the Mulholland scenic corridor; and develop historic sites, hiking and riding trails, scenic overlooks, and visitor facilities.

The Santa Monica Mountains are considered a botanical island, which includes chaparral, coastal sage, oak grasslands, oak woodlands, southern coastal salt- and freshwater marshes, and tidepools. Much California native wildlife still survives in the mountains, including a small population of mountain lion and golden eagle.

Hiking and riding trails are available within existing parklands. Camping, fishing, surfing, National Park tours, as well as a variety of special events and other recreational activities, are available within the National Recreation Area.

An information center at park headquarters provides trip planning advice and information on weather and trail conditions for national parks throughout the system.

The project heads Secretary Watt's hit list. Congress rejected the Reagan Administration's effort to halt all parkland purchases but agreed to a $14.7 million cut in fiscal 1981. Secretary Watt took $14.2 million of that from the Santa Monica Mountains National Recreation Area land purchase plan. Because of Proposition 13, the state's land acquisitions have been drastically reduced. Developers are busily buying, and the future of this project is in doubt.

HEADQUARTERS: 22900 Ventura Blvd., Woodland Hills, CA 91364.

INFORMATION CENTER: 23018 Ventura Blvd., Woodland Hills, CA 91364; (213) 888-3770.

SCODIE MOUNTAINS
U.S. Bureau of Land Management
About 13,000 acres.

S of SR 178 at Walker Pass, adjoining the Sequoia National Forest.

A portion of the Sequoia National Forest about 10 mi. N-S, 9 mi. E-W, lies SE of the main body of the Forest. SR 178 crosses between them, touching this separate portion at Walker Pass. The portion contains the Scodie Mountains, part of the S Sierra Nevada. The BLM land adjoins the Forest on its E and S boundaries, where the E slopes of the Sierra drop down to high desert. The landform is mountain ridges flanking deep, winding canyons that penetrate the mountains from the SE. Notable are Cow Heaven, Sage, Horse, and Bird Spring canyons, each of which contains an unimproved road to or beyond the Forest boundary.

This is a transition zone from mountain to desert habitats. Elevation on the desert floor is about 3,400 ft. The long, deep, winding canyons climb to about 5,000 ft. Ridge elevations are about 6,800 ft., within the Forest. Desert plants such as creosote, burrobrush, and shadscale grow in close proximity to such mountain species as pinyon pine, juniper, canyon oak, and digger pine. The lower canyon floors have abundant Joshua tree, cacti, and low desert shrubs. Springs and intermittent streams have produced riparian communities further up. Attractive spring floral displays.

Wildlife is also a mix of mountain and desert species. Species such as the western toad, coast horned lizard, striped racer, California legless lizard, and California pocket mouse have dispersed E through the canyons, while the desert night lizard, banded gecko, and other desert fauna have dispersed W.

The Pacific Crest Trail crosses the area near Bird Springs Pass Road. The area has considerable recreation use, for camping, hiking, rockhounding, hunting, and ORV touring. Because of this and the roads in the several canyons, it is unlikely that any part of this area will be accorded wilderness status. It adjoins a National Forest area that had been recommended for such status.

HEADQUARTERS: BLM, Bakersfield District Office, 800 Truxtun, Rm. 311, Bakersfield, CA 93301; (805) 861-4191.

SEQUOIA NATIONAL FOREST
U.S. Forest Service

288,380 acres of this Forest are in zone 8, several large blocks of Forest land almost surrounding Isabella Lake, although the Forest has no lake frontage and the boundary is generally 3 or more mi. from the lakeshore. Most of the Forest is in zone 7, and the entry appears there.

SHEEPHOLE MOUNTAINS AND VALLEY; CADIZ VALLEY
U.S. Bureau of Land Management
Included in Joshua Tree National Monument.

TOPANGA STATE PARK
California Department of Parks and Recreation
7,830 acres.

From Santa Monica, SR 1 W to Topanga Canyon Blvd. N to Entrada Rd., then every left turn to Park.

A large, new, undeveloped park in the Santa Monica Mountains. Elevations from 200 ft. to 2,100 ft. Steep, rough ridgetops with dense chaparral. About 15% is oak woodland and grassland. As yet little information has been developed on the flora and fauna of the park, but it is much the same as in other coastal chaparral communities of the region.

Because there are as yet no visitor facilities, this is a good place for a hike on the 30 mi. of quiet trails. This would be one of the largest units in the planned Santa Monica Mountains National Recreation Area (see entry). New trails and some camping facilities are planned.

NEARBY: State beaches between Malibu and Santa Monica.

HEADQUARTERS: c/o Will Rogers State Historical Park, P.O. Box 845, Pacific Palisades, CA 90272; (213) 454-8212.

TULE ELK STATE RESERVE
California Department of Parks and Recreation
965 acres.

25 mi. W of Bakersfield. 3 mi. W and S of Stockdale Rd. interchange on I-5, via Stockdale Rd. and Morris Rd.

A 5-acre viewing area is the only part of the Reserve open to the public. When supplemental feeding is required, elk are fed within sight of this area. This usually occurs May through Feb. at about 2 P.M.

Tule elk were numerous in California until the Gold Rush. By 1863 numbers were greatly depleted, and the last remaining range was fast disappearing. Soon only a few remained.

Since 1874, public and private efforts have been made to preserve the species and reestablish adequate herds. The chief problem has been securing suitable habitat. The DPR says that "today the Reserve is no longer a good example of tule elk natural habitat, and for this reason the Department of Parks and Recreation is looking for ways to provide a more spacious and appealing natural environment for the elk."

Numerous efforts have been made to establish tule elk herds elsewhere, with varying degrees of success. A 1980 summary reported herds at Camp Roberts, Fort Hunter Liggett, Lake Pillsbury, Mount Hamilton, Concord Naval Weapons Station, Point Reyes (see entry, zone 3), and Grizzly Island (see entry, zone 3). The largest herd is in the Owens Valley.

The Reserve is mostly flat, open grassland with a few seasonally flooded ponds and flood channels. Annual precipitation is less than 5 in. The small viewing area is sometimes overcrowded on major holidays.

PUBLICATIONS
(Each is 25¢ at the site, plus postage and handling if mailed.)
Tule elk leaflet.
Bird checklist.
Mammal checklist.

HEADQUARTERS: Rt. 1, Box 42, Buttonwillow, CA 93206; (805) 765-5004.

ZONE 9

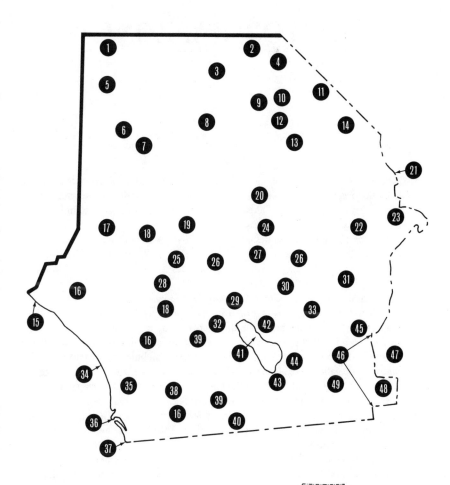

CALIFORNIA, ZONE 9

Includes these counties:

San Bernardino   Orange   Imperial

Riverside   San Diego

This is our largest CA zone and the only one that extends across the state from the ocean to the E boundary. At the Coast, its boundary passes between Los Angeles and Anaheim. Their population has a heavy impact on many of its natural areas.

Few of the public beaches along the Coast met our selection criteria. Planned for recreation, they serve that purpose well, and we have enjoyed them on uncrowded days. Several coastal sites are attractive natural areas, notably Torrey Pines State Reserve.

The mountains E and SE of Los Angeles are largely occupied by the San Bernardino and Cleveland National Forests. Both are heavily used, but both have many attractions and some quiet areas. One can avoid the crowds.

The largest part of the zone, across the mountains, is desert. The California Desert, a region of more than 25 million acres, includes a great variety of landforms: valleys, bajadas, pediments, alluvial fans, mountain ranges, washes, sand dunes, dry lakebeds. Almost half of the area, over 12 million acres, is public domain, administered by the BLM. The area also includes the Anza-Borrego State Park, Joshua Tree National Monument, and Death Valley National Monument, several large military installations, and a number of smaller state and federal sites.

In 1976, Congress directed the Bureau of Land Management to take the lead in developing a comprehensive long-range land use plan for the California Desert Conservation Area. Like earlier plans for National Forests, the theme was to be sustained yield: use of resources without environmental damage. It was a monumental task, requiring acre-by-acre analysis of everything from geothermal potential to Indian artifacts, including flora and fauna. Completed in 1980, the plan identifies potential wilderness areas and other sites that should be protected because of their special natural qualities.

For strangers who wish to understand and appreciate the desert, a good place to begin is the BLM's Barstow Way Station (see entry). The Station is within what BLM calls the High Desert, an area that includes a number of our entries. A leaflet available at the Station describes the area.

Anza-Borrego State Park and Joshua Tree National Monument also have splendid visitor centers and interpretive programs. (So does Death Valley

National Monument, in zone 7.) A few hours in one of these centers makes a visit to the California Desert more fascinating.

The main preface explained how we selected sites within the public domain. The desert sites offer great diversity. No two are quite alike, and some are unique. Some are beside good roads and can be explored in an easy walk. Many are roadless areas, with opportunities for day hikes up attractive canyons. Some are vast and rugged, to be explored only by those who understand the requirements of desert survival.

Water in the desert is always dramatic, creating a palm oasis, a strip of green riparian vegetation, a waterfowl marsh, even a waterfall. We mention streams and springs, where they exist, but one should not assume that all are easily found, or that the water is necessarily safe for drinking.

Canoeing in the desert? Indeed yes, on the Colorado River. Entries for the Cibola and Imperial National Wildlife Refuges describe the opportunity.

ALGODONES DUNES
U.S. Bureau of Land Management
See Sand Hills.

AMARGOSA CANYON-DUMONT DUNES NATURAL AREA
U.S. Bureau of Land Management
See Kingston Range.

AMBOY CRATER
U.S. Bureau of Land Management
3,200 acres.

From Ludlow on I-40, 27 mi. SE to Amboy on Old National Trail Highway. Crater is just W of Amboy.

Amboy Crater is a steep-sided, black, volcanic cinder cone, surrounded by extensive lava flows, an excellent example of a recent volcanic cinder cone, with an unusually flat crater floor. Unlike most other cinder cones in the desert, it has not been mined. It has been designated a National Natural Landmark. Much of the surrounding land is public domain.

HEADQUARTERS: BLM, California Desert District, 1695 Spruce St., Riverside, CA 92507; (714) 787-1462.

ANZA-BORREGO DESERT STATE PARK
California Department of Parks and Recreation
550,000 acres.

85 mi. NE of San Diego via I-8, SR 79 or SR 78.

A huge, unique desert Park with great diversity of topography, flora, and fauna. A National Natural Landmark, containing some of the best examples of the various desert biotic communities in the California Desert and excellent examples of desert geological phenomena. Three principal roads, all scenic, cross the area: S-2, from NW to SE; SR 78, W to E, near the midpoint; and S-22, W to E across the N portion, through Borrego Springs. The Park also has several hundred mi. of backcountry roads, many requiring 4-wheel drive, as well as hiking trails. Although it has conventional campgrounds, primitive campsites (with latrines but no water) are also scattered throughout the Park. You are also welcome to camp anywhere along designated travel routes. "For many people," says the Park leaflet, "this is the *only* way to camp in the desert."

The Salton Sea, a few mi. E of the Park, is 232 ft. below sealevel. S-22, the Borrego Salton Seaway, climbs gradually through sloping, heavily eroded terrain, to an elevation of 580 ft. at Borrego Springs, a town within the Park, site of Park HQ. Continuing W, this route now climbs steeply, with splendid views, topping the mountain ridge at 4,006 ft., the Park boundary.

The western, central, and northeastern parts of the Park are mountainous. Highest point is Combs Peak, 6,193 ft., in the NW corner. Each of the mountainous areas has peaks over 5,000 ft. Several higher peaks are on adjoining BLM and Forest Service land.

Rainfall averages 5 in. a year at Borrego Springs. Large areas of the Park receive much less, the heights of the Santa Rosa Mountains and the Peninsular Ranges somewhat more. Winter rains, when they occur, are likely to be moderate and steady, summer thunderstorms heavy and brief. But desert rainfall is erratic and unpredictable.

Most visitors come in winter and spring, when the climate is most pleasant. Winter temperatures generally range between 35° and 75°F. If rainfall has been sufficient, wildflowers begin blooming at lower elevations in Feb., as late as May and June in the mountains. We saw only a modest display after a wet winter; rangers explained this was a consequence of a succession of wet winters.

Numerous springs in the Park support distinctive plant life as well as both resident and migratory animals. Coyote Creek, in the NW, rises from the ground, flows 2 mi., and vanishes, creating a unique strip of riparian vegetation.

What brings people back here again and again is the infinite variety. This desert is not an endless waste of shifting sands. A few yards off a main road, the dirt track may descend into a dry wash, giving an immediate sense of isolation, and that isolation can be quite real until you find your way back to a paved road again. The landscape includes many dry washes, steep-walled canyons, badlands, dry lakes, bizarre sandstone formations, cliffs several hundred feet high, oases, waterfalls that flow after a rain.

Don't go into the backcountry unprepared. Even experienced desert travelers can encounter problems, but they'll know what to do and have the equipment they need. *The Anza-Borrego Desert Region* (see References section for this entry) has excellent advice.

Plants: Trees are scarce in the desert. A few stands of Coulter and Jeffrey pines occur at high elevations. Pinyon, juniper, mountain mahogany and desert scrub oak on some slopes below 6,000 ft., with manzanita, Parry nolina, desert agave, buckwheat. Usually somewhat lower, but above 3,000 ft. elevation, chaparral community, common species including chamise, scrub oak, ceanothus, manzanita, sumac, Mojave yucca.

The lower slopes and valleys have generally sparse but conspicuous vegetation. One prominent species is the ocotillo, up to 20 ft. tall, which produces small green leaves quickly after rain, drops them in dry weather. Other members of this community include barrel cactus, creosote bush, indigo bush, cholla cactus. Desert washes vary greatly in plant species and density, some of the more common species including smoke tree, ironwood, palo verde, desert willow, mesquite, bunchgrass, desert lavender, loco weed, mistletoe.

A checklist of flowering plants is in preparation. Several hundred species occur here, among them trumpet flower, desert aster, bladderpod, desert lily, verbena, dune primrose, lupine, desert mariposa, blazing star, phacelia, penstemon.

Birds: Checklist available. 206 species recorded, including golden eagle, prairie falcon, mountain quail, scrub jay, raven, red-tailed hawk, roadrunner, Say's phoebe, loggerhead shrike, poor-will, black-throated sparrow; canyon, cactus, and rock wrens; mockingbird, California thrasher, Bell's vireo.

Mammals: Include California ground squirrel, pinyon mouse, desert woodrat, antelope ground squirrel, Merriam kangaroo rat, coyote, black-tailed jackrabbit, cottontail, kit fox, gray fox, mule deer, peninsular bighorn sheep. Ringtail and mountain lion reported, seldom seen.

Reptiles and amphibians: Include western fence, flat-tailed horned, collared, zebra-tailed, and banded rock lizards; chuckwalla, desert iguana, Sonoran gopher snake, red racer, rosy boa, sidewinder, red diamond rattlesnake, shovel-nosed snake, and glossy snake.

FEATURES

The Park leaflet mentions a number of points of interest, among them:
Coyote Canyon, site of a year-round flowing stream. Good birding.
Yaqui Well, a seep that attracts migratory birds.

Split Mountain, high canyon walls, a gorge that carries torrential flash floods after a downpour. Geological interest.

Elephant Trees, a botanical oddity near Split Mountain, with nature trail.

17 Palm Oasis, a dry desert seep. 29 palms now growing.

Calcite Canyon Scenic Area, bizarre sandstone formations.

Palm Spring, another oasis with native palms, good birding.

Some of the following can be reached only with 4-wheel-drive vehicles.

Font's Point, viewpoint in the Borrego Badlands, uplifted by faulting action hundreds of feet. Some say it's the Park's grandest viewpoint. Ancient river sediments nearby recently yielded a million-year-old mammoth skeleton. Check road conditions; 4-wheel drive sometimes required.

Borrego Palm Canyon, several mi. long. Year-round water, hundreds of native palms. Desert bighorn sheep, migratory birds. Hiking trail into canyon mouth.

These publicized features attract many visitors. By all means see them, but this is only a beginning. Backcountry roads and trails lead to many areas no less fascinating.

Anza-Borrego Desert State Wilderness, 46,000 acres, is in the NW sector, SW of Coyote Canyon. Sheep Canyon and Borrego Palm Canyon penetrate the area. Rugged and remote. Water and palms in most canyons. Some 150 bighorn sheep are in the area. Three of the canyons have heavy backpacking use on weekends and holidays, Oct.–May. Horse camp in Coyote Canyon.

Santa Rosa Mountains State Wilderness, 87,000 acres, occupies the mountainous NE sector, E of Coyote Canyon. The highest and least traveled portion of the Park. It adjoins BLM's Santa Rosa Mountains Wilderness Study Area (see entry). Very rugged. Almost no water. Stronghold for peninsular bighorn sheep.

Bow Willow Canyon. A marked road turns W off S-2 about 8 mi. from the SW Park boundary, to Bow Willow Campground and Ranger Station. Nearby is Mountain Palm Springs, a palm oasis. Ask about trails in Bow Willow Canyon. Palm groves in secluded side canyons. With direction from the Ranger, one can hike across the boundary into BLM's Bow Willow Palms area, an isolated fan palm grove.

Bow Willow Palms, 720 acres, at edge of Park in San Diego County. An isolated, undisturbed area of California fan palms, at 2,000 ft. elevation. Part of McCain Valley national cooperative land and wildlife management area. Walk in from Park.

INTERPRETATION

The *visitor center* is unique, a million-dollar project built with much local support. A fine audiovisual presentation, exhibits, publications, information.

Campfire programs, Oct. 15–May 30. Notices in campgrounds and local newspaper.

Guided hikes, Oct. 15–May 30. Notices posted.

Nature trails: Narrows Earth Trail, Bow Willow Nature Trail, Borrego Palm Canyon, and Elephant Trees Discovery Trail. Leaflets.

Self-guided auto tours, with leaflets: Erosion Road and Southern Emigrant Trail.

ACTIVITIES

Camping: 2 developed campgrounds. 142 sites. Reservations Sept. 28–June 4. 10 primitive campgrounds. Camp anywhere on designated travel routes, subject to park rules.

Hiking, backpacking: Many miles of hiking trails, but one can also hike on backcountry dirt roads and, in many places, cross-country. The book listed in References for this section includes detailed trail information, as well as precautions. The Pacific Crest Trail crosses the NW corner of the Park, runs generally W of the boundary.

Horse riding: About 80 mi. of trails. No rentals or nearby outfitters. A horse camp in the NW sector can be reserved; individual campsites close to corrals.

ADJACENT OR NEARBY

Cleveland National Forest (see entry).
Cuyamaca Rancho State Park (see entry).
Santa Rosa Mountains Wilderness Study Area (see entry).

PUBLICATIONS

Leaflet with map.
Nature and auto trail guides.
Park rules.

REFERENCES

Lindsay, Lowell and Diana. *The Anza-Borrego Desert Region.* Berkeley, CA: Wilderness Press, 1978.

The Anza-Borrego Desert Natural History Association, Borrego Springs, CA 92004, has a number of maps and publications available. Among them:

Parker, Horace. *Anza-Borrego Desert Guide Book.*

HEADQUARTERS: P.O. Box 428, Borrego Springs, CA 92004; (714) 767-5311.

AVAWATZ MOUNTAINS
U.S. Bureau of Land Management
96,600 acres.

At the SE corner of Death Valley National Monument, on SR 127 and the unpaved road that leaves SR 127 5 mi. E of the Monument, turning NW into the Monument along the Amargosa River into Death Valley.

From the dry bed of Silurian Lake on SR 127, at about 500 ft. elevation, the land slopes gradually upward toward the SW to about the 2,500-ft. contour, then steeply to 6,154 ft. The large mass of the Avawatz Mountains, extending about 10 mi. NW–SE, has many colorful, eroded slopes, rugged ridges, and narrow, steep-walled canyons. From numerous viewpoints, one looks N into the Monument.

Vegetation is largely desert scrub. An extremely dense stand of Joshua tree adjoins the mountains. Nine springs provide water for wildlife, including a resident herd of bighorn sheep.

The low area along SR 127 has had considerable ORV use, but the canyons are generally undisturbed.

HEADQUARTERS: BLM, California Desert District, 1695 Spruce St., Riverside, CA 92507; (714) 787-1462.

BARSTOW WAY STATION
U.S. Bureau of Land Management

From I-15, Central Barstow exit. One block N to 831 Barstow Rd.
Open: Daily. Mon.–Thurs.: 7:45 A.M.–4:15 P.M. Fri.: to 5:15 P.M. Sat., Sun., and holidays: 8:45 A.M.–5:15 P.M.

BLM's visitor center for the High Desert area, a region about 200 mi. W–E, 100 mi. N–S. Several of our entries are within this area. (See zone map.)

The Station has exhibits, displays, information, literature. Themes include desert ecology, wildflowers, wildlife, desert safety, ORV areas, camping.

Near Barstow, motorists can tune to a special AM frequency for information. See signs posted on the highway.

PUBLICATION: *High Desert Recreation Resources Guide.*

HEADQUARTERS: 831 Barstow Rd., Barstow, CA 92311; (714) 256-3591.

BIGHORN MOUNTAINS
U.S. Bureau of Land Management
58,500 acres.

At the NE corner of the N unit of San Bernardino National Forest. Part of the N boundary is on SR 247, part of the S boundary on the paved part of Pipes Canyon Rd., which originates at Yucca Valley on SR 62 and runs W into the National Forest.

This area adjoins the Granite Peak Roadless Area of the San Bernardino National Forest (see entry), recommended for Wilderness status. Terrain rises from N to S, from about 3,000 ft. in the valley to 6,000 ft. at the Forest boundary, the highest point 6,265 ft. One of the more scenic portions is Rattlesnake Canyon, a broad canyon in the S part of the area. Landforms include craggy peaks, granitic boulder piles, interior valleys, broad desert bajadas.

Typical desert vegetation at lower elevations: creosote bush scrub, black-brush scrub, sagebrush scrub, with yucca and cacti. Moving up the slopes, this gives way to pinyon-juniper and some ponderosa pine forest. The Granite Peak area of the Forest has many Joshua trees, including the world's largest specimen, and this BLM area also has many exceptionally large specimens, in the Mound Springs area of the SW corner.

The Big Bear Lake resort area of the Forest is also in the NE sector, and for much of the year traffic on Forest roads in this sector is heavy. Hikers and backpackers may well prefer to hike into the Granite Peaks area through the BLM lands. Primitive ways are in some of the canyons, maintained only by the passage of vehicles and subject to occasional obliteration by washouts. Sites on the perimeter of the area are accessible by automobile and have some recreational use: camping, rockhounding, hunting, and ORV action.

90% of the area has been recommended for wilderness status.

HEADQUARTERS: BLM, California Desert District, 1695 Spruce St., Riverside, CA 92507; (714) 787-1462.

BOLSA CHICA STATE BEACH
California Department of Parks and Recreation
84 acres.

3 mi. NW of Huntington Beach on SR 1.

This small, heavily-used beach in the metropolitan area is an entry because it adjoins the 530-acre Bolsa Chica Ecological Reserve. Here the Department of Fish and Game has undertaken to restore a salt marsh in an altered and abused tidal marsh ecosystem. The area was acquired from an oil-refining company in 1973. Although the area has been degraded, numerous bird species nest and visit. A new ocean entrance and public marina were included in the plans. The reserve is across SR 1 from the beach, on the inland side.

BORDER FIELD STATE PARK
California Department of Parks and Recreation
680 acres.

15 mi. S of San Diego via I-5 and Monument Rd.

Over 1 mi. of ocean front. The most southerly CA State Park, on the Mexican border. The salt marsh at the mouth of the Tia Juana River is an outstanding natural area, with good birding all year.

BUENA VISTA LAGOON ECOLOGICAL RESERVE
California Department of Fish and Game
192 acres.

On the Coast between Carlsbad and Oceanside.

A coastal lagoon and freshwater marsh. A young Carlsbad resident initiated the move to make this a bird sanctuary in 1939. By the early 1950s the Buena Vista Lagoon Association had acquired 85 acres of submerged land. Other bits were acquired to bring the refuge to its present size. Over 200 birds species and 50 plant species have been identified. Viewing opportunities from outside are good. Future plans include parking, observation areas, restrooms, as well as construction of islands as nesting sites.

CABRILLO NATIONAL MONUMENT
U.S. National Park Service
144 acres.

In San Diego, S on SR 209, Catalina Blvd. Through Navy gates to the tip of Pt. Loma.
Open: 9 A.M.–5:15 P.M.; to 7:45 P.M. in July and Aug. (subject to change without notice).

A small site, but except for the walkways and overlooks in a natural condition. The peninsula has rocky coastal cliffs, overlooking San Diego Harbor and the CA and Mexican coast. Upland areas have desert and chaparral vegetation. Highest point is 420 ft. On the ocean side are tidepools, best observed at low tides in winter. Bayside Trail is a 2-mi. hike. A whale-watching station is a good place to observe gray whales in the Dec.–Feb. migration. Theme at the visitor center is historical.

PUBLICATION: Leaflet with map.

REFERENCES
From Cabrillo Historical Association, P.O. Box 6670, San Diego, CA 92106:
List of publications.
Numerous books on natural history.
Bird checklist. 10¢.
Walker, Theodore J. *Whale Primer.* $3.95.

HEADQUARTERS: P.O. Box 6670, San Diego, CA 92106; (714) 293-5450.

CHEMEHUEVI MOUNTAINS
U.S. Bureau of Land Management
Included in Havasu National Wildlife Refuge.

CHUCKWALLA MOUNTAINS
U.S. Bureau of Land Management
140,100 acres.

S of Desert Center on I-10. Bounded by I-10, Graham Pass Rd. on E, Chocolate Mountains Aerial Gunnery Range, and Bradshaw Mountain Rd.

From about 500 ft. elevation along I-10 in the Chuckwalla Valley to the NE, the bajada rises gradually to the mountain base at about 1,500 ft. The valley to the SW, between the Chuckwalla and the Chocolate Mountains, is about 1,000 ft. higher. The Chuckwalla Mountains are a range of colorful rock ridges, boulders, and hills, rising to several peaks over 3,000 ft., the highest 4,504-ft. Black Butte. Numerous canyons wind into the interior, penetrating the mountain mass, notably Corn Springs Wash from the NE and Ship Creek from the E. Wide-open spaces and large interior valleys give a feeling of spaciousness, while rugged, narrow canyons and jumbles of rocky spires and ridges give a sense of isolation. Water is relatively abundant; many springs, but quality is untested.

The Chuckwalla Bench in the S is a transition zone between Colorado and Mojave Deserts, with an unusual assemblage of plant species: clusters of ocotillo, cholla cactus gardens, yucca, thick stands of creosote, barrel cactus, nolina. The Munz cholla, largest cholla in the California Desert, is found only here and in the Chocolate Mountains. Several other rare plant species occur.

Corn Springs are in a canyon deep in the mountains. The spring supports a rich riparian vegetation including about 20 fan palms, a dense thicket of gnarled mesquite, catclaw, desert willow, and smoke tree. The oasis attracts wildlife, including many migratory birds. It is one of the few CA sites where the elf owl is known to have bred. The area has petroglyphs and other artifacts. It has been designated an Area of Critical Environmental Concern. The canyon has attracted many visitors, and the BLM is considering ways to manage or eliminate vehicle traffic and control other damage.

The route from Corn Springs to the Red Cloud mine is said to be scenic and provide access to good rockhounding sites. St. Augustine Pass is also mentioned as scenic. Hunting for deer, rabbit, and quail is considered good, by desert standards.

Parts of the area have been heavily used for ORV activities. The BLM has recommended that about 1/3 of the area be given wilderness status, excluding these affected areas.

Camping: 27 tent sites at Corn Springs. 8 mi. E of Desert Center via I-10 and follow signs.

HEADQUARTERS: BLM, California Desert District, 1695 Spruce St., Riverside, CA 92507; (714) 787-1462.

CIBOLA NATIONAL WILDLIFE REFUGE
U.S. Fish and Wildlife Service
1,255 acres in CA; 8,208 in AZ.

IMPERIAL NATIONAL WILDLIFE REFUGE
U.S. Fish and Wildlife Service
7,958 acres in CA; 17,806 in AZ.

PICACHO STATE RECREATION AREA
California Department of Parks and Recreation
4,880 acres.

ADJACENT DESERT LANDS
U.S. Bureau of Land Management
115,000 acres.

Along the Colorado River from Blythe to a point near the Mexican border. W to SR 78 and S34.

The two refuges extend for about 50 mi. along the Lower Colorado River, narrow strips of land on both sides. The Picacho State Recreation Area is on the river at about the midpoint of the Imperial National Wildlife Refuge. The BLM lands are generally adjacent on the W.

Cibola National Wildlife Refuge, at the N end of the area, about 20 mi. long. It includes the river, a lake, marshes, river bottomland, and a small fringe of desert ridges and washes. A dredged and diked channel was created before the site became a refuge. The old channel is canoeable. The refuge was established to mitigate wildlife losses caused by 50 mi. of stream channelization. Unlike Imperial and a third National Wildlife Refuge, Havasu, 100 mi. N, Cibola does not have extensive wetlands. However, it does have 2,000 acres of cropland where wildlife feed is cultivated.

Entrance to Cibola on the CA side is from SR 78, 3 mi. S of Palo Verde. Visitors may drive on the dikes on both sides of the dredged channel. A bridge just N of the access road crosses to the AZ side. However, the best way to see the area is by boat. Power boats operate on the river. They can be launched nearby, not in the refuge. Traveling by canoe is even better. This section of river has no white water. If one has the time, launch at Blythe and make the 60-mi. run to takeout at the S end of Imperial National Wildlife Refuge. Camping is not permitted within the refuges, but one can camp between them and at Picacho State Recreation Area.

Mission of the refuge is to maintain Canada goose and field-feeding ducks such as pintail and mallard in the winter season. The refuge is habitat for the endangered Yuma clapper rail. Species of interest include snow and white-fronted geese and sandhill crane, and such occasional visitors as brown pelican, wood stork, and roseate spoonbill.

Most visitors come in summer, for fishing and boating. Best period for visiting is Dec.–June. Management warns that traffic is light and roads unimproved, with low and sandy places. No road service is nearby.

Imperial National Wildlife Refuge, S of Cibola, includes 30 mi. of the river with adjacent backwater lakes. For most of its length, its width is about a mile, becoming broader at the S end. Elevation at the river is about 185 ft. The highest point within the boundaries is about 1,000 ft. Road access is on the AZ side. The map shows no roads to or within the refuge on the CA side. A road N from Winterhaven leads to Picacho SRA. Boats can be launched there, and much of the adjacent area can be explored on foot.

Like Cibola, most of the Imperial National Wildlife Refuge is river bottomland. Vegetation is largely mesquite, willow, arrowweed, screwbean, and salt cedar. In the marshes, cattail, bulrush, marsh cane. On the desert hills: ironwood, palo verde, mesquite, smoke tree, creosote bush, bear-sage, lycium, various cacti.

A marina is on the AZ side, 4 mi. S of the refuge. Boats can be launched and rented there. For birding, Dec.–June is the best period. Summer visitors are usually interested in fishing and boating.

Picacho State Recreation Area is reached by driving 24 mi. N from Winterhaven over a steep, winding, unsurfaced road. The site has about 8 mi. of frontage on the Colorado River. Terrain is much the same as in the Imperial National Wildlife Refuge: river bottomlands, rising to sparsely vegetated hills and the colorful Chocolate Mountains. The HQ campground has 50 sites, piped water. Reservations are available Sept. 29–June 18, indicating this is the popular season. Summer temperatures average over 100°F. The site has two boat-in camp areas, 4 and 8 mi. upstream.

BLM lands: Most of the land to the W of the National Wildlife Refuges is public domain, although part of the area is checkerboarded with private holdings. Four roadless sections were designated Wilderness Study Areas, and these are the subjects of this entry.

W of Cibola are the *Palo Verde Mountains,* in which the highest point is 1,795 ft. Rolling hills and steep, jagged, colorful volcanic peaks. Small, narrow canyons lead into enclosed basins and small, isolated valleys.

Vegetation is generally sparse. Large stands of ironwood in Milpitas Wash. A small palm oasis at Clapp Spring. Bighorn sheep have a transient range in the mountains. Prairie falcon have one eyrie in the area. This is also desert tortoise habitat. Deer, quail, and chukar are present. The area is of interest to rockhounds.

The Indian Pass area has SR 78 and S34 as its W boundary, Indian Pass Rd. on the S. Highest point is 2,177-ft. Quartz Peak. Most of the area is flat to rolling, cut by washes, some wide and deep. Scattered, rugged low mountains and canyons. River bottomland vegetation extends up many of the washes: creosote, mesquite, smoke tree, catclaw. The S portion of the area is the most scenic, with jagged buttes, spires, lava-capped mesas, in rich colors.

Bighorn sheep use the mountainous area. Deer, quail, and rabbit are primary game species.

Adjoining BLM land is used for ORV activity, and some of this extends into the Wilderness Study Area. Rockhounding and camping are also primary activities.

The *Picacho Peak Wilderness Study Area* is adjacent, across Indian Pass Road. Elevation of the peak is 1,947 ft. This area adjoins the State Recreation Area. Terrain is varied, including vegetated washes, deep canyons, volcanic rock, rolling hills, flat desert, mountains.

The *Little Picacho Peak* area lies immediately S of the State Recreation Area, bordering the Imperial National Wildlife Refuge. Within its 260 sq. mi. are flat, meadowlike areas, low rolling hills, table-top mountains, rough and jagged peaks, deep canyons, and washes. Vegetation is varied near the river and lakes. The Wilderness Study Area evaluation gave the highest possible score to the scenic qualities of the N portion. It is the only area where we have seen "painting" noted as an important visitor activity.

Birds: This list is compiled from National Wildlife Refuge checklists. Seasonally common or abundant species include eared and pied-billed grebes, white pelican, double-crested cormorant, great blue heron, great and snowy egrets, Canada goose, mallard, gadwall, pintail, green-winged and cinnamon teals, American wigeon, northern shoveler, redhead, lesser scaup, bufflehead, ruddy duck, common merganser, turkey vulture, Cooper's and red-tailed hawks, Gambel's quail, sora, common gallinule, American coot, killdeer; spotted, least, and western sandpipers; long-billed dowitcher, black-necked stilt, Wilson's phalarope, ring-billed gull, Forster's and black terns, mourning and white-winged doves, roadrunner; screech, great horned, and western burrowing owls; lesser nighthawk, Costa's hummingbird, common flicker, Gila and ladder-backed woodpeckers, western kingbird; ash-throated, willow, Hammond's, and western flycatchers; black and Say's phoebes; tree, rough-winged, barn, and cliff swallows; verdin, house and long-billed marsh wrens, mockingbird, crissal thrasher, black-tailed gnatcatcher, ruby-crowned king-let, water pipit, phainopepla, loggerhead shrike, warbling vireo; orange-crowned, yellow, yellow-rumped, MacGillivray's, and Wilson's warblers; western meadowlark, yellow-headed and red-winged blackbirds, brown-headed cowbird, western tanager, black-headed and blue grosbeaks, house finch, Abert's towhee; savannah, chipping, Brewer's, white-crowned, and song sparrows.

Mammals: Include leafnose and pallid bats, western pipistrel, Mexican freetail bat, black-tailed jackrabbit, cottontail, Yuma and white-tailed ante-lope squirrels, roundtail ground squirrel; little, longtail, desert, rock, and spiny pocket mice; Merriam kangaroo rat, beaver, western harvest and cactus mice, hispid cotton rat, desert woodrat, muskrat, coyote, kit fox, gray fox, ringtail, raccoon, striped skunk, bobcat, burro (feral), wild (feral) horse, mule deer, bighorn sheep.

Amphibians and reptiles: Include zebra-tailed, collared, leopard, desert spiny, side-blotched, long-tailed brush, ornate tree, and desert horned lizards; western whiptail, banded gecko, desert iguana, chuckwalla; Great Plains, red-spotted, and Woodhouse's toads; bullfrog, leopard frog, spiny softshell turtle, western blind snake, coachwhip, western patch-nosed snake, glossy snake, gopher snake, kingsnake, long-nose snake, checkered garter snake, western ground snake, western shovel-nosed snake, spotted night snake, west-ern diamondback, sidewinder, Mojave rattlesnake.

ACTIVITIES

Camping: Prohibited in the National Wildlife Refuges. 50 primitive sites at Picacho State Recreation Area. Camping at any suitable place on BLM land. (Wilderness status would close certain areas to vehicles.)

Hiking, backpacking: Few trails, but much opportunity for cross-country hiking, with possible campsites in isolated basins and valleys.

Hunting: Deer, quail, rabbit.

Fishing: River. Largemouth bass, crappie, catfish.

Swimming: No supervised areas.

Boating: Commercial facilities N and S of the National Wildlife Refuges.
Canoeing: Entire section of river; rentals at Walters Camp, P.O. Box 31,
Palo Verde, CA 92266. Float trips usually originate at Walters Camp (near
Blythe). Usual float trip is one day to Picacho State Recreation Area, next
day to Martinez Lake or Imperial Dam.

PUBLICATIONS
Cibola: Leaflets.
  Public use regulations, with map.
  Bird checklist.
  Mammal checklist (Imperial's, with changes).
  Reptile, amphibian checklist.
Imperial: Leaflets.
  Hunting map and regulations.
  Bird checklist.
  Mammal checklist.

HEADQUARTERS: Cibola: P.O. Box AP, Blythe, CA 92225; (714) 922-2129.
  Imperial: P.O. Box 2217, Martinez Lake, AZ 85364; (602) 783-3400.
  Picacho: P.O. Box 1207, Winterhaven, CA 92283; no telephone. BLM,
  California Desert District, 1695 Spruce St., Riverside, CA 92507; (714)
  787-1462.

CIMA DOME
U.S. Bureau of Land Management
50,000 acres.

From Baker on I-15, 26 mi. E to Valley Wells. Area lies S of Valley Wells,
W of the Cima Rd., which runs S to Cima. The area is crossed by local and
ranch roads.

The Dome is high, broad, and rounded, flanked by rocky ridges. The slopes
of the Dome are gentle, rising from surrounding valleys and washes at about
3,500 ft. elevation to the top at 5,701 ft. Teutonia Peak, rising sharply from
the slopes of the Dome, reaches 5,755 ft. The Ivanpah Mountains extend to
the NE, nearby Kessler Peak reaching 6,163 ft. To the NW, the slope of the
Dome descends into Shadow Valley.

The Shadow Valley-Cima Dome Joshua tree forest is outstanding, dense
stands extending over a considerable area. The thick undergrowth includes
many varieties of cholla cactus with associated shrubs and annuals. Elsewhere
the vegetation is typical of the Mojave Desert: creosote bush scrub, hopsage
scrub, and big galleta scrub steppe.

Wildlife of interest includes golden eagle, Swainson's hawk. This is said to be the only CA area where Bendire's thrasher and gilded flicker are known to breed (a distinction partially lost when taxonomists decreed that all three flickers shall henceforth be "common flicker").

HEADQUARTERS: BLM, California Desert District, 1695 Spruce St., Riverside, CA 92507; (714) 787-1462.

CINDER CONES
U.S. Bureau of Land Management
65,000 acres.

S of Halloran Summit on I-15, W of the Cima Dome area (see entry). W boundary is the paved road from Baker on I-15 to Kelso.

Terrain includes flat valleys, rugged lava flows, and the cinder cones. Numerous large washes cross the area. Several springs create limited areas of riparian vegetation.

The complex includes over 30 cinder cones, dark red and black, symmetrical, rising about 300 ft. above white, sandy washes and black lava flows. It includes cones of ash and cinder, parasitic cones, breached cones, collapsed lava tubes, and other volcanic features, their age estimated between 1,000 and 5,000 years.

Vegetation includes good stands of Joshua tree; cholla, barrel, and hedgehog cacti; creosote bush, low desert shrubs, and grasses.

The site has been designated a National Natural Landmark and Outstanding Natural Area.

HEADQUARTERS: BLM, California Desert District, 1695 Spruce St., Riverside, CA 92507; (714) 787-1462.

CLARK MOUNTAIN
U.S. Bureau of Land Management
15,000 acres.

N of Mountain Pass on I-15 near the NV border. Access by local roads.

An island mountain with exceptional flora and fauna. The mountain, a prominent regional landmark, rises to 7,929 ft. from a base at about 3,500 ft. The mountain mesa has steep-walled, colorful rock formations. Terrain surrounding the mountain includes rolling, rugged hills, narrow canyons, sloping bajadas dissected by washes.

The mountain is biologically distinctive, with eight plant communities. They include a large relict stand of white fir, about 1,000 trees, many specimens over 250 years old; a Joshua tree forest; an exceptionally rich cactus population, including a cactus garden below Pachalka Spring; pinyon-juniper woodland; big galleta scrub steppe; and creosote bush scrub. Fine seasonal flower displays.

Wildlife is also abundant and diverse. Comments gathered in the wilderness study process mentioned outstanding birding and unusual bird species, but without details. Two golden eagle eyries. Breeding area for hepatic tanager and Virginia's warbler. Populations of bighorn sheep, mule deer, Panamint chipmunk, hoary bat, small-footed myotis, desert tortoise.

A local road leads to Pachalka Spring, a perennial water source, and this area attracts some campers, hikers, birders, and rockhounds, but visitor use days are fewer than 600 per year.

Designated an Area of Critical Environmental Concern.

HEADQUARTERS: BLM, California Desert District, 1695 Spruce St., Riverside, CA 92507; (714) 787-1462.

CLEVELAND NATIONAL FOREST
U.S. Forest Service
419,841 acres of National Forest land; 566,781 acres within boundaries.

Three separated parts. (1) SE of Anaheim; S of SR 91; W of SR 71; crossed by SR 74. (2) At Palomar Mountain. S and W of SR 79; crossed by SR 76. (3) About 50 mi. E of San Diego, crossed by I-8.

Planning a visit to the Cleveland requires a bit of study. Its three parts (four, counting a slightly detached part of the Palomar District) have irregular shapes and each contains many inholdings. All three include mountains that lie between the desert and the sea, but not a continuous ridge, nor are the mountains very high. The northern part, the Trabuco Ranger District, covers the Santa Ana Mountains, in which the highest peak is 5,687 ft. Palomar Ranger District, the central part, includes Palomar Mountain, 6,140 ft. elevation, and neighboring hills. Descanso Ranger District, the southern part, includes the Laguna Mountains and the highest point in the Forest, 6,271 ft.;

most of that range is considerably lower. Terrain is complex, with many canyons and interior valleys. On the E side, it drops off sharply into desert. Climate is Mediterranean, though with much local variation. On the W side at low elevations, rainfall is as little as 10 in. annually, though generally a bit over 15 in. On the highest slopes it may exceed 30 in., with a marked seasonal pattern and sharp year-to-year differences. Most streams are seasonal. Several reservoirs are near or within the Forest boundaries, but most of the land around them is private, and they are subject to marked seasonal drawdowns. Snowfall on the high slopes is sometimes sufficient for ski touring and snow play. However, most of the Forest, close to several large cities, is available for hiking when the High Sierra is closed by snow. One reason for the popularity of these Forest campgrounds in summer is that most are at the high elevations, several at 6,000 ft., many over 4,000 ft., where it is cooler than in the valleys below. Large sections of the Trabuco and Palomar Ranger Districts are subject to fire closure after July 1.

In the Trabuco Ranger District, much of the visitor recreation use is on or near SR 74, which runs through the San Juan Canyon. However, the Forest map suggests that many visitors, familiar with the area, enter by various unpaved roads and foot trails around the perimeter, most of them proceeding up small canyons.

Palomar Mountain is known as the site of what may still be the world's largest optical telescope. This Ranger District is irregular in shape, about 40 mi. long, from 2 to 8 mi. wide, with many inholdings. A detached portion is across SR 79; this portion includes about 5 mi. of the Pacific Crest Trail. The Palomar Mountain area has some concentration of recreation facilities, including state and county parks and commercial resorts. The NW corner of the area is the Agua Tibia Wilderness.

The Descanso Ranger District is the largest of the three, 30 mi. from N to S, 24 from E to W, but irregular in shape and with more inholdings than the others. Visitation is greatest in the E sector, the highest country and the coolest in summer. Here 7 campgrounds, including two with over 100 units each, are at or above 5,600 ft. The Pacific Crest Trail runs through this sector. It is permanent throughout the Forest, although these permanent sections are connected by a temporary section between the Pioneer Mail Picnic Ground, at the N end of the District, and the town of Warner Springs.

The Laguna Mountain area, so named because of the small seasonal lakes in the high country, receives more snow than other parts of the Forest. Traffic jams are common on winter weekends when the snow is good, and the Sunrise Highway, S1, is occasionally closed because all roadside parking is full.

Plants: Most of the hillsides are covered with chaparral. Species include mountain mahogany, California buckwheat, several manzanita species, scrub oak, Coast and interior live oaks, white sage, chamise, toyon, coastal sagebrush, willow, sycamore, wild rose, holly-leaved cherry. Valley woodlands include cottonwood, live oak, sycamore, willow, poison oak, wild rose. On the higher slopes, conifer forest, with Jeffrey pine, Douglas-fir, black oak, white fir, incense cedar, Coulter pine. Throughout the Forest there are interesting riparian zones, oak woodlands, and meadows. Flowering plants include ceanothus, slender sunflower, monkeyflower, wild hyacinth, Humboldt lily, penstemons, lupine, wild sweet pea, virgin's bower, yerba buena, yucca. Fire in chaparral burns fiercely and spreads quickly in dry weather. In Sept. 1979, the Laguna fire burned 180,000 acres. Now the E sector of the Descanso Ranger District, together with adjoining private and public lands, is a demonstration area, testing ways to manage chaparral areas. One of the problems is that successful fire suppression causes a gradual buildup of fuel, so that fires become more destructive and more difficult to control.

Birds: No current checklist. Species include California and mountain quail, red-tailed and marsh hawks, common flicker; Nuttall's, hairy, and acorn woodpeckers; western and Cassin's kingbirds, Say's and black phoebes, wood pewee; tree, violet-green, cliff, and barn swallows; spotted owl, Steller's and scrub jays, bushtit, common crow, plain titmouse, horned lark; canyon, Bewick's, and rock wrens; white-breasted nuthatch, mountain and western bluebirds, golden-crowned and ruby-crowned kinglets, phainopepla, Hutton's vireo; yellow, yellow-rumped, orange-crowned, and Wilson's warblers; hooded and northern orioles, western tanager, black-headed grosbeak, brown towhee; savannah, lark, chipping, golden-crowned, white-crowned, fox, and song sparrows.

Mammals: Include voles, kangaroo rats, woodrats, California ground squirrel, northern flying squirrel, western gray squirrel, Merriam chipmunk, brush rabbit, cottontail, black-tailed jackrabbit, ornate and gray shrews, valley pocket gopher, long-tailed weasel, beaver, ringtail, opossum, badger, raccoon, striped and spotted skunks, bobcat, mountain lion, coyote, gray fox, mule deer.

Reptiles and amphibians: Include tiger salamander, small-scaled tree lizard, western toad, California and canyon tree frogs, gopher snake, mountain kingsnake, western diamondback.

FEATURES

Agua Tibia Wilderness, 15,934 acres, NW corner of Palomar Ranger District. Often closed in fire season, beginning July 1. Elevations from 1,400 ft. in canyon bottoms to 5,400 ft. at the crest. Most of the area is in chaparral —but with a difference, for this area has had no major fire in the past century. Dense vegetation with plants of exceptional size: treelike manzanitas with 3-ft. trunks, red-shank chamise with 25-ft. spreads. Some shrubs 14–16 ft. high. Conifer forest at the crest. Best travel time is winter and spring. No overnight use of horses. Water is scarce.

San Mateo Canyon, 29,500 acres proposed for wilderness status; a larger area recommended by conservation groups and included in a House bill. Springs and intermittent streams feed the San Mateo River, which has cut a winding canyon through the Trabuco Ranger District. Its crooked course flows through about 10 sq. mi. of the Forest before it becomes a perennial stream near the S edge.

Side walls clad with oaks and sycamores slope up to rounded hills. Chaparral in the drier spots. Many wildflowers, birds, and mammals.

The road leading NE from the coast near San Clemente ends at the Forest boundary. Some mi. upstream and outside the proposed wilderness area, another road comes in from the E and follows the canyon N. Fisherman's Campground, located at the point where that road enters the canyon, was burned in 1980 and will not be rebuilt. It will remain an access point, possibly a trailhead.

Pine Creek Roadless Area, 13,100 acres, proposed for wilderness designation. SW portion of the Descanso Ranger District. The area drained by Pine Creek and its numerous tributaries, all intermittent. Relatively gentle slopes, from 2,000 ft. elevation in the S to slightly over 4,000 ft in the N. The area has no notable peaks. Plant cover is chaparral, reestablishing after the 1970 fire. Riparian vegetation along Pine Creek.

INCLUDES: Palomar Mountain State Park (in Palomar Ranger District). See entry.

INTERPRETATION
Campfire programs at four of the campgrounds. Schedules posted. Summer season. *Guided hikes,* also in summer.

A small *visitor information center* in the Laguna Mountain area.

Nature trails in each Ranger District. At Trabuco, the El Cariso Trail. At Palomar, Inaja nature trail, through chaparral. Also the Observatory Trail, a 2 1/4 mi. hike, in conifer forest. In the Laguna Mountain area, four trails, each with a theme.

Ask about *star parties, auto tours, night hikes, horseback interpretive tours, junior naturalist programs.*

ACTIVITIES
Camping: 15 campgrounds, 521 sites. Most open all year. Reservations are needed for some campgrounds. These may change from year to year, so inquire. One may camp almost anywhere in the Forest, except closed or posted areas, subject to Forest regulations. A Remote Area Camping permit is required.

Hiking, backpacking: This is not the wildest backcountry. In the Agua Tibia Wilderness, one is usually within a mile or two of the boundary. Nonetheless, there are attractive trails, including some where one can hike all day and encounter few signs of development. Ask a Ranger.

Hunting: Deer, quail.

Horse riding: Several stables in the Mt. Laguna area.

Ski touring: Mt. Laguna area. Some winters, usually Jan.–Mar.

ORV's are limited to posted routes and designated cross-country areas. Some unpaved roads are closed in wet weather to protect roadbeds.

ADJACENT: Anza-Borrego Desert State Park and Cuyamaca Rancho State Park (see entries).

PUBLICATIONS
Forest map. $1.00.
Visitor guide for each Ranger District.
Remote area camping leaflets, for each Ranger District.
ORV maps and regulations, for each Ranger District.
Nature trail guides.
Mammals of the Cleveland National Forest.

HEADQUARTERS: 880 Front St., Rm. 6-S-5, San Diego, CA 92188; (714) 293-5050.

RANGER DISTRICTS: Trabuco R.D., 34 Civic Center Plaza, Rm. 526, Santa Ana, CA 92701; (714) 836-2144. Palomar R.D., 332 S. Juniper St., Escondido, CA 92025, (714) 745-2421. Descanso R.D., 2707 Alpine Blvd., Box 309, Alpine, CA 92001; (714) 445-6235.

COXCOMB MOUNTAINS
U.S. Bureau of Land Management
Included in Joshua Tree National Monument.

CRONESE LAKES
U.S. Bureau of Land Management

N of I-15, about 16 mi. SW of Baker.

These two intermittent lakes, East and West, shown on many highway maps, are at the foot of the Soda Mountains, just off I-15. East Cronese often contains water and provides habitat for wintering and migratory waterfowl and shorebirds, attracting raptors. The Yuma clapper rail has been seen here.

HEADQUARTERS: BLM, California Desert District, 1695 Spruce St., Riverside, CA 92507; (714) 787-1462.

CUYAMACA RANCHO STATE PARK
California Department of Parks and Recreation
24,677 acres.

9 mi. N of I-8 on SR 79.

High in the Peninsular Range, about 40 mi. E of San Diego. It adjoins the Descanso Ranger District—more specifically the Laguna Mountain Recreation Area of that District—of the Cleveland National Forest and is a short distance W of the Anza-Borrego Desert State Park (see entries).

Terrain is rugged, mountainous, from an elevation of about 3,400 ft. in the S end to 6,512-ft. Cuyamaca Peak near the midpoint of the W border. SR 79, the only auto road through the Park, follows a stream valley from Cuyamaca Lake, just outside the N end of the Park, at about 4,600 ft. elevation, leaving the Park at the 3,800-ft. contour at the S end. Several peaks are over 1 mi. high.

Especially if one has just come from the desert area just E of Cuyamaca, it is surprising to find a richly forested area here. On SR 79, much of the vegetation is mature forest, exceptionally large black and canyon live oak; willow, alder, and sycamore along the stream, dense stands of tall incense cedar, white fir, and pines: Coulter, Jeffrey, sugar, and ponderosa. In fact, however, SR 79 is the approximate boundary between plant zones: woodland areas on the W, chaparral on the E.

Most developments are along SR 79: campgrounds, picnic areas, an interpretive center, history museums, Park HQ, and trailheads. Fire roads lead back into the hills, but they are closed to private vehicles, open to foot and horse travel.

Apr. through Sept. is the big visitor season here, although campgrounds and other facilities are open all year. Occasionally winter snow provides enough depth for ski touring and snow play.

Plants: About 1/3 of the site is forested. Tree species include California live oak, Kellogg oak; Jeffrey, Coulter, sugar, and ponderosa pines; incense cedar, white fir, California sycamore, white alder, Fremont cottonwood, leatherleaf ash, interior live oak, arroyo willow. Somewhat more than one third is covered with chaparral, typical species including chamise, manzanita, sumac, buckwheat, buckthorn, ceanothus, coffeeberry. Most of the balance is grassland, although there are scattered pockets of desert vegetation: cacti and agave.

Birds: Birding is outstanding, with nearly 300 species observed in the Park. Although the streams are seasonal and the park has no year-around wetlands, the checklist includes such species as American wigeon, bufflehead, canvasback, common goldeneye, mallard, pintail, redhead, ring-necked duck, ruddy duck, shoveler, blue-winged and cinnamon teals, great and snowy egrets, Canada goose, eared and least grebes, great blue heron. Other species reported include Cooper's, marsh, red-shouldered, red-tailed, sharp-shinned, and Swainson's hawks; golden and bald eagles, osprey; barn, great horned, pygmy, and screech owls; California and mountain quail, band-tailed pigeon, red-breasted and yellow-bellied sapsuckers; Nuttall's, white-headed, acorn, downy, hairy, and ladder-backed woodpeckers; violet-green, cliff, tree, and barn swallows; California thrasher, hermit and varied thrushes, ash-throated and olive-sided flycatchers, empidonax, common bushtit, lesser and Lawrence's goldfinches, roadrunner, horned lark, pygmy nuthatch, gray and Hutton's vireos. Warblers include orange-crowned, hermit, yellow-rumped, black-and-white, black-throated green, Wilson's, Townsend's. Also pine siskin; chipping, golden-crowned, lark, sage, savannah, song, and white-crowned sparrows.

Mammals: Include big brown, evening, and long-eared bats; Merriam chipmunk, nimble kangaroo rat, deer mouse, desert wood rat, dusky-footed wood rat, Botta pocket gopher, broad-footed mole, opossum, cottontail, black-tailed jackrabbit, raccoon, California ground squirrel, western gray squirrel, long-tailed weasel, ringtail, spotted and striped skunks, coyote, bobcat, mountain lion, mule deer.

Reptiles and amphibians: Include alligator, sagebrush, side-blotched, western fence, western whiptail, and granite spiny lizards; western toad, Pacific and canyon tree frogs, ensatina, western skink, racer, western ringneck snake, gopher snake, common and mountain kingsnakes; red diamond, speckled and western rattlesnakes.

FEATURE: *Cuyamaca Peak,* reached by a 3 1/2-mi. trail, offers vistas of the Pacific Ocean, Mexico, Salton Sea, and desert.

INTERPRETATION
Interpretive center has exhibits on native flora and fauna.
History Museum, near HQ, depicts the lives of early residents.
Campfire programs and *guided hikes* in summer. Notices posted.
Two *nature trails,* self-guiding.
Exhibit at *Stonewall mine,* large gold mine closed in 1892.

ACTIVITIES
Camping: 3 campgrounds. 182 sites. All year. Reservations Apr. 6–Oct. 1.
Hiking, backpacking: 130 mi. of trails. Trails into Cleveland National Forest and Anza-Borrego Desert State Park. Two trail camps, 6 and 7 mi. from trailheads; registration required before departure. No trailside camping.
Horse riding: 90 mi. of trails. Riders may use trail camps, registering in advance. Special campground for auto campers with horses.
Ski touring: When snow is sufficient; not every year.

ADJACENT OR NEARBY: Cleveland National Forest and Anza-Borrego Desert State Park (see entries).

PUBLICATIONS
Leaflet with map.

Information on use of trail camps.

Checklists of plants, bird, mammals, reptiles, and amphibians.

HEADQUARTERS: Route 1, Box 2700, Descanso, CA 92016; (714) 765-0355.

EAGLE MOUNTAINS
U.S. Bureau of Land Management

Included in Joshua Tree National Monument.

FORT PIUTE
U.S. Bureau of Land Management

44,200 acres.

On the CA-NV border, W of US 95, E of Lanfair Rd., about 12 mi. N of Needles. Access by local roads.

The area includes part of the Castle Mountains to the N. The Piute Range runs N–S between the Lanfair and Piute valleys. High point in the range is 4,909 ft., above the base at 3,000 ft. on the E side, 3,500 on the W. Mountain vegetation is sparse, mostly creosote and sagebrush.

Visitors are attracted by the Piute Gorge, near the S end of the range. Piute Springs is the source of a perennial creek. Because of the water supply, a fort was built here in 1867–1868, of which only traces remain. The spring and stream support lush riparian vegetation, above which rise steep, red canyon walls. Plants include willow, cattail, watercress, mesquite. The water attracts wildlife as well as visitors.

Good rockhounding in the Castle Mountains. Hunting for chukar, quail, dove.

HEADQUARTERS: BLM, California Desert District, 1695 Spruce St., Riverside, CA 92507; (714) 787-1462.

GOLDEN VALLEY
U.S. Bureau of Land Management

33,800 acres.

E of Johannesburg on US 395. Bounded on N and S by local roads: Randsburg Wash Rd. and Steam Well Rd. E boundary is Mojave Range, Naval Weapons Center.

BLM ranked this area third among 137 CA Wilderness Study Areas. It was rated high on scenic values. It includes the Lava Mountains, Golden Valley, Almond Mountains, Summit Range, Teagle Wash, and Spangler Hills. The Lava Mountains rise about 1,700 ft. from the desert floor, to a high point at 4,985 ft. Canyons in the mountains have walls with spectacular, multicolored sedimentary layers. Golden Valley has a rolling floor about 8 mi. long, 2 mi. wide, between the Lava and Almond mountains. Just N of the Lava Mountains are the sand hills of the Summit Range, with a Joshua tree woodland. The land then slopes down to Teagle Wash, at 2,800 ft. elevation along the W boundary to 2,000 ft. near the Randsburg Wash Road.

Vegetation is typical of the Mojave Desert, mostly creosote bush and allscale, with many seasonally flowering annuals. The area includes 13 sq. mi. of desert tortoise habitat, two prairie falcon and one golden eagle eyrie, a population of the rare Mojave ground squirrel. Good populations of game species: quail, dove, rabbit, chukar.

Teagle Wash has been used for motorcycle racing, and shows it. The Summit Range and other areas W of the Lava Mountains also show erosion and other effects of ORV activity. These areas have been excluded from the wilderness recommendation. The Golden Valley has been less affected, although it shows some vehicle tracks as well as the effects of heavy sheep grazing. Wilderness designation would exclude further vehicle entry.

HEADQUARTERS: BLM, Bakersfield District Office, 800 Truxtun, Rm. 311, Bakersfield, CA 93301; (805) 861-4191.

HARPER DRY LAKE; RAINBOW BASIN-OWL CANYON
U.S. Bureau of Land Management
About 4,000 acres.

Rainbow Basin-Owl Canyon is 5 mi. N of Barstow via Camp Irwin Rd., then 5 mi. W on Fossil Beds Rd. Harper Dry Lake, shown on most highway maps, is several miles farther NW, crossed by a local road.

Rainbow Basin was so named because of its spectacular display of colorful sedimentary rocks. The area is also a rich source of Miocene vertebrate fossils, including fossilized camel tracks. Fossil Canyon is nearby. There is a road loop through the area. The campground is in Owl Canyon.

Harper Dry Lake is no longer dry, because of irrigation on neighboring farmlands. Usually there is some standing water, and a good marsh has developed, attracting waterfowl and shorebirds. Species reported include the endangered Yuma clapper rail and bald eagle. The BLM is cooperating with the CA Department of Fish and Game to develop a habitat management plan. The BLM plans a boardwalk, observation tower, and interpretive program.

Camping: 31 tent sites.

HEADQUARTERS: BLM, California Desert District, 1695 Spruce St., Riverside, CA 92507; (714) 787-1462.

HAVASU NATIONAL WILDLIFE REFUGE
U.S. Fish and Wildlife Service
7,747 acres in CA; 35,323 acres in AZ.

Along the Colorado River between Needles, CA, and Lake Havasu City, AZ. Crossed by I-40.

The refuge was established in 1941 to compensate for the wildlife habitat flooded by Parker Dam. Somewhat to the dismay of wildlife managers, portions of the refuge and adjacent areas have become popular with motorboating enthusiasts. On the whole, the birds and boaters coexist, using different parts of the refuge and at different times. Bird populations are greatest in winter and during migrations; the boaters come mostly in summer. Waterbirds favor the shallows and marshes; boaters choose the scenic river canyon.

The refuge has three units. *Topock Marsh* lies between Needles and Topock, AZ, where I-40 crosses the river. The channelized river is its W boundary, as well as the CA-AZ boundary. The E side of the marsh is a 4,000-acre lake. The marsh is cut by a network of channels and ponds.

In floating the river, one can choose the river or the marsh, the latter requiring a couple of short portages. To visit the marsh by boat, one can launch at either of two concessions, Five Mile Landing or Catfish Paradise. The marsh has numerous stubs and snags, menacing to propellers.

The route through the marsh is about 13 mi., assuming no detours. Camping is prohibited in the unit, so one must plan to be at Five Mile Landing, about the midpoint, or Catfish Paradise, at the S end, before dark. Concessions at both places accommodate campers. Portions of the marsh are closed seasonally; the main route is open. Those who choose the river route have only a 10-mi. run to Park Moabi, a county park, 1 mi. N of the Topock bridge, where camping is available.

Topock Gorge extends S from the Topock bridge to Lake Havasu, a 16-mi.

trip. Some enthusiasts call this the most scenic section of the Lower Colorado. Others limit this superlative to the 7 mi. of colorful rock cliffs in Mohave Canyon. The 16 mi. can be made by canoe in a day, if one starts early. There is little choice, because camping is prohibited in the Gorge, and sundown is no excuse. Takeout is at Castle Rock, on the AZ side, unless one is continuing on through Lake Havasu, inadvisable in windy weather. Beyond the buoys marking the end of the Gorge, camping is allowed on the AZ side, except at Mesquite Bay.

At one time the refuge included Lake Havasu. It now includes only a bit of the upper end, to a point about 3 mi. S of the Gorge boundary. On the AZ side of the Gorge, the refuge includes part of the Mohave Mountains. The Needles are a series of pinnacle-shaped volcanic plugs. Highest point is Powell Peak, just over 2,200 ft. elevation. Part of this upland area has been proposed for wilderness status.

The CA side of the Gorge is the E edge of the Chemehuevi Mountains. The strip of desert upland on the W side of the river, generally less than 1 mi. wide, is the only land area of the refuge in CA. However, much of the adjacent land is public domain, also proposed for wilderness status (see "Adjacent" section for this entry).

The Colorado River is unchannelized through the Gorge. The dam has created a number of backwater bays that are good wildlife habitats. Motors are allowed on the river, but the land area of this unit is closed to all motor vehicles.

Bill Williams River Delta, the third unit, is near Parker Dam at the S end of Lake Havasu. Take AZ SR 95 N from the dam to Bill Williams River. Turn SE on Planet Ranch Rd., which parallels the unit and crosses parts of it. The unit, 6,105 acres, includes four major habitat types: high, rocky desert with scant vegetation; mesa desert floor, with creosote bush-ocotillo association; pockets of saguaro cactus and blue palo verde; river bottomland with open water, extensive cattail marsh, and cottonwood groves. This unit has a greater variety of flora and fauna than the other two. It is best explored on foot.

Elevation at the river is about 500 ft. Annual precipitation is about 4 in. Rainfall occurs chiefly in early spring and late summer during violent thunderstorms.

Plants: Extensive areas of bulrush and cattail. Bottomland in the Bill Williams unit has one of the last large stands of Fremont cottonwood on the Lower Colorado. Desert plant communities include creosote bush, ocotillo, brittle-bush, palo verde, saguaro, white bur-sage, desert lavender, desert holly. Cacti include saguaro, cholla, jumping cholla, barrel, beavertail, hedgehog. Wildflowers include phacelia, evening primrose, desert trumpet, snapdragon, globe mallow, golden aster, California poppy, lupine, milk vetch, desert lily, sand verbena.

Birds: Of the 276 species recorded, only 64 are known to nest on the refuge. Most are seasonal visitors. Best period to see waterfowl is Oct. to mid-Mar.

Wintering snow and Canada geese usually arrive early Nov. An observation tower near the levee road in the Topock Marsh unit offers a view of geese grazing on the refuge fields. Migrating bald eagles are sometimes seen at the marsh during winter and early spring. Active rookeries of great blue heron and double-crested cormorant can be seen here between Feb. and May. Western grebe colonies are best seen in the backbays of the Gorge in summer. The refuge is a major nesting area for the endangered Yuma clapper rail, but these solitary, secretive birds are seldom seen.

Checklist available. Seasonally common or abundant species include eared, western, and pied-billed grebes; white pelican, green heron, great and snowy egrets, black-crowned night heron, least bittern, mallard, gadwall, pintail, green-winged and cinnamon teals, American wigeon, shoveler, redhead, ring-necked duck, lesser scaup, bufflehead, ruddy duck, common and red-breasted mergansers. Also sora, common gallinule, American coot, snowy plover, spotted sandpiper, willet, greater yellowlegs, least sandpiper, long-billed dowitcher, western sandpiper, marbled godwit, avocet, black-necked stilt, Wilson's and northern phalaropes. Raptors include Cooper's, sharp-shinned, red-tailed, and marsh hawks; kestrel. Upland species include Gambel's quail; white-winged, mourning, and Inca doves; roadrunner, lesser nighthawk, white-throated swift, Costa's hummingbird, common flicker, Gila and ladder-backed woodpeckers, western kingbird; ash-throated, willow, Hammond's, and western flycatchers; western wood pewee; violet-green, tree, rough-winged, and cliff swallows; common raven, verdin, house and rock wrens, long-billed marsh wren, black-tailed gnatcatcher, ruby-crowned kinglet, phainopepla, loggerhead shrike, starling, warbling vireo. Warblers: orange-crowned, yellow, yellow-rumped, MacGillivray's, yellow-throat, yellow-breasted chat, Wilson's. Also western meadowlark, yellow-headed and red-winged blackbirds, hooded and northern orioles, western tanager, black-headed and blue grosbeaks, house finch, Abert's towhee; savannah, black-throated, sage, Brewer's, white-crowned, Lincoln's, and song sparrows.

Mammals: Include California myotis, western pipistrel, Mexican free-tailed bat, black-tailed jackrabbit, cottontail, antelope squirrel, roundtail ground squirrel, valley pocket gopher, pocket mice, Merriam and desert kangaroo rats, beaver, western harvest mouse, canyon mouse, cactus mouse, deer mouse, hispid cotton rat, white-throated woodrat, muskrat, porcupine, coyote, kit fox, gray fox, ringtail, raccoon, badger, striped skunk, bobcat, feral burro, feral horse, feral hog, bighorn sheep, mule deer.

Reptiles and amphibians: Include desert banded gecko, desert iguana, western chuckwalla; zebra-tailed, collared, long-nosed, yellow-backed spiny, desert side-blotched, western brush, tree, Mojave fringe-toed, and southern desert horned lizards; Great Basin whiptail, many-lined skink, Gila monster; spadefoot, Great Plains, red-spotted, and southwestern toads; canyon tree frog, leopard frog, bullfrog, Texas and spiny soft-shelled turtles, Sonoran and yellow mud turtles, western worm snake, desert rosy boa, glossy snake, western shovel-nosed snake, spotted night snake, California kingsnake, common whipsnake, spotted leaf-nosed snake, gopher snakes, western ground snake, desert and Mojave patch-nosed snakes, checkered garter snake, Arizona lyre snake, desert sidewinder, Mojave rattlesnake, western diamondback rattlesnake.

ACTIVITIES

Camping: At the concessions on Topock Marsh. No camping in the refuge except boat and tent camping on the AZ shoreline below the buoys marking the S end of the Gorge; no camping in Mesquite Bay.

Hiking: On refuge roads. No marked trails, but numerous areas are suitable for hiking, including the upland E of the Gorge. On the CA side, hiking into the BLM area (see "Adjacent" section).

Hunting: In designated areas, subject to federal and state regulations.

Fishing: In all waters except as posted. Largemouth and striped bass, bluegill, crappie, catfish, rainbow trout.

Swimming: Except where restricted. No supervised area.

Boating: On all waters except as posted. Water skiing on the river only, and not in the Gorge. Boat traffic has become so heavy at peak periods that regulations have been adopted to minimize accidents. Boaters should be aware of these before launching. Launching at commercial facilities: Topock Marsh, Park Moabi, Catfish Bay.

Canoeing: Mar.–Apr. is the best time to canoe the Gorge. Power boat traffic is slight. Desert plants bloom. Climate is good. Power boat traffic is heavy on summer weekends.

ADJACENT

The *Chemehuevi Mountains* (BLM), 95,400 acres, lie between US 95 and Topock Gorge. Access from US 95, Lake Havasu Rd., or on foot from the refuge. From the Colorado River, the mountains rise abruptly through a convoluted series of highly eroded washes, vegetated with smoke tree and mesquite. The mountains form a high ridge with 18 peaks over 2,500 ft. Chemehuevi Peak is 3,697 ft. The W side of the ridge drops abruptly to the desert floor of Chemehuevi Valley. The upper edge of the valley is rocky, irregular, eroded, densely vegetated with Bigelow and buckhorn cholla, barrel cactus, small cacti varieties. Numerous ocotillo. The mountains are habitat for a small herd of bighorn sheep.

Rugged terrain makes the mountains inaccessible except on foot or horseback. The cliffs, high canyons, washes, and ridges offer ample opportunities for solitude. Deer hunting is considered fair. Rockhounding fair to good.

There appear to be no springs in the area, and streams are intermittent.

PUBLICATIONS (refuge)

Public use regulations; information; map.
Leaflet.

Partial plant list.
Bird checklist.
Mammal list.
Fish, amphibians and reptiles lists.
Hunting information.
Fishing information.
Canoe and float trip information.

HEADQUARTERS (refuge): P.O. Box A, 1406 Bailey Ave., Needles, CA 92363; (714) 326-3853. BLM, California Desert District, 1695 Spruce St., Riverside CA 92507; (714) 787-1462.

IMPERIAL NATIONAL WILDLIFE REFUGE
U.S. Fish and Wildlife Service
See Cibola National Wildlife Refuge.

IMPERIAL WILDLIFE AREA
California Department of Fish and Game
2,047 acres.

Finney-Ramer Unit: 8 mi. N of Brawley, on SR III. Wister Unit is at SE corner of Salton Sea. Visitor permits for Wister at Davis Rd., 1/4 mi. S of SR III, 5 mi. NW of Niland.

The *Finney-Ramer Unit* is S of the Salton Sea, in the Imperial Valley, a natural habitat enclave surrounded by broad, flat farmlands. The refuge serves the dual purpose of supporting waterfowl populations and lessening their consumption of farm crops. The area is about 175 ft. below sea level, with sandy saline soil, in a hot desert climate. Water from the Colorado River flows in through irrigation canals, maintaining Ramer and Finney lakes, each about 2 mi. long, and four small ponds. Lakes and ponds are surrounded by thick riparian vegetation. Common vegetation of the site includes mesquite, palo verde, tamarisk, palm, arrowweed, willow, salt cedar, cattail, cane.

The Unit is a strip almost 10 mi. long, about 1 mi. wide. bordered and crossed by public roads. Headquarters and visitor registration are on the E side of Ramer Lake, near the midpoint of the site. Two campgrounds are on Finney Lake, to the S.

The *Wister Unit,* 4,700 acres, is at the SE corner of the Salton Sea, not far from the Salton Sea National Wildlife Refuge (see entry), close to the shore but with no frontage. Acquired in 1956, much of the land was then raw desert.

The Department has created 2,700 acres of ponds, 1,000 acres of ponded watergrass and bulrush. Feed is grown on about 1,000 acres of irrigated land. Colorado River water is purchased.

Birds: Up to 50,000 ducks and 20,000 geese winter here. Checklist is available for the Finney-Ramer Unit. This and the checklist for the National Wildlife Refuge are applicable to the Wister Unit. Over 260 species identified here, including whistling swan, sandhill crane, roseate spoonbill, white pelican, bittern, wood ibis, herons, egrets, rails, terns, snipe, dowitcher, dunlin, yellowlegs, phalaropes, fulvous tree duck, roadrunner, killdeer, Gambel's quail, doves, a dozen hawk species, owls, swifts, woodpeckers, and songbirds.

The first flights of returning ducks arrive in late July or early Aug. The main flights of snow and Canada geese arrive in late Nov. or early Dec. Duck and goose numbers peak in Feb. Most are gone by late Mar. Shorebirds are most numerous in winter, marsh birds in summer.

Summers are extremely hot, temperatures to 120°F. Winter weather is delightful.

ACTIVITIES

Camping: Two primitive campgrounds at Finney-Ramer, one at Wister.

Hunting: At Finney-Ramer, waterfowl and upland game. Because of treacherous lake bottoms, hunting from boat only. Quota of 60 hunters. At Wister, permit and fee required; quota. Hunting 3 days per week and certain holidays, in season.

Fishing: The principal visitor activity. Warm-water species: channel catfish, bluegill, largemouth bass, carp.

Boating: Small boat ramp on Ramer Lake. No motors.

All users must have permits, available by self-registration at entrances.

PUBLICATIONS

Leaflets with maps, both units.

Site maps.

Bird checklist, Finney-Ramer Unit.

HEADQUARTERS: Star Route 1, Box 6, Niland, CA 92257; (714) 384-2493.

IN-KO-PAH MOUNTAINS
U.S. Bureau of Land Management
29,700 acres.

On the Mexican border just E of Anza-Borrego Desert State Park. S of Ocotillo and Coyote Wells. I-8 and SR 98 are the N boundary.

Already declared an Outstanding Natural Area, this site was ranked 5th among 137 Wilderness Study Areas in the CA Desert and recommended for wilderness status. The mountains rise from the Yuha Basin to the E and extend to the NW beyond the limits of this BLM site. The basin is between sealevel and 500 ft. elevation. Most terrain within the site is under 2,500 ft., with one peak in the SW rising to 4,548 ft. Landforms include pinnacles, spires, steep-walled canyons, and the gently sloping Davies Valley, strewn with huge granite boulders. Five springs are in the W portion of the area.

Vegetation is mostly creosote bush scrub. Several small palm groves are scattered in Davies Valley, and the Valley also has extensive stands of agave and ocotillo. A palm oasis is at Mountain Springs with a blackbrush enclave nearby. The Smuggler's Cave area has an extensive growth of southern chaparral.

The site includes both permanent and transient bighorn sheep range, a mule deer population, foraging areas for golden eagle and prairie falcon, chukar, quail.

Davies Valley and Meyers Valley are moderately popular camping areas. Several rockhounding sites.

HEADQUARTERS: BLM, California Desert District, 1695 Spruce St., Riverside, CA 92507; (714) 787-1462.

JOSHUA TREE NATIONAL MONUMENT
U.S. National Park Service
547,790 acres.

At Twentynine Palms on SR 62. S entrance from I-10 on Cottonwood Springs Rd., 25 mi. E of Indio.

The visitor center at Twentynine Palms, just outside the Monument, is the best introduction to the area, worth a stop for at least an hour or two. The center includes a self-guiding trail through the Twentynine Palms Oasis, where the birding is lively. With this orientation, the Monument itself becomes an introduction to the southwestern desert. No one who has spent a few days here is likely to consider any desert region dull or monotonous.

This is high desert, in the transition zone between the Mojave and Colorado Deserts. Unlike the below-sealevel Death Valley and Imperial Valley, elevations range from 1,000 ft. in the Pinto Basin in the E to nearly 6,000 ft. in the Little San Bernardino Mountains in the W. The weather here is usually pleasant, especially so in spring and fall. At Twentynine Palms, elevation 1,960 ft., temperature peaks above 100°F about 80 days per year. Even then, nights are cool, and days are considerably cooler at higher elevations. Average annual rainfall is less than 5 in., but with considerable variation. At Twentynine Palms the driest year on record had only 1/4 in. of rain, the wettest more than 11 in. and once almost 4 in. fell in a single day.

Many visitors make a 40-mi. tour, entering at Twentynine Palms, turning right at Pinto Wye Junction, and returning to SR 62 at the town of Joshua Tree, 15 mi. W of their starting point. Others make the 49-mi. N–S crossing to I-10. These are the principal paved roads in the Monument, winding and narrow in places, adequate for trailers and large RV's with care in driving. Several dirt roads are satisfactory for autos in dry weather. Others are marked for 4-wheel-drive vehicles. No motor vehicles are permitted off established roads, and all must be registered and street-legal.

Large areas of the Monument are roadless, reached only by foot or on horseback. This includes most of the high country in the Little San Bernardino Mountains as well as the Pinto Mountains in the NE. Indeed, 467,000 acres of the Monument have been designated as wilderness.

Plants: The Joshua tree, a giant yucca, is abundant in the higher W half of the Monument, where elevations are generally over 3,000 ft. It attains heights of 40 ft. When it blooms—in Mar. and Apr., but not every year—it bears clusters of cream-white blossoms at branch tips. The similar Mojave yucca has much longer leaves, grows at lower elevations.

The Colorado Desert area, lower, in the E half, is characterized by abundant creosote bush with small stands of ocotillo and jumping cholla. A third ecosystem is the oasis, found where water is at or near the surface. The Monument has five fan-palm oases. Outside the Monument, a number of communities grew up around such desert oases. Since then the water table has been lowered by pumping from deep wells, and the oases may be doomed.

Those who hike into the W mountains find the upper zone not only cooler but moister than the desert below, with patches of chaparral, the association including manzanita and scrub oak. Nearby are slopes with sparse pinyon pine and juniper.

To many visitors, "desert" means cacti, and many varieties occur here, including holycross and Parish chollas, several pricklypear species, barrel cactus, fringe-flowered nipple cactus, buckhorn cholla, cottontop cactus, hedgehog cactus, mound cactus, Alverson corypantha, dollarjoint.

The blooming of desert wildflowers in spring tranforms the landscape. Among the species found here are desert trumpet, yellow cups, fiddleneck, coyote melon, blazing star, tansy mustard, golden gilia, gold-poppy, liveforever, chinchweed, desert dandelion, eriophyllum, coreopsis, scale bud, woolly marigold, fringed amaranth, sand verbena, filaree, locoweed, desert calico, mitra, Mojave aster, purple mat, desert paintbrush, desert mariposa, desert mallow, amsonia, chia, lupine, desert gilia, Canterbury bell, phacelia, brown-eyed primrose, California primrose, woody bottle-washer, white forget-me-not, wishbone, sand blazing star, jimsonweed, sand mat, desert star, pincushion, tidy-tips.

Birds: Checklist available; 219 species, many of these casual or occasional. Seasonally common or abundant species include turkey vulture, red-tailed hawk, Gambel's and mountain quail, mourning dove, roadrunner, long-eared owl, poor-will, white-throated swift; Anna's, Costa's, and rufous hummingbirds; common flicker, ladder-backed woodpecker, western kingbird, Say's phoebe, horned lark, scrub jay, common raven, mountain chickadee, plain titmouse, verdin, common bushtit; Bewick's, cactus, rock, and canyon wrens; mockingbird, sage and Le Conte's thrashers, robin, western and mountain bluebirds, blue-gray gnatcatcher, ruby-crowned kinglet, phainopepla, loggerhead shrike, starling, orange-crowned and yellow-rumped warblers, western meadowlark; Scott's, hooded, and northern orioles; western tanager, house finch; black-throated, sage, and white-crowned sparrows.

Mammals: Checklist available. Includes western pipistrel, leaf-nosed bat, Mexican free-tailed bat, Merriam's chipmunk, pocket gopher, pronghorn, round-tailed and California ground squirrels, black-tailed jackrabbit, cottontail, Merriam and desert kangaroo rats, woodrat, various mice, shrew, raccoon, ringtail, badger, spotted and striped skunks, kit fox, coyote, gray fox, mountain lion, bighorn sheep. Mule deer occasional in the mountains.

Reptiles and amphibians: Checklist available. Includes banded gecko; zebra-tailed, collared, leopard, horned, desert spiny, western fence, Mojave fringe-toed, long-tailed brush, side-blotched, and desert night lizards; Gilbert's skink, western whiptail, California treefrog, red-spotted toad, desert tortoise, western blind snake, rosy boa, glossy snake, western shovel-nosed snake, night snake, common kingsnake, red and striped racers, spotted leaf-nosed snake, gopher snake, long-nosed snake, western patch-nosed snake, western black-headed snake, lyre snake, western diamondback rattlesnake, sidewinder; speckled, Mojave, western, and red diamond rattlesnakes.

FEATURES

Twentynine Palms Oasis is the site of the Visitor Center and HQ.

Fortynine Palms Oasis is reached only on foot, by a 1 1/2-mi. trail. Trailhead is off SR 62 about 4 mi. W of Twentynine Palms.

Keys View is at the end of the only paved road into the Little San Bernardino Mountains. At 5,185 ft., it offers a magnificent view.

Ryan Mountain, 5,461 ft., is closer to the center of the Monument. The summit is reached by a 1 1/2-mi. trail.

Cottonwood Spring, a palm oasis, is near the S entrance. The area includes a Visitor Center, campground. *Lost Palms Oasis,* reached by a 4-mi trail, has the Monument's largest stand of palms.

INTERPRETATION

Visitor Centers are at the N and S entrances and Black Rock Canyon. The one at Twentynine Palms, the N entrance, is more extensive, the preferred introduction to the area.

Nature trails at several locations: at the Twentynine Palm Oasis; Indian Cove, off SR 62; Cap Rock; Cholla Cactus Garden, on the N–S road; Arch Rock in White Tank Campground.

Motor nature trail, 18 mi., emphasizes geology, early history. The unpaved road, suitable for cars in dry weather, offers some fine views of Monument features.

Guided walks, hikes, and *campfire programs* are scheduled principally in spring and fall. Notices posted.

ACTIVITIES

Camping: 8 campgrounds. 535 sites. All year. Water is available at Cottonwood and Black Rock Canyon campgrounds. Water can be obtained at Twentynine Palms Visitor Center and Indian Cove Ranger Station.

Hiking, backpacking: Many short trails for day hikes. An information sheet describes hikes of 1–13 mi. 35 mi. of the California Riding and Hiking Trail pass through the Monument. Camping in the backcountry is permitted, no closer than 1 mi. to any vehicle route, no closer than 500 ft. to a trail. Backpackers must register. A few areas are restricted; these are marked on maps at Ranger Stations and Visitor Centers. The hiker is responsible for knowing about them. For all but short day trips, hikers should have topo maps, ample water, understanding of desert hiking safety.

Horse riding: Horses are permitted at only one campground, Ryan. Horse travel in the backcountry is permitted, but the Monument has no special facilities. Riders must make their own arrangements for feed and water.

ADJACENT

The *Pinto Mountains* (BLM), 26,800 acres, lie between SR 62 and the Monument N boundary, just E of the Twentynine Palms entrance. Steep, generally rounded hills. Vegetation is mostly creosote bush association; smoke trees and other species in washes. Mojave yucca in interior valleys. Much evidence of past mining activity. About 11 sq. mi. of bighorn sheep range, 3 sq. mi. of desert tortoise habitat. A BLM study concluded this area is unsuitable for wilderness designation. It has had considerable ORV use, and this will probably continue.

The *Coxcomb Mountains, Sheephole,* and *Cadiz areas* (BLM), 194,880 acres, surround the NE corner of the Monument, and extend N across SR 62; Amboy Rd. is part of the W boundary. The area S of SR 62 contains portions of two major mountain ranges. Coxcomb Mountains rise sharply from the desert floor on the E, grade W into an area of small boulder piles. Pinto Mountains, on the W edge, extending into the Monument, are more rounded, although many slopes are steep. Large alluvial fans slope away from the mountains. Rugged terrain. Vegetation is sparse, mostly creosote bush association. Two springs in the E portion of the Coxcomb Mountains are used by wildlife, including bighorn sheep. The BLM rates the scenic qualities of the area high. In part because this area adjoins what has already been designated as wilderness within the Monument, this area will probably be so designated.

The 136,000-acre Sheephole-Cadiz area was considered separately from Coxcomb Mountains because SR 62 divides them. It includes two vast desert valleys bounded by steep granitic mountains: Cadiz Valley is below 1,000 ft. elevation, Sheephole generally above 1,000 ft. Highest point in the area is a 4,613-ft. peak in the Sheephole Mountains. Both valleys have dry lakebeds that attract snowy egret and other birds after heavy rains. Cadiz has a small dune system. Creosote bush, galleta grass, and mixed shrubs are sparse in the valleys. Vegetation is about nil in the lakebeds and on the slopes. One spring in the Sheephole Mountains provides water for a small bighorn sheep herd. Wilderness status has been recommended.

The *Eagle Mountains* (BLM), 55,000 acres, lie on the SE boundary of the Monument. An unsurfaced road from the Monument penetrates the area. The S boundary includes a section of I-10. The Eagle Mountains extend from the SE corner of the Monument to the NE, dropping down into the Pinto Basin. Highest point is Eagle Mountain, 3,969 ft. The mountains are rugged and complex, with many small canyons, interior valleys, steep slopes, washes, large boulders of quartz monzonite, boulder piles. In some portions of the washes vegetation is thick, including varieties of yucca, cacti, palo verde, ironwood, smoke trees, various annuals. Most vegetation is creosote bush scrub, with ocotillo and Bigelow cholla.

Three springs in the mountains support wildlife populations, including bighorn sheep. Chukar and quail occur in fair numbers. The site includes fan palm oases. The area adjoins the designated wilderness within the Monument. Wilderness status has been recommended.

PUBLICATIONS
    Leaflet with map.
    Checklists:
        Cacti.
        Birds.
        Mammals.
        Amphibians and reptiles.
    Information pages:
        General information.
        Twentynine Palms weather.
        Campgrounds.
        Regulations.
        Motorcycle, motorbike rules.
        Desert survival.
        Backcountry rules.
        Hiking trails.

REFERENCES

Publications of the Joshua Tree Natural History Association, 74485 Palm Vista Dr., Twentynine Palms, CA 92277:

Trimble, Stephen. *Joshua Tree—desert reflections*. 1979. $2.00.

Amphibians and Reptiles. 10¢.

A Day at Cottonwood Spring. 10¢.

The Desert Queen Ranch. 15¢.

Mammals. 10¢.

The Natural Landscape. 10¢.

A Guide to the Twentynine Palms Oasis. 10¢.

Palm Oases. 10¢.

Wildflowers. 20¢.

Various topographic maps.

HEADQUARTERS: 74485 National Monument Dr., Twentynine Palms, CA 92277; (714) 367-7511. BLM, California Desert District, 1695 Spruce St., Riverside, CA 92507; (714) 787-1462.

KELSO MOUNTAINS; DEVIL'S PLAYGROUND; GRANITE MOUNTAINS; BRISTOL MOUNTAINS
U.S. Bureau of Land Management
384,500 acres.

Between I-15 and I-40, immediately W of the road from Baker, on I-15, that runs E and S through Kelso.

In the triangle formed by these three roads, a majority of the land is public domain, checkerboarded with nonfederal land in the S and W. This entry describes four adjacent Wilderness Study Areas.

Elevations range from less than 1,000 ft. in the Devil's Playground to 6,738 ft. in the Granite Mountains. Most of the area is between 2,000 and 3,000 ft. elevation. Rainfall is about 4 in.

S of Baker is the dry, alkali-covered Soda Lake Bed, mostly barren, lowest point in the area. Extending to the SE, to a point near Kelso, are the low, sand-blanketed hills of the *Devil's Playground*. N of the Playground is 4,250-ft. Old Dad Mountain, steep-sided, habitat for a herd of bighorn sheep. Vegetation is mostly creosote bush scrub, allscale scrub, and mesquite thickets.

The *Kelso Mountain Unit* extends E to Kelbaker Rd. Highest point is 4,764 ft. The mountains are part of the range for bighorn sheep. This 70,700-acre unit is about 40% alluvial and dissected fans, 35% sand dunes, 20% hills, 5% sandy plains. Vegetation is chiefly sparse creosote bush scrub.

The *Kelso Dunes* are in a vast area, a unit of 161,900 acres, lying W of the Kelbaker Rd. The Kelso Dunes are the tallest in the CA desert, rising 500 to 600 ft. Also within the unit are two large, sweeping valleys and the rolling Bristol Mountains. Most of the vegetation is sparse creosote and mixed shrubs. Over much of the area, one has sweeping views of the rugged Providence Mountains to the E and the equally rugged Granite Mountains to the S. The dunes are noteworthy both for their size and an unusual assortment of plant species, more diverse than the scrub of the surrounding desert. Vegetation has begun to stabilize some of the lower dunes. In relatively wet years, there is a fine floral display, including evening primrose, desert sunflower, and desert lily. The dune area has been closed to ORV's because of damage to fragile vegetation, but enforcement is difficult.

The *Bristol-Granite Mountain Unit,* 93,900 acres, extends S to I-40. Much of this area is mountainous: the Old Dad Mountains, Granite Mountains, and Bristol Mountains. Pinyon pine and juniper cover the upper portion of the Granite Mountains, highest in this region. Some 240 plant species have been identified here. Granite Pass has excellent floral displays in wet years. The area has several small springs.

No comprehensive inventory of flora and fauna is available for this large area, but it is generally typical of the California desert. It includes habitat for the desert tortoise, a few golden eagle. It has enough game to attract hunters, though not in large numbers. Rockhounds have found agates, jasper, sagenite, obsidian, chalcedony, calcite crystals, geodes, banded onyx.

In the wilderness study process, some groups objected to closing these areas to ORV's. Similar sentiments were voiced by people interested in ORV activity not as sport but as a means of backcountry transportation. Desert camping from a 4-wheel-drive vehicle or pickup truck has become increasingly popular. It is probable that only portions of the 384,500 acres will be designated as wilderness, other portions put in categories that are protective but less restrictive.

The area has no campgrounds or other visitor facilities.

HEADQUARTERS: BLM, California Desert District, 1695 Spruce St., Riverside, CA 92507; (714) 787-1462.

KINGSTON RANGE
U.S. Bureau of Land Management
270,360 acres.

From Baker on I-15, N on SR 127. The area lies E of SR 127, from Silurian Dry Lake to Tecopa.

Most land in this region, E and S of Death Valley National Monument, along the NV border, is public domain, the nonfederal land generally 2 sections in each 36. This Wilderness Study Area was delineated by roads and utility rights-of-way. Although only 15% of the area was deemed suitable for wilderness designation, half of the remainder was put in class I, in which management priority is protection of natural, scenic, ecological, and cultural resources, limiting conflicting uses.

The recommended wilderness area is roughly limited to the Kingston Range, lying E of the S end of the National Monument, beyond Tecopa Pass. The rugged Kingstons are the highest mountains of this desert region, Kingston Peak rising to 7,323 ft. To the SW, the mountain slope, steep near the ridges, gradually flattens into the broad Valjean Valley, below 1,000 ft. elevation, and SR 127. S of the Valley are the Silurian Hills, with soft, rolling topography. E of the Silurian Hills and S of the Kingston Mountains— separated from them by Kingston Wash—are the Shadow Mountains. Here the highest point is 4,197 ft. These mountains have smooth ridges, rounded peaks.

The area contains 15% badlands, 25% alluvial fans, 20% hills and mountains, 15% dissected fans, 20% plains, plus sand dunes and other features. Desert climate; less than 4 in. of rain a year, rarely as much as 1 in. in any month. The rainfall pattern is less sharply seasonal than in most of CA. May and June are the driest months, Aug. is the wettest. Below-freezing temperatures are rare in the valleys. Summers are very hot. Water is scarce. The Amargosa River (see following description) has surface running water most of the year.

The chief economic activity has been mining. Most of the past mines have been abandoned, but the region is thought to have good potential, and exploration continues. The Wilderness Study Area boundary was drawn to exclude most disturbed areas, and there are no roads within the boundary. Several primitive ways penetrate it. Wilderness designation would, of course, close that portion to all vehicle traffic, and ORV travel will presumably be restricted elsewhere, with some areas designated for ORV activity.

Plants: In the washes, in the interior valleys, and at the base of the mountains, creosote bush and other low desert shrubs. In the higher interior valleys: Joshua tree, yucca, barrel cactus, cholla. Higher, on steep slopes, pinyon-juniper forest. Some white fir forest at the highest elevations in the Kingston Mountains, a surprising occurrence. Another botanical curiosity is a stand of enormous nolinas, a yuccalike plant, this species growing as much as 15 ft. tall; it is found only here and in the Joshua Tree National Monument. In the SE, the area includes part of one of the densest Joshua tree stands in the Southwest.

Birds: No checklist. Species noted include the California yellow-billed cuckoo, golden eagle, vermilion flycatcher, gray vireo, summer tanager, prairie falcon, Virginia's and yellow warblers, yellow-breasted chat, hepatic tanager. Some 220 bird species are said to visit or reside in the Amargosa Canyon, including pied-billed grebe, great blue heron, green-winged and cinnamon teals, shoveler, ruddy duck; sharp-shinned, Cooper's, red-tailed, and marsh hawks; Gambel's quail, roadrunner, great horned owl, belted kingfisher, common flicker, Say's phoebe; violet-green, tree, and rough-winged swallows; verdin, ruby-crowned kinglet, phainopepla; Lucy's, yellow-rumped, and black-throated gray warblers.

Mammals: Include Amargosa vole, desert chipmunk, desert bighorn sheep, California myotis, western pipistrel, rock squirrel, mule deer, black-tailed jackrabbit, coyote, Merriam and desert kangaroo rats, antelope ground squirrel, cactus mouse. Desert kit fox, ringtail, and bobcat are among those presumably present.

FEATURES

Amargosa Canyon-Dumont Dunes Natural Area, 22,763 acres, extends S for 12 mi. from a point about 1/2 mi. S of Tecopa. An old railroad grade runs through the canyon. One of the few desert areas with a permanent stream and riparian vegetation. The canyon varies in width from about 400 ft. in the N to about 2,000 ft. as it opens in the S on a broad alluvial fan. The greatest depth is 960 ft. midway through the canyon. The canyon was cut through the Sperry Hills, exposing layers of widely different ages and compositions. Most colorful are the China Ranch Beds, midway through the canyon, light-colored, mainly white to brilliant pink.

The canyon is an ecological oasis, isolated from any other watered area. Thus unique species have evolved. At the same time, it is an essential water source for fauna from surrounding areas and for migrants. Hiking and bird-watching are the principal visitor activities.

The Dumont Dunes lie to the S of the canyon, the site boundary extending W to SR 127. Although not enormous, the dunes are considered scientifically and scenically interesting because of their great variety. The dunes are not stabilized, but move with the winds. They have no vegetation except on the lower slopes and the sandy terraces to the N.

Both the Canyon and the Dunes have been heavily used by ORV's, although the Canyon had been declared closed to them. Conservationists urged that the entire area be closed. In BLM's final plan, the Dunes have been declared open to ORV's, the Canyon closed.

Salt Creek, like the Canyon an Area of Critical Environmental Concern, follows SR 127. Salt Spring Hills are N of the Arawatz Mountains (see entry). The creek has an exceptionally large riparian zone—for the desert—about a mi. long, up to 150 ft. wide. It attracts diverse wildlife. 82 bird species recorded.

HEADQUARTERS: BLM, California Desert District, 1695 Spruce St., Riverside, CA 92507; (714) 787-1462.

MECCA HILLS
U.S. Bureau of Land Management
24,100 acres.

E of Indio. I-10 is N boundary. On the S and SE, Box Canyon Rd., which joins I-10 25 mi. E of Indio.

The Mecca Hills are extremely colorful, deeply eroded into a maze of narrow, winding, steep-walled canyons, a badlands labyrinth. The intricate passages give the visitor an immediate sense of isolation. Immense layers have been tilted, folded, uplifted, and exposed by erosion, often presenting color contrasts. Elevations range from near sealevel to about 1,500 ft. Sandy washes dissect the area, with limited stands of ironwood, smoke tree, and palo verde. Scattered ocotillo on the slopes.

Painted Canyon, one of the features, is outstandingly scenic throughout. Good views of the area can be enjoyed along Box Canyon Rd. Riverside County has a campground in the canyon.

HEADQUARTERS: BLM, California Desert District, 1695 Spruce St., Riverside, CA 92507; (714) 787-1462.

MILPITAS WASH-PALO VERDE MOUNTAINS
U.S. Bureau of Land Management
40,400 acres.

SW of Blythe on I-10, near the AZ border. W of SR 78, S of the town of Palo Verde. Milpitas Wash Rd. originates at SR 78 about 12 mi. S of Palo Verde, turning NW, then N to Wiley Well, becoming Wiley's Well Rd. before its junction with I-10.

The Palo Verde Mountains are a low range lying E of the Cibola National Wildlife Refuge (see entry) on the Colorado River. Steep, colorful, jagged peaks, the highest only 1,795 ft. Small, narrow canyons lead into enclosed basins and intimate valleys. Sheer cliffs, caves, arches, often with bright colors. Scenic value was rated high.

Milpitas Wash is a broad drainage S of the mountains, dropping from about 1,000 ft. elevation to about 250 ft. at the Colorado River. It is one of the largest virtually undisturbed examples of Sonoran Desert in CA. The Wash is actually a series of parallel washes separated by thick islands of vegetation. Water collects in temporary pools after rain or infrequent flash floods.

Creosote bush flats cover much of the area. The Wash also has mesquite, ironwood, palo verde, and catclaw. Wildlife includes leaf-nosed bat, several myotis species, kangaroo rats, pocket mice, desert tortoise; numerous snakes, including diamondback rattlesnake. Bighorn sheep and mule deer around the mountains. Quail and chukar hunting. The area has had light to moderate recreational use, chiefly for sightseeing, hiking, rockhounding, and camping.

HEADQUARTERS: BLM, California Desert District, 1695 Spruce St., Riverside, CA 92507; (714) 787-1462.

MORONGO-WHITEWATER
U.S. Bureau of Land Management
About 20,000 acres.

Generally bounded by the N unit of San Bernardino National Forest on the W, I-10 on the S, SR 62 on the E, Pipes Canyon Rd. on the N. Numerous private ownerships are within this area. The entry is concerned chiefly with a block S on Pipes Canyon Rd. and SR 62, another on I-10 between the Forest and SR 62.

On the E slopes of the San Bernardino Mountains. Landforms range from broad bajadas and low, rolling foothills to steep, rugged mountains. Elevations range from 2,500 ft. in the valley to about 6,000 ft. at the Forest boundary. Several deep, steep-walled canyons penetrate the mountains, notably Little Morongo, Big Morongo, Mission, and Whitewater. Each of these canyons is watered by natural springs and creeks that flow all year, at least in their upper sections.

Vegetation ranges from Mojave yucca, Joshua tree, creosote, and mixed desert shrubs, up through a pinyon-juniper zone to ponderosa pine forest. The moist canyon habitats have a rich and diverse riparian plant community, including tall cottonwoods and willows. Scenic qualities of the canyons are rated high, especially Whitewater Canyon, which has highly eroded, colorful ridges above the pale white of the boulder-strewn canyon floor.

The canyons, because of their water, attract wildlife. Mule deer are common, as well as bear, bobcat, raccoon. Whitewater Canyon has two prairie falcon eyries and breeding pairs of summer tanager.

The Pacific Crest Trail enters the area from I-10, following the Whitewater River N along the road to a fish hatchery, then crossing to Mission Canyon, following it into the Forest.

NEARBY: A lower section of *Big Morongo Canyon*, E of SR 62, is a famous birding site. 235 species have been recorded, of which 72 nest. Checklist available. Access is just N of the town of Morongo Valley on SR 62, turning right at the sign for Covington Park, then left after 300 yds. and into a parking area. *Big Morongo Wildlife Reserve* is a 180-acre county park. It adjoins the 80-acre *Big Morongo Canyon Preserve* of The Nature Conservancy. Some of the adjoining land is public domain, and it is hoped that a few tracts of private land can be acquired to round out a cooperative scheme for preservation and management of the canyon.

HEADQUARTERS: BLM, California Desert District, 1695 Spruce St., Riverside, CA 92507; (714) 787-1462.

MOUNT SAN JACINTO STATE PARK AND STATE WILDERNESS
California Department of Parks and Recreation
13,515 acres.

From Banning on I-10, S 27 mi. on SR 243.

This State Park is within the San Jacinto Wilderness of the San Bernardino National Forest (see entry), and shares a trail system, including a section of the Pacific Crest Trail. SR 243 is the NW–SE route crossing the Forest. Park HQ is at Idyllwild, a small community within the Forest. The Park can also be entered by an aerial tramway 3 mi. W of Palm Springs to Desert View at about 8,400 ft. elevation. The tram operates all year, on a reduced schedule June–Nov., and the Long Valley Ranger Station at the top is also manned all year.

Two campgrounds are on SR 243. No roads penetrate the park. All travel is on foot or horseback. The site is 6 mi. E–W, 3 mi. N–S. At 10,804 ft. elevation, San Jacinto Peak is the highest in the range, second highest in S CA. Four other peaks within the park are over 10,000 ft. Most of the site is above 6,000 ft. The NE face of the San Jacinto Range plunges 9,000 ft. in less than 6 mi., one of the sheerest escarpments on the continent, and a good reason to use the aerial tram. The tram, carrying 80 passengers over a 12,800-ft. span with a rise of 5,873 ft., is said to be the world's largest and longest.

Annual precipitation is about 40 in., much of it falling as snow. Snow cover usually lasts Dec. through Apr., depths to 10 ft. at higher elevations. High winds and below-zero temperatures are common.

The area is mostly forested. Incense cedar, white fir; Coulter, Jeffrey, ponderosa and sugar pines over the lower slopes, lodgepole and limber pines above. Flora and fauna are essentially the same as in the surrounding National Forest.

The park is within a 2-hr. drive of both Los Angeles and San Diego. Not surprisingly, permits are required to enter the Wilderness, and permits are on quota. Backcountry camping is in designated primitive sites only.

ACTIVITIES

Camping: 2 campgrounds, 1 open all year. 83 sites. Reservations Mar. 30–Nov. 4.

Hiking, backpacking: Day hiking permits issued on day of entry. Overnight permits can be obtained at HQ or by writing at least 10 days in advance for dates as much as 8 weeks ahead.

Ski touring: Many skiers arrive by tram for day touring or camping. All should be prepared for severe weather.

Horse riding: Grazing is prohibited; horsemen must pack in their own feed.

Dogs are prohibited in the Wilderness.

PUBLICATION: Leaflet with map.

HEADQUARTERS: P.O. Box 308, Idyllwild, CA 92346; (714) 659-2607.

NEW YORK MOUNTAINS
U.S. Bureau of Land Management
82,500 acres.

On the NV border S of I-15. The railroad line from Cima to Ivanpah to Nipton is the NW boundary. The area is crossed by Ivanpah Rd., from Ivanpah S to Cedar Canyon Rd.

The New York Mountains are the highest in the region. From the 1,000-ft. elevation in the Chemehuevi Valley, far to the SE, the land rises slowly through connecting valleys into the Lanfair Valley, where the rise continues from about 3,500 ft. to the base of the mountains at 5,000 ft. Here the slopes become steeper, rising to the highest point, 7,532 ft. This is part of the mountainous central portion of the East Mojave region, the Mid Hills and Providence Mountains (see entry) trending to the SW. Buff-colored, jointed rocks and boulders, vertical walls of lava, steep talus slopes. NE of Ivanpah Rd. are the Castle Peaks, vertical, red-hued spires reaching up to 600 ft. above the surrounding terrain. Broad valleys and canyons penetrate the mountains on the SW side. The scenic and complex terrain of the interior area, combined with dense vegetation, provides many opportunities for solitude in pristine surroundings.

The mountains have exceptionally diverse vegetation. In Fourth of July Canyon is a small, relict stand of white fir, only about 30 trees. A number of relict and unusual fern species have been found in canyons here. Lower slopes are dominated by Great Basin sagebrush, juniper, and Joshua tree. Dispersed pinyon-juniper stands. Further E the cover is chiefly creosote bush scrub and big galleta scrub steppe.

Notable bird life includes golden eagle, breeding here, as do yellow warbler, prairie falcon, gilded flicker. Mammals include bighorn sheep, mule deer, California myotis, western pipistrel, Panamint kangaroo rat, Panamint chipmunk, rock squirrel.

Recreation includes bird watching, hunting, hiking, rockhounding.

HEADQUARTERS: BLM, California Desert District, 1695 Spruce St., Riverside, CA 92507; (714) 787-1462.

PALEN AND MCCOY MOUNTAINS
U.S. Bureau of Land Management
266,531 acres.

E of Joshua Tree National Monument, bounded by I-10, the Rice-Midland road, SR 62, and SR 177.

Between the Joshua Tree National Monument and the Colorado River, several small mountains stand like islands on the desert floor. Elevation of the floor is 500–1,000 ft. The mountains, averaging 10–12 mi. in length, are irregularly spaced, several mi. apart, roughly but not uniformly oriented NW–SE. Ridges are generally under 3,000 ft., a few peaks higher. Much of the area has been disturbed by mining and World War II military maneuvers. The tracks of General Patton's tank corps are still conspicuous, and the BLM warns that part of the area may be contaminated by unexploded ordnance. The BLM has recommended about a third of the area for wilderness status, finding it roadless, pristine, and otherwise suitable. This third includes most of the Palen Mountains.

These low but rugged mountains are in the S central portion of the area, rising from Chuckwalla Valley, the route of I-10. The two major peaks are 3,623 ft. and 3,831 ft. high. Palen Valley, W of the mountains, is a large alluvial outwash plain including dry Palen Lake below the 500-ft. contour, as well as extensive sand dunes. The McCoy Mountains are to the E. An extensive interior valley lies between the mountain masses, extensive rolling bajadas crossed by sandy washes.

The Granite Mountains are N of the Palen, Little Maria Mountains N of

McCoy, and the much small Arica Mountains in the far NE sector. The area offers a variety of desert scenery: jagged peaks, eroded rock formations, deep canyons, washes, valleys, dunes. Vegetation is sparse through much of the area, creosote bush scrub. Sandy washes have communities of ironwood, palo verde, and smoke tree. A small stand of crucifixion thorn occurs at the far S of Palen Valley. Little information on wildlife is available, other than reports of a small bighorn herd.

The area has had some ORV traffic, but outside the proposed wilderness area.

HEADQUARTERS: BLM, California Desert District, 1695 Spruce St., Riverside, CA 92507; (714) 787-1462.

PICACHO STATE RECREATION AREA
California Department of Parks and Recreation
See Cibola National Wildlife Refuge.

PINTO MOUNTAINS
U.S. Bureau of Land Management
Included in Joshua Tree National Monument.

PROVIDENCE MOUNTAINS STATE RECREATION AREA
California Department of Parks and Recreation
5,900 acres.

PROVIDENCE MOUNTAINS AND MID HILLS
U.S. Bureau of Land Management
100,000 acres.

State Recreation Area: from I-40 near Essex, 17 mi. NW on Essex Rd. BLM lands are on the W and N, off the Kelso road.

A visit to this exceptionally attractive State Park is a good introduction to the surrounding desert areas. Leaving I-40 at about 1,700 ft. elevation, the Essex Road crosses a broad, gently rising plain. We saw evidence of recent flash flooding not only in washes but also across the flat, gently sloping desert floor. At the base of the Providence Mountains the paved road begins to climb steeply, reaching the HQ area at 4,300 ft., overlooking 300 sq. mi. of desert and mountains.

Prospecting in 1929, Jack Mitchell came on the caves here, mined for silver, made his home here. He and his wife built the road and the stone houses now in the HQ complex and offered guided tours to visitors. After his death, it became a State Park.

The visitor center has good exhibits and, for someone with serious interests, a reference library. At the time of our visit, the ranger naturalist was a talented graduate student who greeted arriving visitors, sat with them on the terrace, and talked enthusiastically about the flora and fauna of the area.

A 1/2-mi. nature trail near HQ has a printed guide keyed to signs. A hiking trail goes up Crystal Spring Canyon. Tours of the caverns are offered at 1:30 P.M. except during July–Sept., on weekends at 10 A.M., 1:30 P.M., and 3 P.M. all year.

The campground has only 6 sites, limited water, and a magnificent view. If it should happen to be full, one can always camp on nearby BLM land.

Oct. to May are the months most visitors come. In summer, it is considerably cooler here than in the valley below.

Most of the surrounding land is public domain, administered by BLM. This entry includes three Wilderness Study Areas, encompassing the Providence Mountains and the Mid Hills to the NE. The areas are roadless, but they have several roads on their boundaries, in some cases separating them: to the W, the Kelso-Baker road; on the N and E of the central portion, Wildhorse Canyon and Black Canyon roads; at the N of the Mid Hills sector, Cedar Canyon Road.

The Providence Mountains extend NE for about 20 mi. from Granite Pass, S of Kelso, overlooking the Clipper Valley to the E. Highest points in the range are 6,612 ft., near the S end, and 7,094 ft., to the N. Landform varies, from limestone cliffs and caverns to rhyolite crags and peaks, mesas, broad bajadas, with many secluded canyons and valleys. Large, flat-topped Wildhorse Mesa is composed of black volcanic rock. This was the setting for Zane Grey's book *Wild Horse Mesa*. The mountains have interesting color contrasts—the black rock, with shades of red and gray. The area has a number of springs.

The Mid Hills are rolling, appearing rather low because they rise from valleys with floors at about 4,000 ft. elevation. The ridgeline of the Mid Hills is above 5,000 ft., and peaks attain 5,828 ft. and 6,412 ft. The hills have some exposed granite formations and boulders. A large part of the Wilderness Study Area is alluvial fans.

Plants: Much of the area has creosote bush scrub and blackbrush scrub, including yucca and cacti. Higher elevations have a mix of scrub and pinyon-juniper forest. A visit to the State Recreation Area can give the visitor a greater appreciation of desert flora. The landscape, which appears monotonous, has surprising variety when looked at more closely. The area covered by this entry includes natural cactus gardens, areas that show a profusion of flowers in wet years, stands of Mojave yucca, Joshua trees, and a number of rare plant species of special interest to botanists.

Birds: Checklist available. Resident species include turkey vulture, Cooper's and red-tailed hawks, golden eagle, kestrel, Gambel's quail, chukar; barn, screech, horned, burrowing, and pygmy owls; roadrunner, poor-will, ladder-backed woodpecker, raven, pinyon jay, plain titmouse, bushtit, verdin; cactus, rock, and canyon wrens; phainopepla, loggerhead shrike, house sparrow (noted to be uncommon, hard to find), house finch, black-throated sparrow. Many of these are "hard to find." The list of summer or winter visitors and migratory species is also long.

Mammals: List available at HQ. Species mentioned include bighorn sheep in the mountains, California myotis, mule deer, Panamint chipmunk, antelope ground squirrel, rock squirrel, Panamint kangaroo rat, cottontail, coyote, gray fox, bobcat, ringtail.

Reptiles and amphibians: Several areas have populations of desert tortoise. Green collared lizard and banded gecko, on the protected species list, occur along with the more common chuckwalla, and spiny and side-blotched lizards. The Mojave fringe-toed lizard occurs; most numerous are the desert iguana and gridiron lizard. The Mojave green rattlesnake and rock rattler are numerous, and the regal ringneck snake occurs.

FEATURES

The caverns discovered by Jack Mitchell include both the *Winding Stair Caverns* and *Mitchell Caverns,* plus some smaller caves. They feature a wide assortment of stalactites, stalagmites, flowstone, and other features.

Mitchells Caverns is a Natural Preserve within the Providence Mountains State Recreation Area.

Hole-in-the-Wall, on BLM land, has exceptional erosional features in sedimentary materials.

ACTIVITIES

Camping: 6 sites, all year, at the SRA. A BLM campground with 9 sites is at Hole-in-the-Wall, 26 mi. NW of Essex on the Essex Road. Another with 31 sites is 35 mi. NW.

Hiking, backpacking: No marked trails. Opportunities for isolation in many canyons and valleys. The Ranger at the State Recreation Area can advise, or visit the BLM office at Riverside.

Hunting: Shotgun hunting of rabbit and quail permitted in the State Recreation Area; no hunting in the Natural Preserve.

PUBLICATIONS

Leaflet, State Recreation Area.
Geologic Setting of Mitchell Caverns.
Nature trail guide.
Bird and reptile-amphibian checklists.

HEADQUARTERS: State Recreation Area, P.O. Box 1, Essex, CA 92332; no telephone. BLM, California Desert District, 1695 Spruce St., Riverside, CA 92507; (714) 787-1462.

SALTON SEA

From Indio on I-10, SE on SR 111. SR 86 is on the opposite shore.

An ancient lake once filled a huge desert basin almost to sealevel. Over centuries it dried, leaving a barren salt bed that held water only at brief intervals. In 1905, during construction of irrigation works, the Colorado River, in flood, broke through and poured into the basin for two years. When the flow was stopped, the Salton Sea was 45 mi. long, 20 mi. wide, as much as 100 ft. deep. It dried, the level dropping until runoff from irrigated land halted the decline and the lake level began to rise again. For a time there was concern that resort communities on the shore would be inundated, but evaporation has approximated the inflow. The lake surface is now about 235 ft. below sealevel.

The water is slightly saltier than the ocean, and saltwater fish species have been successfully introduced. Average depth is now about 10 ft. The lake area is about 175,000 acres. High winds sometimes sweep the lake, making boating dangerous.

Most of the shoreline is privately owned. Several resort communities have developed, but growth is limited because of the exceedingly hot, dry summers. Boating, fishing, and swimming are popular.

We have entries for the following sites on the lake: Salton Sea State Recreation Area, Imperial Wildlife Area, and Salton Sea National Wildlife Refuge.

SALTON SEA NATIONAL WILDLIFE REFUGE
U.S. Fish and Wildlife Service
37,218 acres.

From Brawley on SR 78, N on SR 111 to Sinclair Rd.

Since 1930, when the refuge was established for protection of waterfowl and shorebirds, the level of the Salton Sea has risen, progressively inundating all but about 2,000 acres in two units, both on the shoreline, about 5 mi. apart.

These remaining areas are saltmarsh, goose pasture, freshwater marsh, completely flat except for Obsidian Butte, Red Hill, and Rock Hill.

The site is about 228 ft. below sealevel, in one of the hottest and driest areas of the continent. Average rainfall is about 3 in. per year, and summer temperatures often touch 120°F. Winters are mild and pleasant.

The birding is extraordinary. Wintering populations include large numbers of Canada and snow geese, great masses of pintail, along with green-winged teal, shoveler, American wigeon, shoveler, ruddy duck, and coot. Other winter residents include eared grebe, great and snowy egrets, white-faced ibis, long-billed curlew, whimbrel, willet, greater yellowlegs, long-billed dowitcher, marbled godwit, avocet, and western sandpiper.

In the annual Christmas bird count, the refuge often has high scores for such species as rough-winged and bank swallows, Scott's oriole, orange-crowned and yellow-rumped warblers, redstart, burrowing owl, mountain plover, and others. White pelican are common in spring and fall. (In spring we saw a flight of at least a thousand, soaring high in the sky, near the Salton Sea.) Summer visitors include the wood stork, fulvous tree duck, black-necked stilt. The refuge has an interesting list of accidentals, including brown booby, magnificent frigatebird, Baikal teal. The refuge has a black skimmer colony.

Best birding areas are off Garst Rd. and Red Hill, from Rock Hill, and along the shoreline of Unit 1.

Hunting: Special rules. Inquire.
No motor vehicles allowed on Refuge roads. No water, toilets, picnic sites.

PUBLICATIONS
Leaflet.
Bird checklist.
Refuge map.
Hunting regulations.

HEADQUARTERS: P.O. Box 120, Calipatria, CA 92233; (714) 348-2323.

SALTON SEA STATE RECREATION AREA
California Department of Parks and Recreation
17,868 acres.

From I-10 at Indio, SE 25 mi. on SR 111.

18 mi. of shoreline on the NE side of the Salton Sea, a narrow strip of land.

A popular site for water-based recreation. We include it because of a note from the manager: "This is a tremendous bird-watching area!" No details, but see the entries for the Salton Sea National Wildlife Refuge and Imperial Wildlife Area.

ACTIVITIES

Camping: 150 developed sites. Reservations Oct. 1–May 28. About 800 primitive sites.

Fishing: Gulf croaker, sargo, corvina, tilapia.

Swimming: Unsupervised.

Boating: Ramp, basin, moorings. Sea is dangerous in high winds.

PUBLICATION: Leaflet.

HEADQUARTERS: P.O. Box 5002, North Shore, CA 92254; (714) 393-3052.

SAN BERNARDINO NATIONAL FOREST

U.S. Forest Service

633,423 acres of Forest land; 810,287 acres within boundaries.

Two sections: (1) N and E of San Bernardino; (2) S of I-10 at Banning. Scenic routes through both sections.

The Forest contains a great diversity of terrain and habitat. Gentle flatlands and rolling hills are dominated by sheer escarpments and rocky peaks higher than anything else in southern California. In some places, snow is a rare visitor; in others it may linger half the year. There are mountain lakes, boggy meadows, quiet brooks, and rushing streams. Often barrel cactus and Joshua trees flourish in close proximity to Jeffrey pines and incense cedars.

Forest statistics say that winter sports are the greatest single attraction here. Also, with 6 million visitor-days per year, this Forest has the heaviest recreation use of any National Forest.

On a Saturday evening in late April, we checked into a commercial campground on Big Bear Lake in the N section of the Forest. Few of the sites were occupied. Early next morning we drove W on SR 18. Lines had already formed at the entrances to the several ski areas, people waiting for the ski slopes to open. Traffic was so heavy we were relieved to find our way out.

The larger of the two sections adjoins and lies E of the Angeles National Forest. About 50 mi. from W to E, it occupies the San Bernardino Mountains and the E portion of the San Gabriel Mountains. I-15 and US 395 cross the Forest through Cajon Pass between the two mountain masses. To the S, I-10 crosses San Gorgonio Pass between the San Bernardino Mountains and the San Jacinto Mountains, occupied by the smaller section of the Forest. The Forest includes 24 communities with over 35,000 homes, a summer population of over 120,000 people. Commercial establishments include the ski areas, campgrounds, resorts, marinas, restaurants, garages, and stores. Most of the land around Big Bear Lake and Lake Arrowhead is privately owned. Also within the Forest are the Silverwood Lake State Recreation Area and Mount San Jacinto State Park and State Wilderness (see entries).

The mountains lie between the agricultural and industrial coastal valleys and the desert. SR 18 is called a scenic highway, but it overlooks a great sea of suburbs, shopping centers, freeways, factories, and railroads. Elevations rise from about 1,300 ft. in the front country to the mountain plateau region of 5,000 to 7,000 ft. Highest point is 11,501-ft. San Gorgonio Peak, highest in S CA. San Jacinto Peak is 10,786 ft., and five other peaks rise above 10,000 ft. Many slopes are extremely steep.

Annual rainfall in the W valleys is about 16 in. per year. Precipitation is heavier on the high slopes, much of it falling as snow, enough to keep ski areas busy into April or later. On the E side, in the rain shadow, desert climate prevails. Most mountain streams are seasonal.

Water is the principal forest product here, the Forest watersheds supplying enough for the needs of a million people. Forest management practices are designed to conserve this resource, and to enhance recreation, wildlife, and other values—not for commercial production of wood.

Fire hazard is high in summer. Fire crews respond to about 238 fires per year, 72 caused by lightning, 166 by man. Burned acreage in recent years has averaged 11,500 acres per year. In 1970, when conditions were especially bad, a single fire burned 53,000 acres between dawn and dusk. Substantial areas of the Forest are closed in fire season.

Both because of heavy use and fire hazard, overnight camping requires a visitor permit, for either a designated campground or backcountry camping.

Plants: About 50% forested, including pinyon-juniper areas. Chaparral covers about 35%, on the lower slopes. Pinyon pine, juniper, and sagebrush cover mid-elevation desert slopes. Conifer and oak forests, with some stands of fine, mature trees between 6,000 and 8,500 ft. elevation. Ponderosa, Jeffrey, sugar, lodgepole, Coulter, and limber pines; white fir, incense cedar, Douglas-fir, and black oak are found here. Above 8,500 ft., lodgepole and limber pines dominate. Some 2,000-year-old limber pines are to be found in the San Gorgonio Wilderness. The Forest claims the widest range of rare plant species to be found in the continental United States. Many of these are in only one mountain range.

Birds: Checklist available. Residents include golden eagle, turkey vulture, 7 owl species, pied-billed grebe, coot; Cooper's, red-tailed, and red-shouldered hawks; kestrel, killdeer, poor-will, flicker; acorn, downy, hairy, ladder-backed, and white-headed woodpeckers; black and Say's phoebes, mocking-bird, California thrasher; pinyon, scrub, and Steller's jays; dipper, brown creeper, blue-gray and black-tailed gnatcatchers, Anna's hummingbird, Clark's nutcracker; Cassin's, house, and purple finches; grasshopper, lark, rufus-crowned, sage, song, and vesper sparrows; white-throated swift, brown and rufous-sided towhees, solitary vireo; Bewick's, canyon, cactus, house, and rock wrens; bushtit, wrentit. Many waterfowl in winter.

Mammals: Checklist available. 61 species identified. Forest lists as common: California ground squirrel, western gray squirrel, deer mouse, striped skunk, black bear, coyote, bobcat, mule deer, bighorn sheep. Many bat species, shrews, moles, mice, rabbit, and squirrels. Less frequently seen are badger, kit fox, ringtail, beaver, mountain lion.

Reptiles and amphibians: Reported as common: Coast horned, collared, and western fence lizards; Southern California salamander, Pacific tree frog, western toad, bullfrog, yellow-bellied racer, western garter snake, western rattlesnake.

FEATURES

San Gorgonio Wilderness, 34,644 acres, in the SE sector of the N unit, N of Banning. Trailheads on SR 38. The summit region of the highest range in S CA. Peaks over 10,000 ft. with sweeping vistas of mountains and desert. Small meadows and lakes, wide expanses of bare rock; conifer forest on the N slopes. Maintained trails cross the area, and hikers are advised that only experienced backcountry travelers should go off the trails; terrain is rough and water scarce. Wilderness permits are required. Because of past overuse, the number of permits issued is limited. A 21,500-acre addition to this Wilderness has been proposed, on the extreme E side, adjacent to the N and S boundaries.

San Jacinto Wilderness, 20,564 acres, in the S unit of the Forest. See the entry for Mount San Jacinto State Park and State Wilderness, which divides the National Forest Wilderness in two and has a common trail system. On the crest of the San Jacinto Mountains. The N portion is somewhat more scenic, overlooking San Gorgonio Pass and across to the mountains beyond. Wilderness permit is required, and here, too, the number issued is limited. Note that the National Forest permit does not authorize entry into the State Wilderness.

Granite Peak roadless area, 10,600 acres, in the far NE corner of the N unit, at the boundary. Proposed for wilderness status. Rolling mountains, rock outcropping, elevations from 5,500 ft. to 7,500 ft. Relatively low elevations and proximity to the Mojave Desert make this area accessible and attractive in winter and spring. Most of the area is covered with chaparral species of California juniper and pinyon pine. Fine stands of Joshua tree at lower elevations. The world's largest Joshua tree is here. Arrastre Creek, an ephemeral stream, forms a large canyon at the N end.

Cucamonga Wilderness, 9,022 acres, on the W side of the N unit. This area adjoins the Angeles National Forest (see entry, zone 8), and a 4,400-acre addition on the Angeles side has been proposed. Rugged terrain. Sharp peaks, steep slopes. Elevations from 5,000 ft. to 9,000 ft. The Middle and North Forks of Lytle Creek flow all year. Otherwise water is scarce. Wilderness permit required. Area is subject to fire closure after about June 20.

Pyramid Peak roadless area, 10,200 acres, in the SE sector of the S unit. About 12 mi. S of Palm Springs. Elevations from 2,200 ft. to 7,100 ft. Rolling terrain in the S; rugged mountains with numerous rock outcroppings in the N. The W boundary meets the Pacific Crest Trail. Live Oak Canyon includes 40-ft. Hidden Falls, flowing most of the year. Palm Canyon has lush riparian vegetation, including fan palm, cottonwood, rushes, ferns, grasses. Numerous springs and seeps attract wildlife.

Black Mountain Scenic Area lies N of Idyllwild, between SR 243 and the San Jacinto Wilderness. It is a popular recreation area with numerous scenic overlooks, trails for day hikes, Indian pictographs, and other points of interest.

Includes: Idyllwild County Park, 202 acres, just N of Idyllwild, has an exceptionally fine visitor center and nature trail.

INTERPRETATION: Nature walks, slide shows, ranger talks. Nature trail in Big Bear Ranger District.

ACTIVITIES

Camping: 34 campgrounds, 1,217 sites. Some open all year; others open between Apr. 1 and June 15.

Hiking, backpacking: 470 mi. of National Recreational Trails, wilderness trails, interpretive trails, and hiking trails. The 2,500-mi. Pacific Crest Trail has 200 mi. within the Forest.

Hunting: Deer, ducks, quail.

Fishing: About 110 mi. of fishing streams, as well as lakes. Rainbow and brown trout; black crappie, bluegill, green sunfish, smallmouth bass, redeye bass, bullhead, white catfish.

Swimming: Lakes.

Boating: Chiefly from private ramps and marinas.

Horse riding: Several horse trails. Horse camp near Heart Bar, another at McCall in San Jacinto Ranger District, off SR 74.

Skiing: 6 commercial ski areas, 3 with snow-making machines.

Ski touring: In the high country, depending on snow cover.

PUBLICATIONS

Forest map. $1.00

San Bernardino National Forest Profile, brochure.

Cucamonga Wilderness, brochure.

San Jacinto Wilderness, brochure.

San Gorgonio Wilderness, brochure.

Lytle Creek Canyon, brochure, Spanish and English versions.
San Bernardino National Forest Vehicle Use Plan.
Gold Fever Trail, self-guided auto tour brochure.
The Arrowhead, The Big Bear, The San Gorgonio, The San Jacinto. District
   Recreation Guides.
Shooting area map.
Bird checklist, San Bernardino National Forest.
Birds of the Idyllwild Area.

HEADQUARTERS: 144 N. Mountain View Avenue, San Bernardino, CA 92408;
   (714) 383-5588.

RANGER DISTRICTS: Arrowhead R.D., P.O. Box 7, Rim Forest, CA 92378;
   (714) 337-2444. Big Bear R.D., P.O. Box 290, Fawnskin, CA 92333; (714)
   866-3437. Cajon R.D., Star Route Box 100, Fontana, CA 92335; (714)
   887-2576. San Gorgonio R.D., Route 1, Box 264, Mentone, CA 92359;
   (714) 794-1123. San Jacinto R.D., P.O. Box 518, Idyllwild, CA 92349; (714)
   659-2117.

SAND HILLS

U.S. Bureau of Land Management
68,700 acres.

Extreme SE of CA. A long, narrow triangle, its base at I-8, between the
Coachella Canal on the W, Southern Pacific Railroad on the E, extending
NW almost 40 mi. Crossed by SR 78.

The area is also known as the Algodones Dunes, one of the largest dune
systems in the United States. It is also the site of one of the most vigorous
conflicts between those concerned for the natural environment and the advocates of ORV sport. Parts of the area have been so heavily damaged by ORV's
as to be disqualified for consideration as wilderness areas. In the N sector,
22,000 acres have been declared a National Natural Landmark, and entry of
vehicles prohibited. In the wilderness review process, conservationists urged
expansion of the protected area, while ORV advocates urged its reduction.
   About 40 mi. long, the dune system is up to 8 mi. wide. Some of the dunes
rise 200–300 ft. above their bases. The system includes transverse, longitudi-
nal, crescent-shaped, and star dunes, many shapes and sizes, some partially
stabilized by vegetation, some migrating. Where vegetation occurs, it is likely
to be thick stands of mesquite and creosote. The area includes several species
of rare, threatened, or endangered plants.

The area is believed to have high potential for geothermal development. The BLM has recommended that a large part of the S portion remain available for geothermal and mineral exploitation and ORV activity, while the protected area in the N is expanded.

Birds: List includes turkey vulture, red-tailed and Swainson's hawks, kestrel, burrowing owl, roadrunner, phainopepla, poor-will, black-chinned and Costa's hummingbirds, white-throated and Vaux's swifts, raven, lesser nighthawk, mockingbird, verdin, Gambel's quail, ladder-backed woodpecker, loggerhead shrike, horned lark; ash-throated flycatcher, crissal and Le Conte's thrashers, western kingbird, white-winged and mourning doves, gray vireo, black and Say's phoebes, black-tailed gnatcatcher; barn, tree, and cliff swallows; Abert's towhee, cactus wren, house finch, black-throated and white-crowned sparrows.

Mammals: Include antelope and round-tailed ground squirrels, pocket mice, deer mouse, western harvest mouse, desert and Merriam kangaroo rats, black-tailed jackrabbit, cottontail, pocket gopher, striped skunk, coyote, kit fox, badger, bobcat.

Reptiles and amphibians: Lizards include zebra-tailed, leopard, desert crested, western whiptail, western banded gecko, flat-tailed horned, desert horned, desert spiny, desert fringe-toed, long-tailed brush, and side-blotched. Desert tortoise, spring soft-shelled turtle, desert toad, Couch's spadefoot toad. Snakes include glossy, branded sand snake, spotted night snake, common whipsnake, spotted leaf-nosed snake, gopher snake, long-nosed snake, patch-nosed snake, western ground snake, lyre snake, diamond rattlesnake, sidewinder.

HEADQUARTERS: BLM, California Desert District, 1695 Spruce St., Riverside, CA 92507; (714) 787-1462.

SANTA ROSA MOUNTAINS
U.S. Bureau of Land Management
136,100 acres.

SW of Indio, on the N boundary of Anza-Borrego Desert State Park; adjoining San Bernardino National Forest on the W. SR 74 crosses near the Santa Rosa summit about 1 1/2 mi. E of its junction with SR 371.

Adjoining the Santa Rosa Wilderness Area of the Anza-Borrego Desert State Park, this area has been characterized as one of the most pristine and spectacular in the desert. This despite the checkerboarding of private ownerships in much of the area. A solid block of about 20,000 acres in the SE corner has been recommended for wilderness status. BLM ranked the area 4th among 137 Wilderness Study Areas in CA.

From the below-sealevel Salton Sea about 6 mi. E, an alluvial fan slopes gradually upward to about the 500-ft. contour. Above that the mountains rise steeply. Much of the mountain mass is above 4,000 ft., with a peak of 6,623 ft. within the site, one of 8,716 ft. just outside the boundary to the N. The mountains are rugged, strewn with boulders, cut by highly eroded canyons and washes, with steep cliffs, sheer faces, several valleys. 19 springs are scattered throughout the area.

Vegetation includes a number of plant communities, from the low desert floor to the ridges: creosote bush scrub, succulent scrub, desert chaparral, juniper-pinyon woodland. Spring floral displays. Wildlife includes an exceptionally large population of bighorn sheep, mule deer, quail, chukar.

HEADQUARTERS: BLM, California Desert District, 1695 Spruce St., Riverside, CA 92507; (714) 787-1462.

SHEEPHOLE MOUNTAINS-CADIZ VALLEY
U.S. Bureau of Land Management
Included in Joshua Tree National Monument.

SILVERWOOD LAKE STATE RECREATION AREA
California Department of Parks and Recreation
2,200 acres.

In the San Bernardino National Forest, on SR 138.

The lake, formed by a 249-ft.-high dam, has a surface area of about 1,000 acres. It is heavily used for water-based recreation. Campground reservations are available all year. The site map printed in the leaflet gives only slight indication of land area around the lake.

But it is within a National Forest, in a setting of chaparral-covered hills, at 3,400 ft. elevation, conifers on some N-facing slopes. About 130 bird species have been identified here, including bald and golden eagles and migrating waterfowl, as well as such mammals as coyote, ringtail, bobcat, beaver, and mule deer, mountain lion, and black bear.

ACTIVITIES

Camping: 95 sites. All year. Reservations.

Hiking: 12 mi. of paved trails. Hiker-biker camp.

Fishing: Trout, bass, bluegill, catfish.

Swimming: Supervised in season.

Boating: Ramps, docks, rentals. Because of heavy traffic, lake is zoned: ski area, no-ski zone, no power boats zone, etc.

PUBLICATION: Leaflet with map.

HEADQUARTERS: Star Route Box 7A, Hesperia, CA 92345; (714) 389-2281.

TORREY PINES STATE RESERVE AND STATE BEACH

California Department of Parks and Recreation

1,086 acres.

On S 21, seaward of I-5, I mi. S of Del Mar.

Open: 8 A.M. to sunset.

Coastal bluffs overlooking the ocean, 4 1/2 mi. of beach, salt marsh, eroded canyons, mesa. Highest point is 400 ft. above the sea. The Reserve was established to preserve the last of the Torrey pines, a species that grows only here and on Santa Rosa Island, 175 mi. away. Most of the mainland stand had been cut down before the Reserve was acquired. About 10,000 of the pines are within the preserve, the oldest about 200 years of age. The Torrey pine is not a large tree, but, especially growing in exposed places, is striking—wind-blown, gnarled, and twisted.

Torrey Sands, the yellow, tan, and white cliffs, are estimated to be 20 million years old. Sandstone along the beach, said to be 40 million years older, contains many fossils.

The Los Peñaquitos Lagoon is at the N end, flowing under a bridge on the Coast Road. A salt marsh and waterfowl refuge is on the inland side.

Plants: The Reserve is botanically rich, more than 300 plant species recorded. List available. Since annual precipitation is only 10 in. and summers are dry, the assortment is limited to species adapted to these severe conditions. Common trees and shrubs include California scrub oak, toyon, wartystem ceanothus, lemonade berry, laurel sumac, mission-manzanita, mountain mahogany, bush rue. Also common: chamise, redberry, flattop buckwheat, redbush monkeyflower, bush poppy, deerweed, San Diego rock rose, golden yarrow, black sage, California sagebrush, Mojave yucca. Barrel cactus, prickly pear, and polypody ferns in shaded canyons.

The spring wildflower display includes sea dahlia, beach sand verbena, mariposa lily, milk maids, live-forever, tidy tips, stinging lupine, beach evening primrose, blue-eyed grass, fishhook cactus.

Birds: Over 200 species recorded. Checklist available. Salt marsh attracts loons, grebes, great blue and green herons, snowy egret, mallard, pintail, lesser scaup, long-billed curlew, whimbrel, and least terns, rare in this area. Upland species include valley quail, brown thrasher, brown towhee, wrentit, scrub jay, roadrunner.

Mammals: Include opossum, cottontail, California ground squirrel, gray fox, mule deer. Gray whale often seen offshore in Jan.–Mar. migration.

INTERPRETATION
Museum theme is natural history. Exhibits; publications.
Guided hikes throughout the year. Schedules posted.

ACTIVITIES
Hiking: Trails through the pines, to viewpoints, down to the beach.
Swimming: Surf, supervised in season. Ocean swimming can be hazardous. Some swimming in estuary, especially at high tide.

Pets are not permitted in the Reserve or on the beach.
Reserve is closed when parking capacity is reached. This happens almost every pleasant weekend. Visitors must stay on trails. No fires, smoking, picnicking, food, beverages, collecting.

PUBLICATIONS
Leaflet with map.
Bird checklist.

HEADQUARTERS: 2680 Carlsbad Blvd., Carlsbad, CA 92008; (714) 729-8947.

TRONA PINNACLES NATURAL AREA
U.S. Bureau of Land Management
19,600 acres.

At Searles Lake, E of SR 178 near Trona.

Searles Lake is a salt desert, barren of vegetation except around the edges. Elevation is about 1,600 ft. The Pinnacles are called the most outstanding example of tufa deposits in the United States. They arose from the lake about 25,000 years ago, formed by the action of algae around hot springs. These deposits of calcium carbonate are up to 100 ft. tall. Their shapes are so bizarre that the site is often used as a setting for science fiction films.

Mining of some pinnacles, souvenir hunting, vandalism, and ORV activity on the lakebed have marred the site. The BLM is considering protective measures. The site is a National Natural Landmark.

HEADQUARTERS: BLM, California Desert District, 1695 Spruce St., Riverside, CA 92507; (714) 787-1462.

TURTLE MOUNTAINS
U.S. Bureau of Land Management
238,200 acres.

Near the AZ border. E boundary is US 95; S boundary SR 62. Part of the N boundary is Turtle Mountain Rd., SW from US 95 a short distance S of Havasu Lake Rd.

Parts of the area around the Turtle Mountains have heavy recreational use. The Parker Dam area often has over 100,000 visitors on a good weekend. Motorcycle races have left permanent scars over parts of the area. More than 70,000 acres in the central mountain area is pristine and recommended for wilderness status, while somewhat less stringent protection is recommended for other portions deemed to retain good natural values.

The landscape ranges from broad, open bajadas to highly eroded red basalt spires. Spires and peaks characterize the scenic, steep NE half of the range, while the SW is steep but rounded. Between them is a large, flat interior valley crossed by many shallow washes. The NE mountains are volcanic, colorful: rocks displaying shades of pink, gold, green, brown, and tan. Highest point in the NE is 3,804 ft., in the SW 4,313 ft., above the valley, which lies at about 1,500 ft.

The area has a number of springs. Notable among them is Mopah Springs, the most N known fan palm oasis. Chemehuevi Wash, in the NE sector, has a number of plant species said to be at the N limit of their ranges, among them ironwood, palo verde, smoke tree, and crucifixion thorn.

Vegetation occurs throughout the area and is relatively lush on the bajadas that surround the mountains. The interior valley has dense stands of creosote, cactus, and mixed shrubs.

The region has a herd of bighorn sheep, extensive desert tortoise habitat, prairie falcon and golden eagle eyries, breeding sites for Bendire's thrasher. The area has several good rockhounding sites.

The central portion recommended for wilderness status has no frontage on any surfaced road. The surrounding area, acting as a buffer, is crossed by numerous ways, some well-used, giving access to the perimeter of the wilderness.

HEADQUARTERS: BLM, California Desert District, 1695 Spruce St., River-side, CA 92507; (714) 787-1462.

WHIPPLE MOUNTAINS
U.S. Bureau of Land Management
85,100 acres

> Near the AZ border, W of Parker Dam, E of US 95. S boundary is the Colorado River Aqueduct and Copper Basin Reservoir roads.

Here is some of the desert's most striking scenery: brick-red mountains, eroded spires, pinnacles, natural bridges of red-brown lava, stripes of deep red sedimentary rock capped with gray-green layers. Highest point is 4,131 ft. Whipple Wash penetrates deeply into the mountains from the shore of Havasu Lake on the NE.

The area also has botanical interest because of the blending of Sonoran species with those typical of the Mojave desert. Several hundred saguaro cacti grow on the steep slope facing the Colorado River, one of only 2 or 3 such stands in CA. Other cactus species include foxtail, Bigelow cholla, Mojave prickly pear. Desert riparian areas are well represented with small areas of mesquite, palo verde, and ironwood.

Because of its exceptional scenic qualities, BLM ranked this site eighth among the 137 CA Wilderness Study Areas.

HEADQUARTERS: BLM, California Desert District, 1695 Spruce St., River-side, CA 92507; (714) 787-1462.

INDEX

ABOUT THE AUTHORS

THE PERRYS, long residents of the Washington, D.C., area, moved to Winter Haven, Florida, soon after work on these guides began. Their desks overlook a lake well populated with great blue herons, anhingas, egrets, ospreys, gallinules, and wood ducks, plus occasional alligators and otters.

Jane, an economist, came to Washington as a congressman's secretary and thereafter held senior posts in several executive agencies and presidential commissions. John, an industrial management consultant, was for ten years assistant director of the National Zoo.

Married in 1944, they have hiked, backpacked, camped, canoed, and cruised together in all fifty states. They have written more than a dozen books and produced more than two dozen educational filmstrips, chiefly on natural history and ecology.

Both are involved in conservation action, at home and abroad. They are board members of several environmental organizations.